Tribal Ecclesiology

Christian Heritage Rediscovered

The Series, as the name suggests, is meant to focus on Christian Faith & Living vis-à-vis topics like Literature & Poetry, Indigenous Philosophizing, Ethical response towards Agriculture, Health & Healing, Science & Technology, Ecofeminist Theology, Sociological approach towards Human Rights, Law & Politics, Arts, History of Ideas, Ancient Civilizations, Cultural Contiguity, Religious Cosmologies & Mysticism, Footsteps of famous Theologians, World Peace & Harmony, Global Capitalism, Network Marketing, Cybertheology, Population & Demographics, Epigraphic Studies, Contextualized Education, and many others. We welcome a Mss. on any topic/s mentioned, whether they are original works, scholarly monographs, collections of conference papers, revised dissertations, or translations of historical documents. Through the Series we, the Publishers, are striving to put forward published works that may help Institutions, Academic Bodies, Researchers, Scholars and the World at large in furthering their respective knowledge and understanding on the concerned subject. We welcome your comments on our efforts and further suggestions on how we can foster the upcoming thoughtful theologically grounded books.

Christian Heritage Rediscovered - 31

Tribal Ecclesiology

A Critical Synthesis of Early Christian Traditions and Cultural Traditions of Northeast India

R. Zolawma

CWI

Christian World Imprints(TM)

First Published in 2016 by

Christian World Imprints™
Christian Publishing & Books from India
H-12 Bali Nagar, **New Delhi-110015**
info@christianworldimprints.com
www.ChristianWorldImprints.com
Phone: +91 11 25465925

ISBN: 978-93-5148-107-2 (HB) ISBN: 978-93-5148-108-9 (PB)

Cataloging in Publication Data--DK
Courtesy: D.K. Agencies (P) Ltd. <docinfo@dkagencies.com>

Zolawma, R., author.
Tribal ecclesiology : a critical synthesis of early Christian traditions and cultural traditions of Northeast India / R. Zolawma.
pages cm. -- (Christian heritage rediscovered ; 31)
Includes bibliographical references.
ISBN 9789351481072 (HB)
ISBN 9789351481089 (PB)

1. Mizoram (India)--Church history. 2. Lushai (Asian people)--India--Mizoram--Religion. 3. Christianity and culture--India--Mizoram. 4. Mizoram (India)--Religious life and customs. I. Title. II. Series: Christian heritage rediscovered ; 31.

BR1156.M59Z65 2015 DDC 275.4166 23

Printed in India.

This book in its original form is the Dissertation submitted to the Senate of Serampore College (University), India, towards the degree of Doctor of Theology and is published with the written permission. The author is responsible for the title, contents and opinions in it.

The original title of the dissertation is 'Towards a Tribal Ecclesiology through a Critical Synthesis of Select Early Christian Traditions and Tribal Cultural Traditions of Northeast India, specially Mizoram'.

The Book

The book is an outcome of exploration of two great traditions - the early Christian traditions and Cultural traditions of Northeast India with a special reference to Mizo society. The author argued that the church is not just an institution characterized by rituals and dogmas alone but, the "church is a called out community" doing God's mission. Having in-depth research, the author argued that the uncritical acceptance of ecclesiology that these tribal churches are inheriting from the Western church traditions has resulted in the proliferation of tribal people in line with different denominations. Also, uncritical rejection of the local cultural traditions has contributed to the superficial character of the church which failed to respond to peoples' problems. Keeping the twin problems in view, the author sought to construct a contextual ecclesiology for tribal Christians, based on the early Christian traditions and Tribal cultural traditions, by adopting a critical synthesis method.

This contextual ecclesiology will draw resources from both, the early Christian traditions and Tribal cultural traditions. This new ecclesiology grounded on the teachings of the Bible is termed as Zawlbuk model of ecclesiology. The author asserts that the tribal churches should follow this model so as to give them a new identity:

as a communion of the local Christian community; as an egalitarian community; and as a community of sharing and service.

This landmark research done for the betterment of tribal people critically analyses the past and present ecclesiology and sketches a blueprint for their future course of action.

The Author

R. Zolawma hailing from Tlabung town, Mizoram; is an ordained minister of the Baptist Church of Mizoram. He is an Associate Professor of Systematic Theology and currently serving as Principal of the Academy of Integrated Christian Studies (AICS).

He underwent a thorough theological training at four prominent theological institutions of India. He joined the Eastern Theological College for Bachelor of Theology, and Serampore College for Bachelor of Divinity. However, due to Tribal students' exodus from Serampore College, he came to the ETC again and completed his BD.

He completed his post graduation in Christian Theology from the United Theological College and later on earned Doctorate in Theology from the Federated Faculty for Research in Religion and Culture (FFRRC).

He has contributed numerous articles (in English) in academic books and national Journals, and have published extensively in Mizo also. He is married to C. Sangi and they are blessed with two beautiful daughters, Rebecca and Deborah.

Foreword-I

This book, proposes an ecclesiology in context of tribal people life-setting in Northeast India, giving special attention to Mizoram. The books is the outcome of exploration of two great traditions - the early Christian traditions and Mizo cultural traditions. The author argued that church is not just an institution characterized by rituals and dogma alone but, the "church is a called out community", who are busy in doing God's mission. Having in-depth research, the author argued that the uncritical acceptance of ecclesiology that we inherited from the Western church traditions which resulted in the proliferation of tribal people in line with different denominations. Also, uncritical rejection of the local cultural traditions has contributed to superficial character of the church which failed to respond to people's problems. Keeping this twin problem, the author sought to construct a relevant ecclesiology for tribal Christians in general, and Mizos in particular, based on the early Christian traditions and Mizo cultural traditions.

The church in the past, due to its over-emphasis on conversion and church planting, often failed to challenge the economic, social, religious, cultural, and political systems which have marginalized some sections of the people in society. We cannot talk about true church without resisting the unjust structure in our political, social and economic system. The existence of the church has no meaning without challenging and transforming the institutionalized and systemic injustices that are taking place in the church, government and other public sectors. How do we make the experience of tribals central in our search for a relevant ecclesiology? How do we integrate traditional value of the early church and tribal communitarian value for strengthening the mission of the church? The author has brought of number of suggestions in this area.

The author adopted critical synthesis method for formulating a contextual ecclesiology. He argued that the two traditions – early church tradition and tribal tradition - must be linked through a critical synthesis. It is imperative that the contemporary tribal ecclesiology draw resources from both, the early Christian traditions and tribal cultural traditions. This process will enable us to construct a new ecclesiology grounded on the teaching of the Bible.

The book uncovers that influenced by Judaism and Greco-Roman civilization, the early church existed as a number of local congregations scattered over the Mediterranean region. The Church was founded in different regions with varying religious influences and social contexts. Yet, Christians were united by their faith in Jesus Christ, the Lord and Son of God. Unity and plurality in ecclesiology was evident during the formative period of the Church. Furthermore, ecclesial structure during these first four centuries developed from a non-structured, simple community of believers to a well established hierarchy.

Koinonia is a core concept in this book. A unique feature of early church was *koinonia,* the heart and essence of the church during the New Testament and also subsequent three centuries. It was possible because it was centred on mystery, a spiritual reality, the body of Christ, the people of God, and the communion with God in Jesus Christ. The inner reality of the church is thus the divine communion in the life of the Triune God in and through Jesus Christ. In the early church, the communion of the Local church was primarily expressed and realized in the Eucharistic celebration. Such participation led to real communion in life by sharing both spiritual and material things as well as building up community at a deeper level through the common sharing of goods and properties.

The author compared the *koinonia* of the early church with Mizo traditional essence of *Zawlbuk*, *Tlawmngaihna* and egalitarianism. He brought out the theological significance of traditional Mizo spiritual resources of those three elements and concluded that they are compatible with the teaching of Jesus Christ, and also with the early Christian faith traditions. The author proposed *Zawlbuk* model of ecclesiology. In this model of ecclesiology, *Tlawmngaihna* becomes the basis of tribal ecclesiology and egalitarianism becomes the model of the church structure. In *Zawlbuk* ecclesiology, the tribal Mizo Church receives a new identity: the church as a communion of local Christian community; the church as an egalitarian community; and the church as a community of sharing and service.

Tribal theologians have been constructing tribal theology almost three decades. Yet, no research at the doctoral level has been done on this subject. The book assumes much significant as it brings new challenges in doing tribal theology in contemporary context as people of God. I would say that this work is a landmark in the development of tribal theology. The author has critically analyzed the past and present practice ecclesiology and challenged the church to engage in a new way as God's called out community. I hope this work will generate new theological thinking and debate in our search for a relevant ecclesiology.

Wati Longchar
September, 2015

Foreword-II

There is a Tribal World in India. It is distinctively different from the dominant society of our country on various aspects. Their tribal languages being to Austric, Dravidian and Mongolic families; their socio-cultural life, as egalitarian; their religion being Adidharma/ Primal religion without any symbols and images, created by human mind and hand; their economy being need based, and eco-friendly. There is nature, man, spirit continuum as the bedrock of their existence and identity, as distinct people. As per our constitution, this world is described as Fifth and Sixth Schedule Areas (partially excluded and excluded area). There are many tribal communities in India. The largest are the Bhils; second largest, the Gonds; third, the Santals (70, 00000) and the Oraon (Kurukh) are positioned at fourth place with around 40, 00000 population in Western and North Central States of India. The North Eastern tribals are spread over all the seven states. Constitutionally tribes of North Central and Western India in nine states are covered in 5th Schedule and the tribes of North Eastern states, i.e., seven sisters are covered in 6th Schedule. The 5th Schedule Area is partially excluded area and the 6th Schedule Area is excluded area. This broadly means that any new laws passed by the Central Government of India are not directly applicable and implemented in these areas. The laws are looked into and discussed by the Tribal Advisory Council and the Governor of the States. If there are points that require any change then the said changes are proposed and sent back to the president for his consent. After the consent is received by the Governor, he notify it and then only it is applied or implemented in the scheduled areas. This constitutional provision is for the safeguard of the tribal socio – cultural traditions and and moral values of tribal communities in India.

Tribal communities/tribal people are not Hindus. Tribal religion Adi Dharma/Primal religion is not at all related to Hindus Sanatan Dharma. In Sanatana Dharma, the images & symbols created by human minds and human hands are integral to Sanatana Dharma. Adi Dharma has no human created symbols. It is purely a belief in a power in, with and under nature.

Due to Hindu mission in many tribal areas, tribes have become Hinduised. This does not mean that the entire Tribal Communities are Hindus in the popular sense of the term. Though they have adopted Hindus faith and practice they are still tribes like the Bhils, Gonds, Santals, Nagas and others. India is a secular country and every citizen has the right to chose a faith he or she wants to follow. No one should be compelled to or faced to or allured by external means to adopt a new faith. Hindu mission among the tribal communities is a recent development. The revival of Hindutva has taken up this mission. The dominant society in India had ample free time to preach and spread Hinduism among the Tribal people. But it did not do till the Christian mission from Europe and America came and began to preach the Gospel of Jesus Christ among the Tribal Communities in North Central, Western and North East India. The protestant missionaries began the mission works in the middle of the 19th Century. The Lutheran missionaries came to North Central (Chotanagpur) in 1845. About the same time the Presbyterian and Baptist missionaries began their mission work in North East India. The Christian missionaries served the tribal communities by establishing Schools, Hospitals, Medical service centre even in the most remote places/villages. The tribal people found the Christian missionaries as their friends and well wishers. Those who came to them before were exploiters. And therefore it was natural for the tribal people to accept the Gospel preached by the missionaries and convert themselves as Christians. The Roman Catholic mission followed the protestant mission in many tribal areas. But their socio-economic services outnumber those of protestant missions. At least this is quite true in the State of Jharkhand. Literacy and education are gifted by the Christian missionary agencies to the tribal people. Before the coming of the Christian mission in tribal communities there was no literacy in the present sense of the term. But surely, there was education among the tribal communities and that is how they survived through the centuries.

In the North Eastern States, literacy and education in the formal sense started with their mother tongue as a medium of primary education. Then they switched over to English. This helped them to compete and rise up early in Government and private services. But the tribal people of the 5th schedule area are still deprived of their mother tongue as a medium of primary education. The missionaries and the Government both did injustices to them. They are not given the human right and constitutional right to get primary education in their mother tongue. Jharkhand tribes are still fighting and struggling to get this right. Even now there is no system of mother tongue as the medium of primary education in 5th schedule areas. This has done great damage to the tribal cultural tradition. And as the language itself is cut at the very root of socio-cultural life, naturally the disintegration of tribal culture has a reaching consequence. When language is cut off in the process of education even at the primary level, the damage done to socio-cultural life of tribals becomes irreparable. Christian tribals are still tribals. They have changed their faith but not their blood and racial characteristics. They have maintained the clan system. But, for these tribes it's problematic to deal with Foreign Christian missionaries as they brought denominational practices and structures of their church to the tribal churches. And, on the other hand, the local tribal traditions were rejected. This has created many problems. First of all, the tribal churches has got a foreign appearance. Secondly, the new faith has not gone deep into the tribal traditional culture and finally, this situation may create lot of practical and theological issues and problems for the church in future. And, also dominant society in our country is leaning to discredit other faiths than Hinduism. So, it is time to wake up and do something about the situation. The members of the church in tribal communities are conscious of these problems. There are attempts to deal with them in different ways. The second Vatican council in the Roman Catholic Church has shaken the catholic faith and practices worldwide. There is a conscious attempt for the contextualization of Christian faith in the local cultural communities. Also, among the protestant believers there is a deep concern to contextualize the Christian faith and quality in the tribal communities in North Central and North East India.

Not without Witness by Bishop Dilbar Hans of the CNI Church is a pioneer work in making the Christian faith relevant to Adivasi (Tribal) Culture. *Tribal Awakening*, published by Christian Institute of Religion and Society, Bangalore (1965); *Pearls of Indigenous Wisdom*, by Bishop Dr. N. Minz published by Indian Social Institute New Delhi (2007); *Adivasi Theology* by Dr. Christ Sumit Abhay Kerketta, Gossner Theological College (2009); and a collection of my writings and more recently of young scholars who are trying to wrestle with the issues and problems in making Christian faith relevant to the tribal social-cultural traditions in Jharkhand. are some good attempts in this direction. Turning to the North East, we can trace a long list of scholars and witness who have engaged in contextualizing Christian theology in the tribal socio-cultural traditions of the Mizo, Naga, Khasi and others tribes in the region. Jorhat Theological College played a leading role in this matter. Dr. Renthy Keitzer was pioneer in this region. Then many others followed. Under Senate of Serampore College, W. Bengal there are many younger scholars who are doing their D.Th. Dissertations on the concerned subject and are getting them published one after another. But, Dr. R. Zolawma doctoral thesis which has now taken shape of a book under the title *Tribal Ecclesiology: A Critical Synthesis of Early Christian Traditions and Tribal Cultural Traditions of Northeast India* is different from all on various counts. One can make critical remarks on all these books and Dissertations which may be helpful and valid. One basic thing about all of them is that most of them deal with general theological or Christological issues and problems in tribal socio-cultural context of their church and society. They are good, and must be encouraged to do so. But very few of them have attempted to deal with the Ecclesiological issue and problems in our tribal context. And Dr. Zolawma should be congratulated for his work on Ecclesiology with the critical synthesis of early Christian traditions and tribal cultural traditions as a methodology.

Making critical synthesis as a model to deal with ecclesiology in Mizo Church is remarkable in this book. And at the same time being critical to this critical synthesis also must be noticed by the readers. There will be other ways of dealing with ecclesiological problems of churches in different parts of India, and that is important for many reasons. For one thing, the theology or Christology we all are discussing in our books and articles have to live and work in the context of the life and work of the church. Without an adequate space given by an ecclesiology, how can a theology or Christology survive and make its head way. Necessary spiritual and moral values in a relevant socio-cultural structure of the church are the things that are required to grow and flourish. This is precisely the situation in the churches of Tribal Communities in India. And the worst of all negative attitudes of the national Christian tribal leaders in this matter makes the situation worse. So an attitude of openness, creativity and critical thinking has to grow under the guidance of the Holy Spirit to make meaningful contribution by young scholars and older leaders of the church in tribal communities of India. And this is the future direction we should concentrate on in our theological scholarship in tribal areas. But more and more researches, field research and library researches are required for the original contribution in this area of our concern. I hope seminars and workshops be organized to discuss this book and its practical implications be accepted by the churches for the growth and its missions in tribal communities and other communities in India today.

I congratulate the author of the book and wish him and the church well in going ahead with the new ideas and concepts of the church in Mizoram.

Bishop Dr. N. Minz
S. P. Colony, Debadih
Ranchi, Jharkhand

Acknowledgements

The undertaking of any serious scholarly venture owes large debts to those who assist in the task and this study is no exception. While many debts are no doubt overlooked or unmentioned, I am thankful to all who have contributed to this work. In particular, I would like to extend special recognition to the following:

I would like to thank Fr. Dr. K. M. George, first and foremost, for both his wisdom and patience in overseeing this research work. His wealth of insight into ecclesiology and careful direction were invaluable for the completion of this project and kept me from many errors. My work has benefited greatly from his sound guidance and support. In addition, special thanks are extended to Fr. Dr. M. John Panicker and Rev. Dr. Jayakiran Sebastian for serving on the Supervisory Committee. They provided important insight and correction at various stages of the project, so to them I offer my sincerest thanks.

I thank Rev. Santanu K. Patro, Registrar, Senate of Serampore College and to the Academic Council for granting me a permission to publish my Doctoral Thesis.

I also extend gratitude to former FFRRC Registrars Fr. Dr. John Panicker and Fr. Dr. John Matthews in addition to the current Registrar, Rev. Dr. K. G. Pothen and Dean of Doctoral Studies, for their encouragement and help with the project.

I am greatly indebted to the Baptist Church of Mizoram and such debt extends beyond the pages of this study. I would like to particularly express my sincerest thanks to the BCM for granting me study leave and financial support. My debt to Rev. Dr. K. Thanzauva, the former General Secretary of the BCM, and Dr. R. L. Hnuni, the then principal of AICS, is apparent throughout this work and I gladly acknowledge it.

Recognition must also be given to Princeton Theological Seminary which provided me the opportunity to live on campus and use its library for a semester. I express my deepest gratitude to the seminary president, Dr. Ian Torrance, for granting me a scholarship covering all my living expenses. In addition, I owe a great deal to Dr. Richard F. Young, Associate professor at PTS. I offer to him my deepest gratitude for his scholarly supervision during my stay in Princeton.

Also to students of the Princeton Theological Seminary, Saun Lancaster, Austin Almanguer, Hilary Ritchie, who sincerely did editing of my work, I expressed my deepest appreciation to all of them.

To my teacher, Rev. Dr. Wati Longchar who inspired me to take up the issues of Tribal for theologizing and his brilliant foreward, which describes my book exceptionally well, I thank him so much. To Very Reverend Bishop Nirmal Minz, the pioneer in doing Tribal theology in India, I expressed my profound thanks and appreciation for his generous and kind words about my writing

Finally, I cannot thank enough my wife, Sangi, and two daughters, Rebecca and Deborah, for their love, friendship, and encouragement throughout this work. Their support helped me to continue my work through both good and bad.

Abbreviations

A.D.	*Anno Domini*
AICS	Academy of Integrated Christian Studies
ATC	Aizawl Theological College
BCM	Baptist Church of Mizoram
BMS	Baptist Missionary Society
ca	*circa* (about)
ETC	Eastern Theological College
FFRRC	Federated Faculty for Research in Religion and Culture
Ibid	*Ibidem* (same source)
KUTS	Kerala United Theological Seminary
MTTS	Marthoma Theological Seminary
NT	New Testament
OT	Old Testament
OTS	Orthodox Theological Seminary
PCM	Presbyterian Church of Mizoram
PTS	Princeton Theological Seminary
UTC	United Theological College
Vol.	Volume
WCM	Welsh Calvinistic Methodist

Introduction

1. Statement of the Problem

This book attempts to search for a contextual ecclesiology[1] for the contemporary tribal churches in Northeast India, with reference

1 Contextual ecclesiology is an ecclesiology, which is culturally conditioned and that which interacts consciously and seriously with the context. Contextualization is concerned with how the Gospel and culture relate to one another. Contextualization is "a dynamic process of the Church's reflection on the interaction of the text as Word and God and the context, as a specific human situation in obedience to Christ and His mission in the World". See Bruce Nicholls, "Doing Theology in Context", *Evangelical Review of Theology* Volume II (1987), 101-106; David J. Hesselgrave & Edward Rommen, *Contextualization: Meanings, Methods, and Models* (Grand Rapids: Ker Book House, 1992), 33. According to Joedhiswara, "contextualization is the capacity to respond meaningfully to the gospel within the framework of one's own situation. It is the process by which a local community integrates the gospel message with the - real context, blending text and context into the single, God intended reality called Christian living". Mikha Joedhiswara, "Holistic Evangelism: On Suffering in the Face of Overwhelming Poverty and Multifaceted Religiousity," *Mission Focus* 2/2 (January 1992), 32-33.

to Mizoram based on early Christian traditions[2] and tribal cultural traditions[3].

The existing ecclesiology inherited from the Western missionaries by the tribal churches in Northeast India in general and Mizoram in particular is today found inadequate to meet the needs and aspirations of the people for two reasons: The first reason is the uncritical application of Western church traditions by the tribal Church, and the second reason is its uncritical rejection or acceptance of the tribal cultural traditions and the experience of the people in formulating the doctrine of the church. Consequently, the church, even after hundred of years of its existence on the soil of tribal people, has not succeeded to incarnate fully in the peoples' cultures. In spite of the

---

2 According to James Cone, Christian Tradition refers to the theological reflection of the church upon the nature of Christianity from the time of the early Church to the present day. He further states that the New Testament itself is a result of it. See James Cone, *A Black Theology of Liberation* (New York, NY: Orbis Books, 1986), 33. The Fourth World Conference on Faith and Order in Montreal (1963) defines 'Tradition' (note capital 'T') as the Gospel itself, transmitted from generation to generation in and by the Church, Christ himself present in the life of the Church. For Tradition is also meant the beliefs of the New Testament community handed down and dynamically developed through the centuries. Along this line, Renthy Keitzar asserts that the Tradition in its written form is the Bible. See Renthy Keitzar, "Tribal Perspective in Biblical Hermeneutic Today", *Indian Journal of Theology* 31/3&4 (July-December 1982), 312; "Group Reports", *Indian Journal of Theology* 31/3&4 (July-December 1982), 282. For John Meyendorff, any theology that is traditional is consistent with Scripture, with the experience of the Fathers and the saints, as well as with the continuous celebration of Christ's death and resurrection in the liturgy of the Church. See John Meyendorff, *Living Tradition* (Crestwood, NY: St. Vladimir's Seminary Press, 1978), 7&21. In this study, Christian Traditions refer to select early Christian ecclesiological traditions up to the Third century.

3 Tribal cultural traditions include the past and present, socio-cultural tradition, customs, religious beliefs and practices. They include myths and legend, folktales and stories, wisdom and proverbs, mores, morals, and songs. These cultural traditions have been transmitted orally from generation to generation. Renthy Keitzar considered the oral tradition of the tribal people as the unwritten "Prime Bible" See Renthy Keitzar, *In Search of a Relevant Gospel Message* (Guwahati: CLC, 1995), 95.

increase in numerical strength and its growth in institutionalization, the tribal churches in general appear to be more and more shallow, hollow and superficial in their adherence to truth and moral values. Besides, tribal Christians have increasingly experienced division into hundreds of denominations and unhealthy competition within the community due to denominationalism. This situation calls for a fresh attempt to engage in reflection on *ekklesia* in critical interaction with both early Christian traditions and tribal cultural traditions.

The proposition of the book is that Tribal ecclesiology has to be a synthesis of early Christian traditions and Tribal cultural traditions through mutually critical interaction. The result will be a lively and dynamic ecclesiology, which will be an authentically scriptural, gospel centered and contextually relevant understanding of the doctrine and practice of the church.

2. Elaboration of the Problem

In the past few decades as inspired by the renewal of theology at the Second Vatican Council[4], we have seen a theological quest to incarnate the church in the culture and context of India. The joint Pastoral Letter of the Bishops of India stated: "The Church in India must be a Church rooted in Indian soil, thoroughly at home in various languages, cultures and ways of life, intimately sharing the joys and hopes, grieves and anxieties of the Indian people, and

4 The dawn of the Twentieth century witnessed many movements within the church, such as the Biblical, liturgical and laity movements. Pope Pius XII was especially alert to the changing cultural, social and political forces. Pope John XXIII, by convoking Vatican Council II, opened a new chapter in the life of the church. The Vatican II documents such as *Lumen Gentium, Gaudium et Spes, Ad Gentes, and Nestro Aetate* gave a new direction to the evangelization of peoples and their cultures. See Joseph Prasad Pinto, *Inculturation through Basic Communities: An Indian Perspective* (Bangalore: Asian Trading Corporation, 1985), 235. The achievement of Vatican II is what some called a *Corpernican revolution* in ecclesiology. For an in-depth treatment and a critical evaluation of this aspect, see J. Francis Stafford, "The Inscrutable Riches of Christ: The Catholic Church's Mission of Salvation," in *A Church for All People*, edited by Eugene La Verdiere (Minnesota: The Liturgical Press, 1993), 35-44.

acknowledged by them not as foreign but very much as their own."[5] This renewal in theological scenario also has inspired the writer to undertake this study.

2.1. Context of the Research

This research is undertaken in the context of Mizoram, Northeast India. Northeast India[6] is a cluster of seven States, which include Arunachal Pradesh Assam, Manipur, Meghalaya, Mizoram, Nagaland and Tripura in the eastern most part of India. In spite of its "geo-ethnic character"[7] within the tribes, there exist fundamental commonalities[8] in terms of their history, heritage, colour, culture,

5 Jacob Manathodath, *Culture, Dialogue and the Church: A Study on the Inculturation of the Local Churches According to the Teaching of Pope Paul VI* (New Delhi: Intercultural Publication (P) Ltd., 1990), xiii.

6 Northeast India (hereafter NEI) is a homeland of a heterogeneous mass of population embodying people of great diversity in terms of ethnic components, linguistic affinity and lifestyles. NEI covers an area of about 2,55,082 sq. km, it accounts for 7.7% of the total geographical area of the country and has over 200 scheduled tribes. See "Foreword", in *Impact of Christianity on North East India*, edited by J. Puthenpurakal SDB (Shillong: Vendrame Institute Publications, 1996), xi; S. K. Singh, *Tribal Situation in India*, Vol. I (New Delhi: Manokar, 1982). 405; Lalsangkima, "In Search of a Context for a Contextual Theology: The Socio-Political Realities of "Tribal" Christians in Northeast India," *Indian Journal of Theology* 39/2 (1997), 2-16.

7 Ananda C. Bahagabati, "Emergent Tribal Identity in Northeast India," in *Tribal Development in India: Problems and Prospects*, edited by B. Chaudhuri (Delhi: Inter-India Publications, 1982), 218. Also see Lalsangkima Pachuau, "Tribal Identity and Ethnic Conflicts in Northeast India: A Tribal Christian Response," *Bangalore Theological Forum* XXXI/1 (July 1999), 159; Renthy Keitzar, "Tribal Theology in the Making", *Tribal Theology: A Reader*, edited by Shimeringam Shimray (Jorhat: TSC, 2003), 212-215.

8 See Paticia Mukhim, "Christian Impact on North East India and National Integration", in J. Puthenpurakal, ed., *Impact of Christianity on North East India*, 67-68; O. M Rao, *Focus on North East Indian Christianity* (Delhi: ISPCK, 1994), 4. 14: A. Wati Longchar, "Tribal Theology: Issues, Method and Perspective," *Journal of Tribal Studies* IV/2 (July-December), 80-83.

religion and experience, which keep them different from the tribes of the rest of India.[9]

Tribal people embraced Christianity and planted churches as a result of the Euro-American missionary enterprises[10]. Excepting very few, the Western missionaries who came to NEI thought of spreading Christianity in terms of transporting the institutions of their Euro-American churches. They showed little or no respect to tribal cultures and religions. Anything that did not conform to the Western Christianity was rejected as 'devilish,' 'pagan, 'devoid of rationality', 'devoid of truth', 'uncivilized', and 'animistic'. Ignoring the richness of tribal cultural traditions, everything in relation to the church was imported from the "mother churches". Like many other churches in Asia, the newly planted tribal churches uncritically followed the western ecclesiology brought by missionaries. In so doing tribal Christians become dependent on western experience, thought

---

9 Ambedkar noticed the difference between the tribes of Northeast India and those in other parts of India when the Indian Constitution was framed. He stated that while the tribes in other parts of the country were more or less Hinduised and assimilated into the culture of the people among whom they lived, this was not true of the tribal in Northeast India. Ambedkar still found that the tribes in Northeast were still rooted in their own cultures, with their own laws of inheritance and marriage, their own customs, which were very different from those of their neighbours. Accordingly the Sixth Schedule was promulgated in the constitution for the administration of the tribes in Northeast, whereas the Fifth Schedule deals with the tribes of the rest of India. See R. N. Prasad, *Government and Politics in Mizoram* (New Delhi: Northern Book Centre, 1987), 98; Also K. Thanzauva, *Theology of Community*, 5-6.

10 The British Baptist Missionary Society through the Serampore Mission made the first significant contact with NEI in the early part of the 19th century. In 1841, the American Baptist Mission took over the Assam field and the Welsh Presbyterian Mission stepped into the Khasi field. Later on, the American Baptist Mission entered into Nagaland and Manipur, the Baptist Missionary Society and the Welsh Calvinistic Methodist Mission Society started their work in Mizoram from the later part of the nineteenth century. See detailed Mission agencies in the region from Laldena, *Christian Missions and Colonialism* (Shillong: Vendrame Institute, 1988); F. S. Downs *Christianity in North East India* (Delhi: ISPCK, 1983).

forms and symbols to express their faith and worship[11] and the life and witness of the church. The ecclesiologies of various confessional families in the region were directly or indirectly borrowed from their respective mother churches. Renthy Keitzar has rightly asserted that tribal Christianity (church) is still a "Xerox-copy of American Baptist, or a duplicate of western Presbyterianism, or a carbon copy of the charismatic movement of Pentecostalism, or even a replica of Roman Catholicism of Pre-Vatican II."[12] In short, we may say that the ecclesiologies in tribal areas in Northeast India are alien to the tribal socio-cultural context.

2.1.1. *The Churches of Mizoram*

The Churches of Mizoram are the offspring of the mission agencies from Europe, namely Arthington Mission, the Welsh Calvinistic Methodist Church and Baptist Missionary Society (BMS) and the Lakher Pioneer Mission.[13] The churches in Mizoram, in terms of their organizational structure, are slightly different from the churches of other tribal groups in the region. It was probable that the outcome of the effort on the part of pioneer missionaries to Mizoram. J. H. Lorrain wrote:

> Our experience has taught us that the Lushais (Mizo) are born Methodist...We are not here to make them Eastern

11 Observing Christian Worship in the churches of NEI, Razouselie Lasetso laments, "What went wrong that the tribals shun their own culture and rich heritage for which they should be proud of?" He found not one item in the worship service, which would express the living culture of the people; nothing is different from the Western way of worship. See Razouselie Lasetso, "Pauline Perception of Religion and Culture as Revealed in Corinthians 9:19-23 and Its significance for Constructing a Viable Contextual Theology: A North East Indian Perspective," *Journal of Tribal Studies* X/2 (July-December 2006), 58.

12 Renthy Keitzar, "Tribal Perspective in Biblical Hermeneutic Today", *Indian Journal of Theology* 1/3&4 (July-December 1982), 310.

13 The early history of the church in Mizoram was dealt by C. L. Hminga, in his book, *The Life and Witnesses of the Churches in Mizoram* (Serkawn: The Literature Committee, Baptist Church of Mizoram, 1987).

> duplicates of Western Baptist... but ... to so guide them that they shall develop along their own national lines into a strong Lushai church of God... We look forward to the time when the Lushai Church shall be a happy blend of all that is best in Baptist, Presbyterian and Methodist, with something added perhaps which no Western denomination can supply.[14]

In fact, today there are different denominations existing in Mizoram, and most of them adopt a similar ecclesial structure, which is, for K. Thanzauva and Mangkhosat Kipgen, a blend of the Western Methodist, Presbyterian, ecclesial structure and the Mizo traditional patriarchal social structure.[15] The fundamental weakness of this type of ecclesial structure lies in its uncritical synthesis or adoption of western church structure and tribal traditional patriarchal social

14 Bold mine. *The Annual Report of BMS on Mizoram* 1904-1938 (Serkawn: Mizoram gospel Centenary Committee, 1993), 99. It was in 1894, the two pioneer missionaries, J. H. Lorrain and F. W. Savidge came to Mizoram. Very soon, the missionaries from the Welsh Calvinistic Methodist Church who took over the field from the pioneer missionaries. In 1903, the Baptist Missionary Society entered into the Southern part of Mizoram. Thereafter, the two missions worked side by side with mutual understanding and cooperation. In the beginning, there were only two denominational churches, namely, the Baptist Church of Mizoram established by the Baptist Missionary Society in the Southern part of Mizoram and the Presbyterian Church of Mizoram in the north under the Calvinistic Methodist Foreign Mission. However, today the church in Mizoram is being divided into different denominations, and the question of organic union or ecumenism is hardly heard in the church and considered as not urgent matter.

15 See K. Thanzauva, *Theology of Community* (Aizawl: Mizoram Theological Conference, 1997), 105; O. M Rao, *Focus on North East Indian Christianity* (Delhi: ISPCK, 1994), 10; Sebastian Karotemprel, "The Impact of Christianity on the Tribes of North East India", in *Impact of Christianity on North East India*, 38; Mangkhosat Kipgen, *Christianity and Mizo Culture* (Jorhat: The Mizo Theological Conference, 1996), 4. Mangkhosat Kipgen argues that the interaction between Christianity and the traditional Mizo culture produced a unique Mizo form of Christianity. But this has not yet happened in the doctrine of the church.

structure which results in a strong patriarchal ecclesial structure excluding half of its members, especially women from the ordained (priestly) ministry of the Church. Except in its organizational set up, other aspects of cultural traditions have not been incorporated in their ecclesiological discussions. Just for an instance, the meaning of *koinonia (*the true communion)[16], which is the core of the self-understanding of both the Church (Christian community) and the traditional tribal community, is not revealed in the life and witness of the churches in Mizoram. The church is rather tempted to the direction of institutionalism, hierarchy, power, and individual piousness. Therefore, the urgent need of the tribal Christians in Mizoram is an authentic ecclesiology, a critical synthesis of Christian traditions and tribal traditions.

2.1.2. *Concerns and Challenges*

The tribal churches in NEI in general are faced with various problems, which threaten the unity of the church and disturb the community existence. The common problems that call the church for a self-introspection and retrospection are as follows:

2.1.2.1. Divisions and rivalries among tribal Christians: Christianity, at first sight, was considered the agent of change in tribal societies, and it has contributed to the tribal communities a sense of tribal solidarity. At the same time, Christianity, the church to be precise, has also become an agent, which divides the communities on denominational lines. It is not mistaken to say that the Christianity that the tribal Christians embraced was a very divided, in doctrine, history, catechesis, and ethical standards. For over many decades,

16 Synonyms for Communion include '*koinonia*', 'participation', 'sharing'. It is sharing in being, having all things in common, being in unity, being bound by love (Acts 2: 44-47). According to the tribal sensibility communion is based on the equality of all and mutuality. See Thomas Neendoor, *Communion* (Kottayam: Oriental Institute of Religious Studies India Publications, 1998), 135-141; Paulos Mar Gregorios, *The Church and Authority: Reflections on the Nature and Life of the Church* (Delhi: ISPCK, 2001), 18; K. Thanzauva, *Theology of Community*, 145.

there was much hostility, intolerance and mutual recriminations among the churches due to denominationalism.[17] Historical rivalries that were common in Europe and America were transferred to tribal society. Such rivalries and mutual discrimination have slowed down the momentum of progress, development and integration of the tribal people among themselves and with the rest of India. In addition to this, the proliferation of sectarian groups, which may be called neo-tribalism, is becoming common. The joy of the great community, of believers has been lost in the bickering, rivalries, and misunderstandings of divided sects.

2.1.2.2. Cultural revivalism[18]: The second half of the twentieth century witnessed the process of cultural revivalism in tribal society. The process of Christianization has brought about division not only among tribal Christians but also within tribes; especially non-Christians tribal people began to feel threatened by the rapid pace of

17 Different Missions from the west introduced Christianity in NEI that led to the creation of separate denominational churches in the region. F. S. downs testified that it was due to a historical fact: "We belong to our present denominations due to the accidents of history and birth. The overwhelming majority belongs to the denominations they do because their parents did. The various Protestant groups in the area are organized into separate bodies simply because the mission that established them came from different countries." See F. S. Downs, *Church Union: Theological and Non-Theological Factors* (Shillong: The Church Union Committee of the NEICC, 1965), 1-2. In such a way the Christian community in NEI was divided into several church traditions. Each denomination remains loyal to its own ecclesiastical set up and becomes hostile to others. Denominationalism has over a period of time become the problem of the tribal Christians, which causes enmity, attacks, 'sheep stealing', competition, distrust and disrespect between different Church traditions.

18 The term, 'revivalism' is defined as a conscious, deliberate and organized effort on the part of some members of the society to create a more satisfying culture. Its aim is to return to a former era of happiness, to restore a golden age, to revive a precious condition to social virtue. See *International Encyclopedia of the Social Science*, Vol. II and 12, 75-76. Tribal cultural revivalism is used here to denote organized movement on the part of a section of the tribal people to restore and to maintain traditional culture, faiths and beliefs of the society against exogenous influences.

Christianization. Movement in Arunachal Pradesh especially among the *Adis* and *Nishings*,[19] *Seng Khasi* movement in Meghalaya[20] and Bru Liberation movement in Mizoram[21] are examples of how Christians and non-Christian tribals have grouped themselves around the traditional tribal cultures.

2.1.2.3. Ethnonationalism[22] and Ethnic conflict[23]: What seems to be more dangerous for the tribal people in NEI is ethnic conflict, the

19 Atul Chandra Talukdar, "Tribal Cultural Revival in Arunachal Pradesh", in *Impact of Christianity*, 484-490. *Adis* and *Nishings* are separate tribal groups of Arunachal Pradesh.

20 *Seng Khasi* is a tribal solidarity movement that revives the traditional Khasi culture, started at the end of the 19th century. Christianity, accompanied by western cultural influence disparaged everything that was indigenous. This tendency of the Christian mission coupled with the sense of deprivation arising from the relatively low position of traditional Khasi in relation to the British and the converted Christians, led to the revival of traditional Khasi religion and culture. See V. Xaxa, "Sociological Impact of Evangelization in North-East India," in *Mission Today: Subaltern Perspectives, Vol. II*, edited by Jesudas M. Athyal (Thiruvalla: Christava Sahitya Samithy, Mission Evangelism Study Project, 2001), 72-73; Frederic S. Downs, "Tribal Ecumenism in North East India: The Christian Role in Soliditary Movements", in *Good News for North East India: A Theological Reader*, edited by Renthy Keitzar (Guwahati: CLC, 1995), 8; O. L. Snaitang, *Christianity and Social Change in Northeast India* (Shillong: Vendrame Institute, 1993), 1.

21 Bru is one of the tribes of Mizoram, since 1998 Bru Liberation movement has demanded from the Government of Mizoram for the Constitutional Rights of the people especially a special political and economic package for the Bru tribe.

22 For Lalsangkima Pachuau, "ethnonationalism" is regional or sub-national reactions and resistance to what is seen as an over centralized and hegemonic state. He clearly states that the phenomenon of political movement in NEI, which is launched on the basis of ethnic identity, is the outcome of tribal ethnonationalism. For more detail, see Lalsangkima Pachuau, "Tribal Identity and Ethnic Conflicts in Northeast India: A "Tribal" Christian Response. *Bangalore Theological Forum* XXX/1 (July 1999): 157-167.

23 A Christian sociologist, V. Xaxa has mentioned the factor responsible for this inhuman act, as he states, "the sharpening of ethnic identity has simultaneously sharpened the hostility of one ethnic group against others.

violent war between different tribal groups, which is almost similar to tribalism. Even Christians from two different tribes may kill each other for the sake of their respective ethnic concerns just as tribals before Christianity. Belief in the universal fellowship of the church initially once broke down the barrier of tribalism. But today, the same demonic spirit resurfaces in the form of ethnocentrism that results in ethnic conflict and disintegrates the churches and destabilizes the fabric of tribal society. The Christian faith, which teaches values that transcend caste, race or ethnicity, has found itself time and again in a helpless position vis-à-vis the ethnic position.

2.1.2.4. Another area that calls for the church's attention is the status and place of women in the church, taking into account the cultural and theological constraints that distort the church's life.[24] Most of the tribal churches in NEI have yet to address themselves to the question of the ordination and consecration of women. If ecclesiology is indeed to be people-oriented and Christ centered, then it need to be re-examined from the point of view of those who, for one reason or another, seem to be excluded from or have limited participation in the total life of the church.

This has resulted from time to time in the occurrence of ethnic conflicts culminating in violence, arson, looting, and even death. Even people sharing the same faith, but of different ethnic communities have not been spared from such violence...This is a dilemma which the Church has yet to resolve". See V. Xaxa, "Sociological impact of Evangelization in North East India", *Indian Missiological Review* 13 (1991), 21. Wati Aier referring to the Nagas states, "Conflict, fragmentation, mistrust and enmity are at the center of the Nagas." Wati Aier, "Facing Truth" in *Crusade on Naga Morality* (Kohima: CNBC, 1996), 112.

24 With regard to the status and place of women in the church, R. L. Hnuni, one of the prominent tribal theologians, has stated, "Discrimination is more common in the Church than in secular circles. There are high-ranking women officers, M.L.A and even a women minister in the secular sector. It is in the church circle that leadership of women is not fully accepted whereas it should be the other way around. Fully trained women are denied their ordination, and with respect to leadership, administration, policy making and so on, they are expected to play assisting roles only." Quoted by K. Thanzauva, *Theology of Community*, 210.

2.1.2.5. Crisis of moral values: Tribal communities had been known for their simplicity, honesty, truthfulness and their concern for others and love for community, as they believe in cosmic oneness[25]. For a tribal person, community means in one sense commonality in which diversity exists but unity prevails in the long run. Community means the sense of oneness, a sense of entity, which extends to the whole territorial society. Community also means that the culture sets values that orient behaviour in the direction of common interest.[26] However, today the tribal world appears to be a very different setup. In the context of globalization and with the introduction of private property, consumer values are replacing community values, mutual exploitation is replacing mutual support, and the tribal societies are passing from communion to competition. The moral ideals in personal and social life are fading, and consequently, the tribal communities today are facing ethical problems like, the marginalization of poor people, consumerism, increase of violence, drug addiction, HIV/AIDS epidemic, and corruption. The present moral catastrophe depicts the lack of an effective and common ethical standard in the tribal churches and their failure to live as moral communities.

These are serious concerns and challenges, which deserve due attention in ecclesiological reflections. Therefore, the task of the research work is to answer the following questions: What does it mean to be a true Church for tribal people? What does it mean to be a fully tribal and authentically Christian church? How helpful are

---

25 Taylor argued that an essential feature of primal religion (tribal religion) was the sense of cosmic oneness and said, "Not only is there less separation between subject and object, between self and non-self, but fundamentally all things share the same nature and the same interaction one upon another-rocks and forest trees, beasts and serpents, the power of wind and waves upon a ship, the power of a drum over a dancer's body, the power in the mysterious cave of *kokola*, the living, the dead and the first ancestors, from the stone to divinities of hierarchy of power but not of being, for all are one, all are here, all are now. See John V. Taylor, *The Primal Vision: Christian Presence and African Religion* (London: SCM, 1977), 54.

26 Robert Redfield, "The Folk Society," *American Journal of Sociology* Vol. 32 (1947), 293. Cited by K. Thanzauva, *Theology of Community* (Aizawl: MTC, 1997), 108.

the contemporary understandings of the church in being faithful to the gospel in the present tribal context? Does the church function as God's instrument and respond to the demands of the contexts in which they are placed? If not, in what way can we construct a tribal ecclesiology?

3. Importance of the Problem

The importance of the proposed research work may be broadly mentioned at least in three ways:

This study will make a significant contribution to academic studies of ecclesiology in general, and particularly with relation to the tribes of the NEI. In search of meaning and relevance for tribal people in NEI, efforts have been made by some tribal theologians to get to the roots of tribal culture not only to understand the depth of tribal thinking and conceptualization, but also to incorporate these elements into theological exercise in terms of acceptance, accommodation and interpretation[27]. As a result, a large number of

27 One of the attempts has been in terms of indegenisation and incultruration leading to adaptation of tribal values. Nirmal Minz and Renthy Keitzar represent this approach of contextualization and indigenization. See Nirmal Minz, "The Study Tribal Religion in India", in *Revisioning India's Religious Traditions*, edited by David Scott and Israel Selvanayagam (Delhi: ISPCK, 1996); Nirmal Minz, *Rise Up My People, and Claim the Promise. The Gospel among the Tribes of India* (Delhi: ISPCK, 1997); Renthy Keitzar, "Tribal Theology in the Making", in *New Horizons in Ecumenism: Essays in Honour of Bishop Samuel Amirtham*, edited by K. C. Abraham (Bangalore: BTESSC & BTTBPSA, 1993); Renthy Keitzar, "Decontextualized", in *An Exploration of Tribal Theology*, edited by Wati Longchar (Jorhat: Tribal Study Centre, 1997). Another attempt has been to find parallel for some aspects of the tribal religion and history in the Judeo-Christian history and tradition, for example, as in creation stories. This approach in general attempts to trace some the gospel values in Tribal traditions. For instance, T. Hembrom examines the creation stories found in Genesis and in the Santal tradition to find parallels. See T. Hembrom, The Santals, *The Anthropological-Theological Reflections on Santal and Biblical creation Traditions* (Calcutta: Punthi Pustak, 1996). Another attempt is to find values and norms, which can find relevance in our theological enterprise to bring about creation, redemption, and transformation. K. Thanzauva's theological basis for social transformation

writings appeared that expressed the inadequacy and inability of the inherited theology from the west to address the political, social and religious problems of the tribal people in NEI. The writings also showed the need and feasibility to develop a theology that is rooted in the tribal cultures. However, no serious theological reflection has been done with regard to ecclesiology in relation to the tribal context. Tribal theology without tribal ecclesiology is incomplete. Many of those writings on tribal theology remain in academic levels or perhaps are irrelevant to the people. Because the churches in the tribal areas are, as already noted, the eastern duplicates of the Western church in terms of its doctrines, worship life and its art and architecture, therefore the church fails to be the "privileged locus" of tribal theology. This book makes a modest attempt to offer a contextual investigation of the nature and function of the church.

It is also concerned to contribute to a better understanding of the identity and mission of the church for the tribal Christians. As Jesus Christ (the Word) enters in depth into the roots of each culture by being born in a particular time and a particular community[28], the church likewise locate itself in particular times and particular communities as a continuation of Christ's incarnation. Incarnation is the opposite of foreignness. Therefore, "the church cannot be alien to any people; she is bound to make herself native to every clime, culture and race. She must feel at home everywhere."[29] The Mission Congress at Manila rightly affirms: "The church becomes a church only when she is incarnated in a people and culture, in a particular

---

and Wati Longchar's Creation Centered theology are the examples of this approach. K. Thanzauva, *Theology of Community* (Aizawl: Mizo Theological Conference, 1997); Wati Longchar, *An Emerging Asian Theology: Tribal Theology. Issues, Methods and Perspective* (Jorhat: Tribal Study Centre, 2000).

28 The God who has become human in Jesus of Nazareth is not only the Word made flesh in the individuality of the human body, but also the Word made flesh in the particularity and complexity of an economic, social, cultural, and religious world. Elizabeth Schussler Fiorenza, *In Memory of Her* (New York, NY: SCM Press, 1983), 227-230.

29 Jacob Manathodath, *Culture, Dialogue and the Church* (New Delhi: Intercultural Publications, 1990), 17.

place and time. The mystery is one, total and universal, but its concrete realization is varied, multiple and particular."[30] In a similar vein, Kazoh Kitamori has said: "Christianity should not be bound by Western forms. The incarnation is for all nations, embracing all human life and thought, Christianity in Asia should be based not on Greek but on Asian ground and Asian Christians should find their depths in their own ways."[31]

This presentation will also contribute to a fresh knowledge of the community aspect of ecclesiology. Today, the community aspect of ecclesiology is more than ever before threatened with fragmentation. The human community is frustrated and obstructed by the oppressive systems of patriarchy, class, caste, colour, ruthless capitalism and maddening consumerism and a culture of unhealthy competitions. There is a tendency towards monoculture, threatening the rich diversities of indigenous cultures. The social problems like abuse of drugs, escalations of crime, and corruption can be attributed to the disintegration of community life. In the midst of this fragmentation, one can see the communitarian character and sense of solidarity, something that is very much part of the life of the traditional tribal society[32]. In this direction, the importance of the proposed research is very explicit; to align with the quest of communitarian ecclesiology. It has a definitive relevance to the contemporary Church and society.

---

30 Quoted by Pinto, *Inculturation*, 238.

31 Quoted in Cecil Hargreaves, *Asian Christian Thinking* (Delhi: ISPCK, 1972), 24.

32 Larry Davis has clearly mentioned the importance of the sense of community in tribal culture: "The strong sense of community rooted in tribal cultures is a wonderful asset to be shared with postmodern in a westernized, individualized world of people who have lost a sense of corporate identity and life. The goal of finding an integrated wholeness of relationships with God and other persons reflects much that is deeply needed in contemporary life. In fact, trends in postmodern thinking have been moving in this direction for some time, but there has been no widespread movement to make positive application". See "Can Tribal Theology Succeed?: One Outsider's View", in *In Search of Identity and Tribal Theology*, edited by Wati Longchar (Jorhat: TSC, 2000), 126-127.

4. Definitions

1. *Ecclesiology:* The term "ecclesiology" covers both doctrine pertaining to the church and theological discussion of the nature, function, and structures of the church. The word "ecclesiology" comes from the Greek "ekklesia" and the word "logy" or *logos* which, when combined, denotes a study of the "ekklesia" or the teachings, doctrines, and science about the church.[33] Ecclesiology is the branch of Christian theology which systematically deals with the doctrine pertaining to the church, its origin, its nature, its role in mission, and its leadership. In short, ecclesiology "seeks to express the understanding of the nature and function of the church in a coherent manner from biblical, historical-theological and systematic-contextual perspectives."[34]

2. *Tribe:* The term, "tribe" is used as a blanket term or generic identity, which includes multiple indigenous groups in India. The term "tribe" is said to be taken from the Latin word *tribus,* literally means 'to be three'. The term *tribus* was used to identify the three basic divisions of the Roman people, *Tintienses, Ramnenses* and *Luceres* who were so classified for the purpose of taxation, military conscription and census taking. [35] K. Chattopadhyaya defines "tribe" as "a social group usually with a definite area, dialect, cultural homogeneity, and unifying social organization."[36] The term "tribe" is used by

---

33 Donald K. McKim, "Ecclesiology", *in Westminster Dictionary of Theological Terms* (Louisville: Westminster John Knox Press, 1996), 85; Monica K. Hellwig, "Ecclesiology", in The Modern Catholic Encyclopedia, edited by Michael Glazier and Monica K. Hellwig (Bangalore: Claretian Publications, 1997), 261.

34 O. V. Jathanna, "Ecclesiology in Context: Reflections from an Indian Perspective in the Light of Current Ecumenical Deliberations," *Bangalore Theological Forum* XXXVIII/3&4 (September-December 1996): 3. cf Kuncheria Puthil, *Theology of the Church: New Horizons* (Bangalore: Dharmaram Publications, 2006), 8.

35 K. Thanzauva, *Theology of Community*, 1.

36 K. Chattopadhyaya, *Tribalism in India* (New Delhi: Vikas Publishing House, 1978), 1.

anthropologists to denote "a group of people speaking a common language, observing uniform rules of social organization, and working together for some common purposes such as trade, agriculture, or warfare. Other typical characteristics include a common name, a contiguous territory, a relatively uniform culture or way of life, and a tradition of common descent".[37] The definition of the word "tribe" by the tribal Christians themselves can be seen in the findings of a Consultation held in Shillong, in 1962, which runs thus: a "tribe" is an indigenous homogeneous unit, speaking a common language, claiming a common ancestry, living in a particular geographical area, backward in technology, preliterate, loyally observing social and political customs based on kinship.[38]

5. Limitations

The book highlights the perspective of the tribal Christian in Mizoram.

Concerning tribal traditions, those elements that are common treasures for tribal people which are also constructive, innovative, liberative (may be called the gospel values in the culture) and pregnant with ecclesiological implications will be taken into consideration. More effort will be made to examine the cultural elements, Communitarianism,[39] Egalitarian principle[40], and Tribal

37 Quoted from "Tribe," in *Encyclopaedia Britannica*, Vol. X (1979, p. 115) by K. Thanzauva, *Theology of Community*, 1. A detail treatment of the terminology and meaning of the Tribe will be seen while dealing with the Tribal context in the second chapter of the study.

38 M.M Thomas and R. W. Taylor, eds., *Tribal Awakening* (Bangalore: CISRS, 1965), 2-3.

39 "Communitarianism is a concept and life principle of tribal community in which they live together sharing their joy and sorrows in mutual love and care." Communitarianism is not social determinism in which individual freedom is subsumed; rather true community includes members with many different points of view and creates an atmosphere of freedom to express themselves. See Thanzauva, *Theology of Community*, 106.

40 Tribal society is basically egalitarian. This can be seen in all aspects of community life. One of the marks of this egalitarian principle is sharing.

Home[41] How far can these cultural elements challenge, supplement and enrich the traditional ecclesiology?

With regard to the aspects of ecclesiology, the research is limited on two areas: the nature and function of the church, and the study of ecclesiology in early Christian Traditions being limited to the ecclesiology of the first four centuries starting from the ecclesiology in the New Testament till fourth century with the aim at keeping the unbroken continuity of the apostolic community and its beliefs and

---

The land is owned and shared in common. For instance, the principle of life adopted by the Mizo tribal in the past is remembered as "Thih leh ruam khatah, dam leh tlang khatah" (in death in the same valley and in life in the same hill); "Sem sem dam dam ei bil thi thi" (sharing you live, greedily eating you die). The Haves knew that they were to take care of the Have nots, it was their moral responsibility. See P. Lalnithanga, "Modernising Trends in Mizo society", *Administrative Review: Annual Journal of The Indian Institute of Public Administration Mizoram Regional Branch, New Delhi* (1998), 44.

41 It is a social institution commonly found among the tribal societies all over the world. It is a large house built in the heart of the village. The *Zawlbuk* (Mizo social institution) was constructed on the largest open space in the center of the village, usually close to the chief's house. In large village there could be more than one, in which case the one nearest the chief's house was usually the biggest and was considered the most important. The *Zawlbuk* could easily be distinguished from other buildings due to its distinctive shape and large size- it had to be spacious enough to accommodate all the young men boys of the village. See a detailed description, Mangkhosat Kipgen, *Christianity and Mizo Culture* (Jorhat: MTC, 1996), 61- 64; N. E. Parry, *A Monograph on Lushai Customs and Ceremonies* (Aizawl: Tribal Research, 1976), 8-10. K. Thanzauva has named this social institution as "Community Home". See a detailed theological treatment of the "Community Home", K. Thanzauva, *Theology of Community*, 134-147. In this study, I prefer to use the term "Tribal Home". The reason is that the idea of a community itself is that of a home. Yet homes are of two kinds. One of these is made of bricks, wood, stones, or concrete. It connotes the souvenirs, dreams, or ambitious attaching to the places where we have lived happily. The other sort of home everyone tries to build around himself; it is made of human beings united in a community of friendship. Tribal Home supplies both material home as well as the spirit of community or the spiritual nature of the community.

practices.[42] While dealing with the ecclesiology in the early Christian traditions, the research is limited to explore (1) the ecclesiology from the Gospel traditions, Acts and Pauline Letters from the New Testament Writings, and (2) selected theologians, Ignatius and Irenaeus in the second century, Tertullian, Origen and Cyprian from the third century; Augustine from the fourth century. The selection of these theologians was made on the basis of their contributions towards ecclesiology and representation to both the East and Western Church traditions.

6. Previous Research

There is a considerable body of literature dealing with Northeast India and the Hill tribes. The writers are political scientists, sociologists, anthropologists, economists, missiologists, historians, journalists and recently theologians. However, it is attempted here only to show some of the writings, particularly books that form the conceptual and theoretical background of the this book.

Despite the plethora of writings about the tribal people, and Christianity, there are only few books that deal with ecclesiological issues arising from the tribal context. K. Thanzauva's books, *Theology of Community* (1997)[43] and John Mundu's *The Ho Christian Community: Towards A New Self-Understanding as Communion,* (2003)[44] are worth mentioning. In *Theology of Community*, K. Thanzauva has devoted one chapter (chapter seventh) in searching for a theological basis for Tribal ecclesiology. Nevertheless, the intent of the book is not to give a thorough ecclesiological reflection, but rather to articulate a theology of community from the perspective of tribal people. John Mundu has attempted to relate the concept of

42 The importance of studying the past or traditions for Christians is clearly given by Rowan Williams, *Why Study the Past? The Quest for the Historical Church* (London: Darton, Longman and Todd, 2005), 9.

43 K. Thanzauva, *Theology of Community* (Aizawl: Mizo Theological Conference, 1997).

44 John Mundu, *The Ho Christian Community: Towards a New Self-Understanding as Communion* (Delhi: Media House, 2003).

communion in the *Ho* Community, one of the tribal communities in Chhotanagpur (outside Northeast India), and the communion in the Christian tradition.

The most comprehensive treatment of Christianity in Mizoram is that of C. L. Hminga (1987)[45] written from the perspective of Church growth. His treatment of the subject is mostly chronological history. He examines the growth of the churches in different denominations. The work is a valuable source of information particularly because of his lengthy quotations from primary sources. However, the secular side is sketchy and generally lacks information from primary sources. This book is useful as a study of the numerical, organic and qualitative growth of the churches, and it probably will remain a major work in that subject even for the time to come. However, the work is limited to the activities of missions and churches, Presbyterian, Baptist and Independent Church of Maraland.

Mangkhosat Kipgen's book, *Christianity and Mizo Culture*[46], has adopted a different paradigm to assess the interaction between Christianity and Mizo culture. Kipgen, unlike other authors, argues that Mizo culture has shaped Mizo Christianity rather than the reverse (Western culture). A new look at the historiography of the Mizo is introduced in Vanlalchhuanawm's book, *Christianity and the Subaltern Culture: Revival Movement as a Cultural Response to Westernization in Mizoram.*[47]

The novelty and difference of the present work from the previous ones can be greatly seen in its objective, scope, sources, and method.

45 Hminga, C. L. *The Life and Witness of Churches in Mizoram* (Serkawn: The Literature Committee of Baptist Church of Mizoram, 1987).

46 Mangkhosat Kipgen, *Christianity and Mizo Culture* (Jorhat: MTC, 1996).

47 Vanlalchhuanawma. *Christianity and the Subaltern Culture: Revival Movement as a Cultural Response to Westernization in Mizoram* (Delhi: ISPCK, 2006).

7. Methodology of the Research

7.1. Method for Collection of Data

Apart from engaging in library research a field research methodology, such as empirical method involving a social research method of questionnaire was employed.

7.1.1. *Field research: Questionnaire*

The questionnaire is one important method used for data collection. It can be administered directly or personally by the researcher or sent them by mail. The respondents alone must supply the information without the interference of the researcher.

In order to obtain genuine information for the third chapter of the book, "A Critique of the Contemporary Ecclesiology of the Churches in Mizoram", two hundred questionnaires were distributed to various sections of people in the church, e.g., church leaders (pastor, elder & deacon), women fellowship leaders, and youth leaders of both urban and rural churches. Out of two hundred questionnaires, one hundred sixty were returned to the author. The questionnaire was structured in Mizo and translated by the author.

The structured questionnaire has two main sections and each section is divided in area wise. The division of section are as follows:

The first section is titled as "Profiles of Respondents". It consists of the first six questions on respondents' details, such as respondents' age group, gender status, educational qualification, marital status, economic status and present position in the church. The second section contains questions pertaining to the relevance of the existing ecclesiology of the churches of Mizoram. This section is sub-divided into four, such as, (1) The churches of Mizoram and the early Church traditions (2) The churches of Mizoram and the Western Missionary Church tradition (3) The churches of Mizoram and Contextualization (4) The churches of Mizoram and Mizo cultural traditions.

In order to analyze and evaluate the data, the author has used coding and tabulation method. The percentage is taken by comparing the number of answers to the total number of respondents.

7.1.2. *Library research*

In order to gain insight from the writings of scholars about the theories and practices of the church during the first four years of Christianity, and about the tribal church particularly the churches of Mizoram, a comprehensive library research was done.

Apart from the libraries of the three Theological seminaries under the Federated Faculty for Research in Religion and Culture (FFRRC), the researcher has visited five different theological libraries in India and abroad, namely, the Princeton Theological Seminary library, USA; The library of Tribal Study Centre (Eastern Theological College), Jorhat; Academy of Integrated Christian Studies library in Aizawl; The library of United Theological College, Bangalore; The library of Aizawl Theological College and Mizoram University library.

7.1.3. *Others*

In addition to these, folktales, folklores, Mizo proverbs, ecclesiastical documents, constitution, reports of both the Baptist and Presbyterian Churches of Mizoram are extensively explored. All the sources are critically and systematically analyzed and interpretation was done carefully and thoughtfully.

7.2. Method for the Construction of Tribal Ecclesiology

A method of "critical synthesis[48]" is employed for developing a contextual Ecclesiology for the churches in Mizoram. The term

48 It was, among the philosopher, George Wilhelm Friedrich Hegel (1770-1831) who introduced the thought of synthesis. In his thought, we can find thesis, antithesis and synthesis. For Him, Jesus was the man who first perceived and embodied the reality of this unity (synthesis), the unity of finite and infinite. See Sinclair B. Ferguson, David F. Wright, eds., "Hegel George Wilhelm Friedrich (1770-1831)", *New Dictionary of Theology* (Leicester: Intervarsity

synthesis was used as a description of a theological approach, which has the sense of integration; the blending of theological ideas from different cultures into a coherent whole. The synthetic model tries to preserve the importance of the biblical message and the heritage of traditional doctrinal formulations, while at the same time acknowledging the vital role that culture has played and can play in theology. The synthetic model also reaches out to the resources of other cultures and other theological expressions for both the method and content of its own articulation of faith. In this way, a synthesis develops between one's own cultural point of view and the points of view of others. For Stephen B. Bevans, the synthetic model is a "middle-of-road model"[49], as it appears in midway between emphasis on gospel tradition and cultural tradition. This work adopts Bevans' synthetic model as a point of reference but with an addition of the word "critical". By critical here we do not mean carping or cutting down. We do not mean belittling or demeaning. We do not mean a spirit of fault-finding. Rather, we mean "the effort to see a thing clearly and truly in order to judge it fairly."[50]

The choice of this critical synthesis method is based on the assumption that tribal contextual ecclesiology has to be not just a synthesis of Christian Tradition and tribal cultural traditions but it should be the outcome of the mutually critical interaction of the two traditions. In other words, a synthesis here is not in the sense of simply a merger or amalgamation of Christian tradition and tribal

Press, 1988), 288-289. Friedrich Schleiermacher was the first to make an attempt to unite two traditions, the orthodox and the humanist tradition in a framework of synthesis. Paul Tillich's method of correlation may also be considered as the method of synthesis. See Paul Tillich, *Biblical Religion and the Search for Ultimate Reality* (Chicago: The University of Chicago Press, 1955), 57. A detailed explanation of the method of critical synthesis is done in chapter four.

49 Bevans has identified five models or approaches of contextual theology, they are: Translation model, Anthropological model, Praxis Model, Synthetic model; and Transcendental model. See Stephen B. Bevans, *Models of Contextual Theology* (Maryknoll, NY: Orbis Books, 2000), 81f.

50 "Critical" from Webster's Oxford English Dictionary

traditions, but the result of "the ongoing dialogue between faith and culture or cultures".[51]

This book aims at constructing a contextual ecclesiology for tribal Christians, an attempt will be made to bring the cultural elements that are constructive, innovative and liberative. However, there is a rejection of elements of the culture that are contrary to the gospel, as well as a critique of and removal from the church of those elements that are not the genuine gospel but Western interpretations not attuned to local cultures. A "fusion of horizons"[52] through mutually critical interaction will be the intended result of this work in order to arrive at a meaningful and effective contextual ecclesiology for tribal churches in Mizoram.

8. Structure

This research work consists of four chapters excluding the Introduction. The introduction contains the statement of the problem, elaboration of the problem, importance of the problem, definitions, limitations, previous research, method of the research, and the structure of the research.

The first chapter deals with ecclesiology in select early Christian Traditions with a view to provide a biblical and theological understanding of the nature and function of the church and it also serves as one of the bases to critique the existing ecclesiology of the tribal churches and to challenge and enrich tribal traditions.

---

51 A. Shorter, *Toward a Theology of Inculturation* (Maryknoll, NY: Orbis Books, 1988), 12.

52 The concept of "fusion of horizons" was developed by Gadamer as an alternative to the notion, characteristic of nineteenth century historical theory, that is, the interpreter can and must relinquish his or her own historical horizon and enter that of the author. Gadamer maintained that this is neither possible nor desirable. The "fusion of horizons" refers to the mutual relationship between the horizon of the text and that of the interpreter in the act of interpreting. In hermeneutical theory "horizon" is used metaphorically to denote the limits of thought which are dictated by a given viewpoint or perspective. See Gadamer, *Truth and Method* (New York, NY: Sheed & Ward, 1975), 273-274.

The second chapter has two major parts. The first part analyzes the context of tribal in India with a detailed study of the context of Mizoram. And the second part analyzes at length the Mizo cultural traditions. In this chapter, special effort is made to investigate three fundamental aspects of the tribal traditions, they are, communitarianism, egalitarianism and *Zawlbuk*, with the expectation of finding their significance for the development of Mizo tribal ecclesiology.

The third chapter critically evaluates and assesses the existing ecclesiology of tribal churches, the Baptist Church of Mizoram and the Presbyterian Church of Mizoram from a biblical theological and contextual perspective.

The fourth chapter examines the method of critical synthesis and attempts to find out the viable approach in order to synthesize the early Christian traditions and Mizo cultural traditions.

The fifth chapter proposes a tribal ecclesiology, by interpreting and integrating the Mizo cultural traditions with the help of the doctrine of the church in the early Christian traditions. The chapter also concludes the research by highlighting a summary of findings.

Contents

Foreword-I xi

Foreword-II xv

Acknowledgements xxi

Abbreviations xxiii

Introduction xxv

Chapter 1: Ecclesiology in Early Christian Traditions 1

Chapter 2: Tribal Cultural Traditions with Reference to Mizoram 65

Chapter 3: A Critique of the Contemporary Ecclesiology of the Churches in Mizoram 139

Chapter 4: A Critical Synthesis of the Ecclesiology in the Early Christian Traditions and Mizo Cultural Traditions 223

Chapter 5: Towards a Tribal Ecclesiology: *Zawlbuk* as a Model of Tribal Ecclesiology 259

General Conclusion 269

Appendix 273

Bibliography 279

Chapter 1

Ecclesiology in Early Christian Traditions

1. Introduction

This chapter critically examines ecclesiology in early Christian traditions particularly during the first four centuries. However, it is beyond the scope of this research to exhaustively investigate all aspects of ecclesiology in this early Christianity, our inquiry is limited to the essential nature and function of the church.

We shall explore the historical and theological interpretations of the church in order to help us perceive how changing socio-political cultural factors and ecclesiologies have influenced its self-understanding. And to understand the church in its universal and local dimensions, it is limited to some important time frames: the New Testament and the patristic era. There are two reasons for the choice of the early Christian Traditions in the present research work:

Firstly, the church must be faithful to its origin and keeping the unbroken continuity of the apostolic community and its beliefs and practices.[1] God's salvific act in Jesus Christ is the origin of the Church. So the real church can never simply leave its origins behind or ultimately distance itself from them. Those origins determine what is permanently true and constantly valid in the church, despite all historical forms and changes and all individual contingencies. Loyalty to its original nature is something the church must preserve through all the changing history of that world for the sake of which the church exists.

Therefore, the church must constantly reflect upon its real existence in the present with reference to its origins in the past, in order to assure its existence in the future. It stands or falls by its links with its origins in Jesus Christ and its message; and it remains permanently dependent, for the ground of its existence, on God's saving act in Jesus Christ, which is valid for all time and so also in the present. The church must never cease to reflect upon those origins. Specifically, it must reflect on the original testimony of faith, which remains constant point of reference for the church in any century. This original testimony is unique, incomparable and unrepeatable and as such it is actively obligatory, binding and normative for the church in all ages. The original witness, the original message, is given to us in the writings of the New Testament. These are writings which the community of the church itself, in a complex process lasting several centuries, has come to recognize officially as the original, valid and true witness to God's saving activity for mankind in Christ Jesus.

Secondly, as we are living in a time when traditional concepts about the church are breaking up and conventional assumptions about the church are subjected to re-examination, it is fitting that we look at the testimony of the New Testament and the early Christians traditions, in order to have a solid and comprehensive basis which

1 The importance of studying the past or traditions for Christians is clearly given by Rowan Williams, *Why Study the Past? The Quest for the Historical Church* (London: Darton, Longman and Todd, 2005), 9.

will enable us to critically evaluate the reality of the church and its expressions in the course of history, especially among the tribal Christians in Mizoram. Moreover, the book also anticipates that an understanding of the past should free us from the burdens of the past and this must also enable us to be true to the original experience on the one hand, and to find the ecclesiology relevant for the present context of the tribal Christians in Mizoram.

2. A Biblical Theological Understanding of the Concept of the Church

Etymologically, *Ekklesia* is derived from the Greek verb *kaleo*, 'call', in its compound form *ekkaleo*, "to summon" or "to call out". This signifies that an *ekklesia* is a gathering of people who have duly been summoned or called out, or an officially summoned body. The term *ekklesia* was used as an official term for the citizens' assembly of the Athenian democracy.[2] It is appropriate to look at the concept of the church in the Old Testament, Septuagint and in the New Testament.

2.1. Ekklesia in the Old Testament

In classical Greek literature where the word originated 'ekklesia' signified the secular meaning of the assembly of citizens of a Greek city-state for legislative and judicial purposes.[3] In the Hebrew Scriptures 'gathering of people' is expressed by two common words *edhah* and *qahal*[4]. Although both the words implied 'gathering', in a general

---

2 Edmund Hill, "Church", *The Dictionary of Theology*, edited by Joseph A, Komonchak, May Collins and Dermot A. Lan (Wilmington: Michael Glazier, 1987), 185. See also Everett F. Harrison, *The Apostolic Church* (Grand Rapids: William B. Eerdmans Publishing Company, 1985), 100.

3 M, Goguel, *L 'Eglise Primitive* (Paris: Payot, 1974), 10, cited by Evelyn Monteiro, SC, *Church and Culture: Communion in Pluralism* (London: ISPCK, 2004), 8-9.

4 The Hebrew word *qahal* appears some 123 in the Old Testament, being translated by *ekklesia* about 73 times, and by *sunagoge* 35 times. Edah in the "P" tradition is used to speak of Israel as the covenant community as a whole

sense, they also appeared frequently in phrases like *edhah/qahal* of Israel or of Yahweh' indicating the religious assembly of the Israelites. The root meanings of *edhah*, appoint, and that of *qahal*, 'call,' indicate that Israel is a people appointed or called by God.[5] *Edhah* and qahal would thus have a theological significance designating a people called or summoned by God to gather for some purpose or event. From the etymological analysis of the term *ekklesia* in classical Greek and in the Old Testament, we can draw some theological inferences. People are gathered together, or summoned to a specific place for a particular purpose that may be secular or religious. It is people (Greek citizens, people of Israel), purpose (legislative or religious) and place (Greek city-states, *Horeb, Moab*, Promised Land) that impart real significance to *qahal* or *ekklesia*. However, what implies a distinctive character, and an aura of sacredness, is the qualitative genitive of God or of Israel, indicating that *qahal* or *ekklesia* was a gathering of God's chosen people (Ex. 19:5), a people set apart (Num. 23: 9) and brought into being by divine initiative to participate in the plan of salvation. *Ekklesia* is a community of the new people of God that continues the mission of Jesus to establish God's reign of justice, harmony, equality and fellowship in the cosmic and human world.[6]

The decisive phases in the history of Israel for the formation of God's people among whom traces of the church are found, began with Abraham, 'the Father of all peoples' (Gen. 17:5) and continued through the exodus in the desert, its primitive habitat under Moses (Exo. 19: 24) to Canaan, the Promised Land, until the centuries following the Babylonian Exile. The dispersions (2Kings 17: 7-23) after the exile strengthen the attachment of the people of Israel to their land (Ps. 137: 1-6). Even in alien lands the *Diaspora* Jews never felt uprooted from the land of the Fathers, the birthplace of their faith and hope. This land was, for the Jews, both a concrete reality and an

---

and it is always translated by sunagoge in the LXX. See Kevin. Giles, *What on Earth is the Church?: A Biblical and Theological Inquiry* (London: SPCK, 1995), 233.

5 Monteiro, *Church and Culture*, 8-9.

6 Ibid.

ideal conception. It expressed a particularity as well as universality through the calling of Israel, for Abraham was to become the 'Father of numerous peoples' (Gen. 17:5f), in him all the families of the earth would be blessed (Gen. 12:3) and to Zion each says, "mother, for in her each one is born" (Ps. 87:5), whether they are of Israel or of other nations.

But as some Fathers of the church suggest, the presence of the church can be traced back even before Abraham, to the beginning of time,[7] as described by Hermas in his vision of the old woman: "She (church) was created first, before all things," that is, "the world was made for her,"[8] Origen also supports this view: "do not believe that the church has existed only since the saviour's coming in the flesh; she exists since the beginning of the human race and since the creation of the world."[9] No matter how far back we trace the beginning of the church in the history of humankind, one always finds a close affinity between the human race and the creation of the world; and subsequently, between the gathering of the people of Israel and their land and worship which in a way prefigures the idea of the church as a localized believing community in Christ.

There are certain significant elements that characterize the people of Israel, the 'church of the Old Testament. Through the Promised Land, Israel establishes an essential relationship with the earth. Bound to the human person from its beginnings, the earth occupies a favoured place in revelation. It remains the centre of the history of salvation from the beginning of time to the hope of the Kingdom to come. From Babylon, where Yahweh calls Abraham (Gen. 11:31-12:1), through Egypt, from where he draws his posterity and into Canaan which God's people inherit, an intimate and lasting bond is formed between the land (earth) and Israel (people). For Israel, the experiences of the land, nature and all creation were divine experiences. In nature and the created order Israel heard the hidden

7 Monteiro, *Church and Culture*, 10-11.

8 Ibid.

9 Ibid.

wisdom of Yahweh. The oak trees (Gen. 18:1), the wells (26:15), and the altars erected bear witness to these divine manifestations.

However, Israel is not 'Church' in the full sense of the word. It has several limitations. It does not look beyond the order of earthly things and beyond the temporal structure of a single particular nation. Its faith in the one, absolute and personal Yahweh, the Lord of all nations and all peoples, does not necessarily imply universalism. Its faith was distinctly ethnic in character. The Israelites prided themselves in being the chosen people and the inheritors of the faith of Abraham, Jacob and Isaac (Amos 9:7). Circumcision and the code of conduct concerning food and marriage were "culture-bound," making their worshipping community exclusive, which Bruce Vawter describes as a general syncretism that prevailed during that period. However, certain traits of church are also present- Israel stands out as a believing and worshipping community of the one, true Yahweh.[10]

2.2. Ekklesia in the Septuagint

In the Septuagint, *ekklesia* appears about one hundred times, of which twenty-two are in the apocrypha. The use of the word *ekklesia* in the Septuagint (LXX)[11] is more significant for an understanding of the Christian use of it. In the Hebrew Scripture the two most common words for a gathering of people are *edhah* and *qahal.* The root of *edhah* means 'appoint' and that of *qahal* means 'call'. These words were used to refer to the congregation or assembly of Israel. The root meaning of the two words would indicate that Israel is here regarded as a people appointed or called by God. In the LXX, *edhah* is uniformly translated by *sunagoge,* literally 'a gathering together'. *Qahal,* however, is translated by *sunagoge* in Genesis, Exodus, Leviticus, Numbers, and in the Prophets; but by *ekklesia* in Deuteronomy, the historical books from Judges to Nehemiah, and in the Psalter. K.

10 Monteiro, *Church and Culture*, 10-11.

11 LXX is the Greek version of the Hebrew Scripture, produced almost certainly in Alexandria during the second century B. C. Its name, the Greek word for 'seventy', derives from the tradition that seventy scholars were simultaneously engaged in the translation. See Giles, *What on Earth is the Church*, 235.

L. Schmidt says that *ekklesia* and *sunagoge* in the LXX both have much the same meaning: "both words are used both technically and non-technically, as underlined by the fact that translation varies between "assembly" and "congregation". Concerning the question, why Christians chose the *ekklesia* rather than *sunagoge* to designate the community of those who believe in Jesus Christ, Schmitd says that the Hellenistic Christians found *ekklesia* preferable, because this word was falling into disuse among Greek speaking Jews. And there seem to have been a tendency to employ *sunagoge* for the local Jewish community and for the building in which they met for worship.[12]

2.3. Ekklesia in the New Testament

The history of the church and also the history of the church's self-understanding began not after but in the New Testament. The New Testament writings, therefore, give us more than just the antecedents and the founding of the history of the church and of ecclesiology. Different images of the church arise not only after the New Testament times, but also in the New Testament itself. Indeed it is possible to say that the different emphases and perspectives tensions and contrasts, which we can see in the ecclesiology of subsequent centuries, reflect to a great extent the different emphases and perspectives, tensions and contrasts in the New Testament itself. We shall now move on to investigate the concept of Ekklesia in the New Testament with reference to the Synoptic Gospels, John's Gospel and Paul's Writings.

2.3.1. *Ekklesia in the Four Gospels*

The four Gospels all came to their final form several decades after the earthly ministry of Jesus. Each of the evangelists recounts the story by keeping to the historical setting of Jesus' lifetime, but at the same time each reflects to some degree individual interests, concerns, and theology, and the problems and beliefs of the Christian community for whom they wrote. As the experience of Christian community

12 K. L. Schmitd, "Ekklesia", *Theological Dictionary of New Testament*, Vol. III, edited by G. Kittel (Grand Rapids: Eerdmans, 1965), 528-9.

life forcefully impinges upon every believer, we should expect that the evangelists would at times betray something of their own church life and seek to address it, and this seems to be the case. It is most noticeable in Matthew's Gospel, but there is something of this to be seen in each of the four Gospels. As four inspired interpreters of the Jesus' story, the evangelists speak in their own right. The material each writer includes, emphasizes, or adds makes their Gospel what it is - namely one of personal accounts of the ministry, death, and resurrection of Jesus. The distinctive emphases to be seen in each Gospel can be considered as significant as that of St. Paul, or any other New Testament author. In recent years, New Testament scholars using 'redaction criticism' have made the delineating of these Gospel theologies a major area of study.

In regard to ecclesiology, Matthew and John's Gospels are the most important because of their more developed understanding of the identity of the Christian community, and for this reason they will be given more attention; however, Mark and Luke cannot be forgotten.

2.3.1.1. Matthew's Gospel

The most distinctive feature of Matthew's Gospel is its Jewishness, which is somewhat surprisingly matched by a fierce antipathy to the Jewish leaders. This is generally explained by arguing that this Gospel reflects a community of conservative Jewish Christians who have broken away from a larger group of Jews with whom they are now in conflict.[13] No more needs to be said on these matters at this point, but as we proceed, the particular context from which Matthew speaks will be constantly relevant and must be kept in mind.

Matthew's Gospel has often been called the 'ecclesiological Gospel' not only because it alone uses the work *ekklesia* (16:18; 18:17), and gives the triadic formula for baptism (28: 19), but also, and importantly, because in a number of places the evangelist quite boldly makes the words of Jesus address issues that were of

13 R. T. France, *Matthew-Evangelist and Teacher* (Exeter: Paternoster, 1989), 95-102.

interest to Matthew's church, and because one of his central concerns was to theologically define the community Jesus had called into existence in distinction from historic Israel.[14] In this last matter, the way he presents Jesus as the fulfillment of the hope of Israel brings ecclesiology and Christology together in a manner only paralleled by John among the Gospel writers. J. P. Meier says, the nexus between Christology and ecclesiology is one of the most typical characteristics of Matthew's Gospel.[15]

It is only in Matthew's Gospel, and not the other three, that the word *ekklesia* appears. The first use of the word is in the famous saying following Peter's confession, "You are the Christ, the Son of the living God' (16:16). In reply, Jesus says that this insight has been given by God, and then adds, "You are Peter, and on this rock I will build my church, and the powers of death shall not prevail against it' (16: 18). The second time Matthew uses the word *ekklesia* is in the context of a discussion about what to do "if your brother sins against you' (18: 15). After speaking personally to the brother Christian, and then along with two or three witnesses and finding no resolution to the matter. Matthew advises, 'tell it to the church, and if he refuses to listen even to the church, let him be to you as a gentile and tax collector' (18:17). In discussing Matthew's theology, the question of whether or not Jesus actually said these things - and, if he did, what Hebrew or Aramaic words he used - does not concern us. The only question of interest to us at this point is what ideas did Matthew intend to convey by these words: what meaning do they hold in the context of Matthew's Gospel.

In Matthew 16:18, almost all scholars are agreed that here the word *ekklesia* is used in what is called 'the universal sense' – the totality of Christians. In this context, the word *ekklesia* has completely lost its classical meaning, 'assembly'. The possibility that *ekklesia* simply means those who assemble together is exclude. Matthew has Jesus

14 Kevin Giles, *What on Earth is the Church?: A Biblical and Theological Inquiry (London: SPCK, 1995)*, 53.

15 J. P. Meier, *The Vision of Christ: Christ, Church and Morality in the First Gospel* (New York, NY: Paulist Press, 1979), 216.

speak rather of building a community, not based on national origin, or the keeping of the law, but on the confession of Jesus as the Christ-a confession first enunciated by Peter. It is not human association that constitutes this church, but the divine action, Jesus, as the Messiah is the builder.[16] Whether or not the following words, 'and on this rock' refer to Peter's confession, or to Peter himself as the leader of the church, remains a matter of debate, but the majority of scholars these days prefer the latter.[17] However, a clear line between the two interpretations should not be made. It may be agreed that the rock is Peter, but Peter is the rock on which the church is built because he makes this confession. If this is the case, then this church is make up of all those who make the same confession as Peter. Jesus goes on to promise "the powers of death shall not prevail against this church/ community (16:18). The threat of death by martyrdom or attack by the forces of the underworld is both possibly in mind. In this community, Peter as the leader is given the "keys of the Kingdom of heaven' (16: 19-20). This means that he has been conferred with authority to regulate doctrine and discipline.[18] In all of the Gospels, Peter is depicted as the leader and spokesman of the twelve, and in the early chapters of Acts this continues; but only Matthew has this commissioning of Peter.

The two uses of *ekklesia* in Matthew 18:17 raise other issues. Here, in contrast to Matthew 16:18, a local community of believers must be in mind. Such a congregation, Matthew implies has a unitary collective identity. This church can be told what has taken place and can speak to the offender. Again it would seem that Matthew has

---

16 Giles, *What on Earth is the Church*, 54. According to Giles, the idea of building a community is drawn from the Old Testament and is seen at Qumran.

17 W. D. Davies and D. C, Allison, *The Gospel According to St. Matthew*, Vol, 2 (Edinburgh: T&T Clark, 1991), 627-628. For the view that the rock is Peter's confession, see R, H. Gundry, *Matthew: A Commentary on his Literary and Theological Art* (Grand Rapids: Eerdmans, 1982), 333-335; and in more detail, C. C. Caragounis, *Peter and the Rock* (New York, NY: De Gruyter, 1990).

18 J. Overman, *Matthew's Gospel and Formative Judaism* (Minneapolis: Fortress, 1990), 139-140.

introduced the term ekklesia into this narrative, the original wording being less specific.[19] This use of ekklesia for the local community of believers parallels Matthew's frequent disparaging comments about 'their synagogues' (4: 32; 9: 35; 10:17; 12:9; 13:54), and 'your synagogues' (23:34) when speaking about Jewish communities. Stanton concludes on this evidence that when Matthew writes, 'ekklesia and synagogue are separate rival institutions'.[20] The basic difference is that in one Jesus is confessed as the Christ, and in the other the law still holds pride of place.

2.3.1.2. John's Gospel

Two distinctive features of John's Gospel bear upon the ecclesiology reflected in this document. The first is the dialectical relationship with Israel. Like Matthew, John is thoroughly conversant with Jewish life and institutions. It has been claimed that John is the most Jewish of all the Gospels. However, again, like Matthew, there is in John an antagonism to Judaism that leads to argue, in his own characteristic manner, that Israel has lost its status as the people of God - this honor now being the preserve of those who believe in Christ. The second is its multifaceted presentation of the gospel story.[21] John merges the past and the present, and frequently gives to seemingly straightforward narratives a symbolic meaning. In John, according to Beasley - Murray, 'the historical ministry of Jesus in Palestine is set in indissoluble relation to the ministry of the risen Lord in the world.[22] As a result, the gospel story is frequently to be understood on two levels. At one level, there is an account of Jesus' words and actions, but at another level the reader is supposed to see a spiritual or symbolized dimension to the story or words. The narrative of John,

---

19 V. Thompson, *Matthew's Advice to a Divided Community*: Mt. 17:22-18:35 (Rome: Biblical Institute, 1970), 151-153.

20 G. Stanton, *A Gospel for a New People* (Edinburgh: T&T Clark, 1992), 126-131.

21 G. R. Beasley-Murray, *John* (Waco: Word Biblical Commentary, 1987), xliv-liii.

22 Beasley - Murray, *John*, xlvi.

chapter 9, has been taken as a good example. Jesus heals the man born blind, and then he speaks of himself as the 'light of the world'. The point is not made explicit, but the reader is to deduce from this that true sight is found in recognizing Jesus for who he truly is: the risen Lord who gives light to the world.

In John's Gospel, we have seen communal imagery. The picture of Jesus as the good shepherd who lays down his life for the sheep brings to the fore John's profound communal understanding of disciples. The background to this imagery, for Kevin Giles, is principally Ezekiel 34, where Israel's leaders are condemned for neglecting the sheep. The Lord declares he will be their shepherd and pasture them on the mountains of Israel, and set over them 'my shepherd David' that is the Messiah.[23] In the words, I am the true shepherd Jesus claims to be fulfilling this prophecy. The unique feature of John's picture of the shepherd is his willingness to die for the sheep. The claim being made is that Jesus is Israel's Messiah and that his disciples are the flock of God, true Israel. Christology and ecclesiology are thus brought together. The shepherd and the sheep belong to each other; into the care of the good shepherd God has entrusted the flock. The good shepherd leads and protects them; he directs them to the pastures of life; and he lays down his life for them. He and they are united in a bond of mutual knowledge and trust (10:14, 27).

Another very important indicator of John's communal understanding of the Christian faith is seen in his treatment of the Holy Spirit. John can think of the Spirit as present with the disciples during the earthly ministry of Jesus (6:63b), but when speaking historically he insists that the Holy Spirit, identified as the paraclete - the helper, advocate, counselor- will only be given when Jesus is glorified (7: 39; 14: 16-26; 15: 26-27; 16: 7-15).[24] He will then take the place of Jesus (14:16). His special work in the life of the church will involve four things: (1) He will make Christ present in the believing community (14:18-20). (2) He will teach the disciples

---

23 Giles, *What is on Earth is the Church?* 66.

24 G. M. Burge, *The Annointed Community* (Grand Rapids: Eerdmans, 1987), 6-44.

and remind them of all that Jesus has said (14:26). This teaching will take place as the Spirit calls to mind Jesus' words.[25] (3) He will guide them into all truth (16:13), but he will only reveal what Christ has given him to say (v.14). Most recent commentators take these words to refer to the ongoing prophetic ministry in the church.[26] (4) He will convict the world of sin and righteousness and judgment (16:8). This is not something the spirit will do independently. He works through Jesus or through the disciples. This rich theology of the Spirit's activity after Jesus is glorified. Burge argues, reflects the rich experience of the Spirit in the Johannine community.[27]

In John's Gospel, historic Israel is viewed entirely negatively, Jesus came as the Jewish Messiah, but as the Jewish rejection was so pervasive, the Jews have now been rejected by God. They are no longer the children of God: this honour is now given to those who believe in Christ. This viewpoint is first introduced in the prologue. John writes, "He came to his own home and his own people received him not. But to all who received him, who believed in his name, he gave power to become children of God" (1:11-12).

What we see in the fourth Gospel is a profound linking of Christology and ecclesiology, Jesus as the Jewish Messiah comes to his own people, but they reject him and so he calls all those who believe to become children of God (1: 11-12). Into a bond of personal communion, knowledge, and love, those who respond are united with Christ. They are the new people of God. Pryor, in his study on the narratives and themes in John's Gospel, argues that these themes reflect Jeremiah's prophecy of the new covenant (Jer. 31: 31-34), indicating that the evangelist is claiming that Jesus has inaugurated this, and thereby brought into existence the new covenant community. John does not use the word covenant, but Pryor is able to demonstrate that covenant ideas pervade this Gospel. He concludes that John presents the Christian community as "The

---

25 R. Schnackenburg, *The Gospel According to St John,* Vol. 3 (New York, NY: Crossroad, 1982), 83.

26 Burge, *The Annointed Community*, 214-215.

27 Burge, *The Annointed Community*, 150.

true, eschatological people of God gathered by their covenant Lord, Jesus."[28] For Pryor, the claim to be "true Israel" means that John wants to show that the Christian community has displayed the old.[29] It is now claiming for itself the exclusive status of the people of God'.[30]

2.3.1.3. Mark's Gospel

Christology and discipleship are the twin themes around which Mark develops his narrative. The evangelist says nothing directly about the church of his own day, but the way in which he presents the disciples, especially in relation to Jesus, discloses something of Mark's own beliefs about the post-Easter Christian community.[31] This community confesses Jesus as the Christ (1:1; 8:31), interpreting his Messiah-ship mainly in terms of divine sonship (1:1, 11, 12-13; 8:27-32; 14:61-64); to this community Jesus has community expects that Christ as the son of Man will soon return (13:28-30; 35-37), although no one knows exactly when this will be (13:32).[32] While Mark allows that many responded to Jesus' call to repentance and faith, he usually has the twelve in mind when he speaks of 'the disciples'. They are the Jesus community in the telling of his story.[33] Between the disciples gathered around Jesus and the Jewish crowds who listen to his teaching, there is a clear line of demarcation (4:34) and often antagonism. Jack Kingsbury has well described Mark as a story about 'conflict'.[34] Jesus main opponents are the Jewish leaders who represent the people of Israel; they oppose him at every point

28 J. W. Pryor, John: *Evangelist of the Covenant People* (Downers Grove: IVP, 1992), 157.

29 Pryor, *John,* 160.

30 Ibid., 166.

31 See H. Kee, *Community of the New Age* (Philadelphia: Westminster, 1977); E. Best, *Discipleship in Mark's Gospel* (ShefieldL JSOT, 1981); C. C. Black, *The Disciples According to Mark* (Sheffield: JSOT, 1989); E. J. Mantera, *What are they Saying about Mark* (New York, NY: Paulist, 1987), 36-55.

32 Kee, *Community of the New Age,* 116-140.

33 Best, *Discipleship,* 243.

34 J. Kingsbury, *Conflict in Mark* (Minneapolis: Fortress, 1989).

and eventually have him put to death. Yet this is not the end of the story. In this final drama he makes atonement for sins, replaces the temple as the place of salvation, and becomes the founder and ruler of God's end-time people.[35]

According to Kee, "in every case the images employed in Mark to represent Christian existence are corporate".[36] The call to follow is made to individuals, but the followers then assume a collective identity. They become members of the eschatological family (3:20f; 10: 28-31); sheep in God's flock (6:34); part of the new vineyard (12:1-11); the community of the new covenant (14:24). Kee concludes from the uses of these titles that the 'central feature' of the Marcan understanding of the identity of Jesus' followers is that they are 'the people of God'.[37] Mark is clear that any leadership given in this community must be modeled on that of Jesus himself, and involve humble self-giving; but apart from this principle, virtually nothing can be discovered about the organization or communal life of the Marcan church.[38] From a sociological perspective, Kee concludes that Mark's community may be described as an "apocalyptic sect': a true Israel, anticipating the end in the near future, firm in the belief that divine truths not known to others had been revealed to them and active in evangelism.[39]

2.3.1.4. Luke's Gospel

Luke's understanding of the church will be treated in detail in Acts; however, at this juncture a few comments on the ecclesiology of the third Gospel are given. Luke is far less critical of the disciples' incomprehension (e.g., Mark 7:18, 8:21; 9:20), and attributes others to the fact that 'the meaning was hidden from them' (9:45; 18: 34), or that it was due to the prophetic ordering of things (Acts. 1:6). He also makes a clear distinction between the inner core of

35 Kingsbury, *Conflict in Mark*, 88.

36 Kee, *Community of the New Age*, 107.

37 Ibid.

38 Ibid., 152.

39 Ibid., 144.

disciples whom he regularly calls 'the apostles (6:15; 9:10), and a much larger outer circle of disciples (6: 13, 17), something not spelt out in Mark. By doing this he prepares for the Acts narrative where the twelve apostles' become the chief witnesses of the life, ministry, death, and resurrection of Jesus and the founding nucleus of the new Jesus community. The Marcan Christological titles are found with some additions in Luke, but he differs from Mark by allowing the characteristic post-Easter confession of Jesus as Lord to define discipleship (2:11, 24:34). The Christian community comprises those who recognize Jesus as the Lord.[40]

In Luke's Gospel, the disciples are clearly differentiated from those who do not respond to Jesus. They are depicted as a distinct community who confess Jesus as Lord, and are called to suffer with him. However, Luke does not suggest that a clear breach with Israel has occurred. Thus he does not have Mark's emphasis on Jesus as the teacher only of the twelve. In Luke, Jesus' proclamation is in the hearing of the people (7:1). In this Gospel, the designation *laos*-the people of God- remains the special preserve of the Jewish people, whether they be followers of Jesus or not. Yet this pro-Jewish orientation' is not the full picture. In a carefully nuanced discussion of Luke's understanding of the identity of the Christian community, Robert Maddox points out that in the third Gospel there is also to be seen an 'anti Jewish orientation' and 'a gentle orientation'.[41] Thus he notes that right from the beginning of his Gospel (1:5-2:40), Luke has Israel being divided in the light of its response to God's visitation in Jesus.[42] This is seen to be taking place in the travel narrative (9:51-19:27), where the recurring theme is the judgment of Israel for its hardness of heart. More recently, Kingsbury has come to a similar conclusion. He writes, "Luke's story is primarily a story of conflict between Jesus and Israel, made up of the religious authorities and the

40 K. N. Giles, "The church in the Gospel of Luke" *SJT*, Vol. 34 (1981), 133-135.

41 R. Maddox,, *The Purpose of Luke-Acts* (Edinburgh: T & T Clark, 1982), 31-54.

42 Ibid., 36.

people. Jesus' conflict with the people is to win their allegiance. Jesus' conflict with the authorities is over "authority" and who rule God's People.[43] It has often been suggested that Luke's Gospel betrays a 'universalistic outlook', not found in other Synoptic Gospels, that is welcoming of gentiles, but this claim needs to be critically examined. It is true that Luke begins his Gospel by anticipating their inclusion within the people of God, Israel, concludes with the command to the disciples to preach repentance and forgiveness of sins 'to all nations' (24:47), and has a few hints of a positive attitude to the gentile mission. Yet it is not true to say that Luke has Jesus initiating the gentile mission before Easter. He leaves this matter until he writes the Book of Acts. If there are these three 'orientations' to be detected in Lucan thought- one apparently affirming the continuing place of Israel in the purposes of God, one speaking the rejection of historic Israel, and one open to the salvation of gentiles- then the relationship between Israel as a national identity and the followers of Jesus as another distinct entity is a complex one. In our discussion of this in the next chapter, we conclude that Luke sees the church emerging out of Israel, with the initial membership of the new community. It is only as Israel hardens its heart and opposes the gospel that Luke has God directing the mission to the gentiles. As a consequence, a new entity emerges that transcends the old division between Jew and gentile, 'the church of the Lord' (Acts 20:28). This conception of the church as restored Israel', Jervell maintains, takes us right to the heart of Luke's unique ecclesiology.[44]

2.3.2. *Ekklesia in the Book of Acts*

The Book of Acts makes a significant contribution to the development of a theology of the church because Luke writes both as a theologian and as a historian. As a historian, he sets out to tell his readers the story of the first decades of the Christian mission, and as a theologian he deliberately brings his own views to the fore. We thus have both a selective account of what took place in the years following the first

---

43 Kingsbury, *Conflict in Luke*, 71.

44 J. Jervell, *Luke and the People of God* (Minnesota: Augsburg, 1972), 95.

Easter, and comment on what Luke thought about this. In putting pen to paper, Luke hopes to confirm the faith of those who have part of the Jesus community, and to help others make the decisive step demanded of those who would be members of this community.[45] The Jesus community, which we call the church, is a prime concern of Luke's writing. He highlights its post-Easter beginnings on the day of Pentecost, emphasizes its empowerment by the Holy Spirit, describes its corporate life, shows how its leadership emerged and developed, and struggles to define it in relation to historic Israel from which it sprang.

One of the special features of the Book of Acts is the collective title for Christians used by Luke.[46] After the brethren and the disciples, the term *ekklesia* is the next most common collective title for believers. Some nineteen times it is used of Christians. In classical Greek, this word was used only of an actual 'assembly' of citizens. An *ekklesia* existed while the people were gathered. In Acts 19: 32, 39, 41; Luke uses the word in this way to speak of an unbelieving mob that has assembled in the stadium at Ephesus. When they went home, this gathering or assembly ceased to exist. The fact that Luke can use this important theological term, *ekklesia*, in a secular context in its classical sense is not at all surprising, for Luke and other NT writers frequently. This means we should no more derive Luke's Christian meaning of the term *ekklesia* from the Acts 19 uses than we should derive the Christian meaning of *sodzo*/save from his usage of this term in Acts 27:20 and 31, where it refers to rescue from drowning.

The early Christians first used the word *ekklesia* simply to refer to their assemblies, and only with the passing of time did the word develop so as to mean those who assemble a local community, and then later, the world-wide community of Christians.[47]

---

45 R. Maddox, *The Purpose of Luke-Acts*, 12-23.

46 Cadbury has listed and discussed nineteen terms, see H. J. Cadbury, "Names for Christians and Christianity in Acts," in F. J. Foakes-Jackson and K. Lake, eds., *The Beginnings of Christianity*, Vol. 5 (London: Macmillan, 1933), 375-392.

47 Cadbury, "Names for Christians and Christianity in Acts," .in F. J. Foakes-Jackson and K. Lake, eds., *The Beginnings of Christianity*, 375-392.

One special feature of Lucan theology should be noted at this point. Luke has what many have called an 'absentee Christology'.[48] This idea must be carefully qualified because Luke insists that Christ is present through his spirit (16:7) and by his word, but it is true that Luke emphasizes that Jesus is now reigning in heaven, He is ascended Lord who rules over and directs the church on earth. Luke certainly believed that Christians went to heaven when they died (Luke 23:43), but he has no conception whatsoever of a heavenly church. Indeed his theology of the risen Christ as the ascended Lord of the church excludes such an idea. For him, Christ is in heaven and the Christian community is on earth. This reminds us that each NT writer must be understood in terms of his own framework of thought.

The first time Luke uses the word ekklesia of Christians in 5:11, he qualifies it with the adjective 'whole' as he does in 15:22; The word ekklesia in 5:11 is introduced to make a contrast between those who were assembled and saw the judgment on Ananias and Sapphire take place, a small group of in a household setting in all probability, with the whole church-that is, all the Christians in Jerusalem who Luke numbers in the thousands (2:41) who later heard about what had happened.[49] The whole is emphatic as it often is in Luke's writings.[50] It does not add anything to the meaning of the word *ekklesia* in this sentence. The whole church mentioned in 5:11 is the same entity that Luke calls 'the whole group of those who believed' in 4:32 at the commencement of this section of Acts.[51] When Luke speaks of the severe persecution against the church in Jerusalem (8:1), he is again using the word to refer to all the Christians in the city. This is made plain by the words that follow. Using the plural Luke says, 'they were all scattered except the apostles'. All the Christians that is the church except the apostles- were forced to flee Jerusalem. This persecution of the church proceeded as Saul entered house after house; dragging off

48 C. E. D Moule, "The Christology of Acts", in L. E. Keck and J. L. Martyn, eds., *Studies in Luke-Acts* (London: SPCK, 1966), 159f.

49 Giles, *What is on Earth is the Church?*, 84-85.

50 Ibid.

51 Ibid.

both men and women (8:3). The whole Christian community would also seem to be the force of the word in 11: 22 and 12:5. Acts 12:1 is of special interest; here Luke says, Herod the king laid violent hands on some who belonged to the *ekklesia*. A parallel is found in Acts 15:5, where Luke speaks of some who belonged to the party of the Pharisees. In each case, Luke alludes to a substantive group of people who form an identifiable community. As the mission moves beyond Jerusalem, Luke continues to use the word *ekklesia* in the singular (11:26), or the plural when speaking of believers in a number of cities or towns to mean the Christians in that place. Thus in 14:27, he says that Paul and Barnabas gathered the *ekklesia,* a specific group of people, which the context identifies as the Christian in Antioch, were brought together. The same verb is used in 15:30, but in this parallel those gathered together at Antioch are called 'to plethos'- the whole community.'[52] This evidence makes it clear that Luke understood the word *ekklesia* to be a term to designate the Christian community as it was found in particular places. In 7: 38, he suggests that this community in its entirety is restored Israel, called into being by Jesus.

2.3.3. *Ekklesia in Paul's Writings*

One of the richest contributions Paul make to the Christian theology is his profound reflection on the church, which he understood as an abstract speculation but as something which resulted from his own personal experience, right from the beginning of his commitment to Christ. In the question of the Risen Lord to Saul "Why do you persecute me?" and his answer: "I am Jesus whom you are persecuting" (Acts 9: 4-5; 22:7-8; 26: 14-15), we may see the seed of Paul's later understanding of Christ in relation to the church, namely, the close relationship between Christ and the believers who constitute the church.

However, Paul nowhere spells out a systematic theology of the church, for all his writings are occasional letters answering particular problems facing the Christians to whom he writes; but time and

52 Giles, *What is on Earth is the Church*, 85.

time again we find him explaining his converts what it means to be a distinct community in a hostile world. Men and women received the gospel as individuals, but always involved, as far as Paul was concerned, a crossover from one community to another. Communal thinking pervades Paul's writings and is expressed in many ways. One key term the apostle uses when speaking of this community is *ekklesia.* Pauline usage of the term *ekklesia* may be discussed as follows:

2.3.3.1. All the Christians in one location

Paul, when addressing a specific group of Christians, he can locate them geographically and theologically. Thus he writes to the "church of God that is in Corinth... in Christ Jesus" (1Cor. 1:2), and to "the church of the Thessalonians in God the Father and in the Lord Jesus Christ' (1Thes. 1:1). The Christians of Thessalonica are not those called to a temporary assembly, but to a permanent union with God the Father and Jesus Christ. In some cases, however, (e.g, 2 Cor.1:1; Rom 16:1), Paul only mentions a geographical marker. The theological status of those called the church is possibly brought out most clearly in 1 Corinthians 1:2. In writing to the Corinthians, he gives this one group of people three titles. They are 'the church of God in Corinth', 'those sanctified in Christ Jesus' and 'saints by God's call'. For Giles, while addressing to the Corinthians, Paul is calling the believing community the true people of God.[53]

2.3.3.2. A Small Christian group who regularly meet together in a home

Just as ten or more male Jews meeting in a home could form a synagogue, so too Paul considered a group of Christians meeting in a home an *ekklesia* (Rom. 16:5; 1 Cor. 16:19). A home setting was the normal context for the early Christians to meet; here, teaching, prophecy, and mutual ministry took place and the Eucharist was celebrated. There were no doubt fraternal relationships with those

53 Giles, *What on Earth is the Church?*, 115.

in other house churches in the one city, and possibly when numbers were small, combined meetings may have taken place; but these house churches were not sub-groups of some larger organized church, like home groups may be today. In Paul's writings the use of the word ekklesia refers to what Protestants would call today 'the local church' or 'the congregation'. The members were an expression of the body of Christ, corporately united with their Lord and united together by the Spirit. [54] For example, he sends a greeting to the church that meets in the home of Priscilla and Aquila (Rom. 16:3-4), and passes on a greeting from the church hosted by the same couple at an earlier period when they were in Corinth (1 Cor. 16:19), and he writes to the church in your house in the epistle to Philemon (Philem. 2).

2.3.3.3. A Christian Gathering

In a limited number of examples, all in the later chapters of 1 Corinthians, Paul uses ekklesia in almost a classical Greek sense, alluding to Christians actually assembled (11:18; 14: 19). He speaks of what they should do when they come together 'in church' – that is, 'in assembly'. Those who minimize the theological content in the word ekklesia usually find here the key to Paul's use of the word.[55] It is argued that from this usage Paul comes to think of the church as 'those who assemble'. This argument is not convincing. Paul has identified the church as true Israel (1:2), as a distinct people in this world (10:32), and the body of Christ (12:12-13). These verses therefore mean 'when you gather together as God's people, when the body of Christ is actualized ... this is how you should behave."[56]

The word *ekklesia* was used by Paul to refer to the gatherings of Christians both in a particular place, such as a house and of all the Christians in a city.[57] In the Acts of apostles *ekklesia* is also used both of

54 Giles, *What on Earth is the Church?*, 116.

55 Ibid., 117.

56 Ibid.

57 Paul sends greetings to Nympha and the church in her house (Col. 4:15). In Thessalonica, he speaks of the church of the Thessalonians (1Thess, 1:1; 2 Thess. 1:1).

believers in a single locality and of believers everywhere. The *ekklesia* in Jerusalem was the local church in the city, but it was also the whole church (Acts 5: 11). As the gospel advances beyond Jerusalem and Judea we find ekklesia used in two ways, of the whole brotherhood and of a local community. In the four Gospels there are only two occurrences of the word *ekklesia,* both in Matthew.[58] *Ekklesia* was first used of the Christian community, which had been gathered at Jerusalem by the preaching of the Apostles.[59] This community consisted of those who, with the Apostles, had accepted the belief that Jesus was the Messiah, had been baptized and had received the forgiveness of sins and the gift of the Holy Ghost. This community continues at first as a sect within Judaism, attending the Temple, but unlike the unbelieving Jews, they are eschatological community, which as such has already received the spirit of the Messiah. In short, we may say that the church is a group of people whose lives had been touched and transformed by the gospel of Jesus Christ. In other words, 'church' means a group of people who find themselves in a new relationship with one another because of their new relationship with Christ. The whole thrust of the New Testament is that the *ekklesia* is the community, fellowship of the risen Christ.

2.3.4. *The Nature of the Church in the NT*

We find nothing in the way of a formal definition of the church. The New Testament is not a textbook of dogmatic theology. Rather we find that certain wide-ranging themes like people of God and fellowship of the spirit are employed in speaking of the relation of the believers to Christ and to one another, and that the various

58 Matthew 16: 18 and Matthew 18: 17. The first text is a text, which later became crucial because of the claim that the primacy, which it appears to give to Peter among the apostles, devolves upon the bishop. The latter text prescribes the role of the *ekklesia* in cases of dispute among the faithful.

59 Jean Danielou and Henri Marrou, *The Christian Century, Vol. One: The First Six Hundred Years* (London: Darton, Longman and Todd, 1979), 12.

writers use different striking metaphors and imageries.[60] This multiplicity of ecclesiology in the New Testament was brought to the notice of Christian leaders at the Montreal Conference on Faith and Order (1963), where Ernst Kasemann gave a lecture on 'Unity and Multiplicity in the New Testament Doctrine of the Church'.[61] In his lecture, Kasemann argued that the New Testament does not present a unified understanding of the church, but rather 'a number of eccleciological archetypes' and 'an incessant process of change'.[62] Raymond Brown, the Roman Catholic scholar, has come to a similar conclusion.[63]

This research has proceeded on the premise that some constants and foundational beliefs can be discovered in relation to the church. In what follows, an attempt is made to draw together some key themes that can give direction and inspiration for a renewing theology of the church for today by summarizing our research of the communal thinking of the contributors to the New Testament.

---

60 The NT is rich in imagery of the church. There is the salt of the earth, a letter from Christ, fish and fish net, the boat and the ark; unleavened bread, one loaf, the table of the Lord, the alter, the cup of the Lord, wine, branches of the vine, vineyard, the fig tree, the olive tree, God's planting, God's building, the building on the rock, the pillar and buttress. Again, there is the mother of the Messiah, the elect Lady, the bride of Christ, virgins, the wedding feast; wearers of white robes or a choice of clothing. To this we can add: citizens, exiles, the dispersion, ambassadors, the poor, hosts and guests, the people of God, Israel, a chosen race, a holy nation, twelve tribes, the patriarchs, circumcision, Abraham's sons, the Exodus, the house of David, the remnant, the elect; a flock, lambs who rule; the holy city, the holy temple. For a detailed list see Geoffrey Preston, O. P., *Faces of the Church: Meditations on a Mystery and Its Images* (Edinburgh: T & T Clark, 1997), 3.

61 The lecture was published in Ernst Kasemann, *New Testament Questions for Today* (London: SCM, 1967).

62 Kasemann, *New Testament Questions for Today*, 255.

63 R. Brown, *The Churches the Apostles Left Behind* (London: Chapman, 1984).

2.3.4.1. The Church as the People of God

George Johnston mentions that the Greek word *laos* "particularly denotes the people of Israel, God's chosen people.[64] But it was not generally adopted: national limitations probably caused as rejection. Hebrews 4:9 and 1 Peter 2: 9-10 are the only New Testament instances of its application to the Christian community. Yet many New Testament writers use language, which suggest that they thought of Christians as the continuance, renewal, and enlargement of God's chosen people. For Paul, those who belong to Christ are 'Abraham's offspring, heirs according to promise' (Gal. 3: 29). The Epistle of James is addressed to the twelve tribes in the dispersion and 1 Peter to the exiles of the dispersion in Pontus, Galatia, Cappadocia, Asia and Bithynia. In 1Peter 2: 9-10 we find several designations of the Church, which are used in the OT of ancient Israel.[65] The Messiahship of Jesus and Paul's image of the olive tree (Rom. 11:17-24) give strong support to the suggestion that New Testament writers conceived of the Christian as the ancient people of God reconstituted, renewed Israel and revivified.

Many scholars have agreed with T. W. Manson[66] in his argument that the New Testament doctrine of the Church rests upon the Old Testament theme that Israel is the elect people of God, bound by a covenant sealed with blood to remain faithful and to keep God's law. The *ekklesia* thus saw itself in continuity with the historical Israelites sense of being called out to be God's own people. A Jew considering joining the *ekklesia* might therefore understand himself or herself called to a commitment parallel to the ancient one establishing a people of God centuries earlier. However, the fundamental difference between the historical people of Israel gathered as ekklesia and that

---

64 George Johnston, *The Doctrine of the New Testament* (Cambridge: University Press, 1943), 43.

65 Compare Deuteronomy 7:6 and 10: 15 with Peter's 'chosen' race; with 'royal priesthood' and 'holy nation' Exodus 19:6; with God's own people Deuteronomy 4: 20, 7:6 and 14:2.

66 T. W. Manson, *The Teaching of Jesus* (Cambridge: University Press, 1931), 234-236.

of Jesus' followers is the criteria for inclusion. It is the case that one of the theological breakthroughs in the early *ekklesia* was that God's people was not based on any kind of inherited social or cultural distinction.[67] As Paul says, "there is no longer Jew or Greek, there is no longer slave or free, there is no longer male or female; for all you are one in Christ Jesus" (Gal. 3:28). The New Testament writers are clear in their understanding that the Jesus event and the coming of the Holy Spirit meant that old boundaries of ethnicity, class and gender had been dissolved. Across every kind of barrier made by human beings, the people of God would understand themselves to comprise a single, worldwide community, responsible for caring and loving each other as Jesus had loved them.

2.3.4.2. The Church as the Body of Christ

Paul in his first letter to Corinthians (12: 12-27) is the earliest passage in which he treats at length the idea of the Church as a body. On the surface it seems that he presents us with a simile- the church is like a body. But there are several indications here that Paul is doing more than suggest a simile. "You are the body of Christ and individually members of it" (v. 27) says more than "you are like a body' or 'you may usefully of yourselves as a kind of body'. The language of verse 12, which opens the passage, is instructive: "for just as the body is one and has many members, and all the members of the body, though many, are one body, so it is with Christ". Paul is saying that Christ possesses many members, those who have been baptized into him and have received the Holy Spirit. Christ is this body. The members, too, are the body of Christ, but only in him; without integration by faith, baptism, and the gift of the Spirit of God they could not be this kind of body, the body of Christ.

There have been many scholarly discussions about whether Paul was using the phrase 'body of Christ' in a simile, metaphorically or analogically. E. Best, who interprets the phrase as a metaphor, provides

67 Wes Howard-Brook, *The Church Before Christianity* (Maryknoll, NY: Orbis Books, 2001), 78.

an example.[68] Whatever difficulties it presents to the modern mind, in reality, Christ, the risen and exalted one is a corporate or inclusive personality. A corporate or inclusive personality is not, indeed, a body which corresponds to any body, animal, human, or societal which can be empirically studied, for it is the body which God has willed before the foundation of the world, the body of the redeemed by and in his eternal son.[69]

The Epistles to the Colossians and Ephesians develop the body of Christ theme further. Colossians declares that God's purpose in the incarnation of his son was the reconciliation with himself of all that is estranged (1: 20). Jesus Christ has done the work of reconciliation in his body of flesh (2:22). In his risen body, 'he is the head of the body, the church: he is the beginning, the firstborn from the dead, that in everything he might be preeminent (1: 18). From this beginning, which is Christ, the body develops, but only as believers hold fast to the Head, from whom the whole body, nourished and knit together through its joints and ligaments, grows with a growth that is from God (2:19). Ephesians at greater length works out the theme of the mystery of God's purpose revealed in Christ and his Church. God's mighty act has brought about that Christ, raised from the dead, has become the head over all things for the church, which is his body, the fullness of him who fills all in all (1:22-23). This body is the body of those who are reconciled to God (2:16), of which Gentiles are now fellow members (3:6). It is a body, which is to grow to maturity, the maturity of Christ the head (4:11-12).

The Church as the body of Christ denotes the *corporate* dimension of the Church. The relationship between Christ and Church is determined in a twofold way. On the one hand Christ is directly united with the body, i.e., the church. On the other, Christ is the head of the church. The church is not static but a living organism. The church is not only founded on Christ; at the same time it has Christ as the one to whom it stands in relation and as the goal of its growth.

---

68 Ernest Best, *One Body in Christ* (London: SPCK, 1955), 98-101.

69 Ephesians 1: 3-10.

2.3.4.3. The Fellowship[70] of the Holy Spirit

"Do you not know that you are God's temple and that God's Spirit dwells in you" (1 Cor. 3:16). The Church as the Lord's temple is a dwelling place of God in the Spirit (Ephesians 2:22). Concerning the bonds of Christian unity and peace Paul mentions the 'one body' and the 'one Spirit' together. Christians are baptized into the one body by the one spirit (1 Cor. 12:13). The idea of the Holy Spirit as the creator of the Church is already implicit here. G. Johnston is right in affirming that the thought of Paul "God is the father of the Lord Jesus Christ; God's Spirit therefore is Christ's Spirit.[71] For Paul the Spirit of God and the Spirit of Christ is active throughout and from the very beginning of the saving process. The Spirit prompts the Christian confession that Jesus is Lord, and the grace of the Christian life is the fruit of the Spirit, because those who belong to Christ possess His Spirit and are temple of the Spirit of the living God. To be in Christ is to be in the Spirit. Christians are led by the Spirit of God and by the same Spirit becomes aware of membership in the community of the sons of God (Rom. 8: 14-17). They believed themselves to be living in the fellowship of the Spirit. The *koinonia,*[72] of the Spirit' does mean 'participation in the Spirit'. The life of the believer originates with the Holy Spirit. Those who are truly in Christ

---

70 The term 'fellowship' had been adopted by first century Christians, which was widely used in secular ways. The word comes from a fairly common root meaning, "to share with some one in something" See F. Hauck, "Koinonia" *TDNT*, edited by Horst Baz and Gerhard Schnieder (Grand Rapids: Wm. B. Eerdmans, 1993,), 804. It signified to participate in something rather than to share out something to others. In the Greek world it had been used of business partnerships, of the intimate relationship, which the worshipper claimed to have with his god. Although the word fellowship was used in the Greek version of the Old Testament, it was never used by the people of Jews of their relationship with God; it was used only with the other people. John F. Balchin, *I want to know what the Bible says about the Church* (Eastbourne: Kingsway Publications, 1979) J. A. Fitzmeyer translates 'koinonia' as community spirit. See in Everett F. Harrison, *The Apostolic Church,* 104.

71 G. Johnston, *The Doctrine of the Church in the New Testament*, 99.

72 Eric G. Jay, *The Church: Its Changing Image through Twenty Centuries,* Vol. 1 (London: SPCK, 1977), 24.

are in the Spirit and led by the Spirit and walk by the Spirit; so the fruit of the Spirit is seen in their lives, joy, peace, patience, kindness, goodness, faithfulness, gentleness, self-control (Gal. 5:22-23).

The Holy Spirit is also the creator and sustainer of the Church. The account of Pentecost in Acts 2:1ff, which is presented as the fulfillment of Christ promise to clothe his disciples with power from on high[73] testifies to the conviction that the Church is a creation through the act of God in Christ; but it is at the same time a fellowship created by the Holy Spirit.[74] This self understanding, as the fellowship of the spirit is another indication that the early Church thought of itself as the people of god, renewed and living in the day of the Messiah. The messianic kingdom is inaugurated; Joel's prophecy begins to be fulfilled (Acts 2:16) with the outpouring of the Spirit on the Messiah's first followers at Pentecost. To those who by faith and repentance subsequently enter the messianic community the Spirit comes and brings his gifts and graces of which the greatest (1Cor 13:13) is that love which binds everything together in perfect harmony (Col. 3: 14), the unity of the Spirit.

2.3.4.4. The Church as God's building

The Church as God's building is seen in the four Gospels, the Acts, the Pauline Epistles, 1 Peter, the epistle to the Hebrews and Revelation.[75] The building image has roots in the Old Testament. The prophets speak of God's people as 'the house of Israel' or of

---

73 It was at Pentecost that the Lord by the power of His Spirit, welded into a Church. See John F. Balchin, *I Want to Know What the Bible Says About the Church*, Eastbourne: Kingsway Publications, 1979, 13. The Holy Spirit, at the commencement of what is called His mission, collected the disciples into a living unity; and this great work of the Spirit is called the Church, the body of Christ, the temple of the Spirit, the habitation of God in Spirit (Eph. 2:22).

74 Gustaf Aulen, *The Faith of the Christian Church* (London: SPCK, 1954), 329, 333.

75 R. J. McKelvey's book, *The New Temple* (Oxford: Oxford University Press, 1969) provides a thorough examination of the passages in which the temple theme is to be detected.

Jacob. Isaiah 28:16 and Psalm 118: 22-23 introduce the idea of God's building containing a cornerstone. The application of this to the person of Jesus Christ by the early Church helped to suggest the image of the Church as a building whose principal stone is the rejected and crucified, but now risen Lord. Paul quite often speaks of building up the church in his letters to the Corinthians. In Ephesians the idea of building up the Church is combined with the idea of the church as a body (4:12,16). Paul tells the Corinthians that they are God's building. He himself has laid a foundation, and that foundation is Jesus Christ (1Cor. 3:9-15).

There is a division of view about the 'cornerstone'. Some take it to be a stone connected with the foundation of a building; other to be the important locking stone at the crown of the archway above the main entrance of a building.[76] The first interpretation presents the picture of a number of foundation stones, the most important of which is Christ, the others being the apostles and prophets. The second identifies the apostles and prophets as the foundation, and likens Christ to a stone that is the last to be put into position, and which secures the whole building. If the cornerstone, which is Christ, is the last be built in, it is suggested that the building of the Church originated in human enterprise. If the cornerstone Christ is a foundation, the image fails to do justice to the concept of the continuing activity of the risen Christ in the life of the Church. 1 Peter, which also employs this imagery, attempts to overcome its inadequacy by speaking of Christ as the living stone (not lifeless stone) and of Christians as living stones (2:4 &5).

The core of the New Testament ecclesiology can be drawn out of two key terms, *ekklesia* and *Kyrios*. In all languages the equivalent term for the church is derived from either of these two terms. *Ekklesia* means the assembly, gathering, community, and *Kurios* refers to the glorified Lord Jesus Christ. The church is therefore the community of those who believe in and proclaim the lord Jesus. It is the community,

---

76 McKelvey, *The New Temple*, 114, and see also G. Kittel, ed., *Theological Dictionary of the New Testament*, Vol. 1 (Grand Rapids, Michigan: Eerdmans, 1964), 792-793.

which belongs to the Lord. Both the *Ekklesia* dimension and the kyrios dimension belong to the essence of the church. There is no church without Jesus Christ and the community.

One of the main goals of this section has been to bring some clarity and precision to the theological meaning of the word church. We began by putting forward the almost obvious proposition that the church should be defined as 'the community of believers in Christ' or Christian community. On this basis, we have undertaken a detailed analysis of the communal thinking of the apostolic writers (Matthew, Mark, Luke, John and Paul). What we have found is that assuming this definition, all the apostolic writings can be explained and integrated. At every point, this theory made sense of what was given in scripture, and what was given in scripture is confirmed by research work.

2.3.5. *The Structure of the Church*

In the beginning Christianity was a reform movement within Judaism, a sort of Christian Israelites. They felt themselves to be the Easter community of the already exalted Messiah. It was very conscious of its ties with Jerusalem and the temple. In spite of the Lord's instruction to go to Galilee, they settled down in Jerusalem.[77] The separation of Christianity from Judaism is, at root, a matter of the emergence of a new identity. If the earliest Jerusalem community had looked on itself as the messianic Israel, mission produced a nascent communion of Jew and Greek, the beginning of a fellowship to be fully realized in history. By the coming of the new man the wall of division between Jew and the Greek is abolished and the two are made into one.

The early church was a pre-institutional religious movement. Its small communities lacked the worldwide organization, uniform pattern of internal authority, socio-political influence, or even a

77 Jacob, Kavunkal, "Evolution of the Understanding of Christian Identity in the course of the Centuries", in *The Church in India in Search of a New Identity*, edited by Kurien Kunnumpuram SJ, Errol D'Lima SJ and Jacob Parappally MSFS (Bangalore: NBCLC, 1997), 85-86.

national or ethnic identity. It was genuinely a minority movement. The primary characteristic of this church was that it was made up of group of people in a place who have received the Gospel of God,[78] and the Gospel of Christ.[79] However, it was a missionary movement. Church and mission were synonymous. The community lived through mission and for mission. The "Letter to Diognetus", written by an apologist about 129 C.E, illustrates the early church's conviction that every believer is so to live in obedience to Christ that others, seeing their exemplary lives, will want to follow Christ also.[80] It was a mission measured by being rather than doing. The whole church is missionary:

> In the course of conversion and yet converting, at once the subject and object of the mission message, involved on the one hand in an uninterrupted process of growth and extension and on the other tirelessly in fostering this process.[81]

The early Christian churches did not have a uniform ministerial and administrative structure. Apostolic ministry quenched to the early churches was exercised and continued in different ways. The Palestinian Jewish Churches continued the Jewish system of Sanhedrin or the Council of the Elders or Presbyters. The Pauline churches followed spontaneous charismatic leadership and structures. The title "Episcopos" emerged in the Hellenistic circles for the leader of the local church. With the Pastoral Letters of Paul we find a gradual fusion of the Jewish and Hellenistic systems and the emergence of a threefold ministry of *Episcopoi, Presbuteroi* and *Diakonoi,* which first emerged in Asia Minor and became gradually normative for all churches by the beginning of the second century,

78 1 Thes. 2:2, 9.

79 1 Thes. 3:2.

80 Norman E. Thomas (ed), *Classic Texts in Mission and World Christianity* (New York: Orbis Books, 1995), 4.

81 Joseph Schmidlin, *Catholic Mission History* (Techny: Mission Press, 1993), 2.

as witnessed in the Letter of Ignatius of Antioch.[82] However, the Episcopos seen in the letter of Ignatius was not a Monarchical Bishop. He decided everything in the council of Presbyters, and the local Christian communities had a decisive role in the major decision in matters regarding the Christian community, especially in the choice of their leaders. In short, the New Testament speaks of various ministries as functions in the church for the common good and for the building up of the community. Inferior and superior, higher and lower are concepts alien to the perspective of the New Testament, which views ministries in their relation to community and in their diversity. In the church each one has his function; not everyone can do everything (1Cor. 12: 27-30).

3. Ecclesiology in the Second Century

The ecclesiology in the second century Christianity can best be represented and understood by dealing with the writings of the two well-known Church Fathers, namely, Ignatius of Antioch and Irenaeus of Lyon.

3.1. Ecclesiology of Ignatius[83] of Antioch (died c. 115)

Ignatius of Antioch is one of the figures of the church of the early second century. Unlike the other Apostolic Fathers he lays bare

---

82 A detailed treatment of the ecclesiology of Ignatius of Antioch is given in the following section.

83 The Apostolic Father, Ignatius is known from his letters. With regard to the number of his letters, there are two findings, seven letters and thirteen. See L.W. Barnard, "The Background of St. Ignatius of Antioch", *Vigiliae Christianae* 17/4 (December, 1963), 193; Robert B. Eno, S. S, *Teaching Authority in the Early Church* (Wilmington: Michael Glazier, Inc, 1984), 32; and Allen Brent, *Ignatius of Antioch: A Martyr Bishop and the Origin of Episcopacy* (New York, NY: Continuum, 2007), 3 &4. Allen Brent's work is worth noting, he show how Ignatius shaped the idea and theology of the office of a bishop in the Christian church. He provides an account of the circumstances and the cultural context in which Ignatius constructed what became the historic church order of Christendom.

his innermost thoughts and feelings. His letters[84], reveal that he is concerned with the practical details of Church life and order, and these letters contain doctrinal importance in several ways, especially for Christology and ecclesiology. Ignatius uses the New Testament images of the Church, and shares Pauline understanding of the catholicity of the Church. Nevertheless, his main concern is for the Church unity and good order.[85] He is the one who describes the bishop's role incomparable well. In his writings we also come across the threefold ministry in the Church.

Ignatius understood the Church as one, and he was the first to speak of the "Catholic Church". This unity, for him, is not because of the harmony or the good feelings of Christians among themselves, but the presence of Jesus Christ himself in the church. This does not mean, however, that unity is a spiritual realm. Contrary to that it is based on a hierarchy that represents God the Father, Christ, and the Apostles. "Similarly all are to respect the deacons as Jesus Christ, and bishop as a copy of the Father, and the presbyters as the council of God and the band of Apostles. For apart from these no group can be called a Church".[86]

He underlined the importance of the bishop in the Church. For him nothing is to be done in the church without the bishop, and he who is not subject to bishop is not subject to God:

> Shun divisions. Follow the bishop and presbyters, and respect the deacons. Do nothing without the bishop. The eucharist is not valid without his consent. Where the bishop

---

84 A corpus of 13 letters according to Allen Brent were as follows: 1. Ephesians. 2. Romans. 3. Trallians. 4. Magnesians. 5. Philadelphians. 6. Syrnaeans 7. Polycarp. 8. Tarsians. 9. Philippians. 10. Antiochenes. 11. Hero. 12. Mary to Ignatius. 13. Ignatius to Mary.

85 J. F. Bethune-Baker, *An Introduction to the Early History of Christian Doctrine to the Time of the Council of Chalcedon* (London: Methuen & Co. LTD, 1962), 357. See also J. N. D. Kelly, *Early Christian Doctrines*, 1960, Revised Ed. (New York, NY: HarperCollins Publishers, 1978), 190-191.

86 Justo L. Gonzalez, *A History of Christian Thought*, Vol. 1 (Nashville: Abingdon Press, 1983), 76.

> is, there should be the laity be found. It is not allowable to baptize or to hold an agape without him. A ceremony so held is displeasing to God and has no validity.[87]

For him the bishop is seen as the focus of the unity of the local church. Concerning the role of presbyters in the Church, he likens them to the apostles. At all events Ignatius uses *presbuterion* (collective noun for presbytery) and his description of them as a council. In the council they would collaborate with the bishop in matters of church policy and discipline and exercise the function which Ignatius states is particularly fitting for presbyters, is "to cheer the soul of the bishop".[88] He also frequently mentions the existence of deacons in the church, but says little about their functions, for him deacons are entrusted with the service of Jesus Christ. In other words, the work of deacons represents the ministry of Christ and the whole church to the needs and sufferings of men. For him this threefold ministry as patterned on the relationship between God the Father, Jesus Christ, and the apostles. He tried to correlate the bishop with the Father, the Presbyters with the apostles, and the deacons with Jesus Christ, as in Magn. VI:

> Seek to do everything in a divine harmony, under the presidency of the bishop, who takes the place of God, of the Presbyters, who take the place of the senate of the Apostles, and of the deacons, who are dear to me, to whom the service of Jesus Christ has been entrusted. So adopt God's principles: love one another in Jesus Christ.[89]

However, Ignatius is silent about the appointment and commissioned of the posts of bishop and presbyters. For instance, how were the bishop and presbyters chosen and commissioned? Ignatius does not make a clear-cut principle of apostolic succession.

87 Lightfoot, *The Apostolic Fathers*, 308.

88 Eric, G. Jay, *The Church*. 34.

89 Jean Daniel and Henri Marrou, *The Christian Centuries*, 117. And also see Lightfoot, The *Apostolic Fathers*, 118.

But he strongly disclaims the suggestion that the pattern of ministry, which he advocates, is no more than a human invention to counteract schism. For Ignatius, appointment of bishops throughout the world, are according to the will of God.[90]

The writings of St. Ignatius of Antioch attest a stage of development in which the monarchical episcopate occupies a very central place in the ministerial structure. The figure of monarchical bishop portrayed by St. Ignatius of Antioch is that of one who presides over a group of presbyters and is assisted by deacons. Now we have seen the development of two-tiered ministry, namely bishop-presbyter and deacon, to a three-tiered ministry, namely bishop, presbyter and deacon. Judy Schindler has rightly stated that Ignatius had almost complete disregard for the New Testament model.[91] In the early centuries, despite the evolution of ministry into a structure, the spiritual dimension of authority and its theological nature were maintained. The office reflected the mystery of the church and manifested the gifts of the Spirit.

3.2. Ecclesiology of Irenaeus (c. 130-200)

Iranaeus was bishop of Lyon in Gaul in the late second century (177?) when Pothinus was martyred in a persecution during the reign of the Emperor Marcus Aurelus. According to F. A. Christie, Irenaeus was essentially the first theologian who constructed the religion of Jesus in terms of Greek thought and the first to formulate that scheme of salvation necessitated the Nicene-Chalcedonian dogma.[92] His principal surviving work was "The Refutation of False Knowledge", which is known as *Adversus Haerese*[93]. It is mainly a refutation of the teaching and claims of Gnostic teachers. His refutation of Gnostic

90 Eric G. Jay, *The Church*, 31.

91 Judy Schindler, "The Rise of One Bishop-Rule in the Early Church: A Study in the Writings of Ignatius and Cyprian," *Baptist Reformation Review* 10//2 (Second Quarterly 1981), 3-9.

92 F. A. Christie, "An Interpretation of Irenaeus", *The American Journal of Theology* 21/1 (January, 1917), 129.

93 Robert B. Eno, S. S., *Teaching Authority in the Early Church*, 42.

teaching led him to the realm of ecclesiology at which he deals with the Gnostic claim to possess a secret tradition derived from the apostles. It is the church, he insists, which possesses the true apostolic tradition. It is not a secret; it is enshrined in the Scriptures, and is contained also in what he calls the canon of truth, taught openly to all who will in sincerity and humility learn from the Church's authoritative teachers. He summarizes this canon of truth as follows:

> The church, though dispersed throughout the whole world, even to the ends of the earth, has received from the apostles and their disciples this faith: (She believes) in one God, the Father Almighty, Maker of heaven and earth, and the sea, and all things that are in them; and in one Christ Jesus, the son of God, who became incarnated for our salvation; and in the Holy Spirit, who proclaimed through the prophets the dispensations of God, and the advents, and the ascension into heaven in the flesh of the beloved Christ Jesus, our Lord, and His manifestation from heaven in the glory of the Father 'to gather all things in one' (Eph. 1:10) and to raise up anew all flesh of the whole human race, in order that ... He should execute just judgment towards all; that He may send... that angels who transgressed... together with the ungodly... among men into everlasting fire; but may, in the exercise of his grace, confer immortality on the righteous and holy... and may surround them with everlasting glory.[94]

Some of his arguments on the doctrine of the church may be presented as follows:

3.2.1. *The Universality of the Canon of Truth*

Ireaneus claims that these doctrines, summarized in the canon of truth are taught everywhere in the church: "The church, having

94 Alexander Roberts and James Donaldson, eds., *The Ante Nicene Fathers*, Vol. I (Grand Rapids: WM. B. Eerdmans Publishing Company, 1956), 331.

received this preaching and this faith, although scattered throughout the whole world, yet, as if occupying but one house, carefully preserves it... Although the languages of the world are different, yet the import of the tradition is one and the same... in Germany... in Spain... in Gaul... in the east... in Egypt... in Libya".[95]

3.2.2. *The Succession of Bishops*

According to Iranaeus, the substantial identity of the church's canon of truth with the teaching of the apostles is further guaranteed by the unbroken succession in the various local churches of those who are the official guardians and teachers of the canon, the bishops: "It is within the power of all... who may wish to see the truth, to contemplate clearly the tradition of the apostles manifested throughout the whole world; and we are in a position to reckon up those who were by the apostles instituted bishops in the churches, and the successions of these men to our own times."[96] He says that if the apostles had known of 'hidden mysteries' such as the Gnostics claimed to be able to impart, they would surely have transmitted them to the men to who they were entrusting the churches.

3.2.3. *Succession of a See*

It is important to recognize that Iranaeus traces the apostolic succession through the previous holders of a see (*kathedra),* and not through bishops who lay on hands in consecrating. He conceives of each of the important Christian centers as having a *kathedra,* a teaching chair, which must be occupied by one who will faithfully and responsibly guard the canon of truth. When the chair falls vacant, through death or for other reasons, the Church must choose a suitable successor.[97] In argument against Gnostics he concentrates on the bishop's role as the official teacher of the church, the guardian

95 Eno, S. S., *Teaching Authority in the Early Church,* 42.

96 Ibid., 45.

97 Ibid., 42.

of the purity of the canon of truth, who has succeeded to the office in a particular church in direct line from the apostles.

In Irenaeus' doctrine of apostolic succession, it must be noted that although there is no doubt that he uses the word bishop in the sense of the monarchical bishop, however, it is not so clear whether he speaks about the apostolic succession of presbyters or he speaks both of a succession of bishops and of a succession of presbyters.

3.3. Evaluation of the Ecclesiology in the Second Century

From the above discussion on the ecclesiology of the Church Fathers, Ignatius of Antioch and Irenaeus of Lyon, during the second century, we may conclude that both of them trace the foundation of the Church to Jesus Christ and his apostles. They stick to the fundamental teachings of the New Testament, they stress the unity of the Church in terms of its doctrine which is contained in the Scripture and which is expressed in a canon of truth or faith, of which the official guardians and teachers are the bishops who occupy their sees in a succession traceable back to the apostles.

4. Ecclesiology in the Third Century

The third century was a turning point in the development of ecclesiology and the history of Christianity. The ties with Judeo-Christianity were broken, and hereafter it was to be engaged in the Hellenistic and Roman world; but this world was varied. We find movements appearing which were to continue in the Christianity of the following centuries. Three great events characterize this period: In the Greek world there was a philosophical revival, represented by Plotinus among the pagan and Origen among the Christians, and the influence of those thinkers was felt in the succeeding centuries; in the Latin world Christianity underwent an extraordinary expansion both territorial and cultural, and became differentiated from eastern Christianity; finally the Judeo-Christian ascetical movement stirred up various doctrines in eastern Syria.[98] We have, in this century, seen theologians like Tertullian, Origen, and Cyprian who provide

98 Jean Dielou and Henri Marrou, *The Christian Centuries*, 181.

a collection of documents, which give us a clear idea of the church institution at this period. We shall now look into the ecclesiologies of these three famous scholars and theologians, Tertullian, Origen and Cyprian.

4.1. Ecclesiology of Tertullian (c. 160-220)

Tertullian of Carthage was a lawyer and the first theologian who wrote in Latin and laid down guidelines and provided terminology for western theology especially in the area of Trinitarian doctrine, Christology and atonement. Concerning the doctrine of the church his ideas and belief may be presented under two sub-points: The unity of the Church and the apostolic tradition.

Tertullian, like other Church Fathers, uses the New Testament images of the Church. In his *Apologeticus,* he uses the New Testament body imagery to express in a simple way the corporate life of the Church to non-Christian audience. It is the body united by a common profession, discipline and, and hope. Christians meet together in a congregation that they may present their unanimous prayers to God. These include prayers for emperors and those in authority. Their corporate life is expressed both in their own discipline and more outwardly in their charitable ministrations to the poor, orphans, aged and prisoners.[99] He uses also the image of the bride of Christ with the closely connected idea of the church as the mother of the faithful. He speaks of 'our lady mother, the Church'.[100] Following Irenaeus he claims that the Church's unity, is its very essence, consists in its possession of a tradition of doctrine, which he usually refers to as 'the canon of faith', received from the apostles through the succession of the bishops. This, canon of faith, is his weapon against the Gnostics: "...all doctrine which agrees with the apostolic churches, those moulds and original sources of the faith, must be reckoned for truth, as undoubtedly containing that which the churches received

99 Apologeticus xxxix. Cited in Eric G. Jay, *The Church*, 50-51.

100 Eno, S. S., *Teaching Authority in the Early Church,* 42.

from the apostles, the apostles from Christ, Christ from God" (De Praescriptione XXI). [101]

Since the church in Carthage could not claim to have been founded by an apostle, he said that recently founded churches derived the tradition of faith and the seeds of doctrine from churches founded by the apostles, hence both are apostolic. In such churches the substance of preaching and the canon of faith will agree with what is preached and taught in churches founded directly by the apostles. For Tertullian, this is the test to be applied to the churches, which are being founded every day. If they hold the same faith as the churches founded by the apostles are to be reckoned no less apostolic than the churches directly founded by apostles. He further states that the churches in Africa, being founded from Rome, where the apostles Peter and Paul were martyred are, rightly called apostolic.[102]

In response to the Gnostics' claim that their teachings have been handed down from the apostles, Tertullian said that the Gnostics have no such lists, and their teachings are evidently not of apostolic origin, for their teaching are so contradictory among themselves and so diverse from the teachings of apostles. On the other hand, the teaching of apostles is well known. It is that 'canon of faith' (Tertullian), identical in substance with the 'canon of truth' (Iranaeus) and the 'teaching of the church' (Origen). However, when Tertullian became a Motanist or sympathizer of Montanism[103], he sees the Church in a different light. He now defines the Church as a society of the Spirit; its members are spiritual men and women.

---

101 Quoted from *The Ante-Nicene Christian Library*, Vols. III & IV, by Eric G. Jay, *The Church*, 51.

102 Eric G. Jay, *The Church*, 51.

103 Round about 206 Tertullian left the Church and joined the Montanist sect, a group of 'puritans', who reacted against what they perceived as lax morals among Christians. They expected the Second Coming to occur soon and emphasized the immediate leadership of the Holy Spirit, not the ordained clergy. See A. Kenneth Curtis, J. Stephen Lang and Randy Petersen, *The 100 Most Important Events in Christian History* (Grand Rapids: Fleming H. Ravell, 2003), 25.

> The very church itself is properly and principally, the Spirit Himself, in whom is the Trinity of the One divinity-Father, Son and Holy Spirit. The Spirit combines that Church which the Lord has made to consist in three. And thus, from that time forward, every number who may have combined together into this faith is accounted a church, form the author and Consecrator. And accordingly the church, it is true, will forgive sins: but the church of the Spirit by means of a spiritual man, not the Church which consists of a number of bishops (De Pudicitia XXI).[104]

In commenting on Tertullian's statement, R. C. Moberly states that while Tertullian's main positive is a truth immovable and of priceless value, his negative inference is an exaggeration and an untruth. According to Eric G. Jay, by the 'positive' means the concept of the Church as the creation of God the Father through the Son in the power of the Holy Spirit to be the body of the Spirit's presence. By 'negative inference' he means Tertullian's apparent conclusion that the ministerial structure of bishops, presbyters, and deacons have no place in the church. Eric Jay does not agree with Moberly to conclude that Tertullian repudiates the Episcopal system. For Eric G. Jay, it is as a Montanist that Tertullian appealed to the principle of apostolic succession against the teaching of Marcion. His conclusion is that "Tertullian was protesting not so much against the idea of ministerial order as such as against the failure of bishops, whether by laxity or by officialism, to be what they should have been. Such protests have been needed."[105] What is obvious here is that as Raymond Panikkar[106] states that to constitute a Church three dimensions, mystical (spiritual), historical and sociological are necessary; it seems that Tertullian's statement lost the balance of these three dimensions and focuses only on the mystical aspect of the Church.

---

104 Cited by Eric G. Jay, *The Church*, 54.

105 Ibid.

106 R. Panikkar, "The Dream of an Indian Ecclesiology", in *Searching for Indian Ecclesiology*, edited by Gerwin van Leeuwen (Bangalore: Asian Trading Corporation, 1984), 24-25.

4.2. Ecclesiology of Origen[107] (c. 185-255)

According to Fred Gladstone Bratton, Origen was trained in the eclectic school of Alexandria, and he possessed a balanced mind in which the intellectual did not destroy the spiritual.[108] In the first half of the third century a new intellectual movement appeared in Alexandria known as Neo-Platonism. Its chief exponent was Plotinus, and his Christian counterpart was Origen, he represents a transition from Middle Platonism to Neo-Platonism.[109] It is generally agreed that most of the Christian Fathers in this period were not interested to contemporary philosophies. It was Origen, who tried to relate Christianity to the science and philosophy of his day. He believed that Greek philosophy was a preparation for understanding Scripture.[110] He made an attempt to interpret and systematize the faith by using well-known principles of interpretation (typology and allegory), philosophical categories to present revelation for the first time in a scientific form.[111]

4.2.1. *The Church as Historical Institution*

He believed that the church as the guardian of the teaching of the apostles which has been passed on through the apostolic succession: "The teaching of the Church has indeed handed down through an order of succession from the Apostles, and remains in the Church even

---

107 Origen is one of the most appealing characters in history. By birth and education he belonged to the Catechetical Christian tradition and his work was one of the most important formulations of that tradition. He represents a transition from Middle Platonism to Neo Platonism. It was under Origen that the school of Alexandria reached its peak. See Williams A Jurgens, *The Faith of the Fathers*, Vol. 1. (Bangalore: Theological Publication in India, 2000), 189-214.

108 Fred Gladstone Bratton, "The First Christian Liberal." *Journal of Bible and Religion* 8/3 (August, 1940), 137.

109 Jean Dielou and Henri Marrou, *The Christian Centuries*, 159.

110 A. Kenneth Curtis, Stephen Lang and Randy Peterson, *The 100 Most Important Events in Christian History*, 27.

111 Peter Stockmeyer, "Early Church", in *Encyclopedia of Theology*, edited by Karl Rahner (Freiburg: Burns and Oates, 1986), 379.

to the present time. That alone is to be believed as the truth... "[112] He prepared 'the teaching of the Church', which is strikingly similar in substance to the 'canon of truth' as made by Iraneaus and the 'canon of faith' of Tertullian.

Concerning ministerial structure, for Origen the Church is an organized community with a properly constituted ministry of priests, to whose appointment the local congregation must give consent, and at whose ordination the presence of the people is required, so that they may all know and be certain that the man elected to the priesthood stands out from all the people in learning, holiness, and eminence in every kind of virtue. Origen has much to way of the responsibilities of the Church's ministers. The bishops who like Peter have received the keys of the Kingdom, the disciplinary authority to bind and loose, must themselves be men of Peter's quality such that Christ may build the Church upon them. On the other hand, 'priesthood of every member of the Church' is expressed by Origen: "Do you not know that the priesthood is given to you also, that is to the whole Church of God, the people who believe?' All therefore 'must offer to God sacrifice of praise, prayers, pity, righteousness, and holiness'.[113]

Origen does not fail to notice the shortcomings of the Church and its members, he says: I can confidently say that the treasury of the Lord is his Church, and in that treasury ... there often lurk men who are vessels of wrath ...chaff with the grain, and fish which have to be thrown out and destroyed together with good fish which have all come into the net (Homillies on Jeremiah XX. 3).[114] In another homily he uses the parable of the tares and wheat in a similar fashion: "It is impossible for the Church to be entirely purified while it is on earth. Open sinners may be excommunicated, but there remain those whose sins are secret."[115] This led him to distinguish between the empirical Church and the spiritual. The latter is the true Church,

112 Williams A. Jurgens, *The Faith of the Fathers...*, 190.

113 Eric G. Jay, *The Church*, 61, quoted from *Contra Celsum* III. 51.

114 Jay, *The Church*, 62.

115 Ibid.

which the Epistle to the Ephesians describes as 'without spot and wrinkle... holy and without blemish'.[116] It is the assembly of the saints whereas the empirical Church is the assembly of believers.[117] For him this true church is also the heavenly Church and he holds that it existed before the creation of the world. He argues that this is implicit in what is said in the Epistle to the Ephesians about the Church. He goes on saying that Paul (Eph. 2:20) says that the Church is built on the foundation of the prophets as well as the apostles. He interprets 'prophets as those of the O.T among whom he includes Adam.[118] Moreover, Ephesian 5:25 ff also implies the preexistence of the Church. Eric G. Jay comments that the Platonic doctrine of Forms (that earthly entities and the institutions are imperfect copies of heavenly realities) has influenced Origen's ecclesiology.

4.3. *Ecclesiology of Cyprian*[119] *(Bishop of Carthage 248-258)*

Cyprian was a contemporary of Origen. Origen and Cyprian represent two divergent trends in Christian thinking, the authority of the spiritual and the authority of office, the Gnostic and the hierarchical self consciousness, Origen associated with the Greek and Cyprian with the Roman tradition.[120] Cyprian became a bishop of Carthage in 248. Throughout his episcopate he was faced with urgent pastoral problems. In his ecclesiology there is tension between the rigorist disciples of Tertullian and the sensitive pastor.[121]

116 Jay, *The Church*, 62.

117 Ibid.

118 Ibid., 63.

119 Caecilius Cyprianus was a wealthy, cultured pagan born around 200. When he became a Christian, he forsook his former life style, gave his goods and money to the poor and took a vow of chastity. He had training in Greek and Roman classics. More detail about him can be obtained from Maurice Bevenot, S. J., *Cyprian De Lapsis and De Ecclesiae Catholica Unitate* (Oxford: Clarendon Press, 1971).

120 Campenhausen, *Ecclesiastical Authority and Spiritual Power*, 265.

121 R. F. Evans, *One and Holy* (London: SPCK, 1972), 64.

Shortly after his election as bishop of Carthage, the persecution of Christian occurred due to the instigation from the Emperor Decius. Even though it was not of long duration, it was very fierce, especially in Rome and North Africa. Under this persecution many Christians had yielded to the demand to throw incense into braziers before the statues of the gods of Rome or the Emperor. When the persecution was over, the question of readmitting the lapsed to communion was vigorously disputed. There were diverse views on this issue in the western churches. In order to solve the problem, Cyprian called a council of North African bishops in 251 at Carthage and he read his landmark work, *On the Unity of the Church,* which had a profound impact on church history. In order to place Cyprian's ecclesiology in its context, it is appropriate to briefly look at Novatian ecclesiology, which compelled Cyprian to work on his ecclesiology.

4.3.1. *Novatian*[122] *Ecclesiology*

Novatians, upholding the full rigour of the ancient disciplinary rules of the Church, argued that a Church that included lapsed or was willing to receive them to communion ceased to be a church because it lacked the mark of holiness. Apostasy corrupts the Church to the point of extinction. This ecclesiology finds the essence of the church in its holiness, and its members determine its holiness. The vulnerability of such an ecclesiology lies in the difficulty of setting a standard of holiness. Novatians placed the emphasis on freedom from apostasy, but they appeared to be unmindful of the seriousness of other forms of ungodliness. It was in this situation that Cyprian says: "This is a worse crime than that which the lapsed seem to have

---

122 Under Cornelius, bishop of Rome, there was a man of outstanding ability, Novatian who challenged the bishop on the issue of the readmission of the lapsed into the communion. At Carthage, there were presbyters, who curried favour with the unrepenting lapsed, formed against the bishop under the leadership of a deacon named Felicissimus. More detail see in J. Jayakiran Sebastian, *"Baptisma Unum in Sancta Ecclesia" A Theological Appraisal of the Baptismal Controversy in the Work and Writings of Cyprian of Carthage* (Delhi: ISPCK, 1997), 47-49. And also Bevenot, *Cyprian De Lapsis and de Ecclesiae Catholica Unitate*, x & xi.

fallen into who nevertheless, standing as penitents for their crime, beseech God with full satisfaction...he who has lapsed has only injured himself; on other, he who has endeavored to cause a heresy or a schism has deceived many by drawing them with him... while the lapsed has sinned but once, he sins daily" (De Ecclesiae 19).[123] We shall now look into the ecclesiology of Cyprian.

4.3.2. *The Unity of the Catholic Church*[124]

The summary of his idea on the Unity of the church may be presented as follows: The Church is a divine institution, the Bride of Christ. Only in the Church can people have salvation; outside it is darkness and confusion. Beyond the church, sacraments and pastors- even the Bible have no significance. An individual cannot live the Christian life through direct contact with God; he needs the Church. Since Christ established the church on Peter the rock, all bishops were in some sense successors of Peter and as such, should be obeyed. His statements like "Outside the church there is no salvation" and "He cannot have God for his Father who has not the Church for his mother" place a great importance.

4.3.3. *The Principle of Unity*

"The authority of the bishops forms a unity, of which each holds his part in its totality."[125] Interestingly, Novatians were theologically orthodox; they accepted the 'canon of faith'. But it was no longer sufficient to insist that the basis of unity was the orthodox faith, the teaching of the apostles. Cyprian now maintains that the basis of unity is the episcopate. Novatianists claimed to have the episcopate; their bishops as well had been validly consecrated. Nevertheless it was Cyprian's contention that they were not bishops. He said that

123 Ibid., Bevenot, *Cyprian De Lapsis and de Ecclesiae Catholica Unitate*, 89.

124 "Cyprian", *Ante-Nicene Fathers*, Vol. V, edited by Alexander Roberts and James Donaldson (Buffalo: The Christian Literature Company, 1886), 421-429. And see also Maurice Bevenot, S. J., *Cyprian De Lapsis and De Ecclesiae Catholica Unitate* (Oxford: Clarendon Press, 1971), 56-99.

125 Bevenot, *Cyprian De Lapsis and de Ecclesiae Catholica Unitate*, 65.

the bishop's throne is not vacant when Maximus was consecrated as a bishop in opposition. It is to be noted that Cyprian is working here with the concept that the succession of a bishop is to be traced not through the bishops who consecrated him, but through his predecessors in office. After disposing of their claim to have bishops, Cyprian insists that it is the possession of the episcopate, which gives unity to the church:

> You ought to know that the bishop is in the Church, and the Church in the bishop; and if any one be not with the bishop, that he is not in the Church. The Church, which is Catholic and one, is not cut or divided but is indeed connected and bound together by the cement of priests who cohere with one another.[126]

Cyprian presents his conception of the Church positively and systematically in his writing. The argument is that for him the Church is one. "The church forms a unity, however far she spreads and multiplies by the progeny of her fecundity."[127] He alludes to Paul's witness to the oneness of the Church in Ephesians 4:4-6, and claims that this unity, first given to the Church in Peter and the apostles, is now manifested in the episcopate. As the apostles formed a corporate body, so also does the episcopate, and the episcopate is one. Concerning the oneness of episcopate for Cyprian is, as commented by J. N. D. Kelly[128], that it is rider to this doctrine that each bishop is entitled to hold his own views and to administer his own diocese accordingly, and that the principle of charitable respect for each other's opinion must be maintained.

Cyprian's concept of the Church and its ministry is a fuller development of what we found in Ignatius of Antioch, Iranaeus, and

126 Ep. LXVIII, & LXVI. These passages strongly implies that Peter and the other apostles were the first bishops. Cyprian took a crucial step in the history of thought about the episcopate: the Apostles themselves were the first bishops of the Church. See R. F. Evans, *One and Holy*, 49.

127 Bevenot, *Cyprian De Lapsis and de Ecclesiae Catholica Unitate,* 65.

128 J. N. D. Kelly, *Early Christian Doctrine* (London: Black, 1958), 205.

Tertullian. Cyprian does not follow the Alexandrians into speculations about an ideal Church; his concern is the empirical, geographical extended Church. In this domain its essential nature and unity must be realized and maintained. This unity is indeed fruitful of great variety. He illustrates this by the sun and its many rays, the tree and its many boughs, the fountain and its many streams. The Church is also the fruitful mother of Christians. But she is also the spouse of Christ who cannot be adulterous (De Unitate). He also uses the Noah's ark image, but in a distinctly new way. He uses this mage for the explanation of the scope of salvation: "If any one could escape who was outside the ark of Noah, then he also may escape who shall be outside of the Church". Thus, for Cyprian the schismatic bodies, whatever reason, separates itself are not part of the Church and outside the possibility of salvation.[129]

4.4. Evaluation of Ecclesiology in the Third Century

In the third century, ministerial structures get firmly stabilized as a hierarchical order. However, the mystical dimension of the church and spiritual character of its ministry dominant in the first and second centuries are not forgotten. They try to harmonize or at least balance the hierarchical order by the conception of the church as a Spirit-filled community of believers. But, in fact, the balance had begun to lean on the side of the hierarchical order. The consolidation or ministerial structures in the third century was very much influenced by the thought of Origin, Tertullian and Cyprian. For instance, to describe the mystery of the Church, Cyprian had recourse to various images and figures of the Bible- bride of Christ, ark of salvation, the flock of Christ. In preference to all these, he employs the image of mother. As mother, the church is a sacrament of unity and it reflects the Trinitarian unity of the Father, the Son and the Holy Spirit. The church is a visible corporate body, system or organization with its proper constitution and structures. In this system, the ministries, especially episcopate, occupy a central place. The church, as Cyprian stated, is built on the bishop and it is in

129 "The Unity of the Church", *Ante-Nicene Fathers*, Vol. V, 423.

the bishop just as the bishop is in the Church. This conception of structure has to be viewed in the light of the situation of the third century. Schismatic and heretical groups posed great dangers to the unity of the Church. In this context the office of episcopate was exalted as a focal point of unity and direction. Cyprian's concept of Church and ministry was to exert great influence in the following centuries. H. Von Campenhausen, in this regard, comments, "the image of Cyprian, the holy bishop and martyr, controls despite some lapses in dogmatic taste, the ecclesiological thinking of the Roman Catholicism to this day".[130]

In the ecclesiological thought of the third century dominated by Cyprian, and Tertullian not only did the tripartite ministry- bishop, presbyter and deacon, but a sharp distinction between the people and those belonging to the sacred order also develop. It was at this time that the word 'priest' begins to be employed widely to refer to those who belong to the hierarchy. Cyprian compared the Eucharist to the Old Testament sacrificial system with the result that the ministers of the Church whose relation to the Eucharist had become by then more defined, were attributed the characteristics of the Old Testament priesthood.[131]

The emphasis is placed now on the visible and the organizational set up of the church and the importance to the priestly dimension contributed to the transformation of the ministerial structure into a predominantly hierarchical structure with higher and lower positions as on a ladder.

5. Ecclesiology in the Fourth Century

The conversion of the Emperor Constantine, and the end of persecution of the Church in the Roman Empire early in the fourth century, brought profound changes in ecclesiastical life. As K. M. George opines, "the situation in which the pagan culture was the dominant power in the face of which the Christian Church as a

130 H. Von Campenhausen, *Ecclesiastical Authority and Spiritual Power*, 266.

131 E. Schillebeeckk, *Ministry, Leadership in the Community of Jesus Christ* (New York, NY: Cross road, 1981), 48.

minority community had to defend itself was reversed".[132] The Emperor, Constantine considered himself 'bishop of external affairs of the Church'.[133] To be able to cope with the state on a more equal footing, the church had to develop, an organizational structure beyond the local level. It was modeled on the administrative structure of the Roman Empire. The Roman Empire has been defined as a mosaic of cities each with certain autonomy. In the same manner the whole of the Catholic Church seems to have been divided into a series of the local communities. In what ways had the church adopted the Roman system of governance? Gerd Theissen, in his book, *Social Reality and the Early Christians*[134] answers comparable well to this question:

Loyalty to the central Authority or supreme Head: Under *Pax romana*: The Romanist conception of authority is that it involves centralization.[135] We have seen people clung to their emperor. So also Christians clung to their *Kurios* Jesus Christ. It is found that Early Christology used the same title of sovereignty as the emperor cult. The titles like *kyrios*, son of God, *soter*, *evangelion* are technical terms in both the early Christian proclamation and in the emperor cult.[136]

In Ecclesiology, just as the emperor is the head who integrates the people of the Roman Empire, the risen Christ integrates Jews and Gentiles into a worldwide community. Theissen comments that these structural analogies do not allow us to make any genealogical derivation to trace Christian conviction back to the emperor cult.[137]

The Roman Empire grew together through supra-regional communications, supported by unified administrations, a centralized

---

132 K. M. George, *The Early Church, Defending the Faith, Witness and Proclamation: Patristic Perspectives* (Geneva: WCC Publication, 1996), 26.

133 John E. Lynch, "Power in the Church: an Historico-critical survey" *Concilium* 197 (April 1988), 14.

134 Gerd Theissen, *Social Reality and the Early Christians* (Minneapolis: Fortress Press, 1992).

135 Charles Gore, *The Holy Spirit and the Church* (London: John Murray, 1924), 201.

136 Theissen, *Social Reality*, 273.

137 Ibid.

legal system, generally spoken languages, Latin and Greek and a network of roads and cities. This proffers Christians to have a well-organized hierarchical ecclesial structure within the empire. The uniform church government in this period was Episcopal form of church government. The canon of Church council dealt with matters of jurisdiction. Canon 6[138] of the Council of Nicaea (325) ratified the bishop of Alexandria's jurisdiction over the bishops of Egypt, Lybya, and Pentapolis, and that of the Bishop of Antioch over the bishops of neighbouring eparchies, and there was a similar custom in the case of the Bishop of Rome. The Council of Constantinople (381), in canon 3 enacted that 'the bishop of Constantinople has seniority of honour after the bishop of Rome because Constantinople is New Rome'.[139] The bishop of Jerusalem had been accorded a precedence of honour and was counted among the patriarchs (a title used only from the sixth century) with the bishops of Rome, Constantinople, Antioch and Alexandria. The adoption of the hierarchical administrative system of the Roman Empire as a model was clearly a departure from that notion of a collegiate for which Cyprian has contended.

Theologians in the fourth century were chiefly engaged upon the doctrines of the Trinity and of the Person of Christ. It was the period of the Arian, Apollinarian, Macedonian, Nestorian, Eutychian and Donatist controversies. In addition to these, we also notice some significant development in ecclesiology during this period. Now we shall move on to examine the ecclesiology of one of the famous among fourth century theologians, Augustine of Hippo.

5.1. Augustine (354-430)

When Augustine became Bishop of Hippo in 396 his diocese had long been split by the Donastist schism. Many of his writings deal with the nature of the Church and its unity. Let us examine some of the issues in his ecclesiology: What is the church? How did he understand the unity of the Church? How did he mean by catholicity and apostolicity of the Church?

138 William A. Jurgens, *The Faith of the Early Fathers*, 283.

139 Jurgens, *The Faith of the Early Fathers*, 400.

5.1.1. *The Church as the Mystical Body*

Fundamental to Augustine ecclesiology is the idea of the Church as the mystical body of Christ. For him Scripture speaks of the one Christ with three points of reference: as the eternal Word, equal to the Father; as the Mediator between God and man (humankind); and as the Church. Basing on Acts 9:4, he says that the head of the Church is Christ, and the Church is the body of Christ; but also the head and body are one in Christ, not because he is not whole without the body, but because he has also deigned to be whole with us, who even without us is whole and entire.[140] In view of this integral unity of head and body Augustine speaks in several passages of the Church as the whole Christ, one man, entire man, one person, perfect man.[141] In one of his sermons Augustine speaks of the Eucharist as that which expresses the unity into which the Christian has entered through the ceremonies of initiation:

> If you wish to understand the body of Christ, hear what the Apostle says to the faithful: 'Now you are the body of Christ, and his members' (1Cor. 12:27). Therefore if you are the body and members of Christ, it is your mystery which is set forth on the Lord's table, ... You hear the words 'body of Christ', and you answer 'Amen'... Thus the Lord Christ has put his mark upon us, willed us to belong to him, and consecrated the mystery of our peace and unity upon his table.[142]

In developing the image of the Church as the body of Christ, he does not neglect the New Testament idea of the Church as the fellowship of the Holy Spirit. As the human body is indwelt and quickened by the soul so the Holy Spirit indwells and quickens the mystical body.

---

140 Cited by Eric G. Jay, *The Church*, 84.

141 S. J. Graowski, *The Church: An Introduction to the Theology of St. Augustine* (London: Herder, 1957), 18-19. And also J. N. D. Kelly, *Early Christian Doctrines*, 413.

142 Cited by Eric G. Jay, *The Church*, 85.

"The spirit by which every man lives is called the soul: you see what the soul does in the body. It gives life to all its members. What the soul is to the body of a man, the Holy Spirit is to the body of Christ, the Church".[143] It is fundamental to Augustine's theology that the Holy Spirit is the bond of love, both in the life of the divine Being and in human relationships. Therefore it may be said that the quickening principle of the Church is love. The Church is a fellowship of love, a fellowship created by the Spirit who is love and a fellowship of those who love both God and the sons of God in Christ. Thus he holds closely together the ideas of the Church as the body of Christ and the fellowship of the Holy Spirit.

5.1.2. *The Unity of the Church*

From the concept of the church as the fellowship of the Holy Spirit of love, Augustine deduces the nature of the Church's unity. Those who do not love God or their fellow Christians separate themselves from the one Church. For Augustine true unity and charity are synonymous, and consequently schism and lack of charity are closely linked. The schismatic actions of the Donatists, their antagonism to the body of which the love of God and man is the very soul, betray their failure in charity. And since the Holy Spirit is the giver of charity he concludes that the Donatists do not have the Holy Spirit.[144] Augustine, unlike Cyprian (to Novatians), was prepared to allow to the Donatists that their sacraments were valid. But he held that it could not be effective for salvation unless and until the recipient was received into the Catholic Church, when he Holy Spirit would make them efficacious and fruitful.

Augustine's ecclesiology, particularly his view that the Holy Spirit is effectively active among people nowhere but within the boundary of the visible Catholic Church seems forgetful of the biblical doctrine

---

143 Cited by Eric G. Jay, *The Church*, 85.

144 Augustine, "The Catholic and Manichaean ways of Life," *The Fathers of the Church*, Vol. 56, translated by Donald A. Gallagher and Idella, edited by Joseph Deferri (Washington, D.C: The Catholic University of America Press, 1966), 40-41.

of the Spirit of God as the giver of life in all its dimensions. His argument also seems to imply that a separated body of Christians, and a member of a separated body, can express or experience nothing of the love of God, of Christ, and of neighbour.

5.1.3. *The Holiness of the Church*

Scripture speaks of the Church as both mixed and as holy without spot and wrinkle. Augustine found a solution of this difficulty in a distinction, appears to have affinity with that made by Origen, between empirical and the essential.[145] He admits that there are, within the church, the covetous, and defrauders, and robbers, and usurers, and drunkards, and the envious. However, the true members are the holy and just. They are the orchards of pomegranates with pleasant fruits of which the Song of Solomon speaks.[146] At this point, Augustine's idea of predestination exerts its influence. The true members of the church are the fixed number of the saints predestined before the foundation of the world, as he says, "there are some also who as yet live wickedly, or even lie in heresies or the superstitions of the Gentiles, and yet even then 'the lord knowed them that are his'. For, in that unspeakable foreknowledge of God, many who seem to be within yet really are without" (On Baptism v. 27).

A distinction between the Church as inclusive of both worthy and unworthy members and the Church's righteous core has given way to a distinction between the visible Church and an invisible Church consisting of a fixed number of people, known to God alone and predestined by him for salvation from before their creation, a doctrine which J. N. D. Kelly contends, means that the notion of the institutional Church ceases to have any validity.[147]

145 Eric G. Jay, *The Church*, 88.

146 Ibid.

147 J. N. D. Kelly, *Early Christian Doctrines*, 413.

5.1.4. *The Catholicity of the Church*

In his controversy with the Donatist, Augustine employs the creedal adjective 'catholic' in its geographical sense. How, he asks, "can the party of Donatus claim to be the Church when it exists in North Africa alone?"[148] Alluding to the accusation that communion between catholics in North Africa and traditores contaminates the Catholic Church throughout the world, he speaks of the folly of pronouncing the whole world defiled by unknown crimes of Africans and the heritage of Christ destroyed through the sins of these Africans by the maintenance of communion with them. The catholicity of the Church consists in communion with the see of Rome and with the universal Church.[149] The church is the *ekklesia* Catholica, and Augustine, especially in his anti-Donatist writings, frequently designates it by the one word *catholica.* For Augustine, the universality of the church is extended not only geographically, but also in time. The body whose head is Christ is co-extensive with all who by grace live in righteousness from Abel to the last elect person.[150]

5.1.5. *The Apostolicity of the Church*

Following his predecessors, Irenaeus, Tertullian and Cyprian, Augustine affirmed that the doctrine of apostolic faith and life of the Church is guaranteed by an unbroken succession of bishops in the sees founded by the apostles. He makes the point that it is futile for Donatists to claim apostolicity for their party since there has never been a Donatist among the successive bishops of Rome, which he regards as the outstanding example of an apostolic see. It seems that he conceives of apostolic succession in the same way as his predecessors: a bishop succeeds to a vacant see, and traces his succession through his predecessors in that see.[151]

---

148 Letters XLIX, 3, cited by Eric G. Jay in *The Church*, 89.

149 Expositions on the Psalms LVI, 13: Contra Faustum XXVIII, 2; Letters XCIII, 7:23, from Eric G. Jay, *The Church*, 89.

150 Eric G. Jay, *The Church*, 89.

151 Ibid., 89-90.

5.1.6. *The Church as Mother*

Augustine also used the metaphor, already used by Cyprian, of the Church as the mother who gives birth and nurtures Christians and provides a safe home for her children: "You are safe who have God for your Father and His Church for your mother".[152] She gives birth through baptism; it is the Church who gives birth to all, either within her pale or beyond it. Augustine also acknowledges that many of the children whom this mother brings forth prove to be sinners. Repentance is always possible and reconciliation always offered. But there is no second baptism; the sinner is purged by faith discipline and truthful confession. He or she returns to his mother.

5.1.7. *The City of God and the Church*

Augustine's best known work, after his Confession, in his *De Civitate Dei,* "On the City of God". It was written primarily to give an answer to the accusation that the calamity of the fall of Rome to the Goths was caused by Rome's desertion of its old gods in favour of Christianity. In providing it Augustine found himself obliged to present what amounts to a history of the world interpreted as the progress of two cities, the heavenly city of God, and a city which revolts from God. The creation of the angels originates the city of God, and the angels form a barge part of it. The foundation of the city which opposes god is laid by the willful disobedience of the angels who fell. With the creation and fall of man the two cities became established in the world. History is interpreted as the intermingling, sometimes the co-operation, sometimes the enmity and always the tension between these two cities, the earthly and the heavenly, both constituted by love, the former "by the love of self even to the contempt of God, the heavenly by the love of God, even to the contempt of self."[153] Augustine undoubtedly identifies the City of God with the Church:

> What is the city of God, but the Holy Church? For men who love one another, and who love their God who dwelled

152 Eric G. Jay, *The Church*, 89.

153 *De Civitate Dei XIV*, 28, cited in Eric G. Jay, *The Church...*, 91.

> in them, constitute a city unto God. Because a city is held together by some law; their very law is Love; and that very law is God; for openly it is written, "God is Love". He therefore who is full of Love is full of God; and many, full of Love, constitute a city full of God.[154]

Nevertheless, in what sense of the word "church" is this identification to be understood? To this question various answers have been given, the empirical Catholic Church; the Church as the mystical body, or bride of Christ; the invisible church of the elect. Identification of the City of God with the empirical church is made difficult in that the latter is a mixed society within which are some who are not predestined to salvation. Complete identification of the mystical body is made difficult in that angels are said to be the first citizens of the city of God,[155] while Augustine never speaks of them as members of Christ's body. A probably conclusion is that the City of God is indeed the Church whose extent and membership are invisible to man, which in its celestial part 'is made up of the holy angels,'[156] and in that part, 'which wanders as a stranger on the earth'[157] consists of those members of the Catholic Church who are the congregation of the saints, persevering in faith and love and predestined at the consummation of all things to enter into the peace and blessedness of God's eternal city. It is not to be forgotten that for Augustine membership of the Catholic Church by baptism is a *sine quo non* of final salvation.

Augustine's influence or a legacy of his theology in the later generations has been immense, as R. W. Battenhouse has remarked:

> The civilization of medieval Christendom was to owe more to him than to any other of the Church Fathers, Gregory the Great turned to him for scriptural commentary and theology, Charlemagne for political theory, Bonaventura

154 Eric G. Jay, *The Church*, 91.

155 De Citate Dei, XI, 9.

156 Encheiridion LXVI, cited in Eric G. Jay, *The Church...*, 92.

157 Eric G. Jay, *The Church...*, 92.

> for mysticism, and Aquinas for elements of scholastic philosophy. Later, with the coming of the Reformation, Luther and Calvin became his disciples, and after them, Pascal-each gathering from the bishop of Hippo fresh stimulus for revitalizing Christian piety.[158]

In regard to ecclesiology, his doctrine of mystical body governed the thinking of the medieval Church. His teaching that the unity of the Church is secured by communion with the see of Rome gave a strong support to the mounting claims of that see to primacy and supremacy. His arguments against the Donatists provide a ready arsenal whenever a sect arose to insist that the Church must dissociate itself from sinners and to claim that it alone was the Church of the Holy. Concerning his understanding of the Catholic Church, not as the local church but as universal, John Zizioulas comments that this interpretation equates catholicity with universality and lends catholicity a quantitative geographical content instead of its original qualitative one.[159] Calvin took up Augustine's doctrine of the Church as the invisible company of the elect in the sixteenth century.

6. Summary of the Development of Ecclesiology in the First Four Centuries

Having examined and investigated the ecclesiology in each century of the first four centuries, we can come to a conclusion by summing up the whole discussion as follows:

6.1. Unity and Plurality of Ecclesiology

The church during the first three centuries existed as a number of local congregations scattered over the Mediterranean region. Church's life was synonymous with the local Christian community. Judaism and the Church of Jerusalem, and later the Grecco-Roman

158 R. W. Battenhouse, *A Companion to the Study of St. Augustine* (Oxford: University Press, 1955), 54.

159 In Joseph Areeplackal, *Spirit and Ministries: Perspectives of East and West* (Bangalore: Dharmaram Publications, 1990), 187.

civilization greatly influenced the form of life of the early Christian communities. The Church was founded in different lands with varied religious and social background. The spreading of the Gospel to the various cultural centers demanded an adaptation to the local culture in the presentation of the message and the organization of the community. However, Christians, irrespective of their race and color, were united in their faith in Jesus Christ, the Lord and Son of God. Unity and plurality were evident during the foundational period of the Church. Their faith in Jesus was based on the witness of Apostles. Charles Gore has rightly mentioned that the unity of the church, as it is seen in the New Testament and in the subsequent history of the church, was guarded especially by the three bonds: "first by the authority of the common faith or word of God, secondly by the need to seek the gifts of God in the sacraments of the society; thirdly, by the obligation of adherents to the Apostolic ministry."[160]

6.2. Ecclesial Structure

In the first three centuries the New Testament pattern of local churches was generally followed. In fact, some local churches grew bigger than others in terms of number and power, yet, the principle was maintained more or less in both the East and the West. The local churches had the same essential faith in Christ: they were all autonomous in administration, shared their joys and sorrows and received each other in a true spirit of hospitality and brotherliness.

However, after the conversion of the Roman Emperor Constantine to Christianity, there arose four major "Patriarchal Sees", modeled on the chief provincial centres of Roman imperial administration in the Metropolitan cities of Rome, Constantinople, Alexandria and Antioch.[161] These four centres or the four Patriarchal Sees became the hot beds of conspiracy, conflict and mutual acrimony. Due to the power struggle between the Patriarchs, they

160 Charles Gore, *The Holy Spirit and the Church* (London: John Murray, 1924), 136.

161 K. M. George, *Interfacing Theology with Culture* (Delhi: Tercentenary Publication, 2010), 72.

became less and less tolerant of diversity. These patriarchs were ready to pronounce anathema on their critics for every little difference and disagreement. "Anathema upon anathema worked its way down the centuries to perpetuate division in the church".[162] This war between patriarchs in the fourth century caused some major divisions in the Body of Christ in the subsequent centuries.

During these four centuries we have seen the process of development of the ecclesial structure, from the "poor believers"[163] of Jesus Christ, non-structured, simple community of believers to well established hierarchical Church structure, which reflected the imperial glory. For Kuncheria Pathil, this hierarchical church structure form of Church government is contrary to the New Testament vision of authority.[164] And Christianity, an exclusive faith, maintaining a strict separation between the Church and the world (state), began to integrate into society, structurally and to a great extent ideologically open to the contemporary philosophies.

6.3. Self-understanding of the Church

It has taken different nuances, interpretations and expressions. At times political changes and cultural considerations compelled the church to redefine its self-understanding. Moreover, heresies and schisms, threatened the Church, consequently, the Church, in order to maintain its unity or orthodoxy, redefined its self-understanding. The early teachers of faith have made efforts to articulate the self-understanding of the church in different imageries to make it comprehensible in varied socio-historical and political context. However, what is obvious is, these metaphors or images do not

---

162 K. M. George, *Interfacing Theology...*, 72.

163 Gerd Theissen, *Social Reality and the Early Christians*, 270. He said that the Christian congregations were socially rooted in the lower classes. He further stated that the development of systems for social relief in the early church, the continued survival of the theology of the poor and the slaves can all be most easily explained if we place the early Christian communities at the bottom of the society. See also K. M. George, *The Early Church*, 23.

164 Kuncheria Pathil, *Indian Churches at the Crossroads* (Rome: Center for Indian and Interreligious Studies (CIIS), n.d.), 5.

express the complete essence of the Church. Because any concept of the church is basically influenced by the form Church takes at a given time in a given context. And it is found that the self-understanding of the church in the first four centuries, finds validation with the word of God, and Apostles' teaching (tradition) and the contemporary ecclesiastical thinking.

6.3.1. The church as communion of believers as well as local churches up to the third century It is reasonable to say, though under a very broad and general classification of the periods of the history of the church, that during the first three centuries of Christianity, i.e., until the emergence of the Constantinian imperial Church, the Church did not have any Primatial and Universal administrative structures. The Church Universal was simply the communion of the different Local Churches, though the term "Local Church" as such did not exist at that time. The church was the community of Jesus' disciples or followers who used to gather in a place or house, such as church in Jerusalem, Church in Antioch, Church in Corinth, Church in Rome, etc. The churches were not considered as units, either geographical or administrative, or a worldwide institution or organization. It may be noted that even today some of the Eastern churches separated from the Roman Catholic Church think that any such universal organization and administrative structure, such as Papacy or Ecumenical Council is not essential to the Church, though they may be beneficial. The church is primarily a mystery, a spiritual reality, the body of Christ, the people of God, the Communion with God in Jesus Christ, which transcends all space and time. But this mystery becomes incarnate and manifest in space and time in the different local churches with their visible outward or signs. The Local churches are marked by their differentiation and individuality with their own identity. The individuality and identity of the Local churches arises out of the diversity of the offered in Christ. This individuality is expressed in the varieties of theologies, liturgies, disciplines, ministerial patterns, administrative structures, spiritualities and popular devotions. No one model of a Local church was normative to other Local churches, though in the history of the church there are plenty of examples of churches that had imposed their own models and way upon other churches.

Communion is the heart and essence of the church in the NT and in the early centuries. The inner reality of the church is the divine communion or participation in the life of the Triune God in and through Jesus Christ. This vertical communion is attained sacramentally in a historical human community on the one hand, and on the other the divine communion is the ultimate basis for the human communion. In other words, the vertical or divine communion leads to the horizontal human communion and vice versa. The communion of the Local church was primarily expressed and realized in the Eucharistic celebration and it led to real communion in life by sharing both spiritual and material things and by building up community at a deeper level common sharing of goods and properties among the early Christian was an expression of the communion at all levels.

In the early church the communion however was never limited to the Local Church. Communion in the Local church led to the communion of the different Local churches. All the NT books clearly attest to the communion among the Local churches. Christian communities spread from the towns to rural villages and when the presbyters took charge of those rural communities, the Bishop of the town used to send part of the consecrated best to the rural communities as a symbol of the one Eucharist and one communion. Mutual visits of Bishops and leaders of the Local churches, praying for one another, exchange of letters and communications, material help to other churches, mutual corrections and interventions in case of heresies and schisms, solicitude for the other churches, common concern for preserving the Apostolic Tradition and the true faith were the regular features of communion among the different Local churches. It was a general custom right from the post-apostolic period that many neighboring Bishops took part in the ordination of new Bishops. It is, therefore, very clear that during the first three centuries the Universal church did not mean an overarching institutional or administrative structure linking the various Local churches. It simply meant the communion of the different Local churches, basically a spiritual communion with the consciousness of One church, Holy, Catholic and Apostolic that naturally led to visible and tangible communion among the different Local churches. The development of ecclesiology in early Christianity may be meaningfully summarized by using the words of M. Schmaus:

> The church is seen as the society of Christians, as that totality in which unity and charity endure (communion of saints). The church exercises a spiritual motherhood...development of the idea of apostolicity and apostolic succession in the church (Irenaeus), of the importance of the bishop and of the bishops' councils (Cyprian), of the idea of the living relation of the church to the whole world (theology of the Greek Fathers) and the independence of the church from the power of the state (Augustine), while at the same time the concept of salvation by force, of the use of the worldly sword (Augustine, Isidore) also emerged. Augustine evolved a theology in which apostolicity was intrinsically bound up with catholicity and in which the validity of sacramental efficacy was established as independent from the person of the individual minister, so preparing the doctrine of the sacramental character.[165]

165 M. Schmaus, *The Church its Origin and Structure* (London: Sheed & Oates, 1974), 71.

Chapter 2

Tribal Cultural Traditions with Reference to Mizoram

1. Introduction

It is generally understood that Tribal communities in India have a rich tradition of culture, values and norms. These cultural values have placed them in good standing and many are gaining relevance in modern society; especially in areas of ecological concerns and community living.

The main intent of this chapter is to examine Mizo cultural traditions, especially those elements that are thought to be pregnant with ecclesiological significance. The choice of the cultural traditions of the Mizo of Mizoram as the locus of this research work is made, on the one hand, with the intention of avoiding the pitfalls of an analysis that is too general, and on the other hand, in order to identify and focus on concrete issues affecting tribal people. There are at two underlying hypotheses which direct this study. The first is that many other tribal groups in Northeast India commonly share both similar problems and common cultural traditions with the tribal people in Mizoram. The second assumes that the cultural traditions of the tribal people of Mizoram can represent most of the tribal groups in Northeast India and that they are also accessible and viable, as the researcher hails from Mizoram.

In this chapter, we will first have a cursory look at the tribal situation in India in general by examining the mind-set of the dominant people in India toward Tribal people as a whole. The research will then turn to the tribal situation of Northeast India and, where appropriate, to Mizoram in particular, including its geographical and socio-cultural isolation and the Tribal policies. The study will then examine the cultural traditions of the Mizo people of Mizoram, with special effort made to consider three essential aspects: the community Home (Zawlbuk), the community ethics (Tlawmngaihna), and the community life principle, egalitarianism. The assumption being that these three elements are the foundational cornerstones upon which the Mizo community is built and that they can be incorporated into ecclesiology. While investigating the Mizo cultural traditions, as far as possible, they will be treated in relation to other tribal groups in Northeast India.

2. Tribal Situation in Northeast India: An Overview

2.1. Tribal Realities in India as a whole

According to Nirmal Minz, tribal reality includes four major components: the people, their homeland, power, and God[1]. It is most pertinent here to examine the first aspect, the people: What is a tribe? Who are tribal people in India?

The term 'tribe' is commonly used in at least three different contexts: (1) Tribe is understood as an objective ethnological category, relevant to the practical problem of classifying social groups. (2) Tribe figures as one stage in an evolutionary sequence, (e.g., band,

1 Nirmal Minz, "A Theological Interpretation of the Tribal Reality in India", in *Readings in Indian Christian Theology* Vol. 1, edited by R. S. Sugitharajah and Cecil Hargreaves (Delhi: ISPCK, 1993), 47.

tribe, chiefdom, and state) stressing the historical transformation of certain features of politics, economy and social organization. (3) Tribe serves as an expression of socio-cultural identity and distinctiveness among descendents of aboriginal social groups now threatened by assimilation, displacement and destruction at the hands of encroaching states.[2]

Since it is hard to find a commonly agreed upon definition of "tribe," it may be more appropriate to highlight some of the salient features denoted by the term tribe. It needs to be noted that various descriptions highlight one or the other aspect and attribute of tribe. As Winthrop notes as classificatory the term tribe denotes a "culturally homogeneous non-stratified society possessing a common territory, without centralized political or legal institutions, whose members are linked by extended kinship ties, ritual obligations, and mutual responsibility for the resolution of disputes".[3] Even though Winthrop's description highlights some of the important characteristics of tribe, it leaves out other important features. Some of these features are included in Aiden Southall's description. According to Southall, the tribe is commonly defined as "a whole society, with a high degree of self-sufficiency at a near subsistence level, based on a relatively simple technology without writing or literature, politically autonomous and with its own distinctive language, culture and sense of identity, tribal religion being also coterminous with tribal society."[4]

In order to understand the tribal situation in India, it is necessary to look at the definition of the word "tribe" given by the tribal Christians themselves at a Consultation held in Shillong, in 1962, it is defined as "an indigenous homogeneous unit, speaking a common language, claiming a common ancestry, living in a

---

2 Robert Winthrop, *Dictionary of Concept in Cultural Anthropology* (New York, NY: Greenwood Press, 1991), 308; see also V. Sebastian, S. J, "Theologising in Tribal Traditions: Relevance of "Worldview" as a Conceptual category," in *Christ among the Tribals*, edited by F. Hrangkhuma and Joy Thomas (Bangalore: FOIM, 2007), 100.

3 Winthrop, *Dictionary of Concept in Cultural Anthropology*, 307.

4 Cf. Winthrop, *Dictionary of Concept* ..., 308.

particular geographical area, backward in technology, preliterate, loyally observing social and political customs based on kinship."[5]

A tribe in India is an administrative and political concept. According to the Constitution of India, the President of India is empowered to specify the list of Scheduled Tribes for each state and Union Territory. Stephen Fuchs, a noted anthropologist, gives the following reasons for the Government of India to consider a group of people as tribe:

> The Indian Government extends the privileges granted to the Scheduled Tribes to those social groups which are not fully integrated into the Indian nation for reasons of economic handicaps, different ecological conditions, different racial origin, and a different mental and religious world outlook and culture.[6]

Hrangkhuma writes, according to the above definition, the following are the major criteria used to differentiate a tribe from a non-tribal:

---

5 K. Thanzauva, *Theology of Community* (Aizawl: Mizoram Theological Conference, 1997), 1-6; M. M. Thomas and R. W. Taylor, eds., *Tribal Awakening* (Bangalore: CISRS, 1965), 2-3; K. Chattopachyaya, *Tribalism in India* (New Delhi: Vikas Publishing House, 1978), 1. Tribal communities are found in small or big groups in different parts of India, they can be broadly divided into two groups, plain and hill tribals. Ambedkar, one of the members of the Constituent Assembly, noticed the difference between the tribes of Northeast India and those in other parts of India. He stated that while the tribes in other parts of the country were more or less Hinduised, this was not true of the tribal in Northeast India. Ambedkar noticed that the tribes in Northeast were still rooted in their own cultures, with their own laws of inheritance and marriage, their own customs, which were very different from those of their neighbours. Accordingly the Sixth Schedule was promulgated in the constitution for the administration of the tribes in Northeast, whereas the Fifth Schedule deals with the tribes of the rest of India. See R. N. Prasad, *Government and Politics in Mizoram* (New Delhi: Northern Book Centre, 1987), 98.

6 F. Hrangkhuma, "Christ and Tribal Culture," in *Christ and Cultures*, edited by Jacob Kavunkal and F. Hrangkhuma (Bombay: St. Pauls, 1994), 140.

- the degree of integration in the national mainstream
- economic position
- environment
- ecology
- origin
- religion[7]

However, unlike the above view, Lalsangkima Pachuau, looks at the term 'tribe' or "tribal" from religious cultural perspective. For him the Constitution of India employed the term "tribal" to designate a whole cluster of diverse non-Indic or semi-Indic communities who are mostly non-Aryan and remained outside the Hindu *Varna*.[8]

Tribal people in India are given different names like *Vanvasi* (forest dwellers), *Vanjati* (forest caste), *Pahari* (hill- dwellers), *Adi-vasi* (original inhabitants of the land), *Adijati* (primitive people), *Janjati* (folk people), *Anusuchit Janjati* (Scheduled tribe) and *Adivasi* (first settlers) by the Caste Hindus. Some educated tribal, especially from Northeast India, are critical of using the term tribe or tribal for all these terminologies carry a derogatory sense and convey the negative attitude of the dominant people towards tribal people. Some tribals do not want to be tribal since the word 'tribal' is defined in terms of backwardness and uncivilized status. According to Lalsangkima Pachuau, the very choice of the term "tribal" points to the marginal existence of the so-called tribal and the oppressiveness of the structure that imposed the identity upon them. The term "tribal" divulges the intent to dominate and oppress the people to whom the nomenclature is imposed. He, therefore, contends that the creation of the tribal identity is artificial; it is done just for the convenience of the administrative system that is thoroughly influenced by the caste

7 Hrangkhuma, "Christ and Tribal Culture," 140.

8 Lalsangkima Pachuau, "Tribal Identity and Ethnic Conflicts in Northeast India: A "Tribal" Christian Response," *Bangalore Theological Forum* XXX/1 (July 1999), 163.

stratification mindset, and politically and culturally controlled by the Hindu society.[9]

The situation of tribal people in India can in short be described as the politically powerless, economically exploited, socially stigmatized, and culturally alienated. Nirmal Minz testifies to the situation of tribal people in India by making the following statements:

> The tribal person is a strange animal to many in our country even today. Our youngest daughter went through a traumatic experience... Her college and hostel mates were surprised to see that she belonged to a tribal community and began to dissociate from her. However, they were willing to associate themselves with her on the condition that she did not declare herself as a tribal[10]

The tribal population of India is considered to be the second largest in the world. In the 1991 census, excluding Jammu and Kashmir where the census could not be held, there were 6,77,58,000 persons identified as tribal. This constitutes 8.08% of the total population of India.[11] The tribal people are broadly classified into three major racial and linguistic groups: the Mongoloid, the Austroloids and the Dravidians. They are spread all over India, but are most concentrated in six major states: 1) Northeast India- Assam, Meghalaya, Arunachal Pradesh, Nagaland, Manipur, Mizoram and Tripura; 2) North Central Regions- Jharkhan, Bihar, West Bengal, Northern Orissa, and Chhattisgarh; 3) Western India-Rajasthan, Gujarat, Western Madhya Pradesh, and Northern Maharastra; 4) North West India- Himachal Pradesh, and part of Jammu and

---

9 Lalsangkima Pachuau, "Tribal Identity and Ethnic Conflicts in Northeast India ..., 162.

10 T. Lakiumong Yimchunger, "Re-Perusal of the Term "Tribe" and Its Redeemable Humanized Potentiality: A Liberative Perspective," *Journal of Tribal Studies*, 7, cited from Nirmal Minz, "Mission in the Context of Diversity-Mission in Tribal Context", *Religion and Society* 36 (1989), 7.

11 Quoted from Thanzauva, *Theology of Community*, 5; see also Longchar, *An Emerging Asian Theology*, 4.

Kashmir; 5) South Eastern Regions- Southern Orissa, North Andhra Pradesh, Southern Madhya Pradesh, and Eastern Maharastra; 6) Southern India- Western Ghats and the Nilgiri Hills in Kerala, Tamilnadu, and Karnataka.[12]

It is believed that the origin of the idea of "tribe" in India goes back to the time of the Aryan invasions.[13] When the Aryans invaded the Indian subcontinent, the resident natives whom they called Dasyus were defeated and scattered. Some of them were assimilated into the Hindus society as the lowest group of the caste system, while others were driven away to remote hills and forests. The assimilated groups are today classified as "Schedule Caste" while the driven- away groups are known as "tribes". Thanzauva believes that the people who are known as tribes today are neither Hindu nor Muslim. They are called "tribes" simply because they are believed to be the descendents of those who lived in the country before the Aryan invasion and they do not belong to the two major religious communities, namely Hindu or Muslim.[14]

The tribal people in India are diverse not only in culture, language and ethnicity, but also in terms of socio-economic development. According to R. R. Prasad, tribal people in India can be classified into four major categories based on their eco-cultural setting, levels of techno-economical development and acculturative influences.[15] The first group comprises communities who may be called "primitive tribes". They inhabit remote, isolated and inaccessible areas. They live a life of pre-agricultural pursuits such as food gathering, hunting, and fishing. The second group represents those tribes who are a little more advanced than the first one, practicing shifting cultivation

12 Nirmal Minz, *Rise Up, My People, and Claim the Promise: The Gospel Among the Tribes of India* (Delhi: ISPCK, 1997), 10. See also Lalsangkima Pachuau, *Ethnic Identity and Christianity: A Socio-Historical and Missiological Study of Christianity in Northeast India with Special Reference to Mizoram* (Frankfurt am Main: Peter Lang, 2002), 40-42.

13 Thanzauva, *Theology of Community*, 3.

14 Ibid.

15 R. R. Prasad, "The Missing Link in Tribal Development: The Cultural Dimension," *Bangalore Theological Forum* XVIII/3 (1985), 70.

and having some contact with the outside world. The third group belongs to those who are partly acculturated. They have contact with the outside world. Their agriculture is more advanced than the traditional shifting cultivation. They are in a transitional stage, likely to respond to development. The fourth group of tribal people is already acculturated communities who have adapted to modern ways and technology. This group of tribal people is more or less indistinguishable from the non-tribal.

The attitude of the non-tribal towards tribal people in India has been very negative. Tribal people are called by various contemptuous names, such as *Vanjati* (caste of the forest), *Vanvasi* (forest dwellers), *Pahari* (hill dwellers), *Adijati* (primitive people), *Adivasi* (first settlers), *Janjati* (folk people) and *Anusuchit Janjati* (Scheduled tribes).[16] In the caste system of the dominant Indian society, tribal people are classified at the bottom of the social structure. They are considered to be an untouchable, servile class, impure and, sometimes, less than human. Thus, according Nirmal Minz:

> The old Hindu political, economic and philosophical writings like Kautilya's Arth Sastra and Manu Smrity did not count the Dalits and the tribes of India as human beings. The Vedas treated them as chandals (anti social people) and Gita and Mahabharata showed them as wild animals like monkeys and Rawans (vultures).[17]

Peter Haokip expressed a similar view in regard to the tribal situation in Manipur, as he says:

> The hill tribes in Manipur (till recently or still today in some places and by some) were called hao (a derogatory designation) and were not allowed to enter the houses of Manipuri Hindus. It was considered to be defilement. If a

16 L. P. Vidhyaarthi and B. K. Rai, *The Tribal Culture of India* (Delhi: Concept Publishing Company, 1977), 25.

17 Minz, *Rise Up, My People*, 8.

tribal wanted to meet a Manipuri Hindu, he could only shout from a distance in front of the courtyard of the house.[18]

Hence, in the sight of the non-tribal or dominant communities of India, tribal people are outcastes and alienated. Tribal people are looked upon and treated as foreigners in their own country. This attitude becomes even more blatant in the case of the hill tribes of Northeast India, to which we now turn.

2.2. The Tribal Realities in Northeast India

Northeast India composes "seven sister states" of the Indian Republic. They are Assam, Arunachal Pradesh, Manipur, Meghalaya, Mizoram, Nagaland and Tripura. The region has an area of 245,993 square kilometers. As most areas of Northeast India are covered by hilly terrain, the majority of the people live in the four plain areas: the Brahmaputra and Barak Valleys of Assam, the Tripura plain and the Manipur plateau.[19] Many tribes and ethnic groups with diverse cultures, traditions and languages inhabit the region. According to Wati Longchar, about four hundred tribes live in Northeast India, speaking hundreds of different languages and dialects.[20] The majority of the inhabitants of the region are of Mongolian racial stock. Though there is no conclusive agreement among scholars concerning the origin of the inhabitants of the region, F. S. Downs has estimated that they arrived in the region during the past three or four hundred years.[21]

Tribal people of Northeast India can be broadly classified into two groups based on geographical location: the hill tribes and the plain tribes.[22] Hill tribes consist of the Mizo-Chin-Kuki group living

18 Quoted in Longchar, *An Emerging Asian Theology*, 3.

19 Frederick S. Downs, *History of Christianity in India, Volume V, Part 5: North East India in the Nineteenth and Twentieth Centuries* (Bangalore: Church History Association of India, 1992), 1.

20 Longchar, *An Emerging Asian Theology*, 14.

21 Downs, *History of Christianity in India*, 1.

22 Thanzauva, *Theology of Community*, 12.

in Mizoram, Manipur, Tripura and North Cachar Hills of Assam; the Naga group in Nagaland, Manipur and Arunachal Pradesh; Khasi and Jaintias in Meghalaya; Garos in Meghalaya and Assam; Arunachalis in Arunachal. Most of the hill tribes of Northeast India are Christians except for the Arunachalis who have been protected from Christian missionaries for many years. Racially they all belong to the Mongoloid stock.

The plain tribal, on the other hand, are scattered in the river valleys of Brahmaputra and

Barak, in Assam, and in the plains of Tripura. They are the indigenous people who formerly had been owners of the land with their own kingdoms, but today they are suffering from landlessness, displacement and assimilation. They are reduced to colonial status. The Ahoms in the Assam plains and the Meiteis in the Manipur valleys are sanskritized (Hinduised) tribes, though they claims to be non-tribal and are not counted as tribal people by the Government of India.[23]

Besides the indigenous tribes, there is another group of tribal communities that may also be considered as plains tribes. They are commonly known as *Adivasis*, working in the tea gardens of Assam. The British tea planters brought these people as labourers to Northeast India between 1840-1961 from Orissa, Bihar and Andhra Pradesh. Their population is considered to be approximately 1.5 million. These people live as bonded labourers and are scattered among the 800 tea gardens of the region. They are the major labour force of the Assam valleys. Although these people originally belonged to a scheduled caste or tribe, the government of India does not give them such status, so that they are not able to enjoy the benefits guaranteed by the Constitution for the Scheduled Caste and Scheduled tribes.[24]

The tribes of Northeast India have experienced a state of alienation throughout their history. They suffered from the British invaders in the past, and they continue to suffer at the hands of the dominant communities of India today. A number of factors, most of

23 Thanzauva, *Theology of Community*, 12.

24 Ibid.

them due to the attitudes and policies of the dominant groups, have contributed to the tribal's alienation. The following are some of the major factors responsible for the tribal problems in Northeast India in general and Mizoram in particular.

2.2.1. *Geographical and Socio-Cultural Contexts*

Northeast India is geographically isolated from the rest of the country. It is connected to the mainland of India through a narrow passage in northern Bengal, of about thirty kilometers in breadth, popularly known as the "chicken's neck". Northeast India has a long international boundary, approximately 5000 kilometers long.[25] To the north are China, Tibet and Bhutan; Myanmar is in the East and South, and Bangladesh is in the West. Because of its geographical setting, Northeast India is politically a very sensitive region. It has been one of the most strategic regions of India. In terms of racial identity, the tribal people of Northeast India are also secluded from mainland India. While the majority of the people in mainland India are of Aryan race, people of Mongoloid stock predominantly inhabit Northeast India.

This geographical and racial seclusion has been an important factor in the rise of a number of socio-cultural and political problems of the tribal people in the region. Because, as Lalsangkima has stated, the region is situated geographically and racially between two great traditions of "Indic Asia" and "Mongoloid Asia" the tribal people of Northeast India are exposed to confusion in regard to their identity. "Whereas they are politically Indian, they are racially and culturally Mongoloid".[26] In other words, Northeast India feels alienated from the rest of the country, thereby revolutionist leaders of Northeast India have felt that the political integration of their region into the union of India was done against their will and approval.[27] Moreover, the caste system espoused by the people of mainland India contributes

25 Longchar, *An Emerging Asian Theology*, 36.

26 Lalsangkima Pachuau, ""Tribal" Identity and Ethnic Conflicts in Northeast India: A Christian Response", http://www.Martynmission.Cam.ac.uk, 4.

27 Longchar, *An Emerging Asian Theology*, 16.

to the isolation of the tribal people because they are now accepted as equal citizens of the country.

The problem goes even deeper than this, however. It is not just that the tribal people of Northeast India find difficulties in being accepted by the dominant society; not infrequently, they are mistaken for foreigners in mainland India. Mr. Lalhmingthanga, the then Finance Minister of the Government of Mizoram, made the following statements in his "Foreword" to Animesh Ray's book, *Mizoram Dynamics of Change*:

> On several occasions of my visit to different places of India like Delhi, Bombay, Madras, etc., sometimes passport (sic) was demanded from me for my identity and when I explained that I am an Indian from Mizoram, it appeared many people do not know that there is a Union Territory called Mizoram in India. Not only this, I have come across a number of Parliament members who cannot locate Mizoram in the map of India."[28]

Many students from Northeast India, including the author, have had similar experiences. Wati Longchar even argues that isolation is one of the main reasons for the Government's negligence and "step-motherly treatment" of the region.[29]

We have seen the geographical and socio-cultural isolation of Northeast India and its impact upon the lives of tribal people who live there. We now turn to analyzing other factors affecting the tribal situation in Northeast India.

2.2.2. *Policies Applied for Tribals*

As noted before, a number of problems facing the tribal people in Northeast India are the products of the policies of the non-tribal or

---

28 Animesh Ray, *Mizoram Dynamic of Change* (Calcutta: Pearl Publishers, 1982), vii.

29 Longchar, *An Emerging Asian Theology*, 16.

the dominant groups for the tribes.[30] Notable among these are the policies of assimilation, isolation and integration.

2.2.2.1. Assimilation

The tribal people in India have been assimilated physically, culturally and religiously through various forms of contact with them. Most of the plain tribes of Northeast India, who at one time had their own distinctive identities, cultures and languages, have today become victims of assimilation through Hinduism. Thanzauva provides a good summary of the situation:

> At some time in history, the various tribes of the Bodi group, Tibeto Burman family, such as Boro, Kachari, Chutyas, Dimasas, Karbi, Lalungs, Mechs, Mishings, Tipperas, Garos, Kochs, Hajongs, Dalus, Rabhas and others in the plains of Assam, all spoke their own dialects, and maintained their own independent cultural and territorial identity. They practiced tribal religions, which are vaguely and perhaps superficially called animism. Today the sanskritized tribals in the plain areas have, in some cases, forgotten their own cultures and languages. The process of sanskritization was carried out in Assam, Manipur and Tripura under royal patronage. Later on, in the plains of Assam, Hindu priest and immigrants mostly did it.[31]

Unfortunately, when they became assimilated into Hinduism the tribal people not only lost their identity, cultures and languages but also were adopted into the Hindu caste system, in which they were assigned the lowest class of the social hierarchy. In the Hindus social system, becoming low caste means becoming a servile class within society.[32]

30 Thanzauva, *Theology of Community*, 14.

31 Ibid.

32 Ibid., 17.

As a consequence of assimilation, though a few people who have been accepted by those of a higher caste after embracing their religion regard themselves as having climbed the social ladder higher than their unconverted fellow tribal's, today thousands of the plains tribals of Northeast India have been reduced to lower social conditions. As Thanzauva observes, in the contemporary situation the yardstick of religious affiliation has already been replaced by educational and economic status. It is therefore, unconvincing to regard a person as belonging to a higher social class just because of his or her religious affiliation.[33] The hill tribes of Northeast India who do not contact Hinduism remain free from the kind of assimilation experienced by the plains tribes.

2.2.2.2. Isolation

The policy of isolation was adopted by the British Government for the purpose of protecting the tribal people from exploitation at the hands of outsiders. The policy prevented non-tribal people from interference in the affairs of the tribes, and separated the tribal areas from the purview of normal administration. It was largely affected by the British Government's deliberate efforts not to develop communication in the tribal areas, which, as a result remained cut off from the rest of the population.[34] Prior to its adoption in India, a similar policy of isolation and indirect rule had already been introduced in some places in Africa and the United States where the tribal people were given the right of self-determination.

In India, the policy began with the enactment of the Government of India Act of 1870. The Act specified a few areas as "Scheduled tracts" in the Himalayan region: what was then Assam, Darjeeling, Kumaon and Garhwal, Tarai Parganas, Jaunsar-Bawar, Lahoul and Spiti; in middle India- Chhotanagpur and Santhal Pargana, Angul Mahal, Chanda, Chhatisgarh, Chhindwara, Manpur (Indore), Jhansi, Mirzapur, ganjam; in South India- Vizagapatnam, Gadvari, and Lakshadeep. With the passing of Regulation XIII of 1883,

33 Thanzauva, *Theology of Community*, 14.

34 Vidhyarthi and Rai, *The Tribal Culture of India*, 413.

Chhotanagpur became the first tribal area to be declared a non-regulated area. Meanwhile the Lieutenant Governor of West Bengal framed the Inner Line Regulation of 1873, which restricted entry of outsiders into specific hill areas. The Scheduled District Act of 1874 gave effect to both the Government of India Act 1870 and the Inner Line Regulation of 1873.[35]

In regard to Northeast India, the whole area was declared a scheduled district with the enactment of the Scheduled District Act of 1874. However, a special arrangement was made for the administration of hill areas within the system through the Assam Frontier Tracts Regulation of 1880. The Regulation adopted a policy of minimum interference in the affairs of the hill tribes, subject only to the maintenance of law and order. It stated that the operation of unsuitable laws should be barred from the hill districts of the region. According to the regulation power to administer the hill area was concentrated in the hands of a single deputy commissioner in charge of each district, who exercised the powers of judge and district magistrate simultaneously.[36]

So in the hill areas of Northeast India, the policy of isolation was systematically implemented. The Inner Line Regulation Act of 1870 was applied to all the hill areas, except in Karbi, Khasi, Jaintia and Garo hills where other regulations that strictly limited residence, business or property transactions by outsiders were enforced. According to this regulation, the Government was empowered to

> prescribe, and from time to time alter by notification… a line to be called the inner line and to prohibit any subject living outside the area from living or moving therein… Beyond this line the tribes are left to marriage their own affairs with only such interference on the part of the frontier officers in their political capacity as may be considered advisable with

35 R. R. Prasad, "Tribal Development in India- Strategies and Programmes," *Journal of Rural Development* 7/1 (1988), 84.

36 Downs, *History of Christianity in India*, 20-21.

> the view to establishing a personal influence for good among the chiefs and the tribes.[37]

The Assam Frontier Tract Regulation of 1880 was applied in 1894 to the districts of Naga Hills, North Cachar Hills, Garo Hills, Khasi and Jaintia Hills, and Mikir Hills.[38] The Bengal Eastern Frontier Regulation of 1873 was applied to Northern Lushai Hills.

Again, in 1919, as a result of reforms suggested by Montague and Chelmsford, certain territories were declared "backward tracts" under the Government of India Act of 1919. The Act did not change the policy of isolation as such, but made certain additions and omissions in regard to the areas. Subsequent discussion following this Act resulted in the setting up of Simon's Commission on November 8th 1927, to study the problems relating to further constitutional reform. As a result of the Simon's Commission recommendation, the Government of India Act of 1935 was passed. This act separated the hill districts into two areas, Excluded Areas and Partially Excluded Areas. Sections 91 and 92 of the Government of India Act, 1935, established as excluded areas the Naga Hills District, the Lushai Hill District, the North Cachar Sub-Division of Cachar District, and the Frontier Tracts (Arunachal Pradesh); and as partially excluded areas, the Garo Hills District, the Khasi and Jaintia Hills District, and the Mikir Hills Tracts of the Nagoan and Sibsagar districts.[39] The main differences between the excluded areas and the partially excluded areas were:

1. The governor functioned at his own discretion in an excluded area, whereas he sought the advice of the ministers of the provincial government in a partially excluded area.
2. The expenditure in regard to the excluded area was non-votable, while the demands in the case of partially excluded area were subject to a vote of the provincial legislature.

---

37 Downs, *History of Christianity in India*, 20-21.

38 Thanzauva, *Theology of Community*, 19.

39 Downs, *History of Christianity in India*, 24.

3. The discussion of any matter regarding the excluded areas needed prior consent of the Governor.

In 1939 Verrier Elwin, Adviser on Tribal Affairs to the Government of Assam, advocated the establishment of a sort of "national park" for the tribal and advised that the tribal's contact with the outside world should be reduced to a minimum.[40] In Elwin's view, tribal people comprised three groups. The first groups were those who had become assimilated into the Hindu hierarchy through continuous and intimate contact with them. The second, those who had been partially Hinduized and had thus suffered moral depression and decay as a result of contact. The third group comprised of those who lived in isolated hill areas and had avoided becoming detribalized. In his view, the national park would be able to provide refuge for the second group and protect the third group.[41] Accordingly, "Elwin's national park" policy of keeping tribal people as "museum specimens" became the model of administration for most hill areas of Northeast India.

Three points can be made in conclusion to this survey of the policy of isolation. First, as F. S. Downs observed, though the policy of isolation did to a certain extent help the tribal people to preserve their land and identity, in the process it reinforced a barrier that had already existed between the hill tribes and their plain neighbours.[42] The gap between the hill tribes and the plains people increased, and the policy of isolation did not encourage communication between them. In the opinion of L.P. Vidhyarthi and B.K. Rai, lack of communication between the hill tribes and the rest of the population of the country, promoted by the policy of isolation, is the root cause of tribal separatist movements.[43]

Secondly, the whole concept of an isolation policy was insufficiently positive. On the one hand, the primary objective of

40 Vidhyarthi and Rai, *The Tribal Culture of India*, 414.

41 Wilkinson, "Isolation, Assimilation and Integration," 19.

42 Downs, *History of Christianity in India*, 22-23.

43 Vidhyarthi and Rai, *The Tribal Culture in India*, 413-414.

the policy was a negative one: to protect the tribal people from exploitation at the hands of the dominant community by means of certain laws and regulations. This focus on protection meant, on the other hand, that it did not give sufficient importance to the development of tribal socio-economic conditions. As Thanzauva comments, "the protection of tribals does not simply lie in the promulgation of laws, but in their socio-economic development.[44]

Thirdly, since the policy adopted an objective approach to tribal problems, there was not sufficient room for the participation of the tribal people themselves in the realization of their dreams and visions. In short, what the tribal people need is not merely protection, but empowerment to make their own economic and political decisions and thus better protect themselves from the various forces of oppression.

In the wake of the Indian nationalist movement, the British policy of isolating the tribal people was regarded as causing a sense of separatism. In the post-Independence era, therefore, the Government of India adopted integration as its major policy towards the tribal people. We now turn to our attention to this phase.

2.2.2.3. Integration

In post independence India, although some administration still preferred a continuation of the policy of isolation, the majority of politicians rejected this policy on the ground that it had become a threat to national integration. Furer-Heimendorf observes:

> While anthropologically minded administration advocated a policy of protection, which in specific cases involved even a measure of seclusion, Indian politician attacked the idea of segregation and seclusion on the grounds that it threatened to deepen and perpetuate divisions within the Indian nation,

44 Thanzauva, *Theology of Community*, 24.

and delayed the aboriginals' (tribals) integration into rest of the population.[45]

The Government of India, therefore, adopted a policy of integration. The main objective of the Government's integration policy was to make the tribal peoples "an integral part of the Indian nation even while maintaining their distinct identity and culture".[46] The policy drew its objectives from Prime Minister Jawaharlal Nehru's *Panchsheel*, five principles of his vision for tribal upliftment include:

1. People should develop along the lines of their own genius and we should avoid imposing anything on them. We should try to encourage in every way their own traditional arts and culture.
2. Tribal rights to land and forests should be respected.
3. We should try to train and build up a team of their own people to do the work of administration and development. Some technical personnel from outside will no doubt be needed, especially in the beginning. But we should avoid introducing too many outsiders into tribal territory.
4. We should judge results, not by statistics or the amount of money spent, but by the quality of human character that is evolved.[47]

In the opinion of the policy makers, tribal protection and upliftment considered was "an integral part of the development of the Indian people as a whole". A sub-committee, under the chairmanship of Shri A. V. Thakakar, a close associate of Mahatma Gandhi, was constituted by the constituent assembly to study the minorities' problems. The committee emphasized the need for protecting tribal economic interests, safeguarding their way of life and ensuring their

45 Christoph Von Furer-Haimmendorf, *Tribes of India: The Struggle for Survival* (Berkeley: University of California Press, 1982), 313.

46 http://www.redif.com/freedom/20bipin.htm, 2.

47 Vidhyarthi and Rai, *The Tribal Culture of India*, 419.

development so that "they might take their legitimate place in the general life of the country".[48] It also recommended "considering the past experiences and the strong temptation to take advantage of the tribal simplicity and weakness it is essential to provide statutory safeguard for the protection of the land."[49]

The concerns of the government's integration policy are expressed in the Constitution of India itself in various ways. Articles 46 states that, "the State shall promote with special care the educational and economic interests of the weaker sections of the tribes and shall protect them from social injustice and the scheduled tribes and shall protect them from social injustice and all forms of exploitation."[50] Article 164 creates provision for the appointment of a minister to look after tribal welfare exclusively; Article 224 creates provisions for special administration; Article 275 provides for financial grants from the central consolidated funds to the state governments for tribal welfare. Article 330, 332, and 334 provide for reservation of seats for Scheduled Tribes in the house of the people and state legislature assemblies. Reservation of jobs for Scheduled Tribes in the government services is provided in Articles 335 and 338. Article 339 makes a provision that the president of India appoints a commission to study and report the welfare of the scheduled tribes at the end of every ten years.[51]

In relation to Northeast India, soon after Independence, the Interim Government of India in 1947 constituted a sub-committee headed by Gopinath Bordoloi, the Chief Minister of Assam, to make an on-the-spot study of the situation. The sub-committee acknowledged the strategic situation of the tribal areas and felt that the tribal people should be granted adequate safeguards so that they might be free from any fear of domination by the more-sophisticated

---

48 S. L. Doshi, "Tribals: An Assimilationist Society and National Integration", in *Tribal Situation in India: Proceedings of a Seminar*, edited by K. Suresh Singh (Shimla: Indian Institute of Advanced Study, 1972), 463.

49 Vidhyarthi and Rai, *The Tribal Culture of India*, 415.

50 Ibid.

51 Thanzauva, *Theology of Community*, 26.

people from the plain. Animesh Ray describes the feeling of the committee:

> Because of the strategic position of the tribal areas, the people living there should be free from any fear of exploitation or domination by the advanced section of people from the plains and that they should have full freedom in respect of their own manners, customs, inheritances, social organizations, village administration, etc., and unless they could be guaranteed adequate safeguard in maintaining their characteristic way of life their bonds with unity with the rest of the country would not be consolidated and strengthened. [52]

Following the recommendation of the sub-Committee, the Sixth Schedule of the Constitution was implemented for the administration of the hill areas in Northeast India. Under the Sixth Schedule of the Constitution, autonomous district councils were created in all the hill areas except in Nagaland, which demanded separation from Assam.[53] Moreover, the Constitution also made provision that, where there were different scheduled tribes in an autonomous district, the governor might divide the areas inhabited by them into autonomous regions. In accordance with this provision, Pawi-Lakher Regional Council was created for the Pawi and Lakher tribes in southern Mizoram.[54] In this way, the new government duly provided statutory safeguards for the protection of the land from expropriation and virtual serfdom under moneylenders. However, a large number of tribal people living outside the areas of such scheduled districts were not protected.[55]

Within a short period after its institution, however, the hill tribes felt that the powers vested in the district council were extremely

52 Ray, *Mizoram Dynamics of Change*, 93.

53 Thanzauva, *Theology of Community*, 23.

54 Ray, Mizoram *Dynamics of Change*, 94.

55 Vidhyarthi and Rai, *The Tribal Culture of India*, 415.

inadequate for the protection and development of their society.[56] As the powers and authority provided in the District council did not meet their aspirations the tribal people started to agitate for their independence from the Government of India. The discontentment eventually led to armed struggle first in Nagaland, and then in Mizoram, and also more recently in Manipur and Assam.[57] A. P. Sinha has observed:

> No responsibility and powers were given to the District Councils, to be established under the provisions of the Fifth Schedule, for development planning and administration of their area. It was more a measure to provide protection (rather) than provide opportunity for experimentation in development. It was in no way different from the earlier British policy of isolation and preservation rather than assimilation and change. The British legacy was maintained.[58]

Despite the government's intention to improve the lot of the tribal people, there was a serious lack of implementation of development policies by the administrative authorities. There was no effective follow-up of government policy and of recommendations made by various study teams to improve the situation of the tribal people. The concerns of the integration policy enshrined in the Constitution, and the visions of policy makers like Nehru, were largely unfulfilled.

As a result, the tribal people of Northeast India began to lose hope and confidence in the Government of India. Add to this, their experience of encounters with the dominant communities of the plains people and the miserable condition of their fellow tribal people who had been assimilated and exploited by the dominant communities, and it is little wonder that the hill tribes of Northeast India should feel that the national policy of integration is nothing but a modern

56 Thanzauva, Theology of Community, 23.

57 A. P. Sinha, "Politics and Economic Development in the Hill District of Assam," in *Tribal Situation in India: Proceedings of a Seminar*, edited by K. Suresh Singh (Shimla: Indian Institute of Advanced Study, 1972), 24.

58 Ibid.

version of assimilation, a policy designed to assimilate them into the dominant Hindu culture. Thanzauva describes the attitude of the tribal people of Northeast India towards the integration policy thus:

> The prejudice that has been created in the tribal mind to Northeast India is that national integration for them means assimilation into Hindu culture at the expense of their own cultural identity. This attitude has developed among the tribals not from the study of what scholars have written about the policy of national integration but from their daily encounter with their neighbouring plain people. In their encounter with plain people in the markets and some other places, they have been the victims of cheating and exploitation. They also saw the miserable conditions of their fellow tribals who were assimilated and exploited by the plain people. These experiences contributed to the development of negative attitude towards plain people which eventually erupted into violent struggle.[59]

In addition to this, another dimension that has often been overlooked in relation to the issue of integration of the tribal people with the rest of the Indian population is racial discrimination. As mentioned earlier, most of the tribal people in Northeast India are of Mongoloid stock; they therefore differ in appearance from the dominant population of India. Any measure of cultural and linguistic assimilation or integration cannot remove the fact that a Mizo or a Naga looks quite different from the Bengalis or from the dominant people of any mainland Indian city.[60] This racial difference, as noted before, has been a key factor in the dominant Hindus' attitude towards the tribal people of Northeast India. Inspite of all the government policy and efforts to integrate the tribal people with the rest of the Indian population, the dominant caste Hindus do not accept tribal people for intermarriage, commensality and intimate

59 Thanzauva, *Theology of Community*, 30.

60 Furer-Haimendorf, *Tribes of India*, 314.

social intercourse. As long as a social barrier is maintained on the basis of caste and race, there cannot be true integration.

2.2.3. *Tribal Development*

The present system of development programmes for tribal areas of Northeast India are sponsored by the central government. In this system, planning is done under the elaborate structure of central guidelines and approvals, and the government controls all the planning and development administration. As a result, the people have no place in the formation or governance of development plans and measures; even in those that affect them intimately they are merely recipients. As Thanzauva has said, the present system of development planning is the government's programme with the people's participation, whereas it is supposed to be the people's programme with government participation.[61] Exclusion of the people from participation in the development process has had very negative consequences within the implementation process, often leading to misappropriation of development funds. When government officials control the whole direction and administration of the development schemes, the poor villagers lack both knowledge about the details of development programmes and an institutional forum in which to express their views and aspirations. By taking advantage of the absence of people's participation, the bureaucrats and their subordinate development officials, together with the local politicians and the rural rich, often monopolize the whole development process. As a result, millions of rupees expended on rural development benefit

---

61 Most of those who have studied tribal development in India have found that the fundamental weakness of the tribal development programmes is the absence of the people's participation in the development process. See L. C. Jain, B. V. Krishnamurthy and P. M. Tripathy, *Grass Without Roots: Rural Development Under Government Auspices* (New Delhi: Sage Publications, 1985), 166-169; L. Jagatdeb, "Tribal Development in India: A Critique", in *Tribal Development in India*, edited by R. N. Pati and Basantibala Jena (New Delhi: Ashish Publishing House, 1989), 151-170: and *Thanzauva, Theology of Community*, 47.

mainly those charged with the delivery of policies and the rural rich. L. C. Jain and his colleagues have commented thus:

> If present arrangements persist they would lead not only to a loss of scarce resources but also to an accentuation of inequality and corruption and an incalculable loss of respect for government as a just and honest institution, worse still, they would extinguish the slender hopes of the poor to see a better future[62].

In most states of Northeast India, development activities are highly politicized and huge amounts of money granted for the economic development of the people are siphoned off for political purposes. Politicians in power, in their bid to survive in electoral politics, often misappropriate development finds to further their political aspirations. Sreeradha Datta, for instance, has noted how huge amounts of development funds were siphoned off through collusive arrangements between politicians and underground insurgents in Nagaland.[63] Such politicization of development schemes not only cripples development work, but also fosters corruption in the region.

In addition to the above limitations, the overriding ideology behind the present tribal development programmes is inadequate. In this regard, R. R. Prasad has pointed out that the main objective of tribal development in India is just, "to make tribals catch up non-tribals in the race for social, political and economic prosperity"[64]. Such a predetermined objective of development both undermines tribal society and also restricts growth. Though it may be quite desirable that tribal people should also come up to the level of the non-tribal in terms of economic development, tribal people do not necessarily need to follow in the footsteps of the non-tribal. What

62 Jain, Krishnamurthy and Tripathi, *Grass without Roots*, 197.

63 Sreeradha Datta, "What Ails The Northeast: An Enquiry into the Economic Factors", cited from http://www.idsa-india.org, 12.

64 R. R. Prasad, "Tribal Development in India: Strategies and Programmes", *Journal of Rural Development* 7/1 (1988), 81-103.

tribal people would wish for is economic development in harmony with tribal society.

2.2.4. *Tribal Uprising*

Northeast India is described by Lalsangkima Pachuau as the "problem child of modern India."[65] Observing the current situation of Northeast India, Lalsangkima, without any hesitation, states:

> The problem child has not shown any sign of becoming less problematic, ...The post-independence history of Northeast India has been infested with conflicts and violence, and the region is plagued with layers of inter-community and inter-ethnic tensions. Excepting a few states, most of the states have experienced armed insurrections costing enormous bloodshed. According to a recent study, in each of the last three years, the death toll due to insurgency reported by the media was more than 1000 each year. The damaged caused by the problem child to the family continue to multiply A recognition of the severity of the child's problem and a careful diagnosis for proper healing is now urgently called for. More importantly, one must also admit that the problem of the problem child does not lie only with the child, but also with the parents and the other members of the family. The healing of the child now includes correcting the way the parents have treated the child and how the entire family members relate themselves to the child. Healing as wholeness demands a wholistic diagnosis and treatment.[66]

---

65 Lalsangkima Pachuau, *Ethnic Identity and Christianity: A Socio-Historical and Missiological Study of Christianity in Northeast India with Special Reference to Mizoram* (Frankfurt am Main et al.: Peter Lang, 2002), 29.

66 Lalsangkima Pachuau, "Toward Overcoming Violence in North East India: A Perspective Drawn from Minority Experience" A Paper Presented at ATTI Conference at ECC, Whitefield (May 2003), 1. Before Lalsangkima, we have also seen two books, that depict the picture of Northeast India like, V. I. K. Sarin, *India's North-East in Flames* (Ghaziabad: Vikas Publishing Company,

The eruption of armed struggle among tribal people in Northeast India was mainly because the Government of India address their sufferings and aspirations, not in proper perspective. For reasons already mentioned above, the tribal people became extremely discontented. They developed a sense of distrust and suspicion towards the dominant communities and the government they represented.[67] All these factors, plus their apprehension about losing their land and identity, have contributed to the tendency of tribal people to take up arms and struggle for political separation. The first of such movements in Northeast India began with the formation of Naga National Council (NNC) in the early nineteen fifties in Nagaland, which was followed by the Mizo National Front (MNF) in Mizoram in the mid nineteen sixties. Others followed.[68]

In most cases, it was the passion for liberation from the impoverished condition of life that compelled the tribal peoples of Northeast India to take up arms and demand political separation. For instance, in the case of the Mizo National Front movement in Mizoram, it was the miserable experience of hunger following the *mautam*[69], and the government failure to respond to their problems, that served as the responsible factor for the formation of the armed revolutionary movement. The widespread discontentment and frustration against the Government of India in general and the

---

1982), and S. K. Ghosh, India' *North-East Frontier: Fifty Turbulent Years* (Titagarh: Linkman Publication, 1997).

67 Animesh Ray, *Mizoram Dynamics of Change* (Calcutta: Pearl Publishers, 1982), 295.

68 A number of other movements erupted later. They are: the Tribal National Volunteer (TNV), Tripura National Army (TNA), All Tripura Tribal Force (ATTF) and Tripura National Army (TNA) in Tripura; United Liberation Front of Asom (ULFA), Boro Security Force (BrSF) in Assam; the People's Liberation Army (PLA), People's Liberation Army of Kanglai Pak (PLAKP), Kuki National Army in Manipur, etc, to name a few of them, see Pachuau, *Ethnic Identity and Christianity*, 46-57.

69 In 1959, a specific tyope of bamboo flowered all over the Mizo Hills and there was an incredible multiplication of rats. When the rats exhausted the bamboo flowers, they attacked and devoured the standing crops, bringing about a great famine, which the Mizo called *mautam*.

Government of Assam in particular eventually led to the formation of the Mizo National Front (MNF).[70]

These revolutionary movements turned Northeast India into one of the most troubled and disturbed area of the country. Hence, it is not wrong to call Northeast India the problem child of India.

2.3. Common Characteristics of Tribals

Tribals, irrespective of different groups of different regions, have maintained some basic commonalities. Their belief systems, habitats, lifestyles and economy have helped them to maintain some common features.

2.3.1. *Interconnectedness of Tribal Cultures and Nature*

There is an inseparable interconnection between tribal cultures and forest. Asangla Lemtur states about the link between tribals and forest that "the tribal treat the forest as their ancestral home, since the forest has been a permanent abode for them."[71] For tribals, forest is their home as every walk of life has deeply attached with forest: the sources of their livelihood is forest, the source of medicine is forest, the place of education is in the forest, and their worship is in the forest. T. Lakshmaiah has rightly stated that "there is a sort of emotional attachment existing between a tribal and forest"[72] while reclaiming the bond of connection of the two.

---

70 John Vanlal Hluna, *Church & Political Upheaval in Mizoram* (Aizawl: Mizo History Association, 1985), 10. MNF signed a historic Peace Accord with Indian Government on June 30, 1986 and Mizoram was given the status of full fledged Statehood under the Republic of India.

71 Asangla Lemtur, "An Ethical Analysis of the Tribal Ethnic Identity Crises in India: A Feminist Critique," in *Religion and Society* 50/3 (September, 2005), 62.

72 T. Lakshmaiah, "Tribal Tensions" in Buddhadeb Chaudhuri ed., *Tribal Transformation in India*, Vol. III, Ethnopolitics and Identity Crises (New Delhi: Inter India Publication, 1992), 413.

2.3.2. *Centrality of Land*

Land occupies a central place in the life of tribals. A. Wati Longchar is of an ardent advocate of this fact. Longchar argues that for tribals, the land is life as almost every aspect of tribal life is revolving around the land. The land is the source of origin, nourishment, and the land gives identity, "no land, no people".[73]

2.3.3. *Communitarianism*

Another visible common characteristic, in a wide range of tribal societies, is a communitarian way of living together in the village level in which people know each other sharing their joys and sorrows and giving importance to the welfare of community. Community for tribals means commonality.[74]

3. Mizo Cultural Traditions

As we embark upon the cultural traditions of the Mizo community in Mizoram, it will be quite appropriate to first examine the meaning of culture and have an overview of the social and cultural context of the Mizo community in the past, before the introduction of Christianity to the people.

3.1. The Meaning of Culture

The word 'culture' does not refer only to education of the intellect or creation of refined or cultured activities such as art, literature, etc. The classical understanding of culture, which alludes strictly to the inner processes that shape the intellectual, spiritual and aesthetic faculties of a person, has long been discarded.[75] So, too has the widely accepted definition of culture held by the 19th century anthropologist Edward Tylor that, "Culture or civilization is that complex whole

73 A. Wati Longchar, "The Need for Doing Tribal Theology," in *Tribal Theology: A Reader*, 9.

74 Thanzauva, *Theology of Community*, 108.

75 Aylward Shorter, *Towards a Theology of Inculturation* (London: Geoffrey Chapman, 1988), 20.

which includes knowledge, belief, art, morals, law, custom, and any other capabilities and habits acquired by man as a member of society."[76] Culture is a difficult term to define, even describe. No society is strictly mono-cultural. The modern empirical view gives a more comprehensive understanding of culture. Studies on cultural anthropology have brought into focus that the ethnological and social dimensions of culture "includes not only the arts and letters, but also modes of life, the fundamental rights of human beings, value systems, traditions and beliefs."[77] It corresponds to the need of people for full humanity, because culture is "what belongs to the people, it is the people, not something that is bestowed upon them like politics, loans, dams and war."[78] Culture facilitates social harmony, gives meaning, identity and a sense of pride to individuals. Culture, which embeds positive human aspirations, must be valued as the soul of society.

A certain culture, as the lifestyle of a community together with symbols, myths, norms, values, concepts, language, and meaning, can be in conflict with another culture of a different social group. Cultural differences characterize and dissociate peoples, groups, races and nations, indicating singular worldview, ethos, genus, history and beliefs. This broad anthropological idea of culture makes it a dynamic, all-embracing and evolving reality, open to diversity and conflicts.

Culture as the totality of ideological (thought and value systems) and structural (social economic, political, historical, and ethical) processes that characterize a people in a given cultural space is what concerns our discussion. For us, it is important to understand that the symbolic system people construct for making their world, life and society meaningful is rooted in faith and hope. On the one hand, that construct influences their worldview and value system, which

---

76 Edward B. Tylor, *Primitive Culture*, Vol. I (London: John Murray, 1903), 1.

77 S. Ramanathan, "Will culture make the difference?" Intergovernmental Conference on Cultural Policies for Development, Stockholm, 1998, quoted in *The Hindu Magazine* (July 14, 2002), 1.

78 Monteiro, *Church and Culture*, 44.

in turn conditions individual behaviour, community relationships and organization. On the other hand, worldviews can animate cultural expressions, customs, rituals, structures and institutions. S. Ramanathan writes, "Human behaviour gets defined by its culture, and culture and community borders get defined as much by difference and multiple identities, as by commonality."[79] Culture provides questions and answers to the human condition. It is not made up of merely verifiable behavioural patterns. It may also feature certain patterns, values and goals constructed on emotional grounds. The idea of culture as understood today encompasses every aspect of human life material, spiritual, social, political and emotional.

3.2. Political, Economic, Social and Cultural milieu of Mizoram

As has been stated earlier, the tribal people in Mizoram are of Mongoloid stock. Nevertheless, due to the absence of written records for many years, it is almost impossible to trace their relationship with the other people of Mongoloid stock. They lived in the Chin Hills of Myanmar, which lie in the area neighouring Mizoram for nearly four hundred years before settling in Mizoram.[80]

The Mizos are made up of various tribes, which include Lusei, Hmar, Lai, Paihte, Ralte, Mara, etc.[81] It is commonly believed that the various sub-tribes of the Mizos had already organized themselves as a distinct socio-cultural ethnic group of the time when they lived in the Chin Hills of Myanmar. Later, under the strong leadership of the

79 Ramanathan, "Will culture make the difference?" 1.

80 The word "Mizoram" is also a new name given to the land formerly known a Lushai Hills or Lushai District. In 1954, when the District Council was formed, through the Legislative Act, the Lushai district was changed into Mizo district. When the Mizo district was granted Union Territory after years of struggle for independence from the Indian Union, the Mizo district officially became known as Mizoram. Mizoram is now one of the states of the Indian Union. It is located in the southern tip of the northeast India. Bounded by Burma in the east and south and by Bangladesh in the west, Mizoram has more than 500 kilometers of international boundary.

81 B. C. Allen, *Lushai District Gazetteer*, Vol. X (Allahabad: The Pioneer Press, 1906), 48.

Lusei tribe, the Mizos were supposed to have organized themselves into one political and economic unit. The process appears to have been gradual and the final shape of it took place with the annexation of the land by the British in 1880. The Mizos speak one common language called Mizo. According to the 1901 census, the population of Mizoram was 82,434 of who about 99% were Mizos.[82]

3.2.1 *Political Set Up*

Before the advent of the British, the Mizos did not have a political organization for the entire tribe. For the purpose of conquest, that is to suppress other clan chiefs within their area and to defend their land against encroachment in the foothills, the chiefs would occasionally organize joint action. But this was not permanent. Mizo polity was village- based. The Mizos lived in villages, which is the basic unit of their society. They are a close-knit society with no caste system or class distinctions. Miss E. Chapman who worked in Mizoram as a missionary was right when she said that there is a strong sense of unity among the Mizos.[83]

3.2.1.1. The Lal (chief) and Council of Elders

A village was a well-knit community over which the *Lal* or chief and his council of *Upa* or elders ruled. The British were amazed to find numerous and efficiently run village administrative units entirely independent of each other. Apart from a number of *Pawi*, *Mara* and Fanai chiefs who ruled mainly in the southern hills, most chiefs belonged to the *Sailo* family of the *Lusei* clan who established themselves as the principal chiefs throughout the northern and central areas of what came to be called Mizoram. The Sailo clan had gained this position of dominance by eliminating the lesser chiefs before the advent of the British.

---

82 Allen, *Lushai District Gazetteer*, 48.

83 E. Chapman and M. Clark, *Mizo Miracle* (Madras: CLS, 1968), 10.

A number of scholars have described the way in which the Sailo chiefs ruled their villages.[84] The chief owned the village and its land. The inhabitants of the village were his subjects and were implicitly bound by customary law to obey and execute his commands. The chiefs were generally wise and shrewd, knowing how to make their people loyal to themselves. The people themselves willingly fought for their chief and carried out his errands. The chief also had great responsibility for his subjects. As the guardian of the village he was responsible for defending it from enemies. He was the leader in war as well as the dispenser of justice. His attitude towards his subjects was paternalistic; they were treated as his children, whom he helped when in need, chastising the guilty and rewarding those who had achieved something noteworthy. The chief was respected, admired and loved by his subjects. Very seldom did the subjects disregard his rulings. If they did, they would almost certainly be expelled from the village and their property confiscated.

Even though the chief theoretically held power, in fact the government of the villages had democratic elements. This was due to the appointment, by the chief, of Upa (Elders) to assist him in the administration of the village. The chief was free to appoint whomever he deemed fit, but usually they were chosen from among the *thangchhuah*, who were reputed public figures and representatives of the different clans found in the village.[85] Thus, while the position of the chief ensured stability to a mobile society the participation of the elders in the decision-making process provided a broader representation of the people's interests. While in theory the chief

84 See N. E. Parry, *Monograph on Lushai Customs and Ceremonies (1928);* N. Chatterji, *The Mizo Chief and His Administration (1975);* Vanlawma, "Mizo Lalte leh an Khua leh Tui," *Mizo Zia-Rang* (1975).

85 Thangchhuah was an honorific title given to a man who had distinguished himself by killing a certain number of different animals in the chase or by giving a certain number of public feasts culminating in the Khuangchawi feast. See "thangchhuah" in J. H. Lorrain, *Dictionary of the Lushai Language* (Calcutta: The Asiatic Society, 1940, reprinted 1975), 447. A detailed discussion about *Thangchhuah* can be obtained from Kipgen, *Christianity and Mizo Culture*, 120.

could give an order without consultation, and the people would not dare disobey, in practice very few chiefs would attempt to do so for the reasons mentioned above. Thus, for instance, if there was a case involving the chief's own relatives, he would usually leave it for the elders to decide rather than being involved in the judgment himself. Thus, by demonstrating fairness in the way they formed their judgments, the chief and council of elders normally faced no opposition to their decisions. Cases were attended to immediately and justice administered speedily.

3.2.2. *The Economic System*

3.2.2.1. Jhum Cultivation

The Mizo economy was based on agriculture. The agricultural system of jhum, slash and burn, was practiced in Mizoram. Every year a new plot was chosen for the cultivation. Therefore, after about ten years all the land near a village had been used. Since there was unoccupied land available elsewhere, after this period of time the entire village would be shifted to a new site.

3.2.2.2. Property

Constant shifting of villages made it impossible to amass wealth in the form of immovable or even substantial moveable property. Members of the family had to be able to carry on their backs what they owned to the next village site. What can be called household property was therefore very limited.

3.2.2.3. A Bamboo-Based Economy

The most important constituent in the Mizo economy was bamboo. Bamboo of various types met many of the essential needs of the people. At every stage of its growth, from shoot to maturity, it served a specific purpose. The new shoots provided food; young bamboos provided material for making baskets and other household implements; and mature bamboo provided the primary building material. Due to these and many other ways in which bamboo was used, the Mizo economy was very much dependent upon it.

3.2.3. *Religious Beliefs*

The traditional religion of the Mizos had been described as animism, which means attribution of soul to inanimate objects or natural phenomena.[86] The term is today generally used to describe the faith of primal or preliterate people depending on memory and oral traditions rather than on sacred literature. It involves belief in all kinds of spirits with a High Spirit, including belief in some form of life after death. In accordance with this definition, the Mizos were certainly animists. They believed that the world was occupied by spirits, some benevolent while others were malignant to human beings. The evil spirits inhabited trees, streams, springs, mountains or any other objects curiously shaped or deformed. They would not attack human unless provoked. When an unwary man encroached on the sacred habitation, they got angry and cause all kinds of illness and misfortunes. To recover from the illness these evil spirits had to be placated by the sacrifice of appropriate animals. This was prescribed by the *puithiam* or priest who performed the sacrifice when the required animals and other materials were obtained. He killed the animals with the suitable chants, cut the extremities off and placed them on a bamboo platform. This was the share of the evil spirit to whom the sacrifice was made, the extremities representing the whole animal. The meat was cooked and all of it had to be eaten on the spot, usually on the outskirt of the village.

The most important sacrifice a Mizo had to perform was the 'sakhaw biak' (worship to the family or clan god). Every family had to always keep castrated pigs and the largest of them was reserved for this purpose. "Sa" means animal and "khua" means nature or weather. The combination probably means "life principle or basis. *Sakhua*

86 Zairema, "The Mizos and their Religion", in *Towards a Tribal Theology: The Mizo Perspective*, edited by K. Thanzauva (Aizawl: Mizo Theological Conference, 1989), 32.

was the family or clan god.[87] Clan here is used to describe a group of blood related people speaking the same dialect within a larger tribe descended from some ancestors not too far off in the history. If one neglects this sacrifice *sakhua* may get angered, in which case he might withdraw his protection. The family would then be more vulnerable to the attacks of evil spirits.

Another important spirit to who sacrifice was made at one stage or other in life was *Khaltu* (one who plays with), who can be described as a guardian angel of individuals. *Khaltu* was not as exalted as *sakhua* or other spirits, however, was intimately connected with the life and welfare of individuals. A person's *khaltu* is said to belong to the opposite sex.

What is interesting with regard to Mizo religion is that each clan had its own family god and each individual had his or her own guardian angel. What is more interesting in Mizo religion is their belief in the existence of multiple spirits comprising both males and females. This, the belief in gods and goddesses, sanctioned freedom for worship to the people irrespective of sex. Every Mizo had the right to worship his or her *sakhua* and had an access to salvation. There was no discrimination on any bases; everyone was free to embrace any *sakhua* according to his or her wishes. Some of the features, which are worth noting in the Mizo religion, are: (1) their belief in a supreme spirit (2) communitarian understanding of God.

3.2.3.1. Belief in a Supreme Spirit

Belief in the existence of a supreme being had already developed among the Mizo people before the coming of Christianity. J. Shakespear mentioned that practically all the sub-tribes of the Lushei-

87 According to J. H. Lorrain, in his dictionary of Lushai Language, the term 'sakhua' is given three meanings: (1) an object of worship, a god; (2) ancient ancestors who are worshipped by the Lushais; (3) the spirits who presided over the house or household. See, J. H. Lorrain, "sakhua", *Dictionary of the Lushai Language* (Calcutta: The Asiatic Saciety, 1940).

Kuki family believed in the supreme spirit called "Pathian"[88] who was supposed to be the creator of everything and the benevolent being, but had, however little concern with men,[89] as A. G. McCall also stated that "all Lushais (Mizos) believed mutually in the existence of one supreme God, a God of all humanity and goodness."[90]

3.2.3.2. Communitarian Understanding of God

It is interesting to note that the Mizo understanding of God or gods can be explained as communitarian, in the sense that there is no hierarchy in their understanding of the family gods. Even though they have the idea of a supreme spirit and spirits, these spirits had been remembered according to their functions. This communitarian understanding of God has some similarity with the doctrine of the Trinity in Christianity, particularly, with regard to the functions of the three gods, *Pathian* (Holy Father) *Khuanu* (goddess) and *Vanchung nula* (maiden or daughter). Hminga has commented that the Mizos seemed to think of *Pathian* as living in the heaven with a family just like a human family, *Pu Vana* (the grandfather Heaven), *Khuanu* (Pathian's wife or Mother goddess) and *Vanchung nula* (maiden in heaven above):

> ...just like the Christian doctrine of Trinity-Father, Son and Holy Spirit, the traditional Mizo concept had a triune god idea in the Pathian family-grandfather, a wife and a daughter.[91]

---

88 "Pa" means father and "thian" or "thien" means "holy"; 'Pathian' is the combination of the two words, 'pa' and 'thien', which means "Holy Father' holy in the sense of pure and unmixed. See Zairema, " The Mizos and their Religion", 39.

89 J. Shakespear, The Lushei Kuki Clans, London: Macmillan & Co.Ltd, 1912), quoted in C. L. Hminga, "The Traditional Mizo Concept of God", in *Towards a Tribal Theology: The Mizo Perspective*, edited by K. Thanzauva (Aizawl: Mizo Theological Conference, 1989), 46.

90 Quoted from A. G. McCall, *Lushai Chrysalis* (London: Lusac and Company, 1949) by C. L. Hminga, "The Traditional Mizo Concept of God", 46.

91 McCall, *Lushai Chrysalis*, 46.

It is reasonable to presume that believe in this communitarian God (reality) have deeply influenced the Mizo people to sustain a communitarian spirit in society.

3.2.4. *Mizo Understanding of Humanity*

The Mizo understanding of humanity may be presented in two ways: the human being as a unitary being and the human being as a social being.

The Mizo people perceived the world in terms of relationship. In their understanding of human nature, there was no dichotomy between body and soul, or between sacred and secular. They believed that every human being had a soul, and yet the soul and physical body were related inseparably to each other. If the body felt sickness or pain, the soul also suffered. The Mizos believe that if a person underwent a frightening physical experience, such as being mauled by a wild animal or being captured by an enemy, the soul was similarly frightened. In order to restore a proper or normal life to such an endangered person a sacrifice had to be made. Sometimes the soul was believed to have detached itself from the person and then to wander around. A sick person might dream that she or he was still in the place where they had been before they had gotten sick. In such a case, the soul was believed to have failed to return to the person and must be called home.[92] In this way, body and soul formed inseparable parts of the same personal reality in the traditional tribal worldview.

Traditional tribal religion had a concern for the total human being, both physical and spiritual because of this concept of the unity of the human person, In traditional Mizo society, the sacrifices people offered to the evil spirits were made primarily for the purpose of recovering from physical illness. Because of this, Zairema has suggested that the word "sacrifice" in the Mizo context should be

---

92 Zairema, "The Mizos and their Religion", in *Towards a Tribal Theology: The Mizo Perspective*, edited by K. Thanzauva (Aizawl: Mizo Theological Conference, 1989), 37.

more appropriately understood as "ceremonial cure"[93]. In traditional Mizo belief, attainment of a place in paradise, or *pialral,* in the life after death was integrally connected with providing food to the people. In order to get a place in paradise, one had to become *thangchhuah* by providing a series of feasts to the community. Hence, in the traditional tribal worldview, faith in God and service to others were integrally related as soul to body; one could not attain paradise without attending to the physical needs of others.[94]

Humanity among the tribal people was perceived more in terms of the community, rather than of the individual. For tribal people, a person's humanity could not be realized unless she or he was in community. In traditional tribal society, those who lived in one village usually belonged to one particular tribe or clan. They were closely related to one another, and maintained a particular system of social organization based on family ties and blood relationship. Particularly among the Mizos, every village had a chief, under whose leadership the village became a well-knit community. The chief ruled over the village and a council of elders, appointed by the chief himself, assisted him in the administration. Although the chief held absolute authority over the village, his mode of life and dress were not different from those of the common people. Similarly, though chieftainship was hereditary, there was not a particular chiefly clan among Mizos. Any person could become a chief provided he had followers. Therefore, among the Mizos, if the chief acted "in a cruel manner, his subjects would be likely to migrate to another village with a more benevolent ruler".[95]

Usually, the chief acted as a father to his subjects, helping them when they were in distress and in need. Therefore, the tribal people lived together as one family in the village. They developed a strong sense of community and oneness. It was in the community that a tribal found his/her true humanity. In former times, if someone asked

---

93 Zairema, "The Mizos and their Religion", 37.

94 L. H. Lalpekhlua, *Contextual Christology: A Tribal Perspective* (Delhi: ISPCK, 2007), 158.

95 Kipgen, *Christianity and Mizo Culture*, 59.

a tribal where she or he came from, the tribal would reply that she or he came from such and such a person's village, citing the name of their chief rather than the name of their village. So, in the traditional tribal society, the individual person's identity was subordinated to the community identity.[96]

To be a human in the traditional tribal worldview was to live in relation with others in a community. In traditional tribal society, there were no written constitutions, rules or regulations; the system of life was based on interpersonal relationship. People lived together in mutual trust and respect for one another. Their houses had no locks and keys and yet theft was hardly known. In the traditional Mizo house, a firewood stick was simply placed to obstruct the doorway, and it was quite sufficient to keep any person from entering the house.[97] This community consciousness, or understanding of humanity in relation to community, had been developed in a long process and kept alive by their cultural traditions. In what follows, we shall look at some of the vital cultural traditions that uphold and strengthen the community consciousness among the Mizo people.

4. Select Mizo Socio-Cultural Traditions

The cultural traditions of Mizo society include the past and present, socio-cultural traditions, customs, religious beliefs and practices. They include myths and legends, folktales and stories, wisdom and proverbs, mores, morals, and songs. These cultural traditions have been transmitted orally from generation to generation. However, in this study, we shall look into only three aspects of Mizo cultural traditions, namely, the community home (*Zawlbuk*), the community ethics (*Tlawmngaihna*), and the life principle of the community (*Egalitarianism*). For the Mizo community, it may be said that all other cultural traditions revolve around these three aspects; in other words, the integrating principle of the tribal communities in general and the Mizo community in particular is communitarianism, which

96 Kipgen, *Christianity and Mizo Culture*, 59.

97 Ibid.

is the final outcome of the harmonious blend and functions of these three triangulating aspects of the culture.

Each of these Mizo cultural traditions, *Zawlbuk, Tlawmngaihna* and Egalitarian principle of life, have been theologically treated by quite a number of theologians, like K. Thanzauva[98], Mangkhosat Kipgen[99] and Lalpekhlua[100]. However, it is beyond the scope of their inquiries to critically examine the relevance and potentiality of each of these cultural elements for the development of Mizo tribal ecclesiology. Therefore, in this section, the main purpose is to explore these three essential aspects of Mizo cultural traditions with the expectation that the insights from these traditions can be resourceful for our investigation of tribal theology in general and ecclesiology in particular.

People who have worked in close contact with tribal communities will certainly admit that the strength of the tribal people is their community-centered life known as communitarianism.[101] The fundamental idea of communitarianism is that human beings are, by nature, social beings. As Robert Redfield explained the characteristics of tribal a community, which he called "The folk Society", as follows:

> Such society is small, isolated, non literate, and homogenous, with a strong sense of group solidarity. The ways of living are conventionalized into that coherent system we call "culture". Behaviour is traditional, spontaneous, uncritical, and personal, there is no legislation or habit of experiment and reflection for intellectual ends. Kinship, its relationships

---

98 K. Thanzauva, *Theology of Community: Tribal Theology in the Making (*Aizawl: Mizo Theological Conference, 1997).

99 Mangkhosat Kipgen, *Christianity and Mizo Culture* (Jorhat: MTC, 1996).

100 Lalpekhlua, *Contextual Christology: A Tribal Perspective* (Delhi: ISPCK, 2007).

101 Communitarianism is a concept and life principle of tribal community in which a homogenous people live together sharing their joy and sorrows in mutual love and care. See a detailed description of communitarianism in Thanzauva's book, *Theology of Community*, 136-145.

> and the familial group are the unit of action. The sacred prevails over the secular; the economy is one of status rather than the market.[102]

As Thanzauva has stated, Redfield had used modernization as the sole criterion to judge the tribal society and failed to notice the good aspects of tribal society.[103] One of the common characteristics, in tribal society, is the spirit of communitarianism, or the practice of a communitarian way of living together in the village level, in which people know each other, sharing their joys and sorrows. For tribal people, community means in one sense a commonality in which diversity exists but unity prevails in the long run. Community means that the sense of oneness, a sense of entity, extends to the whole territorial society. Community means that the culture sets values that orient behaviour in the direction of common interest.[104]

One may question how such a communitarian society actually operate in the complex "mix" which is life- be it in primitive or sophisticated; whether the nature of community described above is a reality of the past; or a romanticized construct. For Thanzauva, it is more than a reality of the past; it is to a great extent the actual life of the tribal community even today.[105] Then, in what follows, we shall examine the factors or agents that uphold the tribal communitarian way of living.

As has been stated, for Mizos, there are three factors that are most essential for communitarian living, they are, the Community Home, *Zawlbuk*, community ethics, *Tlawmngaihna*, and Egalitarian principle. We shall now turn to a comprehensive look at each of these factors that have upheld and sustained the Mizo community throughout the centuries.

---

102 Robert Redfield, "The Folk Society," *American Journal of Sociology,* Vol. 32 (1947), 293. Cited by K. Thanzauva, *Theology of Community* (Aizawl: MTC, 1997), 107.

103 Thanzauva, *Theology of Community*, 107.

104 Ibid., 108.

105 Ibid.

4.1. Zawlbuk

The *Zawlbuk* was a Mizo social institution, which met the socio-cultural and educational needs of the community. In English translation, a *Zawlbuk* is described as a community house, dormitory, bachelor house, village house, and community hall. It is common practice of various tribes in the world to construct a large house in the village for the community, particularly for bachelors to sleep together.[106] S. E. Peal observed that the system of a community home in the tribal society was found to exist from Bhutan to New Zealand and from the *Marquesas* to Nigeria.[107] Most of the tribes in Northeast India used to have a community home, for instances, *Kichu* for Angami, *Ariju* for Aos, *Dikha* Chang for Sumis, *Longshim* for Tangkhuls, *Nokpangte* for Garos, *Zawlbuk* for Mizos. The *Zawlbuk* in the Mizo community was used for a community home, mainly for bachelors. Literally *Zawlbuk* means "House in a flat ground". *Zawl* means flat ground, *buk* means a hut or a temporary house.[108] However, the meaning of the *Zawlbuk* is much deeper and greater

106 K. Thanzauva, "Theology of Zawlbuk", in *Towards a Tribal Theology: From the Mizo Perspective* (Aizawl: Mizo Theological Conference, 1989), 99.

107 S. E. Peal, The Communal Barrack of Primitive Races, cited by K. Thanzauva, *Theology of Community*, 134. See also S. S. Shashi, ed., *Encyclopaedia of Indian Tribes*, Vol. 10: Tribal culture, custom and Affinities (New Delhi: Anmol Publications Pvt. Ltd., 1994), 132f. These social institutions flourished in their full glory only in the past and now have almost completely disappeared as a result of the impact of modern civilization and the influence of Christian missionaries.

108 The *Zawlbuk* was constructed on the largest open space in the center of the village, usually close to the chief's house. In a large village there could be more than one, in which case the one nearest the chief's house was usually the biggest and was considered the most important. The *Zawlbuk* could easily be distinguished from other buildings due to its distinctive shape and large size- it had to be spacious enough to accommodate all the young men boys of the village. See a detailed description from H. L. Malsawma, *Sociology of the Mizos* (Guwahati, Delhi: Spectrum Publications, 2002), 55; and Mangkhosat Kipgen, *Christianity and Mizo Culture* (Jorhat: MTC, 1996), 61-64; K. Thanzauva, *Theology of Community*, 134-147; N. E. Parry, *A Monograph on Lushai Customs and Ceremonies* (Aizawl: Tribal Research, 1976), 8-10.

in its significance than what can be understood from such a simple meaning. It was the most useful institution for social education. It was not only the abode of the youth physically, but was indeed a place in which youth were shaped into becoming responsible adult members of the society. The life of a *Zawlbuk* also insured that a child, as he grew to maturity, was not at any time suddenly forced into a different world than what he was accustomed to living in earlier days. It was not just a place of austerity with a rigid set of rules; it was more well-evolved machinery built up through intuitive recognition of society's needs and demands in harmonious blend with the instinctive urges of the individual.

4.1.1. *The Genesis of Zawlbuk*

It is difficult to trace the origin of the *Zawlbuk* in Mizo society. Some writers are of the opinion that it is a survivor of the community house, which were the first stage in the development of homes when the whole village lived together. Lalbiakthanga in his book entitled, "The Mizos" describes the origin of the *Zawlbuk* and argues that it was introduced after the Mizos migrated from Burma to Mizoram.[109] According to H.L. Malsawma, Zawlbuk seems to have existed at first in Khawnglung village in Mizoram around 1860 AD.[110] Even though nobody knows for certain the origin of the *Zawlbuk*, it is reasonable to believe that it arose out of necessity. The people lived in fear, not of the *huai* (spirit), but of enemies and wild enemies. Consequently, there were occasions when the sudden united action of the young men was needed. To meet these needs, the people probably developed the *Zawlbuk* where all the unattached bachelors would be together. In short, we may say that it came into existence to serve the needs of the society as conceived by the Mizo chiefs and continued to function as the most important social unity.

---

109 Quoted in V. S. Lalrinawma, *Mizo Ethos: Changes and Challenges* (Aizawl: V. S. Lalrinawma, 2005), 38-42.

110 H. L. Malsawma, *Sociology of the Mizos* (Guwahati, Delhi: Spectrum Publications, 2002), 55.

4.1.2. *Description of the Building of Zawlbuk*

The *Zawlbuk* was usually built near the chief's house invariably at the most central place in a village. Situated within a stone throw of the chief's residence, it used to be a very large dwelling place capable of accommodating all young men and boys in the village. It was constructed by the united labour of the villagers at the command of the chief. It was to be built by all the male inhabitants in the village, from boys ten to eleven years of age to the elderly people, came out with their implements like *daos* and took part in the construction. It was generally built on a steep hillside so that the natural fall of the ground might allow ample room for domestic animals. The entire breadth of the *Zawlbuk* at the end facing the roadside functioned as its entrance and it started about four feet inside the edge of the platform on which the *Zawlbuk* was erected. At the point of the entrance a bamboo wall was fixed up with the entire roof breadth wise, leaving about five feet below it over the platform. The vacant space between the wall and the floor was popularly known as "Awk paka'. A big log sufficiently long to cover the entire breadth of the *Zawlbuk* was placed on the platform about four feet inside the bamboo woven entrance wall thereby leaving an open space as verandah. The dwellers had almost to roll over the log to find their place within the *Zawlbuk*. This log used to be called 'bawhbel'[111]. On one side of the open platform in front of the entrance, there used to be a large bare room, varying according to the size of the village, with a square earthen hearth in the center on which a few logs were always smouldering. At the far end there was a raised sleeping platform extending the width of the building[112]

4.1.3. *Zawlbuk Discipline*

The internal organization of the Zawlbuk as a social institution and an institution for providing educational growth of the inmates may

111 'Bawhbel' means rising on something with a very smooth surface. The resemblance of the picture of the *Zawlbuk* is shown in the Appendix B.

112 Malsawma, *Sociology of the Mizos,* 55; N. Chatterji, *The Earlier Mizo Society* (Kolkata: Tribal Research Institute, 2 Reprint, 2008), 69-71.

now be elaborated. The *Zawlbuk* had strictly maintained a logical order for its self-government. In order to administer the *Zawlbuk*, the chief recognized, but did not appoint, a leader called the *Val Upa*[113] (like Knighthood). The chief's recognition or acceptance was based on qualities such as industriousness, efficiency, courage and success as a hunter. The chief was the titular head, leaving the details of administration to the *Val Upa*. However, the only person in the village who held unbridled authority to prevent any such slovenly behaviours on the part of *Zawlbuk* inmates was the chief, who would usually show his disapproval by throwing a stone on the roof of the *Zawlbuk*. The *Val Upa* was responsible for organizing the group to take up definite responsibilities in looking after the welfare and exercising all round vigilance over the needs of the village. He would appoint a number of monitors under him with the charge of day-to-day vigilance and service on earmarked roads in the village with all the habitations along the same. For the orderly conduct of the inmates, the word of *Val Upa* was law. He was responsible for training the boys and young men under his charge in hunting, arts and in teaching ethics.

Even though there was separate a dormitory for women found in many tribal societies, the Zawlbuk was meant exclusively for men. The inmates were divided into three different categories: (1) The Val Upa (senior bachelors) (2) The Tlangval (bachelors) and (3) the Naupangte (boys).[114] The adult who constituted the higher and the more responsible group in the Zawlbuk were called "tlangval" (bachelors) while those of the lower group used to be called 'thingnawifawm[115]' (boys who had not yet attained puberty). The latter were duty-bound to carry out the orders of the "tlangval" in washing their shirts, running on different errands, collecting and carrying wood for the Zawlbuk fire as also bamboos and stones when graves were dug by the tlangval. In case of the failure or negligence on their part in carrying out duties assigned to them by the tlangval

113 The Val Upa was a senior and experienced bachelor.

114 Thanzauva, "Theology of Zawlbuk", in *Towards a Tribal Theology*, 101.

115 Boys who were assigned to collect firewood for the Zawlbuk.

the 'Val Upa' would inflict punishment to the offender in proportion to the nature of offence committed. In order to have the smooth functioning of the institution, strict rules were enforced; some of them are as follows:

1. No girl was allowed to enter into the *Zawlbuk*.
2. No drinking of rice beer or drunkenness was allowed.
3. No interference of outsiders was tolerated.
4. Theft of any article, big or small was regarded as very disgraceful.
5. No person was allowed to throw a stone at the Zawlbuk except the chief of the village.
6. All inmates should be always ready for war and emergency.[116]

Systematic inculcation of desirable habits and cherished values was a fundamental consideration in organizing the activities of the Zawlbuk and any socially unacceptable action or even slight departure from the established social norms of behaviour and conduct used to be severely dealt with. The disciplined life in the *Zawlbuk* taught them effectively the opposing claims of self-assertions and self-negation and to accept willingly and joyfully the demands of society on them over those of their own selves.

4.1.4. *Functions of the Zawlbuk*

The *Zawlbuk* served multifarious needs of the village. Since it was the time when human enemies and wild animals perpetually threatened the villages, and besides these, there was no formal educational system, the importance of the *Zawlbuk* in the life of the Mizo community cannot be overemphasized. The function of the institution of the *Zawlbuk* was multiple. The main functions may be portrayed as (i) Refuge of the Village (ii) Educational Institution (iii) Recreational Center (iv) *Zawlbuk* was the guardian of social ethics (v) Forum for discussing issues.

116 Thanzauva, "Theology of Zawlbuk", in *Towards a Tribal Theology*, 101-102.

4.1.4.1. *Zawlbuk* as the Refuge of the Village

In fact, it was social necessity that led to the formation of the institution of a community home. Therefore, the primary function of the community home was to ensure the security and peace of the village.[117] In time of inter-village feuds, head hunting, sudden attack of wild animals upon their domestic animals and human beings as well, it was the task of the young men in the Zawlbuk to protect the people in the village. The community home enabled young people to keep vigil and protect the village at any time.

4.1.4.2. *Zawlbuk* as Educational Institution

The *Zawlbuk* functions as a useful institution for training young men in their social and other duties. Even though the *Zawlbuk* had not formal arrangement for the education of its inmates, the practical life activities enjoined on them throughout their stay in the *Zawlbuk* gave them very vigorous training for playing an effective role in their own lives and in the society of which they were to form integral part in their lives to come. Thanzauva has rightly said that that *Zawlbuk* was the Mizo educational institution,[118] which provided different kinds of learning which were necessary for the community to live in the society and be self-sufficient. It was essentially a training institute for young men and boys to learn the art of singing, dancing, oratory, handicrafts, techniques of war, wrestling. The *Zawlbuk* education intended to offer all-round development.[119]

4.1.4.3. *Zawlbuk* as Recreational Centre

Zawlbuk was a centre of recreation, a kind of retreats where men could have some time by themselves away from the usual tasks. It was also a place of recreation for old folks who occupied the *Zawlbuk* almost all the time except in the night after the young men came home to sleep. The *Zawlbuk* was the place where villagers gathered together

---

117 Kipgen, *Christianity and Mizo Culture*, 62-63.

118 Thanzauva, *Theology of Community*, 174.

119 Ibid.

to sing, dance and do wrestling. Village comedians would tell stories and made all kinds of fun by acting and imitating others.[120]

4..1.4.4. *Zawlbuk* was the guardian of Mizo social ethics, *Tlawmngaihna*

The foundation of community-based life was laid in and by the *Zawlbuk* by sowing the seed of the wonderful philosophy of life expressed in *Tlawmngaihna.*[121] And, *Zawlbuk* was a place for giving instructions to the younger generations by the elderly people about manners, ethics, traditions, customs, religions and all essential things for their lives in their own context. Mizo social ethics, *Tlawmngaihna* can, at best, be given an operational definition expressing the various types of activities embracing *Tlawmngaihna* and summing up, though inadequately, as community over the self wherein self sacrifice for the needs of others was to come in spontaneously as a natural part of one's life. In the *Zawlbuk, Tlawmngaihna* was inculcated and also demonstrated in their day to day activities. Their way of life in *Zawlbuk* provided built in support for the basic philosophy of their life and the sustaining coherence to their community based organization. In short, we may say that the institution of *Zawlbuk* was the guardian of Mizo social ethics, *Tlawmngaihna.*

4.1.4.5. The *Zawlbuk* also offered the community a forum to discuss various issues relating to village welfare, security, relationship, hunting, inter-village feuding, head hunting, cultivation and their own history. The elders of the village used to visit in their leisure time to share their experience with the bachelors and sometimes narrated to them their myths, about their legendary heroes.[122] According to Thanzauva's assumption, in the *Zawlbuk,* informal consultations and seminars seemed to go on every day.[123] The *Zawlbuk* constituted

120 Thanzauva, *Theology of Community*, 174.

121 The Mizo philosophy or ethical code *Tlawmngaihna* will be discussed in the next section.

122 Thanzauva, *Theology of Community*, 174.

123 Ibid.

the hub of the village, functioning simultaneously like the present day hotel or motel; strangers from other villages who had no friends or relative in the village were usually entertained in the community home of the village. When the first missionaries came to Mizoram it was in the *Zawlbuk*, community home that they often preached the gospel and taught Christian hymns.[124]

4.1.5. *Critical Estimation of the Zawlbuk*

It has been explained how the institution of *Zawlbuk* in a Mizo village acted magnificently as its nerve centre. It may not therefore be irrelevant to attempt here a critical analysis of this as a social and educational institution from the perspective of gender equality.

The most important social fact that flows from the institutional assemblage of all able-bodied young men of the village in the *Zawlbuk* is the prominent place Mizo youth occupied in the shaping of the social mores and the upholding of traditional customs. The Mizo society, as it then existed, was a thoroughly male-dominated organization, the female folks being considered more as a chattel belonging to the male folks rather than complementary units. Their accepted place in the society was in the home to rear children, perform various domestic tasks and offer such physical assistance to the male folks as demanded by them in their jhum cultivation. Under no circumstances could a woman, young or old, visit a *Zawlbuk*. They were neither expected to offer any guidance or direction for the society's growth and development, nor did they themselves look for any more prominent place than what they enjoyed in their society.

124 Edwin Rowlands, in his report, *The Report of the Lushai Hills, 1897*, mentions, "there are also advantages for mission work; one special advantage is the Zawlbuk system in the village. The Zawlbuk is a large building where the young men, the bigger boys and strangers sleep; and here, at evening, an audience may always be found. Here, in olden times, it is said, they used to discuss their plans for raids and wars, now they recite here their folk lore and traditions; and here too, they hear the Gospel of the living Christ." See K. Thanzauva, comp., *Reports of the Foreign Mission of the Presbyterian Church of Wales on Mizoram* 1894-1957 (Aizawl: The Synod Literature and Publication Boards, 1997), 7.

Theirs was a subservient role and their acceptance of the same without any question prevented cracks in their social organization. Therefore, we may say that *Zawlbuk* as an institution strengthened the domination of male folks in the tribal society and trained them to adjust themselves without tension to the various constraints and restraints of their social mores and customs.

From our discussion about the *Zawlbuk*, what is very clear is that the *Zawlbuk* was a very potent instrument in the sustenance of all the peculiarities of the Mizo society. Even though there was a gender bias in itself, *Zawlbuk* was indeed a very powerful institution in the village organization and exercised perhaps the greatest influence in establishing the social norms and customs as also in perpetuating the highly cherished values of the Mizo people. It is not possible to understand the development and nature of Mizo culture without giving centrality to the role of the *Zawlbuk*.

4.1.6. *Abolition of the Institution of Zawlbuk*

The reason why and how this important social institution or community home has completely gone out of existence today requires some explanation and it is appropriate to examine the forces contributing to such total extinction of the *Zawlbuk* and its consequences.

According to H. L. Malsawma, the British administration and the introduction of formal education by the Western missionaries were responsible for the abolition of the institution of *Zawlbuk*. For him, as long as the chiefs succeeded to hold their powers over the people the institution of *Zawlbuk* occupied the centrality in the community life. However, after the subjugation of the then Lushai Hills by the British in later part of the nineteenth century, as also to the advent of the missionaries, disintegrating forces began to operate to undermine the stability of the *Zawlbuk*.[125] As the chiefs became the subjects under the British administration, the villagers dared to challenge the power of their chiefs, especially the parents of school children refused to send their male children to the *Zawlbuk* on the

125 Malsawma, *Sociology of the Mizos*, 61.

plea that home was a better place of study. Besides, as they had a contact with outsiders and exposed to other cultures, they were led to think that their past way of life with their *Zawlbuk* discipline was little conducive to their development. Those, who had been influenced by the Western culture, began to feel that the only way to improve their lot was to break away from their old ways of living and imitate the Westerners by embracing Christianity and copying their ways of life. For Malsawma, the outcome of all this was a fast erosion of the *Zawlbuk* life.[126]

The first significant open challenge from the church to the *Zawlbuk* institution came with the third revival which started in 1919 and continued for four years.[127] This third revival enormously strengthened the church both in size and influence. Everywhere new churches and mission schools sprang up and the confidence of Christian leaders was greatly enhanced. Church leaders, pastors and teachers began to criticize the disciplines and practices of the *Zawlbuk*.[128] The result of this attack was deterioration of the influence of *Zawlbuk* and it finally disappeared along with its patron-institution, chieftainship the latter was abolished by an Act of the Government of Assam in 1954.[129]

The British Official, Superintendent and one of the BMS missionaries, F. J. Raper made some efforts to revive the institution of *Zawlbuk*, however, due to the fast spread of education made it difficult to maintain it again.[130] F. J. Rapers succeeded to a certain extent in mobilizing the youthful energies of young men to charitable works, [131] but he failed to revive the age-old institution of the Mizo social cultural symbol due to a strong reaction from the indigenous church leaders. Those who opposed to revive the *Zawlbuk* argued

126 Malsawma, *Sociology of the Mizos*, 61.

127 Kipgen, *Christianity and Mizo Culture*, 179.

128 Kipgen, *Christianity and Mizo Culture*, 179.

129 L. B. Thanga, *The Mizos: A Study in Racial Personality* (Guwahati: United Publishers, 1978), 14.

130 Kipgen, *Christianity and Mizo Culture*, 182.

131 Malsawma, *Sociology of the Mizos*, 61.

that the institution of *Zawlbuk* need not be revived because the the church has taken the place of *Zawlbuk*.[132]

4.1.7. *Zawlbuk and Christianity*

Thanzauva argues that when the interaction between the gospel and the indigenous culture took place, it entailed rejection, adaptation and transformation of many elements of the receiving culture. Some elements of the Mizo culture were totally rejected, some were adapted and some were transformed or synthesized. With regard to *Zawlbuk*, the community home, for Thanzauva, the physical structure and traditional form of the community home is no more but the spirit of the community home was transformed into the Christian church and the educational hostels. He further comments that, in the process of interaction with other forces, some of the essential aspects of the *Zawlbuk* were lost and for him, the lost elements need to be rediscovered and incorporated into the existing ecclesiology.[133]

4.2. Tlawmngaihna: The Mizo Social Ethics

Tlawmngaihna is Mizo community ethics, and it is the life of the Mizo as well. Mizo tries to show this finest character in social life and activities. The spirit of *Tlawmngaihna* has been infused in the minds of the Mizo young boys and girls. Boys and girls learn *Tlawmngaihna* from their parents and elders. Outsiders who did not understand the concept of *Tlawmngaihna* often thought the *tlawmngai* Mizo foolish. Hrangkhuma Fanai described Mizo *Tlawmngaihna* in the sight of other cultures by using the incident in Shillong, Meghalaya. He said that when young Mizo men first studied at Shillong (outside Mizoram), they showed *Tlawmngaihna* by digging graves as they did in Mizoram. The local people, Khasi, used to say, "the Mizo like to dig graves". They did not understand that *Tlawmngaihna* required one to do something as if she/he enjoyed doing it.[134] When someone

132 Kipgen, *Christianity and Mizo Culture*, 181.

133 Thanzauva, *Theology of Community*, 140.

134 Hrangkhuma Fanai, "Mizoram Transformational Change: A Study of the Processes and Nature of Mizo Cultural change and Factors that contributed

offered them something to eat, a *tlawmngai* Mizo would say "Ka chak love" (I do not want) or "I am not hungry". It is not that they did not want the food offered to them, neither was it a refusal. It was a polite manner expressed in *tlawmngai* words. Or, an injured person would say "it is nothing" and refuse help, but other *tlawmngai* understood and helped. *Tlawmngai* persons did not want to trouble others, and be a burden to them.

The most important contribution of the community home, *Zawlbuk* to Mizo society was the development and perfection of *Tlawmngaihna*. *Tlawmngaihna* is the term used for the Mizo "code of morals,"[135] a "highly prized virtue"[136] and "a wonderful philosophy of life"[137], which is too rich in meaning to render it in any single word or phrase of another language. J. H. Lorrain, in his monumental *Dictionary of Lushai Language,* gives a comprehensive meaning of *Tlawmngaihna*, which is widely used by contemporary writers, parts of which are given below:

1. to be self-sacrificing, unselfish, self-denying, persevering, stoical, stout-hearted, plucky, brave, firm, independent...
2. to put one's own inclinations on one side and do a thing which one would rather not do, with the object either of keeping up one's prestige, etc., or of helping another, or of not disappointing, etc.
3. to do whatever the occasion demands no matter how distaste or inconvenience it may be to oneself or to one's own inclination.[138]

---

to the change" (Ph.D. Thesis, Fuller Theological Seminary, 1989), 61.

135 N. E. Parry, *A Monograph on Lushai Customs and Ceremonies*, 19.

136 J. Meirion Lloyd, *History of the Church in Mizoram* (Aizawl: Synod Publication Board, 1991), 4.

137 N. Chatterji, *Zawlbuk as a Social Institution in the Mizo Society* (Aizawl: Tribal Research Institute, 1975), 15.

138 J. H. Lorrain, *Dictionary of the Lushai Language* (Calcutta: The Asiatic Society, Reprinted, 1975), 513.

A person who possessed *Tlawmngaihna* was to be obedient and respectful to the elders, courteous in dealing with the weak and the lowly; generous and hospitable to the poor, the needy and the strangers; self-denying and self-sacrificing at the opportune moment in favour of others; ready to help those in distress; compassionate to a companion who falls sick while on a journey, or became victim of a wild beast in the hunt, by never abandoning him to his fate; heroic and resolute at war and in hunting; stoical in suffering and in facing hardship under trying circumstances; and persevering in any worthwhile undertaking however hard and daunting that might proved to be. A *tlawmngai* person would do whatever the occasion demands no matter how distasteful or inconvenient that might be to oneself or to one's own inclinations. Its dimensions covered both personal and collective levels of activities wherein self-interest was subordinated to the interest of others individually and collectively. Chatterji stated, "*Tlawmngaihna* to a Mizo stands for that compelling moral-force which finds expression in self-sacrifice for the service of others".[139] Without the principle of *Tlawmngaihna,* it would not be possible to build a communitarian society and it would not be possible to build a harmonious society where members of the community practiced decision by consensus, sharing their joy and sorrows, and caring for one another.

As *Tlawmngaihna* has multiple characters and it is more of practical than theoretical, therefore, it is quite fitting to narrate some stories of the undisputed Hero and legend of *Tlawmngaihna.* There are no doubts, a number of folk tales and folklores that remember the acts of legendary heroes of *Tlawmngaihna*. Hence, in what follows we will observe the two stories of the hero of *Tlawmngaihna*, namely, Chhurbura (more prominent as Chhura). Chhurbura who by his life and actions demonstrated what *Tlawmngaihna* is. Because of *tlawmngaihna* the character of Chhurbura is depicted in many folk tales as the silliest of all simpletons among the Mizo folk characters. And at the same, he may be considered in many tales as the cleverest of all the wise. Here are just two of his stories.

139 Chatterji, *Zawlbuk as a Social Institution in the Mizo Society*, 15.

(1) "Digging Jungle Potatoes"

On a certain sunny day Chhura and Naa (his friend) went to the Jungles in search of wild potatoes. Naa, as usual, was too lazy to dig out good ones. He could not dig deep and he collected only some of poor quality and under grown sizes. Chhura selected only full grown ones. On their way home, Naa suggested that it would be good to clean their potatoes in the stream. So, they washed their potatoes, Naa up stream and Chhura down stream. Naa now and then would say to Chhura, 'some of my good potatoes' have just been washed down by the current." Naa would then take away the best and better potatoes from Chhura who at last was left with the diseased and under grown ones. However, Chhura made no complaint at the time and he took home whatever Naa gave him. On the next occasion when Naa invited Chhura to go to the jungles in search of wild potatoes, Chhura refused by saying, 'No, for I cannot dig the good ones with you, I better go alone." Naa remained silent knowing that to dig wild-potatoes without Chhura would be a great failure and he never out alone.[140]

(2) "Chhura's Magic Horn"

There lived a brave and interesting man called Chhura in a certain village. His best friend was Naa. Both Chhura and Naa were jhum farmers. Their paddy fields lay adjacent to each other at a fair distance from the village.

At the bottom corner of Naa's plot there was a big hollow tree where many birds used to come and rest for a time to find their next food. Naa could not tolerate those cheerful birds and used to hunt them by throwing stones or by

140 This folk tale is one of the most popular tales which is narrated to children. The English Version is taken from Laltluangliana Khiangte, *Folktales of Mizoram* (Guwahati: LTI Publications & Art & Culture Department, Mizoram, 1997), 28.

shooting them with an indigeneous. Mizo original catapult called "Sairawkherk'.

Fortunately or unfortunately the stones that he threw hit the very hole of a hollow tree that a hobgoblin /phungpuinu uses as a shelter for her young ones. The spirit became very angry and threatened to take revenge on him using her supernatural powers; and then shen chanted certain unintelligible words of an unknown language, which she repeated to threaten her attacker. Naa was scared out of his wits to hear such utterances and thought that if the ownership of the field could be changed then any harm that the female spirit could do would fall on the new owner and he would be saved from the danger. Keeping this in mind, he came to Chhura and proposed that they should exchange the ownership of their plots of jhum land. By showing his plot from the ground level to Chhura he told him to go and look at his own field from a tree for Naa was sure that he had convinced Chhura.

As told by Naa, he saw the tree where there were many birds on the upper branches. And since he also wanted to eat some birds he started to throw stones at them. As usual, the female spirit reacted quickly with her mysterious utterances once again and warned him to stop throwing stones because he was hurting her children. Obviously, Chhura did not heed the warnings. He ignored the bobgoblin and attacked the tree by throwing some more stones. Reading that the new owner could not be scared away and summed to be very brave the spirit steadily escaped from one corner and went down to the brooke. In the meantime Chhura had reached the big hollow tree to verify the spot from where mysterious utterances came. He now realized the exact situation. Looking into the hole and not finding the mother of the young ones, he forced them one by one to swallow hot ash and as a result all of them were killed. Having done that he left the hollow tree immediately and hid himself in the farm hut.

The female spirit wept constantly for the death of her children. Meanwhile, Chhura made a plan to capture the mother spirit. He made a swing in his farm hut and pretended to have gone home in the evening but hid himself on the roof. After sometime, the female spirit came to the hut and sat on the swing thinking that Chhura had gone home and began singing a mourning song. Without delay, Chhura seized the hair of the spirit and pulled it hard, threatening to take her home to be paraded for the pleasure of the village children. The spirit begged him not to be so cruel and promised to give him a sword if he freed her. Chhura replied and said that he already had an axe. And then the spirit promised to give him a hoe, which Chhura again refused because even that hoe required the use of human strength. The female spirit dared not imagine what her plight would be once she was in the village. So she made a last offer and that was her most precious possession, a magic horn (Sekibuhchhuak). Chhura automatically accepted the last offer for he knew that the magic horn could produce delicious food from one end and cooked meat from the other end without human effort. After confirming the real value of that magic horn, Chhura set her free for good and went home happily with his new found possession. Having the precious horn, Chhura and his family now stopped working and lived without much care, getting free supply of the best food of the day.

Naa was always cunning when he came to know about the horn, he was filled with jealousy over the precious possession. Naa cheated Chhura with a trick and took the magic horn away from Chhura.[141]

141 Laltluangliana Khiangte, *Folktales of Mizoram,* 16-19.

The plain truth in these tales is that Chhura has a deep concern for his friend Naa who happened to be the laziest of all men.[142] We also have found in many other stories that Chhura was cheated by Naa. However, a careful examination of the story about Chhura in the light of Mizo *Tlawmgaihna*, it was clear that Chhura was not stupid and ignorant, he knew what Naa did to him; however, it was his *Tlawmngaihna*, abiding love and affection for his friend that often forgave the misdeeds of Naa. Chhura's *Tlawmgaihna* is in line with what Jesus has said to his disciples, "No one has greater love than this, to lay down one's life for one's friends."[143]

4.2.1. *Genesis of Tlawmngaihna*

Some may question whether *Tlawmngaihna* is possible without compulsion from a higher authority. As it was noted earlier, the pre-modern Mizo society was a close-knit society, it was imperative for each member to show kindness and share his or her wealth or things with other members for a harmonious existence. The factor or motive for this neighborliness, or the spirit of egalitarianism, has been rooted in their socio-religious sanctions found in unwritten code, in myths and folktales. Rokhuma has rightly stated, "Five qualities of character was expected of every Mizo to be revealed in courtesy, hospitality, diligence, integrity, readiness to help others, kindness, unselfishness, patience, physical and moral bravery."[144]

It is difficult to trace when and how the Mizo *Tlawmngaihna* came into practice due to the absence of written records. But we shall try to assess, from whatever sources are available at our present stance, the probable origin and sources of *Tlawmngaihna*.

As the maxim says, 'necessity is the mother of invention,' and the same is true in the origin of *Tlawmngaihna* in Mizo community. The consensus among the tribal scholars with regard to the origin

142 Laltluangliana Khiangte, *Folktales of Mizoram,* 14.

143 John 15: 13.

144 Rokhuma, "Moral Degradation and the Role of the Church" in *Ground Works for Tribal Theology in the Mizo Context,* edited by Rosiamliana Tochhawng, K. Lalrinmawia, L. H. Rawsea (Delhi: ISPCK, 2007), 86.

of *Tlawmngaihna* is that the frequent tribal feuds and the practice of headhunting necessitated the evolution of a certain kind of social security system that bounded the community together in times of security demands. They were all forced to stay closely together in order to respond to the dangers from all sides. When a community helped another in times of danger they soon learned to care and love for one another with a deeper sense of feeling for their fellow human beings. Sooner or later, the spirit of selfless sacrifice for others permeated the whole community.[145] Thus, the seed of *Tlawmngaihna* was unconsciously sown in the community.

Primitive Mizo society was a close ethnic group, knitted by blood relationship or the same kinship. By virtue of this close relationship, they were bound to have a deep sense of feeling for others who were also their kith and kin. As life was so closely knitted, no family would own any spoils or others things without sharing with others. Thus the people lived together under the spirit of share and share alike, there was no room for selfish personal gains or materialism. The nomadic type of life, it may be said, had helped evolve and develop the spirit of *Tlawmngaihna* spontaneously. This same spirit was also one of the probable factors that contributed to the fast spreading of the Gospel among the Mizo community. Hence, we may say that Tlawmngaihna is the spin-off of social necessity.

4.2.2. *Cultivation of Tlawmngaihna*

How, and in what way, was this high quality character of Mizo youth developed into maturity through the *Zawlbuk* system of discipline? The simple forms of education for life evolved, as a follow up, in the *Zawlbuk* through their various activities, codes of conduct and modes of living. These ensured healthy reciprocity between different age groups and the elders, so also between the claims of the family as a social unit and the wider society as an organic whole; preventing,

145 See P. L. Lianzuala, "Tlawmngaihna: Towards a Theology of Mizoram," in *Towards a Tribal Theology: From the Mizo Perspective* (Aizawl: Mizo Theological Conference, 1989), 58.

once again, any problem of a generation gap from raising its ugly head as it always does in the more developed societies.[146]

In the task of developing the life and character of the youth, no doubt the elders and the chief of the village played vital roles. The elders, especially those reputed as *Pasaltha*,[147] through acts of *Tlawmngaihna*, would often visit the *Zawlbuk* and recount the heroic past of their lives as young men and of the other *pasaltha* with the aim of driving the message of *Tlawmngaihna* ideals home, to be emulated by the youth. They thus helped in shaping the personalities and aspirations of the younger ones.[148] The ideals thus received from the elders usually helped the aspirants to demonstrate their worth as *pasaltha*. The chief in his turn would uphold the ideals of *Tlawmngaihna* by patronizing the *Zawlbuk* and by giving incentives to the proven *pasaltha*.

Sangliana best expresses the thoroughness of the training given in the *Zawlbuk* and the splendid result manifested in the character of the Mizo youth in meeting the demands of any situation:

> It was in the *Zawlbuk* that all the young boys and lads of the village who slept there at night received their training in habits of obedience, discipline, courage, fortitude, perseverance, self-sacrifice, etc. All other precepts enjoyed by Tlawmngaihna were also inculcated with such thoroughness that young boys and lads who had been inmates of the *Zawlbuk* knew just what to do in case of emergency or in the usual course of events. Most of the social work in the village like cleaning paths, repair of construction of houses

146 Lianzuala, "Tlawmngaihna: Towards a Theology of Mizoram," 5.

147 A "pasaltha" was a brave and manly person or a hero, who had shown his integrity of character by deeds of tlawmngaihna. Pasaltha were held in high esteem not only by their fellow inmates in the Zawlbuk but also by the chief and all others in the village. The credit and honour for such persons was symbolized by a special cup of *Zu* (the Mizo rice beer) offered to them by the chief at special feasts. See Parry, *A Monographn on Lushais Customs and Ceremonies*, 9.

148 Chatterji, *Zawlbuk...*, 16.

> of widows, were carried out by the members of the *Zawlbuk* under the guidance and control of elder ones who also inculcated in the young men a sense of social unity and a feeling of responsibility for the village as a whole. It was in the process of such daily corporate living in the village *Zawlbuk* that a body of rules grew up in amazing uniformity, and the people, both in groups and as individuals, vied with one another in carrying them out to such an extent that the *Zawlbuk* trained youngsters unhesitatingly reacted and acted in accordance with the dictates of *Tlawmngaihna* which had been inculcated in them.[149]

For Sangliana, "A complete Mizo is one who has tlawmngaihna in the fullest measure if that were all possible"[150]. It was *Tlawmngaihna,* which made Mizo life and community agile, attractive and enjoyable.

When gospel of Jesus Christ was preached to the Mizo people its essence of love had been already present in the life philosophy and practice of the Mizo people. Thus, they had no problem embracing Christianity. Khuanga believes that it was due to this principle of life, *Tlawmngaihna* that so much work was done voluntarily.[151]

4.2.3. *The Character of Tlawmngaihna*

4.2.3.1. *Tlawmngaihna* as an Ethical code

The Mizo code of ethics revolves around *Tlawmngaihna.* It is a scale that measures what is wrong or right. It leads to justice and follows the truth. It distinguishes society loving people from dishonest and lazy ones. According to Vivekananda, every act of charity, every thought of sympathy, every action of help, and every good deed is

149 Sangliana, "Tlawmngaihna and the Mizos", Mizoram: News Magazine (1 August 1984), 40, cited by Kipgen, *Christianity and Mizo Culture*, 72.

150 Ibid.

151 Khuanga, "The role of Christianity in the socio-economic praxis of Mizoram", in *Towards a Tribal Theology: The Mizo Perspective* (Aizawl: Mizo Theological Conference, 1989), 97.

taking so much self-importance away from our little selves as the lowest and the least, and therefore, it is all good. [152]

Niskama karma, in the Bhagavad Gita, remains a religious ideal without having much impact on the society while Mizo *Tlawmngaihna* is a principle that pervades the whole Mizo society and is essential to understanding the Mizo cultural life.[153]

4.2.3.2. *Tlawmngaihna* as the Code of Good Work

In Mizo society tlawmngaihna was a rule for good work, as many previous definitions have also indicated. It was the principle of *Tlawmngaihna* that supplied and guided the people to perform good works. The *Zawlbuk* was an institution that defined what *Tlawmngaihna* actually was, and the *Zawlbu*k was very significant for the early Mizo society. There was great competition among the youth because *Tlawmngaihna* itself demanded it. Since good work was the fruit of *Tlawmngaihna*, every one tried to be promoters of peace and harmony in the society.

The Mizo village life depended on the voluntary social service of the villagers. There were times when villagers would contribute their service for the welfare of the village. For instance, the villagers without any question did make foot paths between villages, construction of a house for a widow, the chief's house, the *Zawlbuk* and maintenance of the village water spring. *Tlawmngaihna* functioned as a basis, and means of inspiration, in all the good works rendered by the people.

4.2.3.3. *Tlawmngaihna* as Selfless Service to Others

The word *Tlawmngaihna* had a number of expressions for different situations. In eating, working or hunting it was expressed in the proper manner. It has had a long tradition in the serving of others, where self-denial was very much demanded. Those who had *Tlawmngaihna* never looked down upon people who were in need. No one died of starvation, since people were always ready to help others. When a

152 Thanzauva, *Theology of Community*, 126.

153 Ibid.

dying person had no one to look after them, many *tlawmngai* people went and cared for such persons. If a person died, the youth, out of *Tlawmngaihna*, would do what was needed. The spirit of service was infused among the people through *Tlawmngaihna*.[154] Taitesena was the most renowned man of *Tlawmngaihna*. He was ever ready to help others even at the risk of his own life. Under no circumstances did he excuse himself from the call to service. One of the fields where a man can best exhibit his quality as a tlawmngai person when out for hunting expeditions:

> A hunting expedition offers many opportunities for the exhibition of Tlawmngaihna. A man who possesses endurance and is able to go on all day with very little food, who is courageous in following up wounded wild beasts, who thinks of his friends before himself, takes less than his share of the food, is industrious in building the shelter for the night and in collecting wood for the fire is said to possess Tlawmngaihna and supposed to vie with each other in these respects. If two men one of whom has a gun come up to an animal, the man with the gun, if he follows Tlawmngaihna will offer his friend first shot. If a man gets hurt by a wild animal, his companions must stay and look after him and must not continue the chase and leave him alone. If a man got caught by wounded bear or other animal it would be a fearful disgrace if his companion ran away and left him to his fate, they are bound to stay and help him.[155]

4.2.3.4. *Tlawmngaihna* as a Keeper of Justice and Virtue

Mizo *Tlawmngaihna* upholds justice and virtue in the society. It demands morality and good form. In the early Mizo society there were not many thieves found in the society since people, out of tlawmngaihna, had concern for others. It was shameful to steal the

154 N. E. Parry, *A Monograph on Lushai Customs and Ceremonies* (Aizawl: Tribal Research Institute, 1976), 19f.

155 Ibid., 20.

property of any one. The Mizo society never locked the doors of their houses since honesty was prevalent. The people rejected the practice of injustice, telling lies and cheating. If anyone was found practicing such things they were despised and considered as worthless. Keeping justice, peace and welfare of others was the purpose of *Tlawmngaihna.*[156]

4.2.4. *Tlawmngaihna in Mizo Maxims (Do's and don'ts)*

The Mizo *Tlawmngaihna* is crept in every walk of life in Mizo society including their saying, proverbs and maxims. We shall now look at *Tlawmngaihna* in some of the maxims of the Mizos that are classified in two ways: (1) The Do's and (2) The Don'ts

4.2.4.1. The Do's of Mizo Forefathers

- Respect is to be shown to elders.
- Sharing and giving out is life, eating alone is death.
- You cannot deceive society.
- Always aware the hints of elders in public activities
- Always be on a frontline while having social work
- One has to say, "I'm quite satisfied" while eating at others' house
- A visitor while having a meal be invited always to join
- Next plot cultivators and next-door neighbours are like to be considered as family
- Always clean up your own trash on a road.
- Always help a weary person on a road
- Always take a look around you before you start talking about others
- Always say, 'thank you' while receiving and returning borrowed things[157]

156 Lalthuama, "Tlawmngaihna," *Thu leh Hla,* No. 4 (April 2000): 23.

157 Laltluangliana, *Mizos of North East India,* 90.

4.2.4.2. The Don'ts of Mizo

- Never refuse what an elder requests you to do
- Never criticize your parentage or origin
- Never construct a house to block the path of others.
- A house fly does not alight on anything other than a festering sore.
- Cursing and thoughtless talk should not be practiced.
- Never steal a cloth, a hoe and an axe
- Never start taking a morsel before the elders start taking it.
- Never address to own parents in a stupid manner
- Never talk to other impolitely at anytime
- Never start eating delicious part of the head before your elders
- Never refuse orders of your elders
- They never pollute public drinking water.
- Never block someone's road
- Never speak ill of your own parents
- Never make fun of a handicapped person[158]

The underlying meaning of the above Mizo maxims may be clear without any explanation. The Mizo *Tlawmngaihna* or a communitarian spirit is visible or at least can be sensed in the above maxims as a web that connected all the sayings as the moral guiding principle.

4.2.5. *Impact of Tlawmngaihna on the Later Generations or Modern Mizo Society*

As stated above, *Tlawmngaihna* in the past was the heart and soul of Mizo society as well as the pride of the community. However, as the Mizo society like other societies could no longer exist in isolation, there have been many forces that encountered with *Tlawmngaihna*. As a result, the meaning and function of the *Tlawmngaihna* were bound to change. We have seen today a modified form of Tlawmngaihna or a new version of *Tlawmngaihna*. People who are not satisfied with

158 Laltluangliana, *Mizos of North East India*, 91.

the present *Tlawmngaihna* expressed their wishes to call back the past *Tlawmngaihna*. Their desire for the past *Tlawmngaihna* as well as its great influence was beautifully expressed in the song (poem) composed by one of the famous song writers, Rokunga:

1. Kan tlang kan ram a hring a mawi,
   Tlawmngaihhna pangpar mawi a vul;
   Rangkachak leh lunghlu aiin,
   Chu pangpar chu a mawi zawk e.
   Aw Tlawmngaihna hlu, aw nunna par
   (Chorus) Kan tlang ram nuam hmun sangah hian,
   Kum sang tam tak pawh ral mah se,
   Zamual liam lovin ding reng rawh
2. Ka chawi ang che sakhming hluanin,
   Zo nun par mawi ka ti ang che;
   I mawina rimtui leng velin,
   Ramtin kiltin a fang del del.
3. Hmanah pipu len lai ni khan,
   I hmel ni ang a eng thin a;
   Kan ram kan hnam timawitu kha,
   Thlah hnu chhawl ang a chul zo ta.
4. Tunlai khawvel hun tharah hian,
   Tharin par ang lo vul leh la,
   Kan thiam kan fin timawi turin
   Kan thinlungah lo cheng leh rawh.[159]

Even though the song has four stanzas, the gist is found in its Chorus. The literal translation of the chorus may go like this: O precious *Tlawmngaihna*, O blooming life; Even many thousand years hence; Find a resounding echo; In our dwelling pleasant lofty mountains.

---

159 Rokunga Memorial Committee, *Rokunga Hlate* (Aizawl: RMC, 2000), 9.

4.3. Egalitarianism: Mizo Social Structure

Egalitarianism is one of the essential characteristics of tribal society. In Mizo society, despite its patriarchal social system, there is basic equality between sexes and dignity of women is upheld strictly. Men and women share equal responsibility in family duties, in rituals and festivals. The Mizo society in the past was an egalitarian society where equal rights for all were advocated. Egalitarianism is an absence of racism, caste discrimination, and classism. Laltluangliana Khiangte has rightly expressed the Mizo society in past:

> The Mizo society has no class distinction and no discrimination on the ground of sex. The village exists like a big family and the chief as the father and ruler. Birth of a child, marriage in the village, death of a person or a community feast of any kind arranged by a member of the village and those of yearly festivals were important occasions in which the whole village was involved.[160]

How could that be possible? According to H. L. Malsawma, it was *Tlawmngaihna*, the core and living blood of Mizo social life that knits the individual and family together in an integrated caste-less society where safety is ensured.[161]

In egalitarian society everyone lives freely, nevertheless abiding by a set of rules, customs, and traditions. Amidst the different individualistic societies where the concepts of class and caste rule, the tribal people in Northeast India are proud of being an egalitarian societies. Mizo society is one of them. K. P. Aleaz who is non Mizo scholar has rightly observed, "The Indian tribal culture is egalitarian, democratic and eco-conscious."[162] The underlying philosophy that

---

160 Laltluangliana Khiangte, *Mizos of North East India: An Introduction to Mizo Culture, Folklore, Language & Literature* (Aizawl: L.T.L. Publications, 2008), 22.

161 H. L. Malsawma, *Sociology of the Mizos* (Guwahati, Delhi: Spectrum Publications, 2002), 64-65.

162 K. P. Aleaz, "A Tribal Christian Theology form India", *Journal of Tribal Studies* VII/2 (July-December 2003), 290-305.

runs through the Mizo society is seen in the famous and beautiful saying, "*sem sem dam dam ei bil thi thi*"[163] ("Share, share and live or hoard, hoard and perish"[164]). According to K. Lallawmzuala sharing in Mizo culture is much more than sharing of material prosperity with the needy, it entails sharing of life and labor which is reflected in their generosity, hospitality, and kindness towards others. Mizo people thought that those who did not have the mind of sharing were not worthy to live long in the Mizo society[165] In Mizo society, people helped one another and shared their possessions, success, sorrow and misfortunes. They regarded themselves as *a thlum a al eiza* (eating the sweet and the salty together).[166] If a person constructed a house he would inform the villagers, then at least one person from every family, excepting the widows and the sick, would assist with the construction. If there were widows who could not construct their house, the community would do it for them free of cost. In the same manner, they considered that food was to be shared with one another. When a Mizo villager killed a deer or any animal, he would never keep it to himself. The meat would be distributed to every family. Besides wealth and food, they also shared sorrow and misfortunes. When someone died in the village, the villagers would immediately come to the bereaved family to help and comfort them.

Therefore, they measured the riches of a person not in terms of how much a person has accumulated but in terms of how much he or she spent and shared with others. For Lallawmzuala, even the Mizo social ethics, *Tlawmngaihna* was rooted in this philosophy of

163 Social equity or equilibrium is possible among the people because of this communitarian philosophy. In other words, individualism or selfishness is not tolerated by the Mizo people.

164 Vanlalchhuanawma, "Revival Movement and Mizo Society", in *Ground Works for Tribal Theology in the Mizo Context*, edited by Rosiamliana Tochhawng, K. Lalrinmawia and L. H. Rawsea (Delhi: ISPCK, 2007), 84.

165 K. Lallawmzuala, "Sem sem dam dam, ei bil thi thi" in *Hmatiang Sawnin*, edited by Lalrinawmi Ralte (Bangalore: Bangalore Mizo Association, 2001), 286-287.

166 Lalpekhlua, *Contextual Christology*, 161.

sharing.[167] *Tlawmngaihna* never allows a person who is *tlawmngai* a piece of bread he or she had for his lunch, but gave it to his or her friends who were also hungry.[168]

It was and is this spirit of sharing which keeps in Mizo society communitarianism alive. In other words, sharing is the living soul of Mizo community. Sharing is an opposite of individualism and it dismantles the walls of individualism and opens the being of individuals in the direction of community.

When we say the spirit of sharing, we do not mean that there were no poor people in Mizo society, but the concern for the community, especially the rich people, towards the poor was worth noting. The folk tale, "Lersia and Liandova te Unau" at least partially depicts the Mizo social structure or condition in the past:

> In olden days there was a chief named Lersia in a particular region. He was a just man who when estimating people's worth did not trouble whether they were rich or poor as long as they had kind hearts. One day, he and some of his elders and followers journeyed to a distant village which they never before visited. When about to enter the village Lersia whipped himself and caused large weals to rise on his skin by using a kind of plant which could cause weal on the skin. He also smeared his bod with dust until he looked a very pitiable object. He and his men then went to the centre of the village and sat there. Everyone knew they were from Lersia's village, but no one knew which of them was Lersia. One by one the members of the party were invited to different houses for entertainment until at last the only one left was Lersia himself, who looked so wretched that no one wanted to take him in.
>
> In one of the houses of the village lived two brothers, Liandova and his brother Tuaisiala who were very poor

167 Lallawmzuala, "Sem sem dam dam, ei bil thi thi", 287.

168 L. H. Lalpekhlua, *Contextual Christology: A Tribal Perspective* (Delhi: ISPCK, 2007), 234.

> but very kind. They saw the wretched looking man in rags sitting in the middle of the village street, and one of them went out to him and said, "Friend, we have no food at all as we are very poor, but come to our house so that you can keep yourself warm by our fire. You are welcome to what little we have." Then Lersia went to the house of the two brothers and gladly stayed with them. In the morning he told them who he was, and the other people of the village were mortified when they realized how they had treated the famous Lersia, and they wanted him to go to another house to stay with some rich people. But Lersia would not leave the two brothers who had shown themselves such true friends. He was very kind to them ever afterwards for they had pitied him when he seemed to be in distress. Invited by Lersia they migrated to his village, and he gave them many a cattle and other things, by which they became very rich. And thus was their kindness rewarded. The two brothers were no longer looked down upon by the villagers for they were not poor as before.[169]

This story has testified that poverty was not absent in the past Mizo society. However, what is given most importance by any story-teller is the gracious act of the chief Lersia for the liberation of the two brothers from the bondage of acute poverty and social stigmatization. The story of the chief Lersia is remembered and retold by Mizo people for his kindness and his concern for all the members of the community particularly his concern for the needy.

The community centeredness of the Mizo society did not give any chance for individualism. Every member of the society was absolutely occupied by his or her duties towards the community. Social equity is possible only when and where people have deep concern for others. The egalitarian traits of Mizo society can be seen in almost all aspects of the community life. We now point out the more visible ones:

169 Laltluangliana Khiangte, *Folktales of Mizoram,* 202-203.

4.3.1. *Politico-Economic Egalitarianism*

In the social and political life there were, of course, certain dignitaries who held various offices or duties like the Chief and the Elders (like Council of ministers), the priests, the blacksmith and the village crier (the one who passed information to the public),[170] but they all depended on the basic occupation, jhum cultivation or shifting cultivation. Men and women, young and old, worked together in the field without any discrimination. Unlike many societies where each class or caste has their own properties that only a particular class/caste could use, the Mizo society had community assets shared by all members of the community. The members of the community, all, commonly shared the village wells, the land, the village Blacksmith and the village Priest[171].

4.3.2. *Social Egalitarianism*

The Mizo society, as already mentioned, was deeply community based. Primitive Mizo society was a close ethnic group knitted by blood relationship or the same kinship. By virtue of this close relationship, they were bound to have a deep sense of feeling for others who were also their kith and kin. And there is truth to this even today. This means that no Mizo beggars are found even to this day. Indeed, no Mizo would like to see their fellow Mizo begging but would try to help him in all possible ways so as not to let him beg. At the same time the needy person would not like to shame himself or herself or the Mizo community by begging others even in dire need.

Mizo society has not experienced divisions on the grounds of class or caste. Everything is done together by the people. The society is characterized by the homogeneity of the people. All the privileges and riches are, more or less, shared equally by the members of the community. The people engage in the same kind of work, have the same kind of food habit, are bound by the same socio-cultural traditions and customs, and suffer and bear the same kinds

170 Malsawma, *Sociology of the Mizos*, 14-16.

171 Ibid., 16.

of hardships and problems. Because of all these, it is practically impossible for the Mizos to divide themselves into fragments of classes and build dividing walls on any ground.

However, today, even though these cultural values are very much in line with the teaching of Jesus, due to encounters with various outside forces, these cultural values have been weakened and, in some cases, they have been suppressed or replaced by the alien Western values. Therefore, a rediscovery and incorporation of these values into the teaching of the church is indispensable in order to strengthen the Mizo church.

5. Conclusion

We have analyzed in this chapter the Tribal situation in Northeast India in general and Mizoram in Particular. Tribal people in Northeast India are, as a whole, both linguistically and culturally different from the rest of the people in India. These differences, though they sometimes bring conflicts and cause identity crisis, allow people to keep their own cultural traditions alive in the midst of the plurality of cultures. Among the tribal communities in Northeast India, the cultural traditions of the Mizo people have critically been investigated. Especially the three essential aspects of Mizo culture, *Zawlbuk*, the community home, the community ethics and the community philosophy were revisited and interrogated with the intention of seeing how much these three aspects of the culture have impacted on the society and individual persons. It is found that the aforesaid socio-cultural elements have had far reaching impacts on the society and they are also loaded with social as well as theological potentialities, which can be incorporated in the tribal ecclesiology. The next chapter will examine the existing ecclesiology in Mizoram with the aim of finding out the answers as to how far the Gospel of Jesus has been enriched by the cultural traditions of the Mizo people and how far Mizo cultural traditions play a role in shaping Mizo ecclesiology.

Chapter 3

A Critique of the Contemporary Ecclesiology of the Churches in Mizoram

1. Introduction

In the preceding two chapters, we have discussed ecclesiology in the early Christian traditions particularly the ecclesiology in the New Testament and also in the writings of the early Church Fathers from Ignatius of Antioch to Augustine of Hippo and the traditional cultural traditions of the Mizo community. Those two chapters have been written with the hope of finding new directions for our ecclesiology and challenging and correcting our presuppositions regarding the Church.

This chapter critically examines the contemporary ecclesiology of the churches in Mizoram, especially the ecclesiology of the two Mission churches,[1] the Baptist Church of Mizoram (BCM) and the

1 "Mission churches" is here referred to the Churches founded by the Western missionaries sent by the Baptist Missionary Society (BMS) and Welsh

Presbyterian Church of Mizoram (PCM), against the context of tribal people in Mizoram and in relation to the early Christian heritage. The context of tribal people of Mizoram here refers to two things: they are the realities of the people and their cultural traditions. In our analysis of the ecclesiology of the BCM and PCM, importance is given to the faith and order of the church and ecclesial structure of the said churches.

Hence, we will first situate our analysis with a brief overview of the present day global ecclesial context and the resulting changes that have taken place in the ecclesial context of Mizoram and then analyze in detail the ecclesiology of the Baptist Church and Presbyterian Church of Mizoram and finally offer a critical evaluation of the ecclesiology of the two churches by using the data collected through questionnaire.

2. Wider Context of Ecclesiological Reflections

Each epoch has its own intricacies and challenges. The human race is faced today with problems and threats from various sectors. In such a context of negative experiences and meaninglessness, the Church has a responsibility to provide some credible answers to the question, "What is the body of Christ, the Church, for us today?" This question has been echoed in the writings of many contemporary theologians as they attempt to present the Church in the pluralistic context of the world. How should we, today, interpret and present the doctrine of the body of Christ? That there should be a correlation[2] between

Calvinistic Presbyterian Mission. Those two churches are known as Baptist Church of Mizoram and Presbyterian Church of Mizoram, respectively. The members of these two churches form above sixty per cent of the total Christian population in Mizoram. Except for Independent Church of Maraland, other denominational churches are formed by the break away members from these two churches.

2 Many of the contemporary theologians emphasize correlation as a method for doing theology. For instance, Paul Tillich thinks "it is further necessary to seek a theological method in which message and situation are related in such way that neither of them is obliterated.... It tries to correlate the questions implied in the situation with the answers implied in the message."

the past event of revelation and the present reality of our own faith is well accepted by theologians. In addition, contextualization is not only necessary to understand the Christian faith, but is also part of the very nature of theology itself.[3] Therefore, we cannot overlook the importance of the present day existential condition of humanity in doing theology. As Lucien Richard points out, one can do Christology today only in dialogue with one's cultural setting and, therefore, there exists the need to discern the distinct concerns and anxieties of our situation.[4] Our theological reflection should have a bearing on our daily life because it is in our daily life that we encounter God and try to give meaning to our lives. The Christian doctrine that ultimately matters emerges out of the practical, day-to-day experience of human beings in their attempt to relate their struggles, doubts, fears, sufferings, and pain to the God who is revealed in Jesus Christ. Hence, the main focus of this section is to give an outline of the present day global context and its subsequent impact on Mizo society.

2.1. The Present Day Global Ecclesiological Context

This section points to some of the socio-cultural trends of our society as a setting within which we undertake our ecclesiological reflections. The complexity and diversity of the contemporary context render it

---

Therefore, the task of the theologians is to listen to the questions arising out of the cultural situations and to rethink the tradition in response to these questions. See Paul Tillich, *Systematic Theology*, Vol. 1 (Chicago: Chicago University Press, 1951), 8. For Lucien Richard, the basic contemporary method in Christology is that of "correlation", and by correlation he means "the attempt to harmonize the past tradition and the present situation." See Lucien Richard, *Christ: The Self-Emptying of God* (Mahwah: Paulist Press, 1997), 4. See also Edward Schillebeecks, *Interim Reports on the Books Jesus and Christ, translated by John Bowden* (New York, NY: Crossroad, 1981), 51.

3 Stephen Bevans, *Models of Contextual Theology* (Maryknoll, NY: Orbis Books, 1992), 1. This concern has found wide acceptance among contemporary theologians. See Robert J. Schreiter, *The New Catholicity: Theology between the Global and the Local* (Maryknoll, NY: Orbis Books, 1997), 1-4.

4 Lucien Richard, *Christ: The Self-Emptying of God*, 10.

very difficult to identify its specific features, and most of the trends discussed here are characteristic of the Western European context, or have a Western origin. Nevertheless, they have repercussions in other parts of the world, especially in an age of globalization when everything affects everyone and no country lives in isolation.

The twentieth century witnessed tremendous development and rapid progress in all areas of human life. There were, however, negative aspects as well. Due to the fast developments in communication media and transportation, the world has become a "global village." The fast pace of developments in industrialized countries as well as in developing countries and the resulting transformations that have taken place compel us to understand accurately and urgently the issues at stake and their consequences. We shall briefly outline some of the more prominent trends, such as the secular and technological culture, postmodernity, the processes of globalization and the global experience of negativity, and their impact on the lives of human beings.

2.1.1. *Characteristics of a Secular and Technological Culture*

One of the characteristic features of contemporary culture is its secular spirit; the impact of which is felt not only in the West, but also in other parts of the world. With rapid advances in science and technology, people have become aware that many things formerly belonging to the realm of religion now appear to be manageable without any direct recourse to religion. Religion is thus pushed to the margins of peoples' lives, attempting to depend on their own abilities to solve many problems. Secularization is a complex process, and it is difficult to evaluate its implications because the depth of secularization varies depending on the context and worldview of each culture. In general, however, with the progress of science and technology, superstitious belief in magical powers, spirits and demons has shown a definite decline. There is greater tendency to look for a rational explanation and the generalized scientific outlook, too, is steadily growing.

Secularization has contributed to a sense of a common human kinship beyond national barriers and cultures, beyond the dictates of religion. Some, especially some progressive theologians, view secularization very positively, while others view it as a negative process. In fact, we have to appreciate the positive contribution of secularization in its effort to make human beings conscious of their position in the universe.[5] In some cases, secularization can lead to a search for God instead of rejection, and/or an effort to encounter God in the things and happenings of history instead of the elaboration of a concept of an abstract God having no direct significant for humankind.

However, as understood negatively from a religious perspective, by secularization we mean a phenomenon in which there is a general absence of any reference to transcendence. Harvey Cox believes that, with such secularization, "there was a decline in the impact and centrality of traditional religious institutions in modern societies and a retreat from supernaturalism by the major religious bodies."[6]

---

5 Thomas Kochuthara claims, 'the phenomenon by which religion is pushed out of several areas is healthy one. This should impel religion to discover its real role and fulfill it in a fitting manner. We should not misunderstand the phenomenon as a fight against religion. Factors that seem to work against religion are symptoms of the phenomenon of secularization. These factors have to be critically analyzed for a proper growth of religion. A correct understanding of the phenomenon of secularization can also enhance the mutual relationship between religions, especially in pluralistic setting like ours, and promote the establishment of justice and peace. It can also lead to the discovery of the different dimensions of religion in its relation to society." See Thomas Kochuthara, "Secularism and Secularization: Theological Reflection," *Vidyajyoti* 62 (1998): 245-246. He further states, "in the wake of the process of secularization there is a resurgence of the spiritual. In some cases this quest has led to extreme resistance to the modern, a fall back to on ritualism and a promotion of superstitions and fundamentalism. This trend can be checked only by discovering the proper role of religion." (ibid., 247)

6 Harvey Cox, *The Secular City: Secularization and Urbanization in Theological Perspective* (New York, NY: Macmillan, 1966), 17. However, in one of his later books, he says that "secularization does not actually drive religion from modern society completely. Rather, it fosters a type of private religion that has no real function for the society as a whole." See Harvey Cox, *Religion in*

Religion has become a matter of personal choice, one among several leisure-time activities. Added to that, there is a gradual decline of belief in the supernatural in the everyday concerns of modern humans.[7] It is relevant to note that Cox makes a distinction between "secularism" and "secularization." "Secularization is a historical movement, which is a liberating process whereas secularism is an ideology, a closed worldview, which clips the wings of emancipation and fixes a society on the pin of orthodoxy."[8] According to Peter Berger,

By secularization we mean the process of by which sectors of society and culture are removed from the domination of religious institution and symbols. When we speak of society and institution in modern Western history, of course, secularization manifests itself in the evacuation by the Christian churches of areas previously under their control or influence—as in the separation of church and state, or in the expropriation of church lands, or in the emancipation of education from ecclesiastical authority.[9]

Consequently, human self-understanding and the perception of the nature of human relations with one another has also changed. As Langdon Gilkey points out, the major traits of secularization are contingency, relativity, temporality, and autonomy, with autonomy being considered the most important.[10] Tillich sees a fundamental relationship between secularization and the industrial society. In industrial society, human activities are concentrated upon the methodological investigation and technical transformation of the world, including human being themselves. This results in losing the dimension of depth in the human encounter with reality. The universe

the Secular City: Toward a Postmodern Theology (New York, NY: Simon and Schuster, 1984), 12.

7 Bryan Wilson, *Contemporary Transformation of Religion* (Oxford: Oxford University Press, 1976), 42, 46, 148-149.

8 Cox, *The Secular City*, 75.

9 Peter L. Berger, *The Sacred Canopy: Elements of a Sociological Theory of Religion* (Garden City, NY: Doubleday, 1967), 107.

10 Langdon Gilkey, *Naming the Whirlwind: The Renewal of God-Language* (Indianapolis: Bobb-Merril, 1969), 37-73.

has become self-sufficient and, therefore, appears to be calculable and manageable according to human needs and desires. Then, of course, God is edged out from the scene of human activities.[11]

In today's secular age, people are no longer much concerned about redemption beyond this immanent world order. Scientific and technological developments have caused enormous changes in all realms of the society, and human subjects have become the point of departure and the measure for understanding reality. Owing to an over-optimistic attitude, many think that human reason can find true happiness without any recourse to the Other or the others.

What is of great importance for this study is that the traditional religious models and thought patterns are no longer able to cope with the longings of the present age, and traditional answers have been questioned more than ever.[12] The Church is no longer able to provide satisfactory answers to the questions posed by the present generation,[13] and people find it no longer necessary or useful to belong to the Church. Is our understanding of God and the Church then capable of responding to these challenges? How are we to speak of Jesus and his body, the Church, today? People are searching for meaning in life. The relevance of our ecclesiological paradigm depends on the responses to these concerns of the present generation.

Unless Christology can make sense of the experience of believing Christians in a concrete situation, it remains the preserve of theologically trained elite, a museum piece from the past. Therefore, Christology faces today the challenge of demonstrating that the

11 Paul Tillich, *Theology of Culture* (Oxford: Oxford University Press, 1959), 43-44.

12 Geoffrey Ainger, *Jesus Our Contemporary* (London: SCM Press, 1967), 23.

13 Judo Poerwowidagdo, "The Church, Globalization and Theological Education," *Asia Journal of Theology* 8 (1994): 132-133. For Judo, questions regarding ethical issues "arising out of the development of modern science and technology, such as human genetic engineering, organ transplantations, test-tube babies, surrogate motherhood, sperm-bank, transsexual operations, abortion, euthanasia," etc, the institutionalized church unable to give clear theological and ethical guidance has been rendered powerless against the strength ..."

message that salvation comes into the world through Jesus can make sense out of our twentieth century experience. Failure to dialogue with the present-day context and situation will deprive religion of any voice in the pressing public issues of our time; and the failure to form an adequate image of the scientific, social and political realities of the modern world will force religion into the sphere of private experience.[14]

Hence, our presentation of Christology should address the contemporary problems from within the context of the present world that has its own fears and concerns to contend with. Lucien Richard believes that the characteristics of a culture determine "the fundamental attitude of a whole group towards reality, truth and value, and therefore, even towards religion."[15] Many theologians share the view that the central concern of modern culture is humanization, a search for a new image of humanity at the level of human identity and meaning. This is because the greatest threat today is that of dehumanization, due to the "rise of industrial societies, totalitarian states, mass education and communication, objectifying scientific procedures, bureaucratic forms of organization and militarism."[16] As Donald P. Gray rightly observes:

In the face of these dangers the individual has come to fear that his freedom and hence his unique personhood will be taken away from him. At the same time it has become abundantly clear that there is a strong tendency at work in individuals to enter into a covert complicity with these trends towards depersonalization. While overtly claiming to want freedom and individuality we secretly reject it for the sake of security, approval and anonymity. Man is at war with himself, torn by a desire for freedom and personal integrity which conflicts with his desire for safety and approbation.[17]

14 Ainger, *Jesus Our Contemporary*, 23.

15 George Chalithara, "Prolegomana to Christology: Theological Hermeneutics in Praxis," *The Living Word* 92 (1986), 150.

16 Lucien Richard, *Christ: The Self-Emptying of God*, 10.

17 Donald P. Gray, "Like Us in All Things, Except...," *American Ecclesiastical Review* 168 (1974), 443.

As noted earlier, because of the advance of science and technology, a transformation has taken place in the economic, social and political realms. Tillich perceives technology as a thrust towards a transformation of the world and the self through the progressive acquisition of power. God has become superfluous to those humans who control and predict their own future.[18] For Richard, "technology, by its very nature, leads to domination."[19] Schillebeeckx too speaks along those lines when he points out the dangers of technological culture. He claims that we have introduced science and technology as the historical liberators of humankind to free us from hunger, poverty, tyranny, war and historical fate. Science and technology increase productivity and can be used to meet real human needs if directed in the right way. He further observes that science and technology can work wonders if put at the service of other people's freedom and finally of human solidarity in general. But in reality the sciences function as the instrument of human power, of rule over nature, power over society, power over human beings, both female and male.[20] The problem is not with science and technology, but with the way human beings deal with them, and their non-scientific and absolute claims to offer salvation.

Since the time of the industrial revolution, and largely because of it, human beings have developed a pragmatic view of reality. It appears that today in all realms of life, whether it be political, social, economic and cultural, there is abuse and exploitation. In contemporary society, the primary concern seems to be one's own well-being, health and security. People are seldom encouraged to subordinate one's own needs and interests to the good or well-being of others or to some cause outside oneself. Self-sacrifice and self-abasement are seen as offensive to common sense and injurious to personal health and well-being. Even more, self-concern, self-interest and individual happiness have become the supreme values. As we have noted earlier, today the human subject has become the sole

18 Paul Tillich, *The Theology of Culture*, 44.

19 Lucien Richard, *Christ: The Self-Emptying of God*, 15.

20 Edward Schillebeeckx, *Church: The Human Story of God*, 3.

power and the only meaning-giving agent. This has resulted in a false optimism that causes an explosive situation where there is a growing experience of radical alienation.[21] People have become increasingly aware of the helplessness and hopelessness caused due to the dominating influence that anonymous powers exercise on their lives.[22] Conversely, there is a search for an authentic personal existence, too.

Therefore, today the fundamental questions are: What is humanity? How should men and women define themselves? Authentic humanity is distorted in the secular and technological culture of contemporary society by its insistence on domination and power, by its self-seeking and selfish tendencies. This narcissistic tendency is not only cultural, but it is also innate to human nature. Each person has an inherent tendency to incorporate, expand and protect himself or herself against the world.

In such a context, is there any way out of these selfish, self-seeking powers? Do we have a credible alternative that can challenge and confront them? Where do we look for inspiration? Where can we find fullness and meaning for our life? These are some of the pressing questions that challenge us today.

2.1.2. *Features of a Postmodern Culture*

It is fashionable today to identify our world as postmodern. Different scholars interpret this term in various ways, and there is no absolute clarity concerning the meaning of this terminology. Postmodernity may be conveniently described as a cultural phenomenon that does not appreciate absolute, fixed certainties, or foundation. It takes delight in pluralism and divergence over identity, unity, and strives to analyze the radical 'situatedness' of all human thought.[23] Post modernity is an ambiguous notion which could also be described as the pattern of intellectual outlook originating after the collapse of

21 Lucien Richard, *A Kenotic Christology*, 28-29.

22 Lucien Richard, *Christ: The Self-Emptying of God*, 18.

23 Alister E. McGrath, *Christian Theology: An Introduction*, 2nd edition (Oxford: Blackwell Publishers, 1997), 113.

modernity. Many theologians, however, characterize postmodernity as the radicalization or realization of the insights and achievements of modernity. This is because while simple modernization rested on the rigid application of scientific methods under the aegis of clarity, homogeneity, and universality, the very result of this enterprise was an accelerated production of new commodities.[24] In this sense, postmodernity is the consequence of modernity that was attuned to the formal rhythm of increasing novelty. Moreover, 'there has been a general collapse of confidence in the Enlightenment trust in the power of reason to provide foundations for universally valid knowledge of the world, including God.[25]

One of the traits of postmodernity is a decline of belief in universal theories and a greater commitment to pragmatism in political affairs. Consequently, there is a generalized suspicion of authority and grand narratives, and a concern to encourage diversity and cultural difference.[26] Hence, relativism and pluralism have flourished. Emphasizing radical plurality and particularity it suggests that the same reality can be perceived from various perspectives, and purports that each point of view is then considered equally valuable.[27]

The thrust of postmodernity is to leave behind the classical metaphysical framework, and that means also a rejection of classical ontology. As far as we are concerned, postmodernity challenges

24 George de Schrijiver, "Paradigm Shift in Third-World Theologies of Liberation: From Socio-Economic Analysis to Cultural Analysis," in *Liberation Theologies on Shifting Grounds: A Clash of Socio-Economic and Cultural Paradigm* (Leuven: University Press, 1998), 33.

25 McGrath, *Christian Theology*, 114.

26 Stuart Sim, ed., *The Icon Critical Dictionary of Postmodern Thought* (Cambridge: Icon Books, 1998), 340. See also Jean-Francois Lyotard, *The Postmodern Condition: A Report on Knowledge,* translated by Geoff Bennington and Brian Massumi (Machester: Manchester University Press, 1984), xxiii-xxv.

27 Lieven Boeve, "Critical Consciousness in the Postmodern Condition," *Philosophy and Theology* 10 (1997), 451.

traditional ways of doing theology.[28] There is, moreover, openness to the existing diversities. Some of its specific features are far-reaching relativity concerning value systems and religious traditions, stress on experience as the fundamental criterion in determining all judgments and the determination to celebrate otherness. Although it gives much importance to otherness and difference, postmodern fragmentation means also ghettoizing the socially 'different' into an opaque otherness as long as it keeps itself isolated from richer sources of power.[29] As Konrad Raiser points out, "humanity is obliged to develop ways of acknowledging cultural and religious plurality as a permanent social fact and to move from antagonistic competitiveness to communicative cooperation."[30]

The new cultural climate is characterized by an increasing pluralism. However, what is implied in the acknowledgement of cultural pluralism is that with pluralism we lose the capacity for any one cultural tradition to claim that its perspective offers a superior tradition or viewpoint over others.[31] One of the best options in such a situation seems to be to widen one's consciousness so as to accept the difference of the 'other' not as a threat but as a potential enrichment.

Postmodernity questions any totalization and absolutization. There is a loss of the sense of the transcendent and, therefore, no place for God in everyday concerns of human beings, and the human subject has become the sole power. For the postmodern mind there is

---

28 Douglas Groochuis, "The Postmodernist Challenge to Theology," *Themelius* 25 (1999), 4.

29 George de Schrijver, "Paradigm Shift in Third-World Theologies of Liberation", 72.

30 Konrad Raiser, "The World in the Twenty-first Century: Challenges to the Churches," in *The Future of Theology: Essays in Honor of Jurgen Moltmann*, edited by Miroslav Volf, Carmen King and Thomas Kuchars (Grand Rapids: Wm. B. Eerdmann, 1996), 7.

31 Graig Van Gelder, "Defining the Center-Finding the Boundaries: The Challenge of Re-visioning the Church in North America for the Twenty-First Century," in *The Church Between Gospel and Culture: The Emerging Mission in North America* (Grand Rapids: Wm. B. Eerdmanns, 1996), 29.

no overarching meaning, no coherent worldview informing human on how to live according to an objective, universal principle higher than human himself. In this secularized, pluri-religious, postmodern world too there exists a quest for meaning and love. When confronted with uncertainties, contradictions and the ever escalating fragmentation, we should ask whether the body of Jesus Christ today has the potential to empower people with hope.

2.1.3. *Challenges of Globalization*

Another prevalent trend that characterizes the contemporary society is globalization. Globalization is not a new phenomenon. Its origins can be traced back to the widespread colonization or economic conquest starting from the sixteenth century.[32] It is an economic and socio-political process with no reference points of North and South, or East and West. All such divisions seem irrelevant and geographical distances immaterial. Information and finances recognize no borders.

However, it would be wrong to judge globalization altogether as a negative process. For instance, competition, which is an essential element of its dynamics, has provided impetus to incredible progress in science and technology during the last few decades. For those benefiting from it, the universalization of education provides the means to become conscious of their dignity and to participate in public life. It should be noted that enhancements in public health and education have widespread applicability. Similarly, globalization in the medical field contributes to the possibility of eradicating certain diseases totally. Transport systems and communication media have become more rapid and less expensive. This has opened avenues for knowledge, exchange and development to scale unknown to the past; it has increased the possibilities of physically moving closer to peoples, cultures and countries. Tragedies occurring anywhere in the world are reported instantly and responded to which sympathy and

32 R. Gomez, "Globalization of Indian Economy- A View from the Periphery," *Jeevadhara* 25 (1995), 26-31.

compassion. Thus "a collective human consciousness can speak for justice, freedom, equality and truth".[33]

It should be remembered that "during the last two decades the expansion of trade has been closely associated not simply with third-world economic growth, but with significant improvements in human welfare and the alleviation of poverty and suffering.[34] Advances in overall human well-being and economic progress achieved in the last few decades by the poor around the world have been quite substantial. Thus, globalization as an exchange of information, goods, services and relationships on a global scale can undoubtedly lead to mutual enrichment and growth.[35] If globalization basically means making more available the scientific, the medical, the economic and the sociological advances of our society to every nation and every individual, then it is a blessing and something which should be heralded.[36] What is, however, most alarming is the unequal and unjust distribution of these advantages among peoples and nations. Notwithstanding its many impressive achievements, globalization has also been the hotbed of a host of evils. Therefore, which acknowledging the remarkable contributions of globalization, we cannot but point out its serious harmful consequences and see how they affect society.

What is new, in today's globalization, is the domination of the market economy. This is referred to in recent years as the 'free market, without any significant social or political regulation. It must be pointed out here that the most threatening feature of this kind of free market is the calculated accumulation of capital that inevitably

---

33 John Chathanatt, "Globalization Virus: An Ethical Scanning," *Third Millenium* 3/3 (2000), 20-21.

34 Jay R. Mandle, "Trading Up: Why Globalization Aids the Poor," *Commonwealth* 127 (2000), 15.

35 Michael Amaladoss, "Globalization and Mission in the 21st Century," *Theology Digest* 47 (2000), 52.

36 Theodore McCarrick, "Globalization with a Conscience: Care for the Poor," *Origins* 31 (2001), 54.

regulates human affairs.[37] Deregulation brings increased flexibility and mobility to the system of capital, but eventually the worker becomes a mere instrument in the accumulation process.[38] Thus, under the glamorous exterior of the market there lurks and unequal division of labour according to which certain ethnic characteristics or female features are considered incompatible with the capitalist and productivist work-ethos.[39]

The global market creates unequal relation because the strongest are the ones who impose the regulations. In such an unjust global economic system most of the poor countries of the south fall prey to the economic domination and exploitation of the affluent North.[40] In their attempt to compete with the West, the Southern countries have to enter the very logic of the West. The danger hidden in such a system is that

It has no power against sin, evil and death, despite our pretensions about universal spread and effectiveness. And in many respects, it is a juggernaut that is devouring the lives of people and communities; dissolving civic, national, and state identities, and threatening the life of nature.[41]

---

37 Capital is the fruit of fiction and speculation, functioning all by itself without having to refer to the producing subjects. Understandably, then, functioning as an autonomous system by its own inter dynamism and logic, financial capitalism continues to produce an exclusion of human subjects-more and more people without basic means and without security." Felix Wilfred, "Human Rights or the Rights of the Poor?" *Vidyajyoti* 62 (1998), 739-740.

38 Robert J. Schreiter, *The New Catholicity: Theology Between the Global and the Local* (*Maryknoll*, NY: Orbis Books, 1997), 7.

39 George de Schrijver, "Paradigm Shift in Third World Theologies of Liberation," 72.

40 T. Menamparampil, "Ethics for a Globalized World," *Mission Today* 2/2 (2000), 197-198.

41 M. Douglas Meeks, "The Future of Theology in a Commodity Society," in Miroslav Volf, Carmen Krieg and Thomas Kucharz (eds.), *The Future of Theology: Essays in Honour of Jurgen Moltman* (Grand Rapids: Wm. B. Eerdmans, 1996), 254.

Human addiction to power and to the accumulation of wealth thus, degrades the earth and undermines the lives of generations to come.

Globally linked production of goods leads to the internationalization of finance and capital. The overriding concerns of production and profit making ideology ignore the basic needs of the majority. When the process of globalization does not respect the global ethics and global solidarity, it causes new forms of social evils, while aggravating the already existing ones. This process of globalization is dominating the whole world today, as a consequence of which people become victims, unable to choose and live in dignity.[42] It is appropriate to note how the development strategies promoted by the discourse of the West affect the developing countries:

Through the process, not only the economic but increasingly also the socio-cultural systems of all nations are progressively permeated and appropriated by the socio-economic, cultural and political systems of the capital-advanced countries.[43]

This result in a dominion–dependence relationship between the rich and poor countries:

Though elements such as technology and communications, perceived by some as linked to globalization, can solve many problems including poverty and ignorance if guided in the right direction, in reality the means of production are in the hands of a few who have a vested interest in a system which perpetuates and intensifies poverty, exploitation and domination as a permanent structural practice.[44]

Not surprisingly, it is the local elite who receive the most profit in such a system while the powerless classes are ignored and excluded. As immediate consequence, poverty intensifies, and unemployment

42 Felix Wilfred, "No Salvation outside Globalization?" 136.

43 Rita Noronha, "Emerging Challeges in Contemporary India," *Integral Liberation: A Quarterly Review for Justice, Development and Social Change* 1/1 (1997), 6.

44 Cited from International Seminar on Globalization, "Colonialism to Globalization: Five Centuries after Vasco da Gama, February 2-4, 1998" by Moly Thomas, *Christology in Context: Kenotic Perspectives* (New Delhi: Intercultural Publications, 2005), 14.

increases. With the marginalization of people of the lower strata, the gap between the rich and the poor has widened more than ever.[45] In spite of the fact that the forces of globalization have contributed to a huge improvement in human welfare, raising countless millions out of poverty in recent decades, it is reported that three billion people, almost half the world's population, live on less than $ 2 per day and it is estimated that by 2025, this may grow to four billion.[46] The most horrifying fact here is the poverty inflicted on people against their will, which is deeply dehumanizing. The poor "are often politically powerless, socially discriminated against and culturally deprived. With its concomitant evils of hunger, malnutrition, disease and illiteracy, poverty makes people helpless and dependent.[47] So, for the powerless poor, globalization means to be pushed to the fringes of their own society. Under the guise of uniting peoples, countries and institutions globalization relegates a large section of society from the centre of control to the periphery.[48]

Seen in this light, the hidden agendum of globalization is not the democratization of peoples, but rather "the hegemonisation of the world by dominant capitalist forces."[49] Thus the process of globalization does not in any way express solidarity with the poor. Survival of the fittest and self-interest seem to be the catchwords today.[50] With the policies that support privatization and liberalization, globalization leads to unequal distribution of wealth resulting in economic imbalances. Many communities are fragmented by the dynamic of the market because instead of bringing about

45 Yong-Hun Jo, Globalization as a Challenge to the Churches in Asia Today," *Asia Journal of Theology* 14 (2000), 361.

46 James D. Wolfenohn, "A Call to Global Action," *America* 184 (2001), 8.

47 Kurian Kunnumpuram, "The Church at the Service of the People of India," *Jnanadeepa Pune Journal of Religious Studies* 1 (1998), 150.

48 George de Schrijver, Paradigm Shift in Third-World Theologies of Liberation," 72.

49 Ambrose Pinto, "India: A State Without Sovereignty," *Integral Liberaltion: A Quarterly Review for Justice, Development and Social Change* 1/1 (1997), 15.

50 Felix Wilfred, "Church's Commitment to the Poor in the Age of Globalization," *Vidyaijyoti* 62 (1998), 80.

community among peoples globalization has brought fragmentation and competition and people have been reduced to the status of slaves to machines and markets.[51] The paradox is that, despite its claims of unity with universality, this globalization process simultaneously results in a more unfair and fractured world.

This picture of the global society calls for an adequate Christian response, which can challenge and empower people to awaken from their tiny world of self-seeking, narrow and closed self-centredness, vested interests, and crass individualism to a sense of sharing, generosity, mutuality and outreach to the other, thus promoting a genuine concern for human welfare and global solidarity. What we need today is the liberation of humankind from the enslavement of the destructive aspects of globalization so as to come to true freedom, justice, equality and well-being of all. In a society ruled by market logic, the reality of God's self-giving love, expressed in the logic of grace may appear to be out of place. The materialistic, consumerist and commercial values upheld by globalization have led to the erosion or relativization of traditional values and relationships.

The logic of the market, exchange of commodities and the accumulation of wealth as power gives no space for those biblically narrated relationships and practices that are governed by the excess of gifting, such as mutual self-giving, diakonia and stewardship.[52]

It is quite evident that the world is increasingly interconnected and interdependent by communication of ideas and cultural values, and especially in the economic life the peoples of the world are linked together more than before. This can be a source of hope for deepening a real universal meaning, that all human beings are brothers and sisters in the global family created by God, having a common destiny. This is a great opportunity to become genuinely a connected human family. Therefore, what we require today is to ensure a globalization in solidarity, a globalization without marginalization.

---

51 Michael Amaladoss, "Mission in a Post-Modern World: A Call To Be Counter-Cultural," *Indian Missiological Review* 18/3 (1996), 13.

52 M. Douglas Meeks, "The Future of Theology in a commodity Society," 255.

The positive contributions of globalization must be oriented to divine and truly human values to build a community of sharing and fellowship, mutual love and care, which can lead to the 'one world order' envisaged by globalization, which is also the Kingdom of God Jesus preached. Thus, the eschatological vision of the Kingdom of God provides an alternative form of globalization, where no one is excluded, and greater attention is paid to the weak and the marginalized. In an age of globalization the task of the church is to become a prophetic community of hope and resistance guided by this vision.

3. The Ecclesial Scene of Mizoram

The church in Mizo society needs to reflect on Mizo society as the context of the church and on the position it holds in it. Only in this framework can one fruitfully discuss the functions of the church. If one fails to do this, there is a danger of speculation alienated from reality and of wishful thinking. Therefore, it is imperative to give a sketch of the contemporary context of the Mizo society that determines the context of the church. In the second chapter, we have already given a brief introduction of Mizo culture and traditions; the ecclesial context in this section includes only the present political, social and economic contexts of Mizoram. This is important because the church, in order to be relevant to the people cannot stand still or keeps its distance from the context, rather it has to adapt to the changing situation where it lies. Hence, it is necessary to look at the ecclesial context of the contemporary Mizo church. This will help us see the relevance of the churches of Mizoram on the one hand and on the other hand, it will send a signal to the church informing the need for evaluating its self-understanding or reconstructing its ecclesiology in order to be a vibrant church in the changing context.

As has been stated, churches in general have witnessed tremendous changes in all aspects of their life due to the change of the global context. Especially, in theological circle, the emergence of Liberation Theology, Feminist Theology, and other contextual theologies challenged traditional theologies and are seeking for an alternative that is relevant to set free the oppressed sections in the society. This new development in theological formulation has had no less impact in the life and ministry of the church. In this context the church irrespective of different traditions, particularly in the third world countries is compelled to either restructure or reformulate their ecclesiologies so as to keep its relevance for the people.

The church in Mizoram, even though it is only a hundred years old, has witnessed tremendous changes in all aspects of its life, those changes in the context greatly demand change in the nature and function of the church. It is therefore appropriate to deal with the present contexts and their challenges to the church in Mizoram.

3.1. Political Context

India independence in 1947 opened a new chapter in the political life of the people in Mizoram. The national independence has created a Mizo political consciousness which was materialized in the formation of the first political party, the Mizo Commoners Union (later known as Mizo Union) on April 9, 1946.[53] This was the people's movement against the British Indian Government and also against Mizo Chieftainship, and stood for people's self-determination. After national independence, political administration in Mizoram was in the hands of the elected Advisory Council but soon was transferred to the District Council, which was inaugurated on April 25, 1952.[54] A radical change that was remarkable in politic during this period was the abolition of the traditional chieftainship in 1954,[55] as it was one of the persistent demands of the newly formed political party, Mizo

53 R. Vanlawma, *Ka Ram leh Kei* (Aizawl: M. C. Lalrinthanga, 3rd Edition, 1989), 134; A. Thanglura, *Mizoram Politic Lumlet dan: Bel Keh Phuar khawm Tui Pai Thei Lo* (Aizawl: The Author, 1982), 50; Chaltuahkhuma, *History of Mizoram* (Aizawl: Chaltuahkhuma & Sons, 1987), 90.

54 Vanlawma, *Ka Ram leh Kei,* 225. Chaltuahkhuma recorded the date as April 26, 1952, *History of Mizoram*, 200. The date mentioned by R. Vanlawma is subscribed by other authors, Anismesh Ray, *Mizoram* (New Delhi: National Book Trust, India, 1993), 155; and John Vanlal Hluna, *Church and Political Upheaval in Mizoram* (Aizawl: Mizo History Association, 1985), 75.

55 John Vanlal Hluna, *Church and Political Upheaval,* 79.

Union. Having been inspired by the national independence, which terminated the autocratic rule of the British, the Mizo National Front started an armed revolt on February 28, 1966, for political self-rule, secession from the Indian Union. The elevation of Mizoram to the status of Union Territory in 1972 did not political pacify the people and the armed revolt lasted for twenty years.[56]

In these years of political turmoil, the church could not keep aloof but involved in it[57] and till today the churches in Mizoram takes up its prophetic role in Mizo politics. However, a problem in this regard is the question of the theological basis for the involvement of the church in politics. It was evident that the then President of the Mizo National Front, Laldenga was very much critical of the church's involvement in politics; he strongly urged the church to confine her role to spiritual realms.[58] Lalsangkima Pachuau observed that after that incident the churches were gradually distancing from politics, which had both negative and positive results.[59] The positive result according to Pachuau on this issue is "the churches saved face." The problem of the church on this issue suggests that the ecclesiology of the church needs to be either critically reviewed or construct a relevant ecclesiology in order to address the emerging issues.

---

56 The Mizo National Front and Government of India signed the historic Peace Accord on June 30, 1986, which ended the armed revolt.

57 John Vanlal Hluna's book, *The Church and Political Upheaval* in Mizoram, gives a narrative account of political involvement of the church in Mizoram.

58 Lalsangkima Pachuau, *Ethnic Identity and Christianity in North East India: A Socio-Historical and Missiological Study of Christianity in North East India with Special Reference to Mizoram* (Frankfurt: Peter Lang, 2002), 167.

59 "... the Mizoram churches' gradual distancing had both negative and positive consequences. The churches saved face by distancing themselves from politics, which also created a wide chasm between the political and religious spheres. The chasm prevented the church from playing any meaningful role in the day today political life of the state. The efforts of the Presbyterian Church, the largest denomination, to make a meaningful impact through its "electoral messages" were neither listened to nor heeded. Other attempts to make moral judgment often provoked sharp criticism from politicians." See Pachuau, Ethnic Identity and Christianity, 167.

3.2. Social Context

Along with the political change, Mizoram has witnessed a rapid and radical social change. The Mizo society, a close knitted society was suddenly exposed to other societies; a communitarian society has moved towards individual and impersonal society, illiterate society has now become the most educated society in India. As the people were uprooted from the village as security measures during political turmoil, they were compelled to reside in urban areas and thus the Mizo society today become one of the most urbanized societies in India. A traditional social control system based on consensus was replaced by a sophisticated legal system. The value system that regulates the behaviour of the community as well as individuals is changing from being community oriented to the concern for individual welfare. This drastic social change had resulted various problems in the society.

Christianity has been considered as one of the factors for the change in Mizo society. According to J.V. Hluna's estimation, Christianity is the strongest integrating force of the society.[60] In a similar vein, the former Governor of Mizoram, P.R. Kyndiah said:

> Rarely has a religion affected life of the people in such as comprehensive but amazing way as it does in Mizoram. No facet of spiritual or social life escapes it attention. An individual, family and the community become so involved in the church activities that religion does indeed occupy a pivotal role in the society.[61]

While the church occupied such an important place in society, its contribution towards the welfare and development of society in reality is considerably minimal. What the church spent from its own collection for social work is quite insignificant. However, there is an

---

60 J. V. Hluna, "Contribution of Christianity to Overall Development with Reference to Mizoram," in *Impact of Christianity in North East India,* edited by J. Puthenpurakal (Shillong: Vendrame Institute Publication, 1996), 471.

61 Extract from the speech of His Excellency Shri P.R. Kyndiah, governor of Mizoram, delivered at the 31st College Day celebration of Aizawl Theological College, Durtlang on 22 November 1996, *Presbyterian Review,* Vol. 8 (October-December 1996), 11.

encouraging sign that the church has been increasingly involving in social transformation. After a persistent pressure from the people, the Synod Social Front in the Presbyterian Church and Relief and Development in the Baptist Church of Mizoram, have been made full-fledged departments respectively.

The church exists in the midst of social problems of various kinds. Therefore, the church cannot simply ignore what is happening in society if the church wants to be the witness of Jesus Christ in this world. The existing ecclesiology of both the churches does not allow the church to fully engage in social transformation. A new theological orientation is needed to carry out the church's social mission.

3.3. Economic Context

Christianity was considered as creating a white-collar job in Mizoram.[62] Except such few salaried jobs, the economy depends on traditional jhuming method of cultivation. Under the independent India Five Year Plan was introduced for economic development under which Mizoram also started economic planning in 1951. Due to various reasons the economic planning failed. The traditional system of cultivation (slash and burn system) method has failed due to the insufficiency of cultivable land to meet the population increase and the land also became less fertile. We can assume that around 80 per cent of its population depends on agriculture but they failed to produce the minimum requirement of foodstuffs. Except a few elite groups, the majority people are in acute poverty.

Due to improper economic growth, once an egalitarian society has now become an economically dispersed society. The gap between the rich and the poor becomes wider and wider. Due to this growing economic disparity in the state, the church is compelled to voice the people on this issue.[63] However, it is surprising that the Association

---

62 R. N. Prasad, *Government and Politics in Mizoram* (New Delhi: Northern Book Centre, 1987), 70; See also A. G. McCall, *Lushai Chysalis (London*: Luzac & Co., 1949), 205.

63 K. Thanzauva, "Ralthuam Hlipin Ram Hmasawn Nan Beih A hun Ta (From Armed Armed Struggle to Transformation Struggles)", in Lalrinawmi Ralte

for Mizoram Economic Forum (AMEF) blames the church for developing a spirituality, which dichotomizes sacred and secular, this world and other world that negates this worldly economic development.[64] This is a clear evidence for the need to have a proper theology of the church, which will give us the basis for peoples' economic development.

3.4. Theological Context

One cannot deny the fact that the churches of Mizoram have inherited western theological traditions through the western missionaries who came to Mizoram. A. J. Appasamy's remark concerning the work of western missionaries may also be applied to Mizoram, "Missionaries who were influenced by the Awakenings in their own countries came out to India and did great work here."[65] Those pioneering missionaries were the products of western Evangelical Awakenings in the 19th and 20th centuries. And the church to which they belonged was also the outcome of the Evangelical Movements in the 18th and 19th centuries.[66] Lalbiaktluanga explicitly states that the dominant theology in Mizoram is basically the theology of reformation inherited from the missionaries of the evangelical Awakening in the 19th century. He further state that when the teaching of Justification by faith was first preached in Mizoram, it was found that it was irrelevant to address the existing evils of Mizo society, such as, polygamy, black magic, alcoholism and sacrificial offering to appease evil spirits. Until the 1960s the popular theological trend in Mizoram

---

(comp.), *Hmatiang Sawnin: Chhinlung Thu Thlur Bing* (Bangalore: Shalom Publications, 2001), 62-93.

64 *Zoram Hmasawnna Kailawn* (Aizawl: Association for Mizoram Economic Forum, 1992), 60-68.

65 A. J. Appasamy, "Preface", in J. Edwin Orr, *Evangelical Awakenings in India* (New Delhi: Christian Literature Institutes, 1970), iii.

66 In England the Great Evangelical Awakenings happened in 1773-1788. As a result, the Baptist Missionary Society (BMS) was founded in 1792. See J. *Edwin Orr, Evangelical Awakening in India*, 55ff.

was pietistic and highly ethical in its emphasis.[67] All theological interpretations received by the Mizo Christians are the products of western evangelical spirituality, almost all the religious books and literatures, are the products of western Evangelical tradition.

However, recently, the emergence of contextual theologies in the so-called Third World countries also gave birth to Tribal Theology.[68] This Tribal theology is a challenge to traditional theology, which is inherited from the western missionaries by the churches in Northeast India. It is a conscious attempt to reinterpret the gospel in tribal cultural categories and recover whatever is good in the traditional tribal religions and culture to enrich their faith in God in one hand and to root the gospel in their culture so that Christianity may not be foreign to them. Tribal theology aims at penetrating Christianity into the life of the people, or incarnating the gospel into peoples' culture, so that the gospel becomes more meaningful, and liberating for the people who are striving for the transformation of their society.

3.5. Contemporary Challenges for the Mizo Church

Changes in politics, social and economic life of the people have brought new challenges to the church. The tribal in Mizoram in general are today faced with various problems, which threaten the unity of the church and disturb the community existence. The serious challenges that call the church for a self-introspection and retrospection are as follows:

---

67 Lalbiaktluanga, "Theological Trends in Mizoram", In *Towards a Tribal Theology: The Mizo Perspective*, edited by K. Thanzauva (Jorhat: Mizo Theological Conference, 1989), 69.

68 The first book on Tribal Theology was published by Mizo Theological Conference in 1989, the book entitled, Towards a Tribal Theology: The Mizo Perspective, edited by K. Thanzauva (Jorhat: MTC, 1989). Soon after the publication of this book, Tribal Study Centre was launched by Eastern Theological College under the Principalship of Renthy Keitzar, and K. Thanzauva was the first Dean of Tribal Studies. The Centre has published Journal of Tribal Theology since 1997, which became an important organ of the Centre for developing Tribal Theology.

3.5.1. *Denominationalism*

The existence of the church in denominational fragments should be viewed seriously as a negative development and disobedience of the will of God for the church. Because denominationalism implies a moral surrender on the part of the church to national, racial, ethnic and economic interests that happen to dominate society and it waste the energy that the church needs to proclaim the message of reconciliation. Christianity of Mizoram in the beginning was considered as the agent of unity in Mizo society, because it has contributed to the Mizo community a sense of solidarity or oneness. Nevertheless, Christianity, the church to be precise, soon has become an agent, which divides the communities on denominational lines as seen in the Table[69] below:

Sl/No.	Major Churches in Mizoram	Total Members
1.	Presbyterian church of Mizoram (PCM)	4,40,980
2.	Baptist Church of Mizoram (BCM)	1,28, 386
3.	United Penticostal Church of Northeast India	66,226
4.	Evangelical Church of Maraland (ECM)	35,126
5.	Evangelical Free Church of India (EFCI)	8,733
6.	Fundamental Baptist Church of Mizoram	3,172
7.	Isua Krista Kohhran, Bualpui 'NG" (IKK)	3,500
8.	Church of Jesus Christ	9,800
9.	Isua Krista Kohhran, Aizawl	12,008
10.	Lairam Isua Krista Baptist Kohhran (LIKBK)	23,498
11.	Lalchhungkua-Unity	3,352
12.	Mizo Kohhran (Mizo Independent Church)	4,022
13.	Congregational Church of India, Maraland	3,500

69 V. L. Hruaia Khiangte, comp., *Directory and Statistics of Major Churches and Para Churches in Mizoram 2008* (Aizawl: Research and Development Department of AICS, 2008), 57.

14.	Rinna Kohhran	1,450
15.	Roman Catholic Church	20,500
16.	Mizo conference of Seventh-Day Adventists	23,680
17.	The Salvation Army	52,156
18.	United Penticostal Church of Mizoram	41,036
19.	· Total	8,81,125

In addition to this, the proliferation of sectarian groups, which may be called neo-tribalism, is becoming proverbial. The joy of being communitarian and communion of believers has been lost in the bickering, rivalries, and misunderstandings of divided sects.

3.5.2. *The Issue of Women Ordination*

Another area that calls for the church's attention is the status and place of women in the church, taking into account the cultural and theological constraints that distort the church's life. With regard to the status and place of women in the church, R.L. Hnuni, one of the prominent tribal women theologians, has stated, "Discrimination is more common in the Church than in secular circles. There are high-ranking women officers, M.L.A and even a woman minister in the secular sector. It is in the church circle that leadership of women is not fully accepted whereas it should be the other way around. Fully trained women are denied their ordination, and with respect to leadership, administration, policy making and so on, they are expected to play assisting roles only."[70] Concerning the cause of the subordination of Mizo women in the church, Lalrinawmi Ralte has commented that "the women's exclusion in the beginning of Christianity in Mizoram affects women's subordination."[71] She further comments that women are suppressed by the validity that has been accorded to the Christian

70 Quoted in K. Thanzauva, *Theology of Community*, 210.

71 Lalrinawmi Ralte, *Crab Theology: A Critique of Patriarchy-Cultural Degradation and Empowerment of Mizo Women* (Ann Arbor: U.M.I, 1994), 147.

teachings that now contribute to their oppression.[72] If ecclesiology is indeed to be people-oriented and Christ centered, then it need to be re-examined from the point of view of those who, for one or another, seem to be excluded from or have limited participation in the total life of the church.

3.5.3. *Degradation of Moral Values*

Tribal communities in general had, in the past, been known to others for their straightforwardness, honesty, truthfulness, love for community as well as their deep concern for others, as they believe in cosmic oneness[73]. As already been stated, for a tribal, Community means the sense of oneness, a sense of entity, extends to the whole territorial society. However, today the Mizo society depicts a very different image. In the context of globalization and with the introduction of private property, consumer values are replacing community values, mutual exploitation is replacing mutual support, and the tribal societies are passing from communion to competition. The moral ideals in personal and social are fading, the Mizo tribal communities today are facing serious issues like, marginalization of poor people, consumerism, drug addiction, HIV/AIDS epidemic, and corruption. The present moral catastrophe depicts the lack of an effective and common ethical standard in the tribal churches and their failure to live as moral communities.

---

72 Lalrinawmi Ralte, *Crab Theology: A Critique of Patriarchy-Cultural Degradation and Empowerment of Mizo Women,* 147.

73 Taylor argued that an essential feature of primal religion (tribal religion) was the sense of cosmic oneness and said, "Not only is there less separation between subject and object, between self and non-self, but fundamentally all things share the same nature and the same interaction one upon another-rocks and forest trees, beasts and serpents, the power of wind and waves upon a ship, the power of a drum over a dancer's body, the power in the mysterious cave of *kokola*, the living, the dead and the first ancestors, from the stone to divinities of hierarchy of power but not of being, for all are one, all are here, all are now. See John V. Taylor, *The Primal Vision: Christian Presence and African Religion* (London: SCM, 1977), 54.

These challenges deserve due attention in ecclesiological reflections. The new challenges lead us to raise some pertinent ecclesiological questions: How helpful are the contemporary understandings of the church in being faithful to the gospel in the present Mizo tribal context? Do the churches function as God's instrument and respond to the demands of the contexts in which they are placed? The next section will therefore analyze the ecclesiology of the Baptist Church and Presbyterian Church of Mizoram.

4. Baptist and Presbyterian Church of Mizoram: An Historical Overview

The churches in Mizoram are the progeny of the mission agencies in Europe, namely, The Arthington Aborigines Mission[74] (1894), the Welsh Calvinistic Methodist Foreign Mission[75] (1897), the Baptist Missionary Society[76] (1903) and the Lakher Pioneer

74 Robert Arthington, an English millionaire who had an interest in evangelizing the Mizo (then known as Lushai) and adjacent hill tribes, organized a mission society with his own savings and named it "The Arthington Aborigine Mission". See C. L. Hminga, *The Life and Witness of the Churches in Mizoram* (Serkawn: The Literature Committee of Baptist Church of Mizoram, 1987), 43. (Hereafter, Hminga, *The Life and Witness*).

75 The Welsh Calvinistic Methodist Foreign Mission later became known as, Welsh Presbyterian Mission, was formed in 1843. See John Hughes Morris, *The History of the Welsh Calvinistic Methodist Foreign Mission: To the End of the Year 1904* (Carnarvon: The C.M Book Room D.O/ Brien Owen, Agent, 1910), 25-29; see also Rosiamliana Tochhawng, *A Study of the Ten Articles of Faith of the Presbyterian Church of India* (Delhi: ISPCK, 2007), 11-13. The Welsh Calvinistic Methodist Foreign Mission was operating in Khasi Hills (now Meghalaya) before it adopted Mizoram as its mission field. See Hminga, *The Life and Witness*, 43. See also Saiaithanga, *Mizo Kohhran Chanchin* (Aizawl: The Loch Printing Press, 1969), 8.

76 The Baptist Missionary Society (BMS) was considered as the outcome of William Carey's historic preaching in Nottingham to the Associated Baptists of Mid-east England on 31 May 1792. Carey goaded the people there to "expect great things from God and to attempt great things for God". In the next Association Assembly on 2 October 1792 a Missionary Society was was formed that was known as "The particularl Baptist Society" for the propagation of the Gospel amongst the heathen, which later came to be

Mission[77] (1907). These three Mission agencies were working in Mizoram from the beginning of the twentieth century until the time the churches became self governing and self-supporting in the 1960s. The churches founded by them are known as Mission churches, for they were planted by missionaries from Europe. It is good to note that during the British colonial period in order to safeguard the Mizo people form disintegration and confusion, the British administration did not allow other mission agencies to come to Mizoram.[78]

The origin of both the Baptist and Presbyterian Churches in Mizoram can be traced back to the introduction of Christian faith among the people in the land. In other words, we may say that these two churches are as old as Christianity in Mizoram as they share common parents.

It was on January 11, 1894, the duo pioneer missionaries, James HerbertLorrain and Frederick William Savidge, who belonged to Baptist Church, arrived in Aizawl, Mizoram as sent by The Arthington Aborigine Mission.[79] The two missionaries started the mission work by preaching the gospel, learning and collecting the works of Mizo alphabets and other literature works and teaching those people whom they could gather in their small hut.[80] However, very soon, the two pioneer missionaries had to leave Mizoram due to Arthington's idea that missionaries should not stay among the same

known as "The Baptist Missionary Society". At a meeting on 10 January 1793 held at Kettering, the Society decided to send Carey and the physician John Thomas to India as their first missionaries. See Marina Ngursangzeli, "William Carey and the British East India Company (1801-1830): Implications of their interaction for an understanding of Christian Mission in India Today" (D. Th. Dissertation, Senate of Serampore College, 2005), 54.

77 The Lakher Pioneer Mission was started by Reginald. A. Lorrain, the younger brother of J. H. Lorrain, it is however, not attempted to deal with this topic. More information may be obtained from Hminga, *The Life and Witness*, 105-110.

78 Laldena, *Christian Missions and Colonization*, 47.

79 Hminga, *The Life and Witness...*, 48.

80 Ibid., 50.

group of people for long and the Welsh Calvinistic Methodist Mission took over the field in 1907.[81] During their short stay in Mizoram the pioneer missionaries reduced the Mizo language to written form, and translated the Gospel of Luke and John and the Book of Acts into Mizo. They also prepared a Lushai (Mizo) grammar, a dictionary, a number of small books and a catechism.[82]

It is worth noting about the commitment of the pioneer missionaries particularly to the mission work and their love for Mizo people. They had a great compassion and love for the Mizos. They did not want to leave them without giving them proper education and the Gospel, but it was contrary to their wishes that they had to leave them. Despite they belonged to Baptist denomination, instead of going out of Mizoram, they, out of compassion, expressed their willingness to offer their service to the Welsh Mission even as evangelist as seen in the following excerpts from their writing:

We love the people and country very dearly, and have all along been cherishing the hope that our whole lives would be spent in leading these tribes to Jesus. As you know, we are Baptists and, of course, your Mission would not feel justified in taking us on as regular missionaries, but we have such a longing to remain and work for Christ in Lushai that we would only be too glad if your Mission would accept us as evangelists whose work it would be to preach the Gospel, leaving all church matters to the regular missionaries [83]

81 The first man from the Welsh Calvinistic Methodist Mission who set on the soil of Mizoram was the Welshman, William Williams; he came to Mizoram in 1891 for the purpose of surveying the land for their mission field. He was permitted to stay only one month by the newly established British Administration due to the unsettled conditions of the land. As a result of William's report, the Calvinistic Methodist Church in Wales decided to open a field in Mizoram. But due to the shortage of missionary personnel they could not do so immediately. Meanwhile two missionaries of Arthington Aborigine Mission, J. H. Lorrain and F. W. Savidge came to Mizoram. See Saiaithanga, *Mizo Kohhran Chanchin* (Aizawl: The Loch Printing Press, 1969), 8.

82 Saiaithanga, *Mizo Kohhran Chanchin*, 8-10.

83 This is an excerpt from the letter sent by J. H. Lorrain to Stephens dated Fort Aizawl, North Lushai Hills, 14 May, 1895, cited by C. L. Hminga in his

Even though the Welsh Mission could not accept them as its missionaries even on those terms, Lorrain and Savidge were still pressing them to appoint their own missionaries and send them out as soon as possible so that they may give them a good orientation. When they came to know that Rev. D. E. Jones was appointed for the work in Mizo Hills, they wrote to them:

If Mr, Jones does not sail until the autumn he will arrive here just as we are leaving, and will thus miss the opportunity of availing himself of the aid which we shall be only too glad to give him. We hope to pay a visit to another tribe before we go home on furlough in the spring of 1898, and so shall probably be leaving in December next. We, therefore, would propose that Mr. Jones would come out at the earliest possible date (From Lorrain to Thomas dated Fort Aijal, North Lushai Hills, Assam 29 April, 1897).[84]

The above excerpts clearly indicate that the pioneer missionaries gave more importance to the mission work than their denominational affiliation. On the other hand, this incident also helps us to believe that there were conflicts and competitions between the Baptist church and Calvinistic Methodist Church (later became Presbyterian Church) in Europe; J. H. Lorrain and F.W. Savidge were the victims of it. It was unfortunate that the Welsh Mission could not accept them as their missionaries, had they been accepted, Mizoram would not have been faced with the problem of denominationalism particularly between the Baptist and Presbyterian.

As the Calvinistic Methodist Foreign Mission formally adopted the Lushai Hills as part of their mission field, D. E. Jones, the first missionary of the Welsh Mission arrived in Aizawl on 31st August 1907.[85] After having stayed and worked together with the pioneer missionaries for about three months, the pioneer missionaries eventually handed all the works they initiated over to him and left for England. Since then the whole Lushai Hills was under the mission field of the Welsh Presbyterian Mission.

book, *The Life and Witness of the Churches in Mizoram*, 51.

84 Hminga, *The Life and Witness of the Churches in Mizoram*, 51.

85 Ibid., 52.

During the first half of 1902, things were changed; the Presbyterian Mission Board in Europe had to make a decision as to how the mission field would be looked after. They observed the difficulty of missionaries from northern Mizoram paying frequent visits to south Mizoram on the one hand and the close proximity and easier accessibility of south Mizoram from East Bengal (now Bangladesh) where the Baptist Missionary Society had a Mission Station. Moreover, the Baptist Missionary Society, requested the Mission Board of the Presbyterian Church of Welsh to hand over south Mizoram to their care. Accordingly, in the summer of 1902, the General Assembly meeting of the church in Liverpool agreed to the request and thus, south Mizoram fell into the jurisdiction of the BMS. The BMS asked J. H. Lorrain and F. W. Savidge who were working as missionaries among the Abhor and Miri tribes in Arunachal Pradesh to come to Mizoram for the second time and work among the Mizos who they first loved. They agreed to work among the people on the condition that the BMS should send other missionaries to assist them. Thus leaving Arunachal Pradesh, they came to the southern part of Mizoram via Chittagong and arrived in Lunglei on 31st March 1903.[86] Thereafter, the two mission agencies worked side by side.

It is interesting to note that the two pioneer missionaries in their previous appearance, even though they were aware that they belonged to Baptist, they had no intention to establish a Baptist church. However, in their second coming to Mizoram, as the Presbyterian Church was already born in the north, they also called the newly planted church in south, Mizoram Baptist Church.

The birth of denominational churches was perhaps a necessary evil in that context; J.H. Lorrain still had expressed his vision for the future Mizo Church, as he wrote:

Our experience has taught us that the Lushais are born Methodist... We are not here to make them Eastern duplicate of Western Baptist... but...to so guide them that they shall develop along their own national lines into a strong Lushai Church of God...

86 Hminga, *The Life and Witness of the Churches in Mizoram*, 55.

We look forward to the time when the Lushai church shall be a happy blend of all that is best in Baptist, Presbyterian and Methodist, with something added perhaps which no Western denomination can supply.[87]

The above quotation clearly tells us that for J.H. Lorrain and F.W. Savidge, the church in Mizoram should not be simply an extension of the western church; it should be rooted in local cultures. In other words, for them the body of Christ should incarnate in Mizo culture. Among the native scholars, K. Thanzauva and Mangkhosat Kipgen argue that the vision of the pioneer missionaries has become flesh. For Thanzauva, the ministerial structure of the Baptist church is a blend of the Baptist, Presbyterian and Methodist ecclesiology of the West with the Mizo traditional Village set up (the rule of Elders).[88] As far as the governance of the church is concerned, Thanzauva appears to be true, because, the church in Mizoram is governed by the council of elders (presbyters). However, the vision for one Mizo Church incarnate in their culture for the entire Mizo Christians appears to be still very far away.

We may conclude our discussion about the beginning of the two denominational churches in Mizoram with a note that the geographical feature of the land and the shortage of missionary personnel from the Presbyterian Mission necessitated having two mission agencies from Europe for operating throughout the land and consequently, we have seen the birth of the Mizo Church, manifested into two denominations, the Baptist in south Mizoram and the Presbyterian in north Mizoram.

4.1. The Ecclesiology of the Baptist Church and Presbyterian Churches of Mizoram

We shall now examine in detail the ecclesiology of the two churches. However, the study is limited to three aspects of ecclesiology, they are: 1. The origin and nature of the church. 2. The Mission of the Church. 3. The structure of the church

87 *BMS Printed Report for the Year* 1914, 122.

88 K. Thanzauva, *Theology of Community*, 180-181.

4.1.1. *Ecclesiology of Baptist Church of Mizoram*

4.1.1.1. Baptist ecclesiology: An Evolving History

The Baptist Church of Mizoram as planted by the BMS missionaries belongs to the World Baptist family. Therefore, it is necessary to first look at the historical development of the theology and practices of Baptist church in the West.

The Baptists have understood and articulated their theology and practices in a variety of ways. While there are clear distinctive characters shared by most, if not all, Baptist groups, these distinctive characters are fused in a variety of ways of being Baptist. Bill J. Leonard in his book, *Baptist Ways: A History*,[89] states that those who seek to understand Baptist life and thought might consider the following:

First, any attempt to delineate Baptist distinctive must begin with a confession that any effort to hold certain dynamic, sometimes contradictory, ideals in balance is noble, but nearly impossible task. Some Baptist groups were in the vanguard of the modern mission movements, while others rejected missionary activity altogether. Some have supported the ordination of women, while others have rejected it entirely. Some have demanded various degrees of creedal uniformity, while others have eschewed all creeds and confession.[90]

Biblicism- the attempt to conform to biblical authority and practices has led some Baptists to modify or relinquish certain views when convinced that others were more scriptural. Biblicism has led some Baptists to modify the list of imperatives regarding missions, revivals, foot washing, and the laying of hands. Biblicism has created divisions when individuals and churches differed over the meaning and application of specific texts.[91]

Second, the tension between the individual and the community, between conscience and congregationalism, has meant that schism is an inescapable element of Baptist life. The right of the individual

89 Bill J. Leonard, *Baptist Ways: A History* (Valley Forge: Judson Press, 2003).

90 Leonard, *Baptist Ways: A History*, 14-15.

91 Ibid.

to interpret the nature of the church's life and work anticipated controversy as persons and churches pressed specific doctrines to breaking point. Individuals dissatisfied with one Baptist congregation could simply leave and establish their own church.[92]

Third, Baptist' theological positions remain exceedingly diverse. Like few other denominations, Baptist groups occupy a spectrum that runs from Calvinistic to Armenian, General and Pentecostal Baptist and their heirs maintained a variety of common distinctive-regenerate church membership congregational polity, believer's Baptism, and religious liberty but within a theological framework that was sometimes Calvinist, sometimes Armenian, sometimes a creative and resourceful combination of those and other doctrinal views. Baptist groups that desire to establish a systematic theology can with legitimacy claim various theological traditions for defining Baptist dogma.[93]

Fourth, the compelling ideal that informs Baptist identity theologically and pragmatically seems to be the belief that the people can be trusted to correctly interpret Scripture in the context of community and under the guidance of the Holy Spirit.[94]

Fifth, perhaps a more realistic way of understanding Baptists' origin is to suggest that they exhibit an evolving history, shaped by archetypal beliefs but adapting through a variety of social and cultural contexts. While it is important for all religious communions to understand their origins, they are compelled to acknowledge that movements, like families, are never static. The quest for origin may imply that if contemporary Baptists could simply discover and duplicate what the founders believed, they then would be the true representatives of the Baptist ideal. Given Baptist diversity, that would require delineating which type of original Baptist one wished to be.

Amidst the search for origins, contemporary Baptist groups reflect the impact of multiple trends and experiences. In North

92 Leonard, *Baptist Ways: A History,* 14-15.

93 Ibid.

94 Ibid.

America, for example, many Baptists have been shaped by revivalism, dispensationalism, the social gospel, the civil rights movement, or the mega church phenomenon. In other countries, communism, socialism, Catholicism, and an abiding minority status have shaped the sense of identity in a variety of ways. For instance, while many Baptists in the former Soviet Union apposed communism; other Baptists in Italy embraced it in their dissent against the Catholic establishment.[95]

Studies of Baptist history must take into account the culture of origins that shaped specific Baptist groups. In short, although Baptists share certain commonalities of belief and practice, many being traceable to their seventeenth-century forebears; they also are heirs of their own peculiar historical and social circumstances.[96]

Finally, it is clear that even the writing of Baptist history is not without controversy. In 1890, William Whitsitt, president of the Southern Baptist Theological Seminary, in Louisville, Kentucky, wrote, "I am casting about to begin writing a work on American Baptist History. It is a herculean task, and I must keep it all to myself. Baptist History is a department in which the wise man concealed knowledge. It is likely that I shall not be able to publish the work while I live, but I can write it out in full and make arrangements to publish it after my death, when I shall be out of the reach of bigots and fools."[97]

Those who write and read the elusive history of the Baptists would do well to avoid the fallacy of origins-the belief that one might find authority for contemporary procedures by determining the beliefs and practices of the earliest communities and duplicating them in the present. Even if such replications were possible, Baptist diversity itself requires decisions as to which kind of Baptist tradition might be considered normative. Present and future Baptists are compelled to ask: what kind of Baptists do we wish to be? What historical,

95 Leonard, *Baptist Ways: A History*, 14-15.

96 Ibid.

97 Thomas R. McKibbens, "The Life, Writings, and Influence of Morgan Edwards," *Quarterly Review* 11 (January-March 1976), 68.

theological, spiritual, and communal realities inform the nature of Baptist life in a particular context? Those who wish to discover what it means to be Baptist will be obliged to determine what principles and practices are worth retaining and how best to apply them in the unending transmissions of the church and world.

4.1.1.2. Baptist Polity and Ordinances

The Baptist polity according to F. C. Jonathan, in his book, *Church Organization and Administration: Biblical Understanding Theological Perception*[98] is based on the following principles:

1. Only Christ is the Head of the church. 2. Local church is self-governing. 3. The type of organization and administration is called congregational. 4. Equality of all members.

Baptist churches self-government is not 'democratic'. Administration is not by the pastor or the councils of churches but by the voice of the Holy Spirit in the hearts of local church members. Administration of the church is by the church "belief" that through the church, Christ is administrator. All members have equally received the gifts of the Holy Spirit. Two things arise, a) each member's right and responsibility, b) the guidance of the elected members is gladly accepted. Freedom is not for freedom's sake in the churches. Baptist church's early concept of the freedom is freedom from state power.

Baptists believe in three ordinances. They include- a) Believers' Baptism. b) The Lord's Supper. c) Evangelism. They called these as ordinances because they see power of the command of Christ. These ordinances are not personal but belong to the church.[99]

4.1.1.3. Baptist Identity

The Baptist church identity, as found in the Baptist World Alliance (BWA) declaration is "in every corner of the world there men and women, old and young, who follow the New Testament teachings

98 F. C. Jonathan, in his book, *Church Organization and Administration: Biblical Understanding Theological Perception* (Delhi: ISPCK, 2007), 79.

99 Ibid.

concerning the church being a gathered body of believers who personally confess Jesus Christ as Lord and Saviour and publicly confess that faith by immersion, in the name of the Father, Son and Holy Spirit."[100] In other words, members of the church are those who are born anew, and in Christ receive personal and salvation faith, living in direct acquaintance with and experience of Christ. Only believers can take part in the ordinances.

Baptist Identity has been spelt out into four distinctive and essential 'freedoms'- Bible freedom, the freedom and obligation of Christians to study and obey the scriptures which are central in the life of the individual and the church; soul freedom, the responsibility of every person to deal with God without the imposition of creed, interference of clergy or intervention of civil government; church freedom, the autonomy of local churches, which are free to determine their membership and leadership, order their worship, ordain those whom they perceive as gifted for ministry, and participate in the life of the larger body of Christ; and religious freedom, the freedom of the individual to hold and practice his or her religious beliefs without government interference.[101]

The Baptist World Alliance Study Commission on Baptist Heritage formulated a statement in its meeting in Zagreb, Yugoslavia in July 1989. It discusses the scriptures, the gospel, the church and discipleship, and concludes that Baptists are the following:

> Members of the whole Christian family who stress the experience of personal salvation through faith in Jesus, symbolized both in baptism and the Lord's Supper

100 Denton Lotz, "The Baptist World Alliance", in *Baptist Around the World: A Comprehensive Handbook*, edited by Albert W. Wardin (Nashville, Tennessee: Broadman & Holman Publishers, 1995), xxiv.

101 Richard V. Pierard, "Introduction", in *Baptists Together in Christ 1905-2005: A Hundred- Year History of the Baptist World Alliance*, edited by Richard V. Pierard (Falls Church, Virginia: Baptist World Alliance, 2005), xv.

> Those who under the Lordship of Jesus Christ have bonded together in free Local congregations, together seeking to obey Christ in faith and in life
>
> Those who follow the authority of Scripture in all matters of faith and practice
>
> Those who have claimed religious liberty for themselves and all people
>
> Those who believe that the Great Commission to take the Gospel to the whole world is the responsibility of the whole membership[102]

Based on the above statement, one may say that Baptists are those who emphasize the authority of scripture, salvation through faith in Christ; believers' baptism by immersion; congregational church government; religious liberty and evangelization.

Basic principles that set them aside from the other major Christian bodies may be shown as below: Unlike most other major Protestant bodies, Baptist have had no founder, such as Martin Luther for the Lutherans, John Calvin and Ulrich Zwingli for the Reformed, or John Wesley for the Methodists.[103] In fact, there was John Smyth whom many consider to be the first English Baptist, and Roger Williams whom many regard as the founder of Baptists in America. However, they both left the Baptist faith soon after their baptism as believers. Smyth led his congregation to accept Mennonite doctrine, and Williams became a seeker, rejecting all existing denominations. In addition, Smyth baptized himself, a highly irregular practice, but was baptized by effusion if not sprinkling. [104]

Over the years, Baptist historians have debated the relative influence of Puritan Separation and Anabaptists in the development

---

102 Pierard, "Introduction", in *Baptists Together in Christ 1905-2005: A Hundred-Year History of the Baptist World Alliance*, iv.

103 Albert W. Wardin, ed., *Baptist Around the World: A Comprehensive Handbook* (Nashville, Tennessee: Broadman & Holman Publishers, 1995), 1-2.

104 Ibid.

of the Baptist movement. There is no attempt to resolve the debate here except to note that Thomas Helwys, who broke away with Smyth and established the first General Baptist church on England soil which was Armenian and rejected certain features of both systems. The later particular or Calvinistic Baptists, clearly Puritan in doctrine, accepted believer's baptism by immersion after study of scripture and theywere drawn to the example of the collegians, a group in the Netherlands who practiced it.[105]

Although Baptists have been influenced by the theological currents of their day, they have insisted that they are "People of the Book"[106] claiming Scripture as the sole norm of faith and practice. Besides this, they also have upheld a second principle of the Protestant Reformation "the Priesthood of the believer or soul competency". Whatever one may believe concerning their origins, the Baptist advocacy of these principles clearly places them within the Protestant tradition.[107] On the other hand, from the very beginning they separated themselves from most Protestant of their day by rejecting the magisterial reformation. Protestant reformer, by and large, advocated territorial churches, supported and protected by the state, which incorporated an entire population under its discipline and brought the new born into membership through infant baptism.

With the earlier Anabaptists and Mennonites, Baptist countered by insisting that the local church is composed only of baptized believers and membership must be voluntary, thereby rejecting parish churches and infant baptism, as well as a union of church and State and religious coercion. Such principles thereby place Baptists in what has been denominated as "the Believers' Church," a type of church in which Baptists were historical forerunners.[108]

105 Wardin, ed., *Baptist Around the World: A Comprehensive Handbook,* 1-2.

106 Ibid.

107 Ibid.

108 Ibid.

4.1.1.4. Baptist Church of Mizoram

The Baptist church of Mizoram is part of the Baptist family around the globe. The Baptist Church of Mizoram claims as part of the One, Holy, Catholic and Apostolic Church, the Body of Christ. It is together with other Baptist churches in the world and particularly with the Baptist family in India which acknowledges that the church is the Body of Christ and that its members are the members of His Body.[109] The members are according to the will and purpose of God, who are baptized into the name of the Father, and of the Son, and of the Holy Spirit, they receive the calling and grace of God with repentance and faith, and continue steadfast therein. By the same faith they maintain their vital union with the Head of the Body, though the various means of grace, which He has provided in his church, and through Him they are united in fellowship with one another. The church, therefore, acknowledges that every member has an immediate and direct relationship with God, shown equally by the life of faith and by individual conscience in response to the indwelling of the Holy Spirit. The church shall, therefore, accord respect for the conscientious convictions of the individual members, as long as they are in harmony with the mind of Christ and are not disruptive of the fellowship of His Body.[110]

The Baptist Church of Mizoram holds the faith which the church has always held in Jesus Christ the Redeemer of the world, in whom alone men are saved by grace through faith, and in accordance with the revelation of God which He made being Himself God Incarnate. It worships one God, Father, Son and Holy Spirit.[111]

---

109 The Church of North India, *The Constitution of The Church of North India and Bye-Laws* (Delhi: ISPCK, 2003), 1-2. The doctrine of the church adopted by Mizoram Baptist Church is similar with The Church of North India. For the Baptitsts, a Christian Church is a company of regenerate persons, baptized on a profession of faith in Christ. See Edward T. Hiscox, *Princples and Practices for Baptist Churches* (Grand Rapids, Michigan: Kregel Publications, 1980), 20.

110 *The Constitution of North India and Bye-laws*, 1-2. and *BCM Constitution*, 1-3.

111 Baptist Church of Mizoram. *Constitution and Rules of Baptist Church of Mizoram.* (Serkawn: The Publication Board of BCM, 2001), 3.

The Baptist Church of Mizoram accepts the Holy Scriptures of the OT and NT as the inspired Word of God as containing all things necessary to salvation, and as the supreme and decisive standard of faith. It acknowledges that the church must always be ready to correct and reform itself in accordance with the teaching of those scriptures as the Holy Spirit shall reveal it.[112]

It also accepts the Creeds, commonly called the Apostles' and Nicene as witnessing to and guarding the faith, which is continuously confirmed by the Holy Spirit in the experience of the church of God.[113]

4.1.1.4.1. Baptist Church of Mizoram Polity

As has been stated, the Baptist Church of Mizoram shared with other Baptist churches in terms of faith and practices. However, we have seen its distinctiveness in its polity. Unlike other Baptist families, the polity[114] adopted by the Baptist Church of Mizoram is a combination of the congregational and Presbyterian type of church government. The BCM has a strong centralized structure of church government, and the Headquarters controls the functions of all local churches. Therefore, in a strict sense, the Baptist church of Mizoram is more Presbyterian than congregational; thus, it is not wrong to say that the BCM follows a mild or modified form of Presbyterian polity.[115]

---

112 Baptist Church of Mizoram. *Constitution and Rules of Baptist Church of Mizoram*, 3.

113 Ibid.

114 The system of rules that governs a church is called its polity. While there is an almost endless variety of belief and practice among Christian churches today, church polities can be roughly divided into three basic kinds. They are congregational, Episcopal and Presbyterian. Joan S. Gray and Joyce C. Tucker, *Presbyterian Polity for Church Officers* (Louisville: Westminster/John Knox Press, 1990), 1-5.

115 Under Congregational church polity, each local church directly is governed by the people who make up the congregation. The final authority on any question is the vote of a majority of the members of that particular congregation. Each local church is autonomous; it functions without any outside control. Each congregation has its own bylaws and is sovereign in dealing with matters

4.1.1.4.2. BCM Mission Policy

As evangelism is one of the distinctive marks of the Baptist Church, the BCM has actively been involved in mission and evangelism, carrying out the gospel of Jesus within and outside Mizoram for more than sixty years. The aims and objectives of the BCM in its mission are:

To preach the gospel of Christ to those who have not heard it within and without Mizoram

To discover, innovate and adopt different methods, ways and means for propagating the gospel and employ various instruments to attain its aim.

To emphasize to the people the importance of propagating the gospel within outside Mizoram and therefore, to convince them about their responsibility in this regard, besides to receive gifts from them for the same.[116]

The BCM has spent about fifty per cent of its income every year for mission works operating in different fields and achieved many great things. Its achievement in converting people to Christianity is commendable. However, the scope of its mission and evangelism need to be broadened in order to bring more people to the Kingdom of God.

4.1.2. *Ecclesiology of the Presbyterian Church of Mizoram*

The Presbyterian Church of Mizoram (PCM), as already stated earlier, came into being with the coming of the missionaries of the Welsh Calvinistic Methodist Church. For the first twenty-five years, the church was known as the Welsh Calvinistic Methodist church. It was only in 1924 that the church took the name of Presbyterian Church

---

within its fellowship. However, the BCM is a centralized church government ruled by the elected representatives called presbyters. The final authority is vested in the Assembly, consisting of elected Assembly officers, pastors and elected representatives of local churches.

116 Baptist Church of Mizoram, *Rules and Regulation of ZBM and Working Plan upto AD 2000* (Serkawn: Baptist Church of Mizoram, 1990), 1.

of Mizoram.[117] The Presbyterian Synod (also known as Mizo Synod) was constituted on July 20th, 1924 at a meeting in Durtlang.[118] The Creed and Constitution were formulated on the basis of the Creed and the Constitution of the Welsh Calvinistic Methodist Church, which is now known as the Presbyterian Church in Wales.

4.1.2.1. Presbyterian Church: An Evolving History

In order to have a better understanding of the Presbyterian church of Mizoram, it is important to understand its mother church in Wales. The origin of the Welsh Calvinistic Methodist Church was traditionally traced back to the Methodist movement that started in 1735.[119] The revival movement greatly moved Wales and the prominent leaders were Howell Harris, Daniel Rowlands, Griffith Jones and William Williams. The main concern of these leaders was the spiritual slumbering of the established church and they tried to revive it by calling its members to be actively reborn in Christian living. They felt the need to form some kind of organization and thus a society was formed in each locality under the charge of an "exhorter". A number of societies were grouped together into districts under the care of an overseer and the quarterly gatherings of the representatives of the whole body were called "Associations". But it was not their original intention to found a new church. They continued to be members of the Church of England and they were careful in all measures they took to avoid as far as possible giving offence to Church susceptibility.[120] However, the Church of England became more and more hostile to the members of the movement and they were even persecuted because they gave their loyalty more to the movement than to their church. Moreover, they accept only

117 Saiaithanga, *Mizo Kohhran Chanchin* (Aizawl: The Loch Printing Press, 1969), 83.

118 Ibid., 82.

119 Lefferts A. Loetscher, *A Brief History of the Presbyterian* (Philadelphia: The Westminster Press, 1958), 46.

120 William Williams, *Welsh Calvinistic Methodism: A Historical Sketch* (London: James Nisbet & Co., 1872), 26.

those who were born again as members of the movement.[121] The movement became each year a more organized body and found it difficult to attach themselves to the existing Church. Therefore, in the General Association meeting held at Bala on June 19-20, 1811, they ordained their own ministers for a new denomination- "The Welsh Calvinistic Methodist Church".[122] Initially the newly formed church was called "Calvinistic Methodists in Wales or Welsh Calvinistic Methodists, as they adopt Presbyterian polity and Calvinism they were also known as "The Presbyterian Church of Wales" and both names were used to refer to the same denomination. In the official book of Rules of Discipline and Confession of faith it was put as "Calvinistic Methodists or Presbyterian Church of Wales" in 1900.[123] Finally they adopted the nomenclature, the "Presbyterian Church of Wales" in 1933.[124]

The confession of Faith of the Welsh Calvinistic Methodist Church was formulated in 1823, which was based on the Westminster Confession.[125] According to this Welsh Calvinistic Methodist Church confession, the Presbyterian Church of India (including the Presbyterian Church of Mizoram) adopted its Confession of Faith, which is known as the Ten Articles of Faith in 1926. Vanlalauva has rightly asserted that like all other Presbyterian churches in the world, the Mizoram Presbyterian Church uses the Westminster confession (via the Welsh Confession) as the standard of its faith and as a source of its ecclesiology.[126] 'The Ten Articles of Faith' of the Presbyterian

121 Zairema, "The Fire Must Be Kept Burning", *The Presbyterian Review* VII/26 (April-June 2001), 4.

122 George E. Clarkson, *George Whitefield and Welsh Calvinistic Methodism* (Lewiston: The Edwin Mellen Press, 1996), 100.

123 Rev. Z.T. *Sangkhuma, Kohhran Chanchin* (Aizawl: Synod Publication Board, 1982), 131.

124 Ibid.

125 F. L. Cross & E. A. Livingstone (eds.), "Calvinistic Methodism" in *The Oxford Dictionary of Christian Church* (London: The Oxford University Press, 1958), 224.

126 H. Vanlalauva, "Relation between Calvin's Ecclesiology and Ecclesiology of the Presbyterian Church in Mizoram" (M. Th Thesis, UTC, Bangalore, 1986), 115.

Church of India is used as the main source of data for analysis of the ecclesiology of the Presbyterian Church of Mizoram in the following section

4.1.2.2. Biblical Principles of Presbyterian Church

The Presbyterian Church recognizes that the Scriptures do not contain a detailed plan for church government, in spite of this, however, Presbyterians have always sought to base their polity on principles found in the Bible. The Book of Order states that in the worship and service to God and the government of the church, matters are to be ordered according to the word by reason and sound judgment, under the guidance of the Holy Spirit. In keeping with this idea, the offices of the church, the office of presbyter and that of deacon, are ones for which there is clear precedent in scripture. Acts 6: 1-6 tells of the origin of an office like that of deacon to meet a need in the early church. The scripture establishes this office as one of services to those in need.

Presbyterians believe that the NT uses the words, "bishop" and "elder" to refer to the same office. This can be seen in Titus 1:5 and 1:7 as well as in Acts 20:17, 28. Thus there is no hierarchy of presbyters in the Presbyterian Church; ministers of the word and sacrament and elders differ only in the functions they are called to perform. When functioning together in governing bodies they are equals. At meetings of the governing bodies, all presbyters stand the same footing, and decisions are made by the majority vote of the whole body. Even those elected to be officers of governing bodies, moderators and clerk, have no individual authority outside the body. Their only power is that which has been constitutionally assigned to them for their term of office by the governing body that elected them.

Another principle of this polity derived from the scripture which states power within the church is to be exercised by groups of officers rather than individuals. Both OT and NT refer to a gathering of elders which exercised governance over the people.[127] They believe

127 Deut. 27:1; 2 Sam 5:3; Acts 15:6.

that the Holy Spirit speaks most clearly on matters of government through the prayerful deliberations of groups of presbyters. While the decisions of groups are clearly fallible, Presbyterian polity states that groups are less likely to fall into error than an individual. Therefore, most decisions in the church are made by officers organized into groups called governing bodies.[128]

4.1.2.3. Presbyterian Polity

The name of the church "Presbyterian" refers not to the doctrine or beliefs, but rather to how they govern themselves. Presbyterian polity takes its name from the Greek word for elder. *Presbuteros,* and Presbyterian form of government emphasizes the sharing of power by a group of usually elected elders. There is no single powerful bishop or high priest, the risen Christ is the only head of the church. Each of the congregation is governed by a group of Presbyters elected by the congregation.[129] Herald Schilling's one main argument for this was the Jewish government of the synagogues in NT times. He pointed out that the synagogues were governed by a group of elders, and the Presbyterians claim that the early church took over this polity. Furthermore, for him, Acts 15 is a pillar for Presbyterian polity where we see the apostles and elders assembled to discuss church issue and to decide about it.[130]

4.1.2.3.1. Fundamentals of Presbyterian Polity

At least three fundamental characteristics prevail, without which a system of church government could hardly be called Presbyterian. They are: representative, constitutional and relational. The

128 Joan S. Gray and Joyce C. Tucker, *Presbyterian Polity*, 7.

129 Joan S. Gray and Joyce C. Tucker, *Presbyterian Polity for Church Officers* (Louisville: Westminster/*John Knox Press, 1990),* 1-5. The system of rules that governs a church is called its "polity". Church polities may be broadly divided into three kinds, namely, congregational, Episcopal and Presbyterian.

130 Herald Schilling, Doctrine of the Church (Ecclesiology) (Abak: The Equipping The Saints Trust Samuel Bill Theological College, 1998), 35; see also Pathil Kuncheria, Indian Churches at the Crossroad...,4.

Presbyterian Church is governed by groups of presbyters elected by the people. One of the rights of the Presbyterian is that of electing its own permanent officers. Therefore, no higher governing body can instruct a congregation to install a particular man or woman in a permanent office against their will. The power is exercised under the oversight of the Synod/Assembly/ Session/Presbytery, and in certain cases the presbytery can exercise a "veto power" over the congregation's decisions.[131] The Presbyterian church has a constitution which seeks to put their beliefs and polity into writing. This constitution has two parts: the Book of Confessions and the Book of Order. A confession, or creed, is an authoritative expression of the Christian faith. The book of confessions deals with what they believe, whereas the Book of Order explains the workings of their polity. It seeks to collect and interpret biblical teachings about the church into a system of church government. Most organizations have a set of bylaws to govern the workings of the group. The Book of Order could be seen as the Church's Bylaws; it is one of the standards under which the church makes decisions and carries out its mission.[132] This part of the constitution has three sections, each dealing with a different area of the church's life. They are the form of government, the Directory of worship and the Rules of Discipline. The basic principles and rules of the polity are outlined in the form of Government. The Directory of worship contains their standards relating to worship, the Sacraments, admission to membership in the church and the church service in the world. Rules of Discipline deals primarily with handling conflict within the church. The need for a constitution stems in part from the representative nature of their polity. Officers are elected by the congregation to exercise authority on its behalf. A Constitution that details the precise boundaries of that authority keeps the officers from assuming powers they were never intended to have. The Book of Order is essential piece of equipment for all church officers because it tells them not only the duties they must fulfill but also the powers they can exercise.

131 Joan S. Gray and Joyce C. Tucker, *Presbyterian Polity*, 7.

132 Ibid., 9.

Officers are elected by the congregation to exercise authority on its behalf only as stated in the Constitution.

Another important characteristic of Presbyterianism is its relational character, which is rooted in the belief in the unity of the church. Ephesians 4:5-6 remind us that all Christians have "One Lord, One Faith, One Baptism, One God and Father of us all." Another term for this One Church is the "Church Universal."

The Church Universal consists of all persons in every nation, together with their children, who profess faith in Jesus Christ as Lord and Saviour and commit themselves to live in a fellowship under his rule.[133]

The Presbyterian Church as a particular administration of the church universal tries to reflect this unity through participation in various national and international councils of churches.

4.1.2.3.2. The Powers and Responsibilities of Governing Bodies

The Book of Order says several important things about the power of governing bodies. First, any power that the Church exercises rightfully comes from Jesus Christ. The authority of governing bodies is only ministerial and declarative. This means that the pronouncements and rules of governing bodies should be based on the will of God revealed in Scripture. With regard to governance, Protestant Christians first decided how the church was not to be governed. Then they understood the positive task of designing a system of governance, seeking to follow biblical principles as they were built.[134]

4.1.2.3.2.1. The Office of Elder

Presbyterian Church seeks to follow biblical principles in its governing system. According to Joan S. Gray and Joyce Tucker, John Calvin was faced with the particular task of developing a church organization for the city of Geneva. They further opined that studying the NT, Calvin identified other offices in addition to that of minister which

133 Joan S. Gray and Joyce C. Tucker, *Presbyterian Polity*, 9.

134 Ibid., 34-35.

he considered to be permanent, that is, intended for the church in all times. One of these was the office of elder. Calvin concluded that the NT envisions two kinds of presbyters; some presbyters have the responsibilities of preaching and teaching the word. The other type of presbyter does not have the responsibilities for proclamation, but along with the minister shares the responsibility for governance within the church. Calvin placed particular emphasis on the discipline of personal conduct.[135] Governance was almost synonymous with the correction of error or faults. Elders were charged with the oversight of the daily behaviour of the people. [136]

The influence of Calvin and the church at Geneva rapidly spread throughout Europe and Great Britain; Calvin encouraged his followers to adopt the system of church government begun in Geneva to their own particular situation. Many variations on Calvin's system were developed. Churches throughout Europe developed written constitutions which systematized their ecclesiastical institutions. These constitutions were probably shared among the Reformed family.[137]

4.1.2.4. The Presbyterian Church of Mizoram (PCM)

The creed and constitution of the PCM were formulated on the basis of the creed and the constitution of the Welsh Calvinistic church which is now known as the Presbyterian Church in Wales.[138] Therefore, it is appropriate to first know the constitution of the Presbyterian church of Wales formulated and adopted at the Association of Aberystwyth and Bala in the year 1823.[139] It is also important to note that like

135 Joan S. Gray and Joyce C. Tucker, *Presbyterian Polity*, 34.

136 Ibid., 34.

137 Ibid., 35.

138 H. Vanlalauva, "Relation between Calvin's Ecclesiology and Ecclesiology of the Presbyterian Church in Mizoram" (M. Th Thesis, United Theological College, 1986), 115.

139 D. O' Brien, Owen, *The Historic Constitution, Rules of Discipline and Confession of the Calvinistic Methodist, or the Presbyterian of Wales* (Caernarvon: D.O'Brien, 1900), 83, cited in H. Vanlalauva, "Relation between Calvin's

all other Presbyterian churches in the world, the PCM uses the Westminster Confession as the standard of its confession of faith and as a source of its ecclesiology. The summary of the Article I-X of the confession of faith of the PCM is shown below:

The Scripture of the OT and NT are the word of God the infallible rule of faith and duty. There is only one God, who is a Spirit, Self existent and Omnipotent. In the Godhead there are three persons, the Father, the Son and the Holy Spirit and these are the same in substance, equal in power and glory.

It is the duty of all believers to unite in church fellowship, to observe the sacraments and other ordinance of Christ. At the last day the dead shall be raised and all shall appear before the judgment seat of Christ.

The PCM has also adopted the Invisible and the visible church. Of the church invisible-God is gathering out of every nation great multitude in which throughout the ages, he will show forth the exceeding riches of his grace and wisdom. Of the church visible-it is the whole body of earth, of those who accept Christ as their saviour and who confess Him as their Lord, acknowledging the Father, the Son and the Holy Spirit, one God blessed forever.[140]

Hans Kung has rightly pointed out, "Ecclesiology belongs to the world to which the church also belongs. It is essentially historically conditioned... it is written in various specific places at specific points in history.[141] This is true of the PCM's ecclesiology. As this is the case, the knowledge of the context of Mizoram is always indispensable not only to formulate but also to understand the ecclesiology of the PCM.

The PCM inherits many of the Welsh Calvinistic Methodist Church tradition. In other words, the PCM adopted Presbyterian tradition because of the Welsh Calvinistic Methodist church

---

Ecclesiology and Ecclesiology of the Presbyterian Church in Mizoram", 115.

140 *The Constitution of the Presbyterian Church of Northeast India* (Shillong: Ri Khasi Press, 1984), 1-4.

141 Hans Kung, *The Church* (London: Search Press, 1973)), 13.

tradition through its missionaries. It was the Welsh Calvinistic Methodist missionaries who brought the Gospel to the Northern Mizoram after the first two missionaries, Lorrain and Savidge. Hence, the Creed and the constitution were formulated after the creed and constitution of the Welsh Calvinistic Methodist Church. It also adopted many of the practices of the parent church. Thus the WCM tradition is one of the most important formative influences of the ecclesiology of the PCM.[142] The WCM in Wales came into existence as the result of the revival movement in Wales and England in the 18th and the 19th centuries. Howell Harris, a lay evangelist was the first leader of the movement. Through his labours, the revival occurred in Wales in 1735.[143] Within a few years, Harris organized 30 groups known as societies. These societies were organized into an association, the first meeting of the General association was held in 1743.[144] When the Methodist revival movement under Wesley and Whitefield got under way, the Welsh revival movement went with the former. Whitefield a Calvinistic revivalist had a great influence upon it. Because of the influence of Whitefield and other Welsh leaders who were Calvinistic in their theological orientation, the Welsh Methodist revival movement got separated from the Wesley's Methodist movement in the later part of the 18th century and in 1811 under the leadership of Thomas Charles of Bala, the Welsh Methodist revival movement started what was known as the Welsh Calvinistic Methodist Church.[145]

It was not the intention of the leaders of the Welsh Methodist revival movement to found a new church. They were the members of the Church of England. Although they were involved in the movement, they receive communion in the Church of England.

---

142 H. Vanlalauva, "Relation between Calvin's Ecclesiology and Ecclesiology of ...", 115.

143 Lefferts A. Loetscher, *A Brief History of the Presbyterians* (Philadelphia: The Westminster Press, 1958), 46.

144 Ibid.

145 John Roberts, *The Calvinistic Methodism of Wales* (Caernarvon: The Calvinistic Methodist Book Agency, n.d), 46f.

However, due to an unfriendly attitude of the Church of England, they organized themselves into the church.[146]

It is to be noted that in the new church, WCM, three different traditions were mingled: Anglican tradition, Methodist revival tradition and the Calvinistic tradition.[147] Of all these three traditions, the Calvinistic tradition appears to have been prominent.[148] The new church used the Westminster Confession as the basis of its confession of faith. It was truly Presbyterian in its form of government. The church which used the Westminster confession as the standard of its confession of faith and adopted the Presbyterian form of government and held the theological system associated with John Calvin has become known as the Presbyterian Church in Wales. This is the church born out of the revival movement but grown and developed in the triangular traditions. H. Vanlalauva state the great influence made by the Church in Wales upon the PCM, as follows: "This is the church which had brought across the oceans the Gospel to the land where the name of Jesus and his Church were never known before. Thus one can assume what a great influence the Presbyterian church in Wales exercise upon the people, the Church it had planted.[149]

Like all other Presbyterian churches in the world, the PCM uses the Westminster Confession as the standard of its confession of faith and as the source of its ecclesiology. The Welsh Calvinistic Methodist which planted the church in Mizoram also based its confession of faith upon the Westminster confession.[150] The doctrine of the visible and invisible church in the Confession of the PCM indicates that it has drawn its source from the Westminster confession. The visible refers to the church which exists at present time and comprises of

146 Roberts, *The Calvinistic Methodism of Wales*, 46.

147 Ibid.

148 H. Vanlalauva, *Relation between Ecclesiology of John Calvin and Ecclesiology of the PCM*, 116.

149 Ibid.

150 D. E. Jerkins, "Welsh Calvinistic Methodist," *Encyclopaedia Britanica*, Vol. V (Cambridge: University Press, 1910), 76-91.

its members who are now living. The invisible church is not limited to its present membership but comprises of all those that have been, are, or shall be gathered into one, under Christ the head thereof. The confession also affirms that the ministry is a gift of Christ to the church. The confession also states that the visible church is the eschatological community. It is on the move towards the end. The church is the body of Christ and He alone is the head of the church. The visible expression of the invisible headship of Christ is the affirmation of the absence of any visible head. The communion of saints is the unity which human have with Christ by his spirit and by faith, with one another by love. It involves community in service, edification and works of charity.

The confession affirms complete destination between the church and the state. This is essential for the dependence and the integrity of the church. It also affirms Lord's Supper and Baptism as the Sacraments. They should be administered only by ordained ministers.

4.1.3. *BCM and PCM Understanding of the Church*

The Mizo Churches in general used different terminologies for the Church consisting of the imageries taken from the Bible and local expressions or terminologies of some of those imageries. It is worth discussing the local expressions of the body of Christ, such as, *Eklisia*, *Kohhran* or *Kohhranho*, *Pathian thuawiho* and *Mission Kohhran* or Missionary *Kohhran.*

4.1.3.1. Eklisia

In the beginning, Mizo Christians called the church "eklisia", derived from the Greek term *Ekklesia.* This term was in use among the Mizo Christians for two decades. According to Upa Chalhnuna, this term was first introduced by the Western missionaries, which is the transliterated form of the word "ekklesia."[151] For the missionaries and the Mizo Christians, the church which is called "eklisia" would mean nothing less than the people or community of believers who had been

151 H. Vanlalauva, *Relation between* ..., 127-128.

called out of one setting into another. The first generation Christians were the people from the lower strata of society. After accepting the Christian faith they had to live in a community separated from their socio-cultural and religious context. Despite persecutions met at the hands of their fellow Mizo, they firmly held their faith. They met together on Sunday for worship and prayer. This is eklisia the people of God who had been called out of the traditional socio-cultural and religious world.[152]

4.1.3.2. Kohhran or Kohhranho

Another significant terminology employed till date is "Kohhran" or "Kohhranho". The Mizo word "kohhran" is a combination of two Mizo words, "koh" which means "call" and "hran" or "hrang" which means "to be" separated from or set apart from. Hence, the term "kohhran or kohhranho (plural) may be understood as "called to be different or separated from. Those who are called to live in the community of believers different from those who do not belong to this community are the literal meaning and what the "kohhran" stands for. It must also be remembered that the word "kohhran" and "eklisia" connote the same meaning. In other words, the word *Kohhran* is the literal translation of the Greek word 'ekklesia". Since 1970s, the church has become known to the Mizo as 'Kohhran".[153]

The term *Kohhran* implies that it is a community of believers called out by God to serve Him and to glorify His Name.[154] *Kohhran* is also associated with the idea of keeping distance for society or the world in terms of life style, habit, and behaviour. Owing to the influence of the missionaries, the first generation Christians were completely disassociated with many of the traditional cultural practices.[155] The church also encourages its members to keep a distance with the traditional socio-cultural and religious practices.

152 H. Vanlalauva, *Relation between* ..., 127-128..

153 Ibid., 128.

154 Liangkhaia, *Kohhran leh A Rawngbawl Hna* (Aizawl: Synod Press, 1979), 4.

155 H. Vanlalauva, *Relation between Ecclesiology of John Calvin and Ecclesiology of the PCM*, 129.

The *Kohhran* prohibited participation in traditional festivals, sacrifices and all functions that were related to the traditional faith and culture. It is interesting to note that *Kohhran* prohibited to even singing an indigenous songs. Hence, they kept a distance from their traditional world. This idea of separation and difference in life style was prominent in the conception of the term *Kohhran.*

4.1.3.3. Pathian Thuawiho

Another word for the church is "Pathian Thu awiho" meaning a community or a group of people who believe in the word of God. Saiaithanga clearly states that the term "Pathian Thu awiho" was coined by those who opposed the Christian faith. They applied it to the community of believers in an abusive manner.[156] Later the Mizo Christians used it to identify themselves and then became common usage for the church.

4.1.3.4. Mission Church

Since its inception the Mizo churches has been known as "Mission church" especially this name is applied to the Presbyterian church of Mizoram and Baptist Church of Mizoram. One of the reasons for giving this name is that both of the churches were planted by the western missionaries. The term "Mission Church" became more prominent after the emergence of other denominational churches in Mizoram. By this term, the two churches, PCM and BCM are distinguished from other denominations. Therefore, the name "Mission Church" may be described as the church directly planted by the missionaries.

The name implies that the Mizo Church has been founded and nurtured by the missionaries. Despite some indigenous elements being incorporated into the church, the influence of the missionaries upon the two churches is quite significant. As stated earlier, the church formulated its creed and constitution under the direct supervision of the missionaries. Many pastors who later became church leaders

156 H. Vanlalauva, *Relation between Ecclesiology of John Calvin and Ecclesiology of the PCM*, 131.

received their theological orientation from the missionaries. Since the influence of the missionaries has been very strong in the church, some native leaders who gave emphasis on the indigenous culture and freedom found themselves estranged and alienated and eventually left the Mission Church and formed new denominations. Because of all the above reasons, Vanlalauva, without any hesitation, states that the Presbyterian Church is not more than the extension of the Presbyterian Church in Wales.[157]

4.1.3.5. Other Imageries

Apart from the local expressions of the church mentioned above, the idea of the Church as conceived by the Mizo church can also be known from its use of the Biblical and traditional imageries, of which, the prominent ones with the Churches of Mizoram are: The body of Christ and the people of God.

The Mizo Christians are very much influenced by the Pauline concept of the church. With regard to the concept of the church, the phrase "the body of Christ" is the most popular usage to describe the nature of the church. In describing the church as the body of Christ, the main concern is the unity of the members of the church. Although the various members of the church are bestowed a variety of spiritual gifts to exercise different functions, yet it is asserted, all of them belonging to one body must exercise their respective functions for the edification of the whole body.[158] While speaking of the church as the body of Christ, the influential theologians like Liangkhaia stress the necessity of becoming the members of the church.[159]

Hence, it should be noted that because of the revival movements and of the evangelistic ministry of the itinerant evangelists, there has been a tendency among the believers to privatize their faith. In opposition to this tendency, according to H. Vanlalauva, the Mizo theologians give a considerable emphasis on being a member of the

157 H. Vanlalauva, *Relation between...*, 131.

158 *Kristian Thu Inchhang* (Aizawl: Synod Bookroom, 1972), 66.

159 Liangkhaia, *Kohhran leh A Rawngbawl Hna* (Aizawl: Synod Press, 1979), 11.

church. They also asserted that apart from the church, there is no other way of uniting with Christ.

It should also be noted that the body image is employed not just to emphasize the unity of the members, but the unity with Christ, the supreme head of the church; that the head cannot be separated from the church.

The Christians in Mizoram, right from the beginning, have understood that the church is the people of God. It is only through the people who were actively involved in the evangelistic work that the church grows and develops. It is a historical fact that the whole area of Mizoram is evangelized through the people's movement inspired by the Holy Spirit.[160] To the Mizo Christians, the church should never be made a private and exclusive affair of a few. The church should never be in the hands of a group. The call of God is for the people. There the Church takes the voice of the people seriously in the life and administration of the Church.[161]

4.1.4. *Evaluation of the Ecclesiology of the PCM and BCM*

This section deals with the evaluation of the ecclesiology of the churches of Mizoram by analyzing and interpreting the research data collected through questionnaire. As has been already mentioned in the introduction of the study, 200 questionnaires were distributed to church leaders, pastor, elder and deacon, Women leaders and Youth leaders of Baptist Church and Presbyterian Church of Mizoram both from urban and rural. Out of 200 questionnaires, 160 were returned to the researcher. The research data is divided into six sections: (1) the analysis of the respondents' status; (2) the Churches of Mizoram and the early Church tradition; (3) the churches of Mizoram and the Western Missionary Church tradition; (4) The churches of Mizoram and Contextualization; (5) The churches of Mizoram and Mizo cultural traditions; (6) Proposal for Mizo Christian ecclesiology

160 Saiaithanga, *Presbyterian Kohhran* (Aizawl: The Synod Publication Board, 1965), 3f.

161 Ibid., 3.

In analyzing the research data the researcher uses "quantitative"[162] method to enhance clarity in interpreting and describing the responses for the research questions. All the research data are tabulated, classified and shown in the tables. We shall, first of all, analyze and interpret the data pertaining to the question whether the churches of Mizoram are faithful to the ecclesiology of the early Christian traditions. Secondly, we shall analyze and interpret the data concerning the impact of Western Church traditions in the Mizo Churches. Thirdly, we shall analyze and interpret the data concerning the contextual relevance of the existing ecclesiology of the churches of Mizoram. Finally, we shall analyze and interpret the data pertaining to the Mizo tribal ecclesiology.

4.1.4.1. Analysis of the Profiles of Respondents

Table 1: Distribution of Respondents by Age.

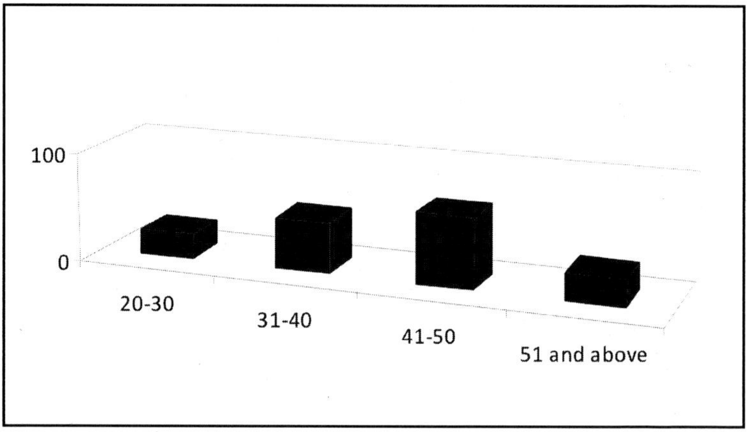

Table 1 shows that out of 160 respondents, 65 (40.625%) are under the age group of 41 to 50, 47 (29.375%) respondents fall in the 31-40, 25 (15.625%) of them are of the age group 51 and above,

162 Quantitative method here is used for providing factual, descriptive information or describing phenomena numerically to answer specific questions. See D. A. de Vaus, *Surveys in Social Research* (Jaipur and New Delhi: Rawat Publications, 2003), 5.

the least number, 23 (14.375%) are of the age group 20-30. The above table testifies that leadership in the churches of Mizoram is in the hands of the age group 41 and above.

Table 2: Distribution of Respondents by Gender.

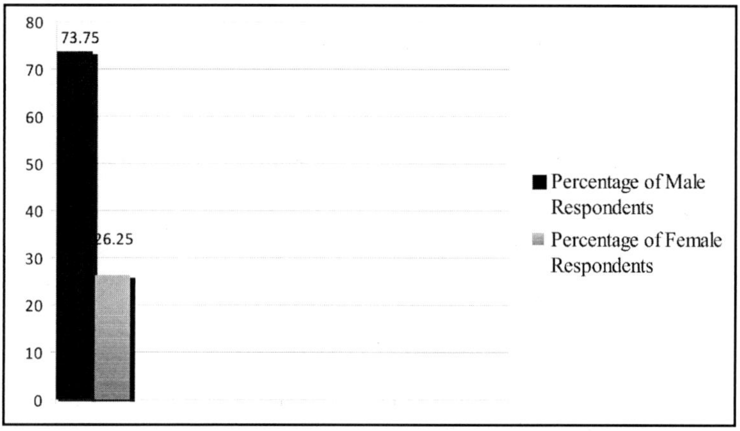

Table 2 shows that 118 (73.75%) out of 160 are male and 42 (26.25%) are female. Even though the selection of the respondents was made randomly, the majority is male; this indicates that leadership in the churches of Mizoram is in the hands of man folk.

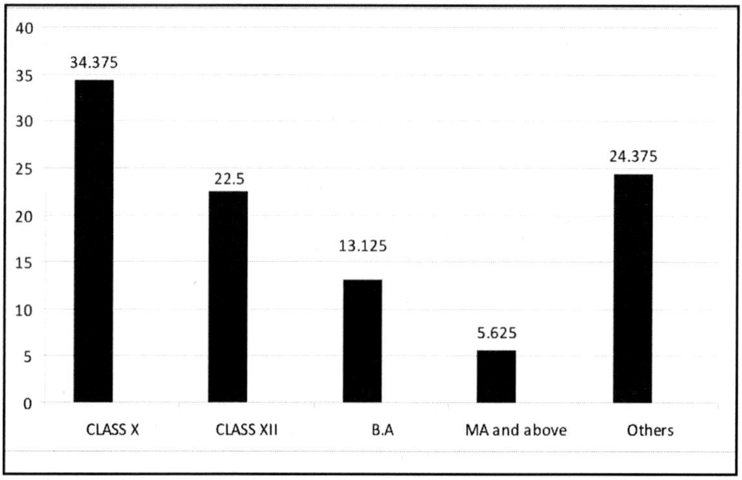

Table 3 shows that the largest number of respondents, 55 (34.375%) out of 160 are of class X level, the next 39 (24.375%) belong to other, which means below class X, 36 (22.5%) are Bachelor degree holders. There are 9 respondents (5.625%) with M.A and above.

Table 4: Distribution of Respondents by Marital Status.

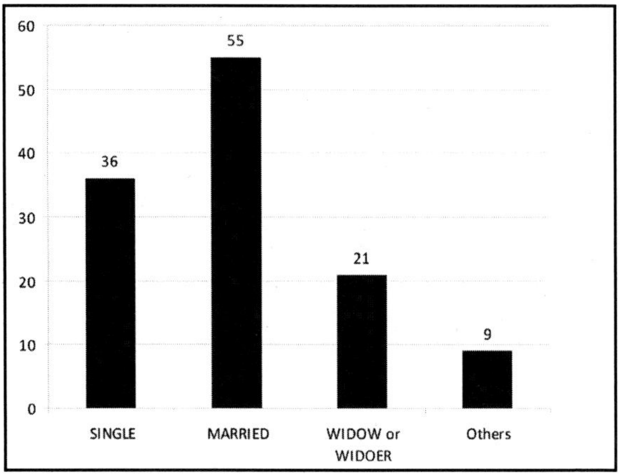

Table 4 shows that 55 (34.375%) out of 160 are married, the next 36 (22.5%) are single, the third largest group, 21 (13.125%) are widow and widower, the least group, 9 (5.625%) belong to other.

Table 5: Distribution of Respondents by Economic Status.

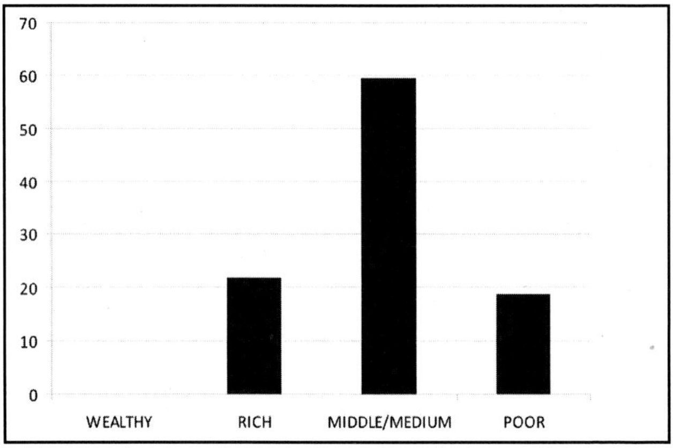

Table 5 shows that among the respondents no one is from economically wealthy family. The largest group, 95 (59.375%) belong to middle class, the next 35 (21.875%) are from rich family, whereas 30 (18.75%) are economically poor. However, it is to be noted that the classification of this economic status is based solely on respondents' answer.

Table 6: Percentage of Respondents according to Current Positions in Church.

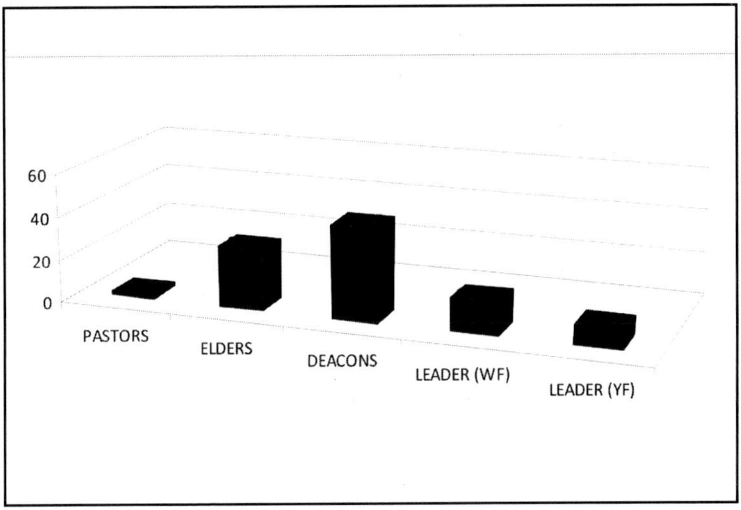

Table 6 shows that the largest number 70 (43.75%) are deacons, the next 46 (28.75%) are elders, the third group, 25 (15.625%) are leaders of Women Fellowship, the least group, 15 (9.375%) are Youth Fellowship leaders. It is to be noted that all leaders of Women Fellowship are female; however, leaders of Youth Fellowship are both male and female.

4.1.4.2. Evaluation of the Ecclesiology of the Churches of Mizoram

1. The Churches of Mizoram and the early Church Ecclesiology

Table 1.1. Distribution of Responses on Mizoram Churches' Continuity with Early Church Tradition.

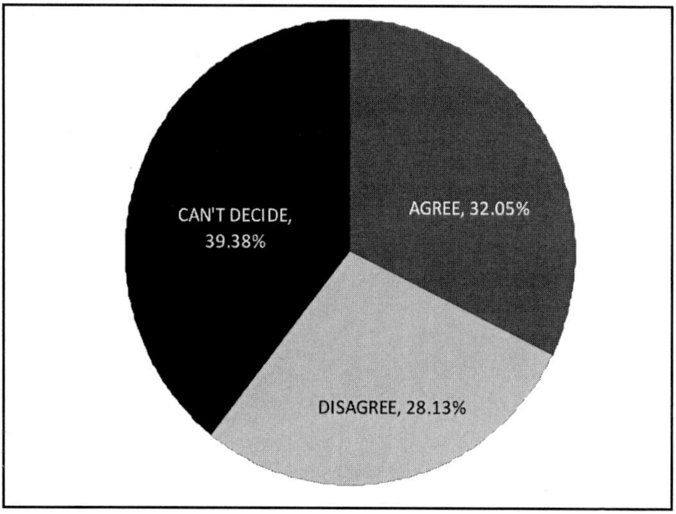

Table 1.1 shows that fifty two respondents (32.05%) out of 160 testify that there is continuity of the church tradition from antiquity; however, forty five respondents (28.13%) see no continuity and sixty three respondents (39.38%) can't decide. From table 1, we can probably say that due to changes took place in course of time; majority of respondents did not find any continuity in the life of the Mizo church.

Table 1.2. Aspects of Mizoram Church identified by Respondents as having Continuity with Early Church Tradition.

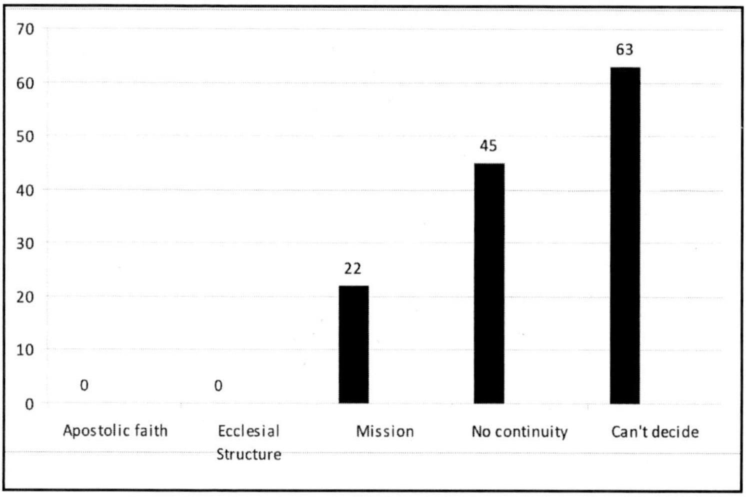

Tables 1.2 shows that thirty respondents (18.75%) out of 160 agree that the churches of Mizoram maintain continuity with the early church by keeping apostolic faith and twenty two respondents (13.75%) have the idea that the mission of the early church is continued by the churches of Mizoram. However, fourty five respondents still do not see any connection between the early church and the churches of Mizoram and a great number, sixty three (39.375%) respondents cannot decide.

Table 1.3. Agreement on Mizoram's Serious Reference to Early Church Tradition for Life and Ministry (Do you agree that the churches of Mizoram seriously take the early church ecclesiology for their life and ministry?)

Table 1.3 shows that fourty respondents (25%) out of 160 say that the churches of Mizoram seriously took the early church ecclesiology for their life and ministry. However, eighty seven respondents (54.375%) disagree to it. And thirty three respondents (20.625%) cannot decide.

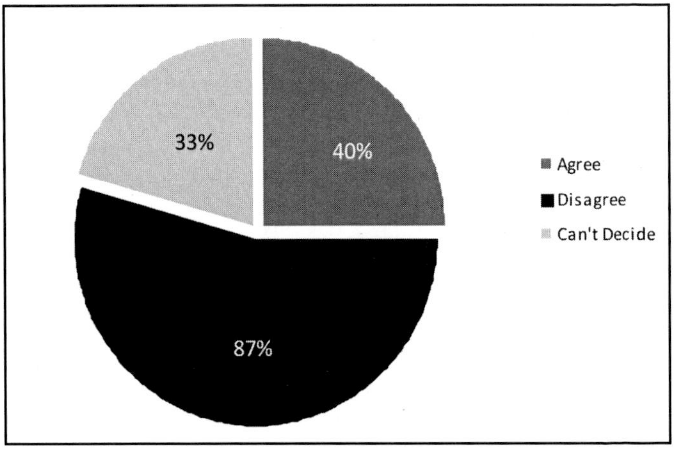

Table 1.4. Distribution of Respondents by Concept of Church.

What do you mean by the Church?

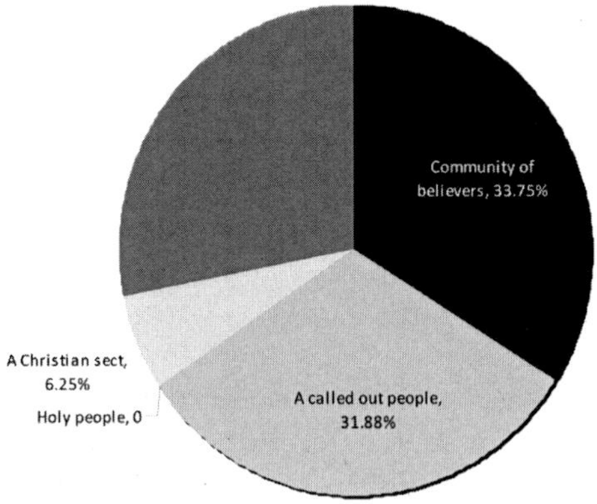

Table 1.4 shows that fifty four respondents (33.75%) out of 160 understand the church as 'a community of believers'; fifty one respondents (31.88%) understand it as ' a called out community'; fourty five respondents (28.13%) understand it as 'Christian Institution and ten respondents see the church as a Christian sect.

Table 1.5. Responses on Necessity for Mizoram to study early Church Tradition.

Do you agree that it is necessary for the churches of Mizoram to study the early Christian Tradition?

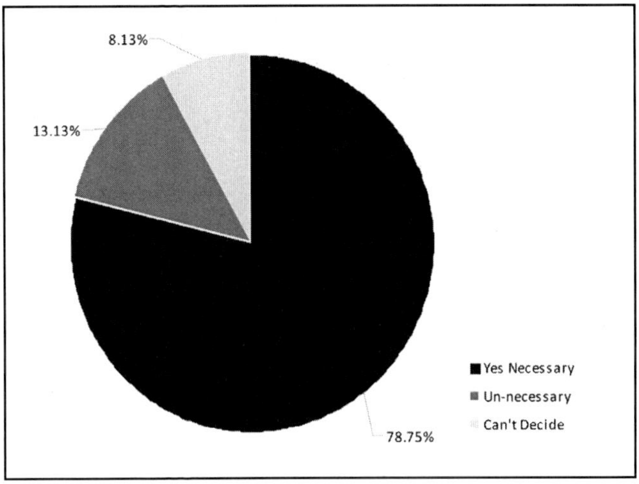

Table 1.5 shows that the majority, one hundred twenty six respondents (78.75%) out of 160 see the need of the early Christian tradition for the life and ministry of the churches of Mizoram. However, twenty one respondents (13.13%) do not see the need for studying the tradition of the Christian antiquity. And thirteen respondents (8.13%) remained undecided.

The whole section, from tables 1.1 to 1.5, testifies that the churches of Mizoram, even after many centuries, still give certain importance to the early church traditions and try to keep unity with the early church. However, in order to be faithful to the early Christian traditions and to the Mizo culture, the churches of Mizoram have to revisit and learn from the early Christian tradition.

2. The Churches of Mizoram and the Western Missionary Ecclesiology

Table 2.1. Responses on the Belief that Mizoram Churches are the Offspring of Western Missionaries.

Do you agree that the churches of Mizoram are the offspring of Western Missionaries?

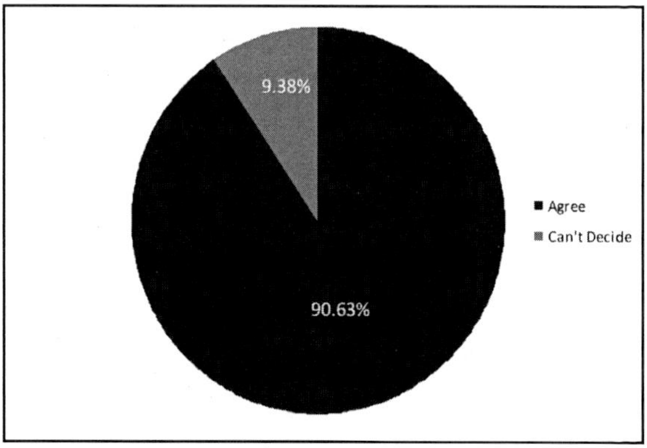

Table 2.1 shows that one hundred fourty five respondents (90.63%) out of 160 testify that the churches of Mizoram are the progeny of the Western churches. No respondent goes against it but there are fifteen respondents who can't decide. This table shows that the churches of Mizoram are well connected to their Western mother churches or counterparts.

Table 2.2. Responses on the Belief that the Churches of Mizoram are Eastern Duplicates of Western Churches.

Do you agree that the churches of Mizoram are eastern duplicates of Western churches?

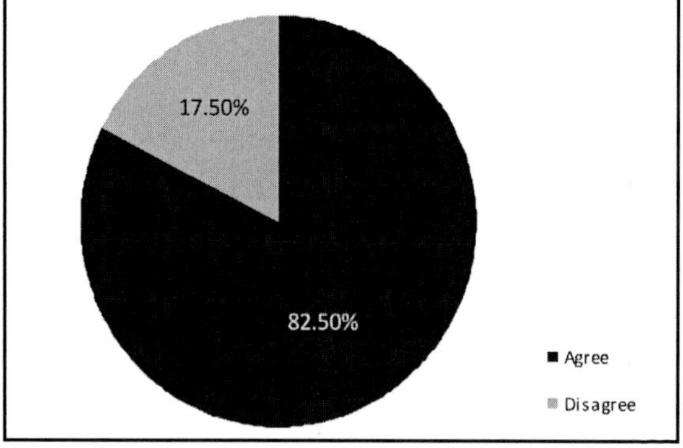

Table 2.2 affirms the finding in table 6. One hundred thirty two respondents (82.50%) out of 160 say that the churches of Mizoram are eastern duplicate of the Western Church. However, there are twenty eight respondents (17.50%) who do not agree to it.

Table 2.3. Responses on the Belief that the Baptist Church of Mizoram (BCM) and the Presbyterian Church of Mizoram (PCM) are Duplicates of the English Baptist Church in England and the Presbyterian Church of Wales respectively.

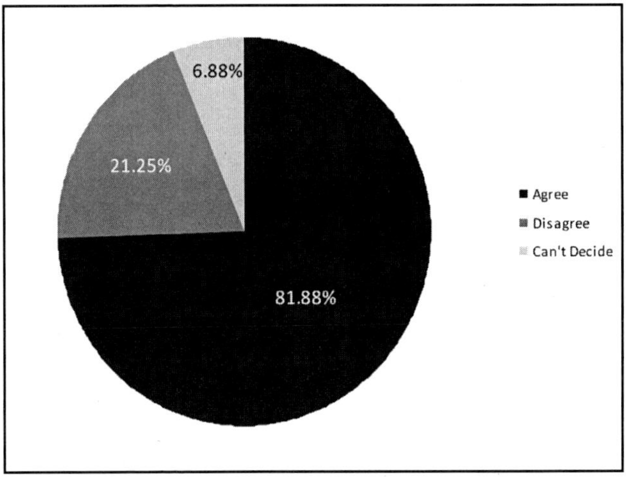

Table 2.3 shows that one hundred eleven respondents (81.88%) out of 160 testify that the BCM and PCM are the duplicates of the English Baptist and the Presbyterian Church of Wales respectively. There are, however, thirty four respondents (21.25%) who do not support it and eleven respondents (6.88%) cannot decide.

Table 2.4. Responses on the Belief that Institutionalism, Individualism and Division in Multiple Sects are Due to the Influence of the Western Missionary Church Traditions.

Do you agree those institutionalism, individualism and division in multiple sects are due to the influence of the Western Missionary church traditions?

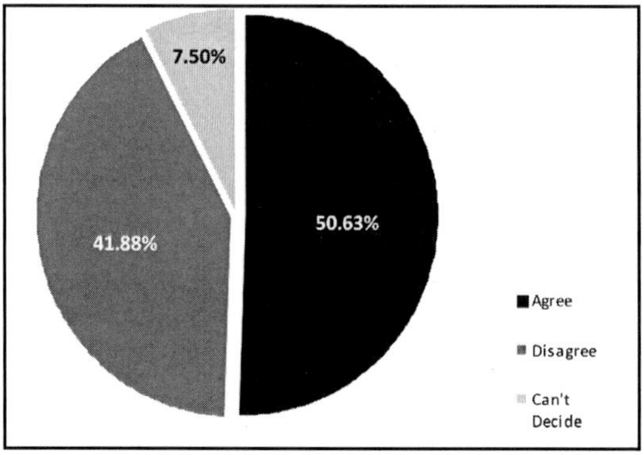

Table 2.4 shows that eighty one respondents (50.63%) out of 160 say that those institutionalism, individualism and division in multiple sects are due to the influence of the Western churches. However, a good number of respondents (41.88%) have an opposite opinion of it. And there are twelve respondents (7.5%) who remained undecided.

Table 2.5. Distribution of Respondents on Agreement that it is good for Mizoram Churches to Follow the Western Churches.

Do you agree that it is good for the churches of Mizoram to follow the Western churches?

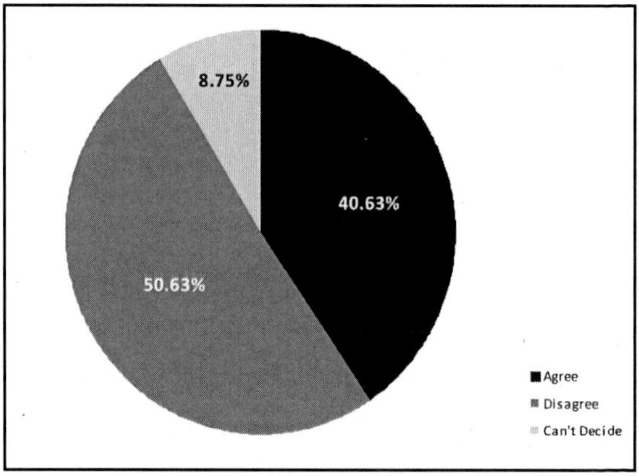

Table 2.5 shows that eighty one respondents (50.63%) out of 160 say that for the churches of Mizoram it is not good to follow the Western Churches. However, sixty five respondents (40.63%) see the need of it, and fourteen respondents (8.75%) remained undecided.

The whole section, from Tables 2.1 to 2.5, reveals that the churches of Mizoram are heavily influenced by the Western church traditions. Even though a good number of respondents are quite happy with the Western church tradition, half of the respondents are critical of it.

3. The Churches of Mizoram and the Mizo context

Table 3.1. Distribution of Responses on Agreement that the Churches of Mizoram effectively address the Problems of the Present Mizo society.

Do you agree that the churches of Mizoram effectively to address the problems of the present Mizo society?

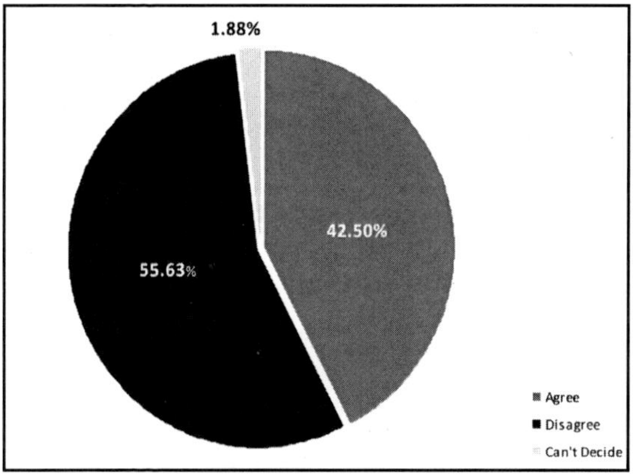

Table 3.1 shows that sixty eight respondents (42.50%) out of 160 agree to say that the churches of Mizoram effectively address the problems of the present Mizo society. However, eighty nine respondents (55.63%) disagree to it, and three respondents (1.88%) cannot decide.

Table 3.2. Responses on the Belief that the Churches of Mizoram are rooted deeply in Mizo Cultures.

Do you agree that the churches of Mizoram are rooted deeply into the Mizo cultures?

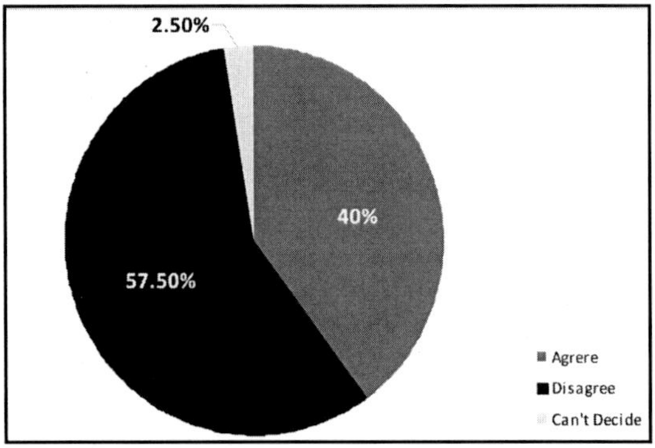

Table 3.2 shows that 92 respondents (57.50%) out of 160 have the idea that the churches of Mizoram are not rooted deeply in the Mizo cultures, the next 64 (40%) say that they are rooted deeply into the Mizo cultures, the least group, 4 (2.50%) cannot decide.

Table 3.3. Distribution of Responses by Preferred Leadership Style for the Mizo Churches.

What type of church leadership do you prefer most for the Mizo Churches?

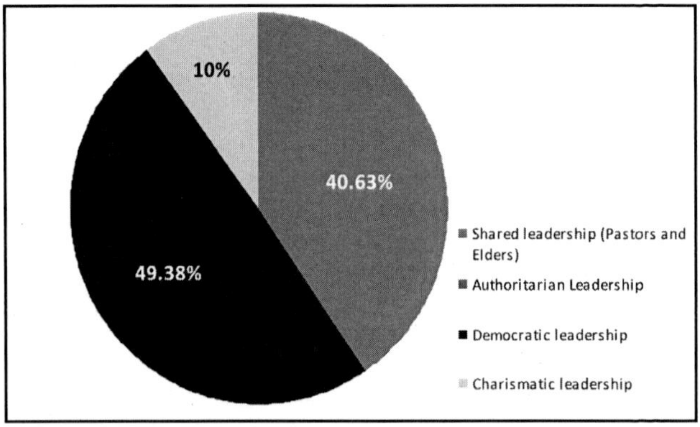

Table 3.3 shows that the largest group, 79 (49.38%) out of 160 prefer Democratic leadership, the next 65 (40.63%) are in favour of shared leadership, the third group, 16 (10%) prefer charismatic leadership. No respondent is in favour of Authoritarian leadership in the church.

Table 3.4. Distribution of Respondents by Belief in Mizoram Churches' Ability to Transform Mizo Society.

Do you agree that that the churches of Mizoram are strong enough to transform the Mizo society?

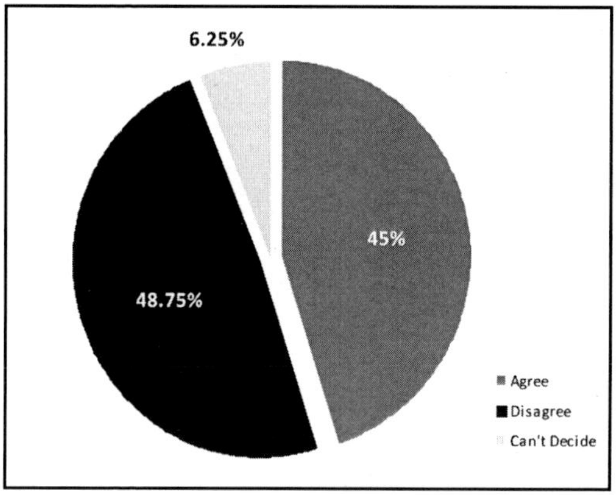

Table 3.4 shows that 78 (48.75%) out of 160 say that the churches of Mizoram are not strong enough to transform Mizo society, however, 72 (45%) accept that the churches are strong enough to transform the society, the least group, 10 (6.25%) cannot decide.

Table 3.5. Ranking of Areas on the Basis of Improvements Most Reportedly Needed.

In which area do you think the churches of Mizoram need to improve most?

Table 3.5 shows that 70 (43.75%) out of 160 have the opinion that the churches of Mizoram need to improve most in worship, the next 58 (36.25%) say that the theology of the church is most needed to be improved, the least group 32 (20%) say that the ministerial structure is most needed to be improved.

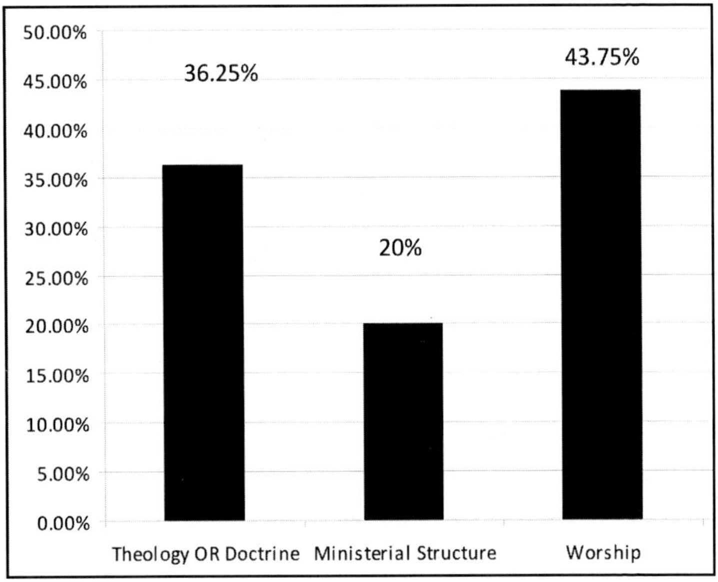

This section, from table 3.1 to 3.5, reveals that the churches of Mizoram are not deeply rooted in the Mizo culture and therefore, they are not very successful in addressing the problems of the society. This section testifies that contextualization of the theology of the church is an urgent need of Mizo Christians.

4. The Churches of Mizoram and Inculturation

Table 4.1. Responses on the Belief That the True Church of God Is Rooted In Local Culture.

Do you agree that the true Church of God is rooted in local culture?

Table 4.1 shows that 105 (65.63%) out of 160 agree that the true church of God is rooted in local culture, whereas 49 (30.63%) disagree and 5 (3.13%) cannot decide.

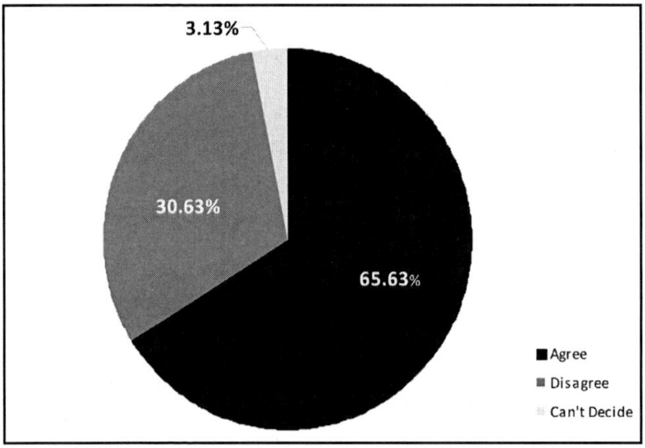

Table 4.2. Areas of Most Prominent Impact of the Church on Mizo Christians.

In your opinion which one is more prominent about the impact of the church on Mizo Christians?

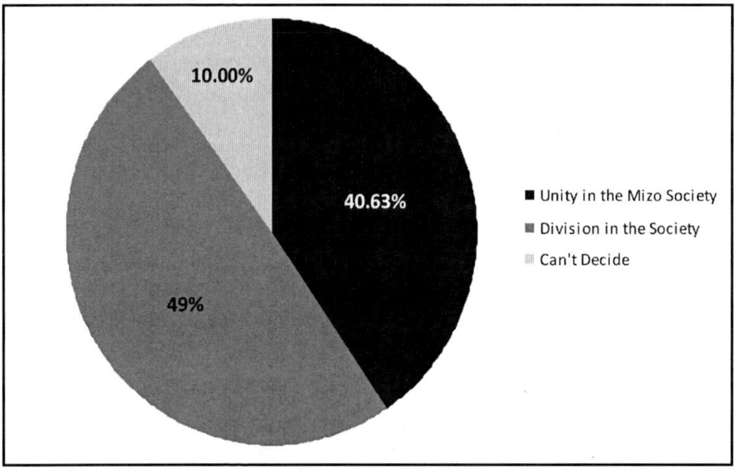

Table 4.2 shows that 79 (49%) say that the division in the church is more prominent than the Unity in the Mizo society, whereas 65 (40.63%) say that it is the Unity in the Mizo society which is more

prominent than the division. There are 16 (10%) respondents cannot decide.

Table 4.3. Responses on the Belief that the Mizo Cultural Traditions should be incorporated into the Ecclesiology of Mizo Christians.

Do you agree that the Mizo cultural traditions should be incorporated into the ecclesiology of Mizo Christians?

Table 4.3 shows that 76 (47.50%) agree to incorporate the Mizo cultural traditions in Mizo Church ecclesiology, whereas 63 (39.38) disagree that the Mizo culture should not be incorporated into ecclesiology. The least group 21 (13.13%) cannot decide.

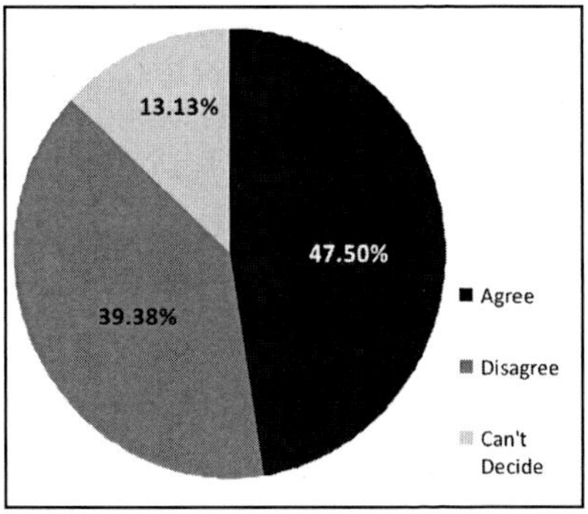

Table 4.4. Responses on the Belief that the Mizo Cultural Traditions, *Zawlbuk*, *Tlawmngaihna*, and Egalitarianism are Compatible with the Gospel.

Do you agree that the Mizo cultural traditions, *Zawlbuk*, *Tlawmngaihna* and Egalitarian trait are compatible with the Gospel?

Table 4.4 shows that 81 (50.63%) out of 160 express their opinion that the cultural traditions, *Zawlbuk*, *Tlawmngaihna* and Egalitarian trait are compatible with the Gospel, whereas 72 (45%) express that they are not compatible with the Gospel. There 7 respondents (4.38%) who cannot decide.

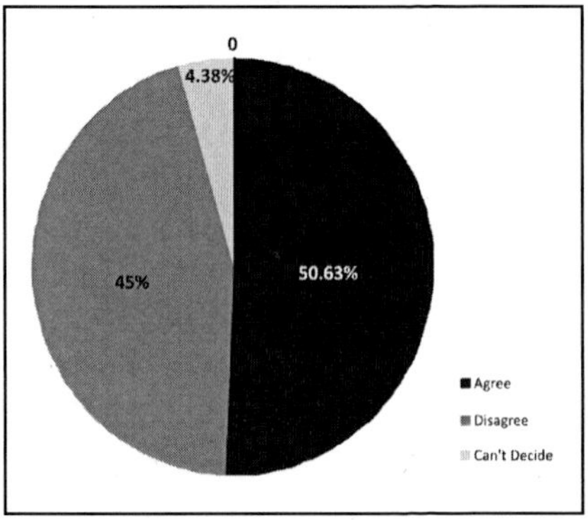

Table 4.5. Responses on the Need for Development of Mizo Christian Theology using Mizo Worldview and Traditions.

Do you agree that Mizo Christians need to develop Mizo Christian theology by using Mizo worldview and traditions?

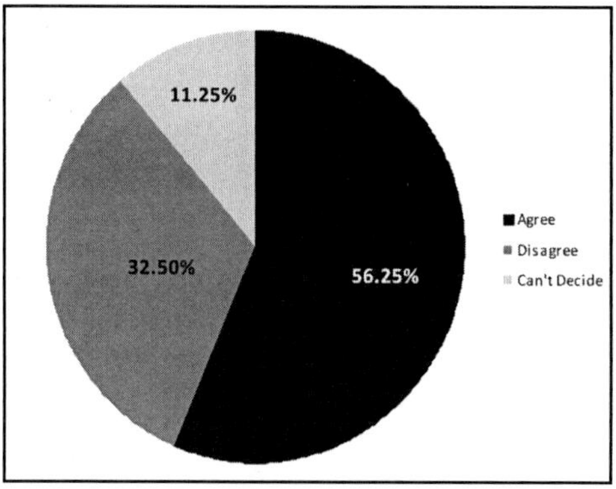

Table 4.5 shows that 90 (56.25%) think that Mizo Christians need to develop Mizo Christian theology by using Mizo worldview and traditions, whereas 52 (32.50%) do not see the need, and the least 18 (11.25%) cannot decide. This section from table 16 to 20 expresses the need of having contextual theology based on Mizo worldview and traditions.

5. Envision for The Mizo Christian Ecclesiology

Table 5.1. Agreement on the Need for Mizoram Churches to Reconstruct Their Ecclesiology.

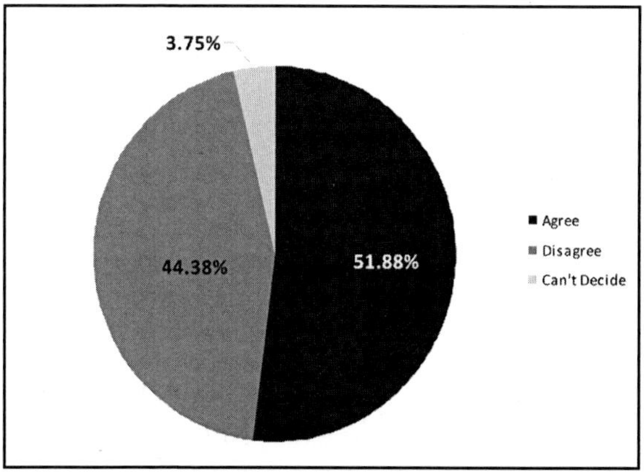

Do you agree that the churches of Mizoram need to reconstruct their ecclesiology?

Table 5.1 shows that 83 respondents (51.88%) out of 160 agree that the churches of Mizoram need to reconstruct their ecclesiology, whereas 71 (44.38%) disagree and 6 (3.75%) respondents cannot decide.

Table 5.2. Responses on the Belief that Mizo Christian Ecclesiology should be Faithful to Early Church Tradition.

Do you agree that Mizo Christian ecclesiology should be faithful to early church tradition?

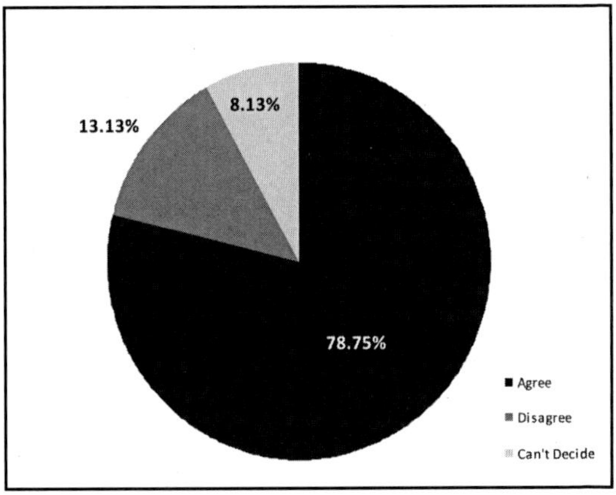

Table 5.2 shows that 126 (78.75%) respondents out of 160 agree that Mizo Christian ecclesiology should be faithful to early church tradition, whereas 21 (13.13%) disagree and 13 (8.13%) cannot decide.

Table 5.3. Responses on the Belief that Mizo Christian Ecclesiology should be Faithful to the Mizo Culture.

Do you agree that Mizo Christian ecclesiology should be faithful to Mizo culture?

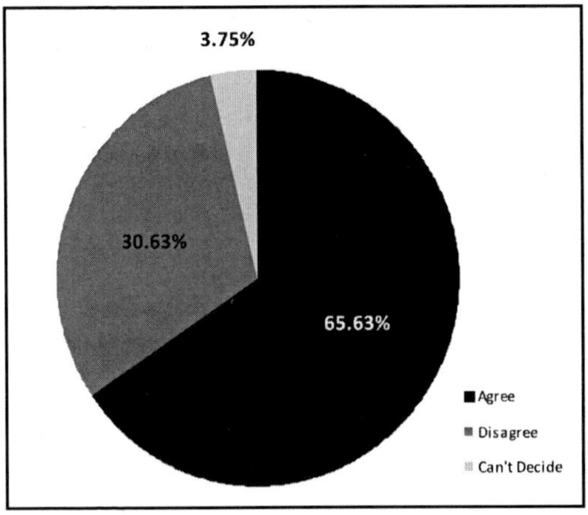

Table 5.3 shows that 105 (65.63%) out of 160 respondents agree that Mizo Christian ecclesiology should be faithful to Mizo culture, whereas 49 (30.63%) disagree to it and 6 (3.75%) cannot decide.

Table 5.4. Responses on the Belief that Mizo Christian Ecclesiology should address the Problems of Mizo Society.

Do you agree that Mizo Christian ecclesiology should address the problems of Mizo society?

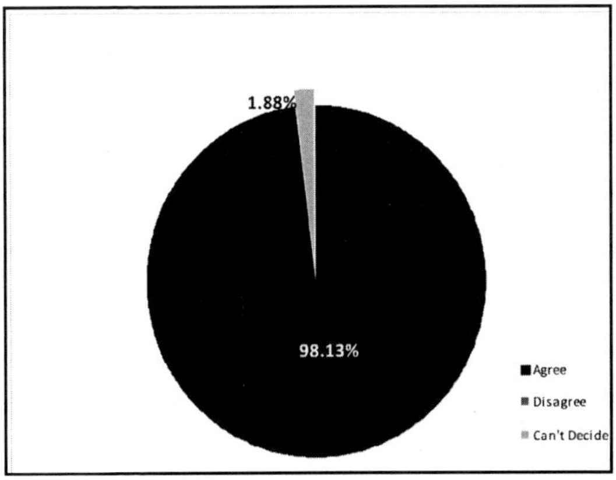

Table 5.4 shows 157 (98.13%) out of 160 respondents agree that Mizo Christian ecclesiology should address the problems of Mizo society, there is no one who goes against it, however, 3 (1.88%) cannot decide.

Table 5.5. Respondents' Priority of the Roles of Missions for Mizoram Churches.

Prioritize the mission of the churches of Mizoram

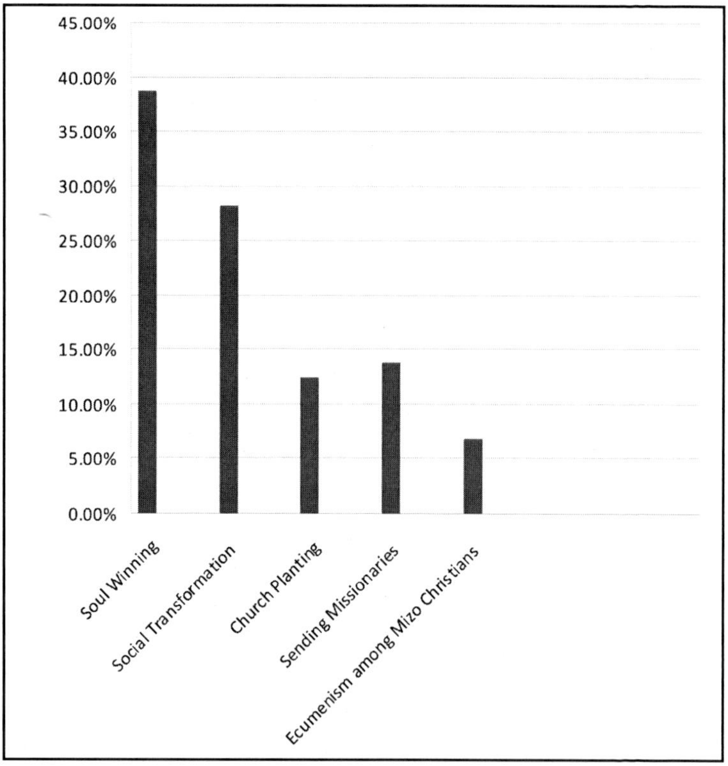

Table 5.5 shows 62 (38.75%) respondents out of 160 say that soul winning most important task of the mission the church, 45 (28.13%) say that transformation of society is the primary mission, 22 (13.75%) say that sending missionaries to other faiths is most

important, 20 (12.50%) give priority to church planting, the least 11 (6.88%) group give priority to ecumenism among Mizo Christians. This table reflects the influence of the Western Evangelical Awakening or the legacy of the Western missionaries who worked in Mizoram.

Findings and Comments

Based on the information received through questionnaire (from tables 1 to 25) we can make a conclusion about the contemporary ecclesiology of the churches of Mizoram as follows:

1. Tables 1.1 to 1.5 testify that the churches of Mizoram, even though they try to maintain continuity, are not faithful to the early church tradition in many respects.
2. Tables 2.1 to 2.5 show that the churches of Mizoram are western church oriented and therefore, they are culturally and contextually not relevant to the people.
3. Tables 3.1 to 3.5 show that the churches of Mizoram are also not faithful to the recipient's culture. Therefore, the churches of Mizoram are not strong enough to address the problems of Mizo society.
4. Tables 4.1 to 5.5 show us the urgent need of the churches of Mizoram, which is contextualization or inculturation of their ecclesiology based on the early church traditions and Mizo cultural traditions.

5. Conclusion

The above analysis and evaluation of the ecclesiology of the two churches in Mizoram helps us to identify its inadequacy for Mizo Christians today. As the churches in Mizoram were founded by the Western Missionaries, the dominant theology in Mizoram is basically the theology of Evangelical Awakenings in the 19th century inherited from the Missionaries as Vanlalauva, in his comment on Evangelical movement in Mizoram, notes, "in Mizo Christianity, the *pianthar* (born again) spirituality is predominantly western. It is something like a carbon copy of the western evangelical spirituality, campaign, crusade and camping which are the means by which *pianthar* spirituality is imparted."[163] Hence, it is not wrong to say that from the very inception of the church in Mizoram until today, the western missionary theology has played a vital role in shaping Mizo Christian theology.

Therefore, it is no wonder that replication has taken place to such an extent that Mizo tribal churches exist like branches of their respective counterparts in the West with attitudes cherished and norms and goals set by their western patrons. We can identify at least three major characteristics as the results of the impact of Western Missionary ecclesiology, which are institutionalism, individualism and division in multiple sects.

1. Institutionalism

The Mizo Churches, as stated, inherited the organizational structures with a slight modification from the Western churches. The church is understood as a power structure, and as institutional existence, therefore, it is often resistant to change. In fact these churches have limited the scope of mission to that of service and charity and institutionalized their mission activities, as if mission is only one of the many things that the church needs to be concerned about. It is true that the church as human entity cannot avoid the inevitable institutionalized existence because of its functions and roles, and because of its response to the stimuli of the environment. But traditions that give identity to institutions are given priority, leaving no space for the fulfillment of the purpose and functions of the church.

---

163 H. Vanlalauva, "Relation between Calvin's Ecclesiology and Ecclesiology of the Presbyterian Church in Mizoram" (M. Th Thesis, UTC, Bangalore, 1986), 115.

2. Individualism

Individualism is a distinct feature of the Western civilization that emphasizes the centrality of human and the assertion of individual freedom as well as individual salvation. In this philosophical ethos, the communitarian dimension of Christian faith, of which the church is a visible sign, has gone through mutations to mean narrow views of community, Christian unity, sin, salvation and the purpose of the church. Tracing the history of the attempts of ecclesiological rediscovery from Peter Waldo of France and Girolamo Savanarda of Italy in the 12th century to Luther and others, through the work of John Wycliff and John Hus, Han Schwarz holds that while opening up bright prospects for the church's rediscovery of centre and periphery, the reformation had heralded the dangers of antagonistic entrenchment and of individualism and secularism. Schwarz further comments that in the name of restoration, the left wing reformation reduced the contours of the church with their narrow definitions of Christian vocation.[164] Thus individualism pushed religion to private realm. So much so, Christian life and discipleship have come to mean indifferent social behaviour and pursuit of self-fulfillment. The reality of poverty, the oppression and marginalization of the weak and the powerless, the increasing fragmentation of the society are seen as outside the sphere of the notion of Christian vocation.

3. Multiple denominations: With regard to possible reason for the increase of the number of denominations as Paul Avis once comments

They rejected corpus *christianum* and embraced corpus Christ. They replaced state-sponsored supported church with tightly knit groups with internal disciplinary sanctions and specific procedures for

164 Hans Schwarz, *The Christian Church: Biblical Origin, Historical Transformation and the Potential for Future* (Minneapolis: Augsburg Publishing House, 1982), 215-219.

admission and compulsion of members. They believed they were the church, the true church and were driven by a spiritual pride.[165]

Each denomination with specific historical and liturgical heritage and theological accent displays this denominational pride. Self-righteousness to certain degrees and operates and functions primarily to perpetuate its continuance and hegemony over the other. The importance of being a church is often asserted through members and institutional might.[166] As stated earlier, historical rivalries that were prevalent in Europe and America were transferred to tribal societies more so in Mizo society. The joy of the great community, of believers has been lost in the bickering, rivalries, and misunderstandings of divided sects.

Our evaluation of the ecclesiology of the churches in Mizoram reveals that the ecclesiology adopted by the churches in Mizoram is inadequate to satisfy peoples' quest for truth and liberation and it also fails to address the contemporary challenges posed by today's global context. The problems with the existing ecclesiology according to our investigation arise due to two major factors: first, its uncritical adoption and application of Western missionary ecclesiology, which hinders the real incarnation of the church in the local culture. Secondly, the wrong attitude towards the local cultural traditions that forbids to incorporate the cultural values into their ecclesiology. Therefore, the ecclesiology of the churches of Mizoram today becomes neither faithful to the Apostolic faith nor to local traditional values, the church stands in-between the Biblical Tradition and Local Traditions.

---

165 Paul D. L. Avis, *The Church in the Theology of the Reformers* (Atlanta: John Knox Press, CLS, 1983), 45 &55.

166 Mathai Zachariah, *Inside the Indian Church* (Delhi: ISPCK, 1994), 105.

Chapter 4

A Critical Synthesis of the Ecclesiology in the Early Christian Traditions and Mizo Cultural Traditions

1. Introduction

In the first chapter we discussed the early Church ecclesiology as community- or communion-centered, and in Chapter Two we examined the tribal community, the Mizo as communitarian. In Chapter Three, we evaluated the existing ecclesiology of the Baptist Church of Mizoram and the Presbyterian Church of Mizoram in the light of the early Christian tradition and the Mizo cultural traditions and found that the existing ecclesiology of the two churches in Mizoram, due to the influence of the Western Missionary ecclesiology, is neither faithful to the early Christian traditions nor to Mizo cultures.

This chapter has two sections. The first section clarifies the nature and approach of the proposed method, a critical synthesis. The second section deals with avenues for synthesizing the ecclesiology in the early Christian traditions and Mizo cultural traditions. Hence, the immediate questions we have to deal with are: How is synthesis used in theological methodology? Is the method of synthesis biblically, theologically and contextually relevant? Why is critical synthesis? What will be the nature and approach of critical synthesis?

2. A Critical Synthesis: Method for Formulating Tribal Ecclesiology

2.1. Synthesis in Theological Method

There are several theological models advocated for constructing contextual theology. Stephen Bevans, in recent times, has shown five basic models for the contextualization of theology, namely, translation, anthropological, praxis, synthetic and transcendental models.[1] In a similar vein, tribal theologian Thanzauva in his book, *Theology of Community*, has classified six different models, namely, transplantation, fulfillment, translation, dialogical, synthetic and praxis models.[2] As the choice of a model is determined by the theological concern of the theologian and the context in and to which theology is addressed, the writer selects the synthetic model for doing tribal ecclesiology. The word "synthetic" is an adjective that means artificial, fake, man-made or manufactured. It derives from the transitive verb "synthesize" meaning to "combine into a complex whole; to make up by combining parts of elements." Used as a description of a theological approach, it has the sense of integration: the blending of theological ideas from different cultures into a coherent whole.[3]

In what follows, we sketch the method of the synthetic model propounded by Bevans and Thanzauva:

---

1 Bevans, *Models of Contextual Theology*, 30-110.

2 Thanzauva, *Theology of Community*, 63-83.

3 Emmanuel Adow Obeng, " Synthetic and Praxis Model in African Theology", in *Theological Method and Aspects of Worship in African Christianity, edited by* Mary N. Getui (Nairobi: J. N. K. Mugambi and Carroll Houle, 1998), 46.

(1) Stephen B. Bevans' Synthetic Model

The synthetic model is for Stephen B. Bevans a "middle-of-road model"[4] In his models of contextual theology, the synthetic model appears in midway between emphasis on cultural/social change and gospel tradition. For Bevans, the Bible came into existence gradually, through a collection of individual books, each of which was formed within the context of contemporary concerns interacting with contemporary culture, neighboring cultures, and ancient traditions. The synthetic model also relies on some passages of the Roman magisterium that try to walk a theological path between mere adaptations on the one hand and a broad culturalism[5] on the other.

The word, synthetic, functions in several other ways as a description of a particular model of theological method. Firstly, this way of doing contextual theology looks to a synthesis of different models. It tries to preserve the importance of the gospel message and the heritage of traditional doctrinal foundations, while at the same time acknowledging the vital role that culture has played and can play in theology, even to the setting of the theological agenda. In addition, the synthesis will include the importance of reflective and intelligent action for the development of a theology that does not ignore the complexities of social and cultural change. Secondly, the synthetic model reaches out to the resources of other cultures and other theological expressions for both the method and content of its own articulation of faith. In this way a synthesis develops between one's own cultural point of view and the points of view of others. Thirdly, and perhaps most profoundly, this model is synthetic in the Hegelian

4 Stephen B. Bevans, *Models of Contextual Theology* (Maryknoll, NY: Orbis Books, 2000), 81.

5 A. Shorter employed this term with precision. See A. Shorter, *Toward a Theology of Inculturation* (Maryknoll, NY: Orbis Books, 1988), 12.

sense of attempting not just to put things together in a kind of compromise, but of developing, in a creative dialectic, something that is acceptable to all standpoints. This is the model that theologians such as Aylward Shorter mean when they speak of the inculturation or interculturation of theology as "the ongoing dialogue between faith and culture or cultures," "the creative and dynamic relationship between the Christian message and a culture or cultures."[6]

(2) Thanzauva's Synthetic Model

The synthetic model is searching for a new theology resulting from the synthesis of the western Christian tradition and the recipient culture. This model holds the view that culture is good and valuable as God has always been working and revealing divine truth in the world, so that the divine presence and activities can be found in every culture in different ways. For practitioners of this model, revelation is something which can be discovered in the context itself, not brought from outside. The presence of God can be perceived in the cultural values, behavioural patterns and struggles of the people for justice and liberation. Hence, Christ is present in every human culture yet in a hidden and imperfect manner.

However, practitioners of this model insist that the truth in human culture is not adequate unless it interacts with the truth revealed in Jesus Christ. That is to say, "The hidden gospel in any culture is not adequate for faith until it is activated by the gospel of Christ." This model, therefore, maintains the need of interaction between Christ of the Judeo-Christian tradition and the local culture in order to formulate a meaningful understanding of Christology. Thus, this model presupposes a synthetic interaction, in which, however, Western cultural forms are necessary to the

6 Shorter, *Toward a Theology of Inculturation*, 12.

> interaction but are not necessarily normative. The source of theology in this model is the interaction of the Christian tradition that has been received via Western culture and with the recipient culture.[7]

This synthetic model is similar to what is also found in the teaching of Pope John Paul II in which he insists on a synthesis of faith and culture. For John Paul II, faith has to penetrate to the core of every culture and purify it, enrich it, and cause it to blossom like the boundless love of Christ.[8] Faith by its very nature possesses its own autonomy vis-à-vis cultures, but paradoxically faith and culture are intimately related and interdependent. Every culture endeavours to express meaningfully the transcendent dimension of earthly existence by the contemplation of every human and cosmic world. Since at the heart of every culture there is a longing for the transcendent, "a faith that does not have a culture, not fully lived."[9] It is intrinsic to faith to inculturate itself, and to synthesize "the human's entire existence around Christ, the wisdom of God. Christ's redeeming love unveils the intrinsic value of natural human limitations, overcomes those elements that are incompatible with the faith and Christian living, raising at the same their values to the mystery of salvation which comes from Christ."[10]

A similar model of synthesis can also be found in Hans Kung's "critical correlation,"[11] a critical correlation of "textuality" and

---

7 Thanzauva, *Theology of Community*, 74.

8 The Pontifical Council for Culture, "Toward a Pastoral Approach to Culture", *Origins* 29/5 (June 1999), 6. See also Monteiro, *Church and Culture*, 172-173. In 1982, Pope John Paul II founded the Pontifical Council for Culture to satisfy the pastoral concern of the Church for the human person and culture and to respond with discernment to the profound and diverse aspirations of the cultures of today.

9 The Pontifical Council for Culture, "Toward a Pastoral Approach to Culture", 67.

10 Quoted in Monteiro, *Church and Culture*, 173.

11 Hans Kung, *Theology of the Third Millennium: An Ecumenical Review* (New York, NY: 1988), 118, quoted by Werner G. Jeanrond, "Hans Kung", in *The*

"contextuality," which means faithfulness to the Gospel as well as the recipient's culture. According to Kung, the first source of Christian theology is the Bible and the second source is the wealth of human experience in the world. These two sources of theology need to be interpreted and they should be critically correlated. However, when biblical and human experiences contradict one another, in such a situation, Kung attributes ultimate normative significance to the Christian message, the Gospel, Jesus Christ himself.[12] Kung's ecclesiology of reform naturally includes the call for a fundamental revision of the role of women in the church. In order that the Catholic Church, whose power structure and ministry are completely dominated by men, might become a church of all human beings, women should be represented in all decision-making bodies and at all levels—the parish, diocesan, national and international.[13]

2.1.1. *Assumptions of Synthetic Model*

The main assumption of the synthetic model is that every culture has elements that can contribute to theological dialogue. These elements may be unique to that culture or may be held in common with other cultures. Both uniqueness and complementarities are emphasized in the synthetic model.

Culture is relevant to the synthetic model. This does not, however, mean that all aspects of culture are good. No culture should be uncritically accepted or rejected, and every culture should be judged from its proven contribution to the progress of society. There are aspects of culture that hinder the progress of societies. Many examples abound in tribal cultures, such as head hunting, tribalism, sacrifice offered to the evil spirit, discrimination of women. Such negative aspects of culture must be rejected since they invalidate the relevance of culture to the synthetic model.

Modern Theologians, edited by David F. Ford (Malden and Oxford: Blackwell Publishing, 1997), 171.

12 Jeanrond, "Hans Kung", 171.

13 Hans Kung, *Reforming Church Today: Keeping Hope Alive* (Edinburgh & New York: 1990), 103.

Another assumption is that God does not manifest Himself in a singular culture. He is manifested in Christian culture as well as in other cultures, but the manifestation may not be the same. The implication here is that all cultures have a concept of God. The concepts may be expressed differently, but on closer examination they show similar, if not the same concept.[14]

The strongest point of the synthetic model is its method of dialogue. It is absurd in our contemporary, postmodern world to believe that truth is the monopoly of a particular religious tradition or culture. Truth cannot be reached by one point of view trying to convince all others that it alone is correct. Such an imperialistic view of truth is not possible within the present world with its radical pluralism and multicultural consciousness. No culture has the ability of capturing truth in its totality within itself. The knowledge and appreciation of positive elements of different cultures enrich one's own. The synthetic model makes this possible. Since the synthetic model involves dialogue, its other strong point is that it is an ongoing process. Cultures are dynamic, and this dynamism is captured through the synthetic model, ensuring changes in theology as culture changes. Another positive aspect of the model is expressed by Robert Schreiter:

> Especially when wielded in the hands of local leaders, it can quickly help achieve the twin goals of some authenticity in the local culture and respectability in western church circles. The theology which emerges from such a model is replete with the categories, names and concerns of a local culture, yet looks like Western theology and is relatively easily understood by Westerners.[15]

---

14 Emmanuel Adow Obeng, "Synthetic and Praxis Model in African Theology", in *Theological Method and Aspects of worship in African Christianity,* edited by Mary N. Getui (Nairobi: J. N. K. Mugambi and Carroll Houle, 1998), 46.

15 R. Schreiter, *Constructing Local Theologies* (Maryknoll, New York: Orbis Books, 1985), 10.

The synthetic model is one way of doing contextual theology, which is essential to our understanding of God's self-revelation. The Incarnation is the ultimate paradigm of the translation of text into context. Jesus Christ, the Word of God in incarnate, as a Jew identified with a particular culture at a limited moment in history though transcending it. In His life and teaching, He was the supreme model of contextualization. The implication of this process is seen in the apostolic witness and the life of the New Testament church. The difference in theological emphasis and method of preaching between Paul's address to the synagogue in Pisidian Antioch (Acts 13:16–41) and his address to the Areopagus in Athens (Acts 7:22–31) is but one notable illustration of the sociological and theological inevitability of contextualization.[16]

2.1.2. *Synthesis of the Gospel and Cultures in the History of Christian Church*

All through the history of the church there has been interaction between Gospel and culture, Christianity and local cultures, with each influencing the other.[17] The first Jewish Christian communities were characterized by loyalty to the Mosaic Law, attachment to the Temple, and experience of election mediated through circumcision. George Soares-Prabu describes the social setting of the Palestinian church as one characterized by a "crisis of colonialism," due to five centuries of Persian, Greek and Roman domination. Christian communities emerging in Palestine had to respond to the economic, cultural and religious crises that affected the Judaic society.[18]

The pioneering step towards incarnating the Christian message and communities among non-Jews may be traced back to St. Paul's

16 Emmanuel Adow Obeng, " Synthetic and Praxis Model in African Theology", in *Theological Method and Aspects of Worship in African Christianity, edited by* Mary N. Getui (Nairobi: J.N.K. Mugambi and Carroll Houle, 1998), 41.

17 K. S. Latourette, *A History of the Expansion of Christianity*, Vol. I-VII (London: Eyre and Spottiswoode, 1938-1945).

18 George Soares-Prabu, "Radical Beginnings: The Jesus community as the Archetype of the Church", *Jeevadhara* 15 (1985), 310.

debate with the Jewish Christians, over the practice of circumcision as an initiation ritual.[19] The Jewish Christian experience of the incarnated Word was that they had to die to their own local limitations of various historical and cultural particularities and rise to a global acceptance beyond Palestinian boundaries.[20] Within a decade of the death of Jesus, the Christian movement had crossed the most rigid cultural separation—from the rural people of Palestine to the urban dwellers of the Greco-Roman cities.[21] In what follows we shall briefly highlight the outcome (synthesis) of the interaction between the Gospel and the local cultures in the history of Christianity.

2.1.2.1. Ancient Era

Dialogue with Judaic-Hellenistic Christian culture and with pagan cultures of Greece and Rome included elements of interaction between the Gospel and culture. Concrete examples of this are the incarnation of the Gospel and faith response of the Gentile converts, linguistic adaptation and integration of the Hellenist and Roman cultures, and emergence of local Christian communities within the pagan milieu of the Mediterranean world.

Later on the incarnation of Christian faith and worship assumed forms of functional substitution.[22] Tertullian used Roman juridical language to explain the rite of baptism as the breaking of a contract with world. St. Ambrose of Milan borrowed the symbolic ritual of anointing from the athletic customs Roman culture.[23] During the golden age of Constantine symbols of the imperial court and of the contemporary political culture were incorporated into the liturgy

19 Acts 15:1-30; 17: 22-28; Gal. 2:1-4.

20 P. Puthanangady, "Theology of Inculturation", *Word and Worship* 20 (1987), 309.

21 W. A. Meeks, *The First Urban Christians, The Social World of the Apostle Paul* (London: Yale University Press, 1983), 11.

22 Gerald Arbuckle, "Inculturation Not Adaptation: Time to Change Terminology," *Worship* 60 (1986), 512.

23 Desmond Crowe, "Inculturation: Challenge to the Local Church," *East Asian Pastoral Review* 3 (1981), 264.

and ecclesiastical structures. Bishop adopted the power symbols of royalty, and priests assumed authoritative roles over the people.[24]

In the second and third centuries, attempts were made to adapt the Christian message to milieus of pagan cultures and religions. To counter pagan gnosis or systematic knowledge, Origen and Tertullian propagated Christological forms—the 'Christ of culture' as a means of incarnating the Gospel. Origen saw Christ as the triumph of culture, while Tertullian advocated the Christ against culture.[25] Clement of Alexandria recognized the contribution of Christian doctrine to pagan tradition and of Greek philosophy to the development of true religion.[26] Most Fathers of the Church were uncomfortable with matters dealing with other religions and philosophies of the time, like the ones represented by the apologists. The Greek Fathers, however, did speak of the values of other religions and cultures and of finding the seeds of God's word.'[27]

By the 5th century, Christianity, which began as an obscure Jewish sect, became chiefly identified with the Mediterranean culture. Before Constantine, the local churches had remained groups of communities having minimum interaction with the surrounding world. With Christianity becoming the official religion of the Empire, multitudes flocked to the Church, bringing with them communities that were largely shaped by the elements in which early Christianity grew and spread: Judaism, philosophic and literary traditions, Hellenistic culture and the mystery cults, popular festivals, the political structure of the Roman Empire, geographical and racial settings—all left their indelible marks on the Church and Christian faith.[28]

Since 431 A.D., the time of the Council of Ephesus, many local churches had developed their own distinctive cultural forms, which

24 Arbuckle, "Inculturation Not Adaptation", 512.

25 P. Schineller, *A Handbook on Inculturation* (New York, NY: Paulist Press, 1990), 51-52.

26 A. Shorter, *Towards a Theology of Inculturation* (London: Geoffrey Chapman, 1988), 138.

27 Monteiro, *Church and Culture*, 54.

28 Latourette, *A History of the Expansion of Christianity*, Vol. I-VII, 361-368.

was particularly evident with the rise of the Eastern churches.[29] During the fifth century, there was a shift from Greek to Latin culture, with the Roman church and Papacy endorsing the Latin language and culture in the Roman Empire, thus closing the doors to ecclesial pluriformity. In contrast to the church's growing non-culturalism, especially noteworthy are the exemplary efforts of Saints Cyril and Methodius in the ninth century, who labored for the Slavonic Church with the celebration of the liturgy, creation of civil and church law codes and translation of the Bible in the Slavonic language.[30]

2.1.2.2. Medieval Age

Incarnating the Christian message in pagan and other religious contexts also involves incorporating emerging philosophical and theological systems with specific cultural-religious traditions. Thomas Aquinas developed a whole system of philosophy based on the Greek philosopher Aristotle. The benefits that pagan philosophy could offer to Christianity, as well as the positive values of other cultures, became better recognized. St. Augustine founded his Christian thought on Plato's philosophy.[31] In the study of scriptures during the Middle Ages, scholastic theologians interpreted the Babel story to imply that ethnic pluralism was largely the result of human sinfulness and estrangement from God. This view, which condemned pluralism, influenced Christian thought over centuries.[32]

Until the fifteenth century there can be observed some openness and flexibility to other cultural, political and religious systems while incarnating the Gospel message among churches. A key principle underlying the interaction between the Gospel and cultures during this period was the assumption that whatever was good should be assimilated and evil rejected. This interaction was primarily restricted

29 Monteiro, *Church and Culture*, 54.

30 Shorter, *Towards a Theology of Inculturation,* 140-144.

31 F. X. Clark, "Inculturation: Introduction and History", Teaching all Nations 4 (1978), 215.

32 B. Anderson, "The Babel Story: Paradigm of Human Unity and Diversity", *Concillium* 1 (1977), 63.

to liturgy, as in the rites of baptism and marriage for which a pagan rite or cultural symbol might be given a new religious meaning. Existing religio-cultural surroundings influenced the philosophical and theological systems of the times and in turn shaped the local churches. In the process of Christianizing cultures, the Christian message penetrated local cultures, although not to the extent of making Christianity the dominant element of people's life or of challenging systems that lacked full compatibility with the Gospel. A compromising approach by the church within certain secular contexts, resulting in an uncritical identification with unjust political regimes, could undoubtedly have adverse consequences for the acceptability of the Gospel.

2.1.2.3. Missionary Period

Beginning in the sixteenth century, the mission of proclaiming the Good News entered a new phase. As governments expanded, the Gospel encountered the major cultures of the world. However, the association of Catholic faith with European culture, transplantation of feudal ecclesial structures in the new world, and the fear of pagan beliefs and practices affecting the purity of Christian faith proved great stumbling blocks for successfully communicating the truth of the Christian message.

Planting of the European church in mission lands without any appropriate adaptation to the culture of the area hindered the Christian faith in its encountering and dialoguing with cultures, and other cosmic and meta-cosmic religions. Dialogue could not take place because the church came to give and to teach, not to receive and to learn. Consequently the church became a ghetto, excluding the creativity of local cultures.

In the sixteenth and seventeenth centuries, efforts to inculturate the Gospel were made by Robert de Nobili and Constantine Beschi in India, Thomas Stephens in Portuguese Goa, Matteo Ricci in China, Pedro Paez in Ethiopia. Their innovative attempts at initiating a cultural exchange between the East and West are an inspiration for many. Ricci effected a real mediation by making himself Chinese among the Chinese and creating conditions to make Christ known and incarnate the Church and the Gospel message in the context of Chinese culture.[33] Nobili undertook the formidable task of accommodating Christianity to the caste redden society of India. He himself adopted the rigid code of *sannyasi* to better interact with the Brahmins.[34]

2.1.2.4. Modern Times

Until the late nineteenth century, the tendency among Christians was to address one culture and one civilization, since multiplicity was feared as the disastrous result of human arrogance, as symbolized by the Tower of Babel.

Pius XII affirmed that the Catholic Church should neither belong exclusively to any particular people nor more to one than to another. He also asserted that faith must be adapted to local customs: "Let not the Gospel on being introduced into any new land destroy or extinguish whatever its people possess that is naturally good, just and beautiful."[35]

In the early twentieth century, adaptation, accommodation and indigenization became the rationale for establishing native churches in mission soil, although efforts in this direction were restricted to recruitment of local clergy. The local church was not yet native, in the sense that it remained to a large extent unconcerned with aspirations and needs of the people already living in the region, and the decision makers were foreigners. Due to several weaknesses in missiological approach and the absence of an alternative theology of the local church, the Western, monolithic image of the church remained unchallenged. Even during decolonization and the rise of nationalism the church was, as ever, alienated from its local context.

---

33 H. Carrier, *Gospel Message and Human Cultures: From Leo XIII to John Paul II* (Pensyvania: Duquesne University Press, 1989), 116.

34 Robin Boyd, *An Introduction to Indian Christian Theology*, Reprint (Delhi: ISPCK, 1994), 11-13.

35 Monteiro, *Church and Culture*, 57.

In the present era when the communication revolution, globalization and post-modernism profoundly influence cultural realities, human relationships and values, religious belief and even faith in God are being redefined. With intense urbanization creating cultural shocks, war and environmental degradation causing mass displacement of people, a new cultural synthesis emerges, and the church cannot ignore these challenges. The prophetic statement of Pope John XXIII, in 1959, that the church does not identify itself with any one particular culture to the exclusion of the rest[36] prepared the way for the Catholic church to open its doors to cultures outside the West.

The fundamental theological justification for the synthetic method is the historic nature of the mystery of God's revelation: God's communicates himself in particular historic-cultural contexts. God's self-communication is history. It is also the primary setting for reincarnating the Good News and Christ, the perfect revelation of the mystery of God.[37] In becoming human, God subjects himself to the most concrete conditions of human history: "The God who has become man in Jesus of Nazareth is not only the Word made flesh in the individuality of a human body, but also the Word made flesh in the particularity and complexity of an economic, social, cultural, and religious world."[38] The historical incarnation of God in Christ Jesus is the reason and justification for synthesis.

To sum up, theological justification for synthesis of the gospel and local culture adheres to the pattern of the Christ event in the economy of salvation: incarnation of the Word in history, *kenosis* of Jesus in his ministry and death, and the glorification of Christ in his resurrection. Likewise, the Christian experience is rooted in the culture of the people where it finds expression in local symbols and elements. In synergistic process culture becomes a force that transforms and animates a local church towards the goal of creating new communion with other cultures and churches.

36 Monteiro, *Church and Culture*, 58.

37 Schniller, *Handbook on Inculturation*, 46

38 Monteiro, *Church and Culture*, 66.

2.1.2.5. A Synthesis of the Western Christian Traditions and Mizo Culture in the Past

Whenever the gospel encounters local cultures, a certain degree of synthesis takes place. Even in Mizoram we have seen a certain form of synthesis that took place when the Western Christian traditions encountered the Mizo cultural traditions. However, it is evident that the synthesis of the Western Christian traditions and Mizo cultural traditions in the past was not satisfactory for two reasons: (1) due to uncritical acceptance of the Western traditions and (2) due to uncritical rejection or acceptance of Mizo cultural traditions. Therefore, it is appropriate in what follows to critically look at the nature and outcome of the interaction between the Western Christian traditions and Mizo cultures in the past based on the data supplied by Thanzauva.[39]

Western Christianity	**Mizo culture**	**Synthesis or Outcome of Interaction**
Ethical teaching	Taboos (*serh leh sang/hrilh*)	Emergence in the form of strict of pietism rules of Sunday observation, respect for the Bible.
Church	*Zawlbuk* (Bachelor's dormitory)	Transformed into church buildings, and educational hostels.
Universal Christian Fellowship	Communitaria-nism within the village	Transformed into Christian community or wider tribal Christian fellowship

39 Thanzauva, "A Theological Basis for Social Transformation: Methodological Implications of Third World Liberation Theology in the Context of Mizoram, North East India", a D.Th Dissertation, Whitley College, Melbourne, 1993, 235.

Christian love and commitment	Social ethics and life philosophy (*tlawmngaihna*)	Adopted into Christianity in the form of self sacrifice, giving and sharing.
Rejection of slavery	Practice of slavery	Slavery disappeared
Patriarchal society	Patriarchal system	Affirmed with certain modifications, atrocities and discrimination against women diminished.
Christian marriage	Mizo marriage ceremony	Transformed into a new pattern, retaining most of the traditional practices except drinking rice beer, and introduced ceremony in the church.
Western Christian hymns and tunes	Traditional songs and tunes	Transformed into a new synthetic tune known as *Lengkhawm zai.*
Christmas	Mizo Kut (Festivals)	Transformed into prolonged community celebration of Christmas; sometimes community feasting and singing together for several days and nights.
Western dance and drums	Mizo traditional dance and drum	Resurgent in the revival movementand a drum which was once rejected was reintroduced in all the churches.
Drinking tea	Drinking rice beer	Christians mostly gave up liquor but today increasingly some Christians particularly young people, are practicing it again.

Based on the above table, Thanzauva came to a conclusion that the outcome of the interaction includes components of rejection, adaptation and transformation. He argued that some dehumanizing traditions and practices of the Mizo were rejected completely, and some of the liberative elements were adapted and some were transformed. For him, in the process of interaction, the new Mizo Christian identity has emerged. In spite of having this view, he did not fail to recognize the lost of even liberative elements of the Mizo culture in the process of interaction. Therefore, he gives emphasis to the need of rediscovery of liberative elements from the tribal cultures.

Thanzauva's view seems to be in line with the general assumption that the tribal cultures in North East India were not completely submerged in the culture of their Western missionaries.

As far as the synthesis of the Western Christianity and Mizo culture is concerned, it is agreeable with Thanzauva that synthesis or inculturation in its simplest form took place in Mizo Christianity. At the same time, it is quite evident that Mizo cultural elements or traditions were not given equal importance or treatment with the missionaries' cultures. We see in the above table that when the church in Western culture encounters with *Zawlbuk* in Mizo cultural tradition, the nature and functions of *Zawlbuk* were totally eclipsed. The structure or shape of the Mizo church building and also the functions of the church we have today are more or less the same as its the western counterpart. It is hard to see how the legacy of the institution of *Zawlbuk* in the life and ministry of the Church has been maintained except in the issue of women. K. L. Khama has rightly mentioned that the only element that has been adopted by the church from the *Zawlbuk* is women's subordination.[40] On the issue of women's participation in the church, the Western patriarchal culture via the Western missionaries reinforced uncritically and accepted Mizo patriarchal culture; therefore, there are no ordained

40 K. L. Khama Chhakchhuak, *Zofate Nunphung danglam zel leh an hun tawn* (Churachandpur: Kawlkhuma, 1993), 56.

Mizo women in the church even after one hundred years of Mizo Christianity.

Hence, we may say that what was adopted from Mizo cultures were only those elements which were benevolent or acceptable to the Western missionaries or similar values with theirs. As this is the case, the makers of the Mizo Church were not the Mizo people; the makers of Mizo Church were the missionaries and pro missionaries. In other words, the Mizo Church is the result of the synthesis of Western ecclesiology and those Mizo cultural elements that are acceptable to Western cultures. Consequently, Mizo Christian ecclesiology is neither faithful to the early Christian traditions nor to the Mizo cultures. This is the reason why we need to search for a viable methodology that will be equally critical with both the Western Christian traditions and Mizo cultural traditions. Therefore, the author proposes a critical synthesis for a new synthesis of the early Christian traditions and Mizo cultural traditions in order to have a harmonious blend of the gospel and the recipient's culture.

2.2. Method of Critical Synthesis

We have just discussed the meaning of synthesis at length and how it has been applied in theological formulations. However, when we speak of critical synthesis, we must also be clear about what we mean by critical.

2.2.1. *Critical*

By critical here we do not mean carping or cutting down. We do not mean belittling or demeaning. We do not mean a spirit of fault finding. Rather, we mean "the effort to see a thing clearly and truly in order to judge it fairly."[41]

A critical synthesis requires engaging the past tradition critically. Only as we grow conscious of the human tradition that has nurtured our faith and shaped the way we read the Bible can we assess that tradition, critique it, renew it, and when necessary move beyond it. Seen in this light, critical engagement with our past

41 "Critical" from Webster's Oxford English Dictionary.

becomes a fundamental part of our faithfulness to it. It also becomes a fundamental task in maintaining our identity as a restoration movement.

When we engage the past critically we do not seek quick and easy condemnation of the past, nor do we seek quick and easy vindication of it. We do not seek to marshal supporting evidence for our own theological position. We are critical in that we seek, as best we can, to understand the past on its own terms, not ours. We approach it with sympathy and imagination and do not shrink from questioning cherished interpretations.

When we engage the past critically we seek first and foremost to understand the past, all the while knowing that we, too, cannot escape fully our own limited perspectives. Even though we see in the past all sorts of intellectual shortcomings and moral failures, we attempt to treat the people of the past with all the respect we can muster, for we sense that we, too, are made of much the same stuff.

Why do we need to critically engage with the past? Critical engagement with the past makes us self-conscious about our dependence upon traditions from the past. The first challenge here, as we have seen, is simply recognizing that we do indeed stand in a human tradition, for our historylessness has blinded us to that fact. Our forbearers often denied any complicity in human traditions, claiming to be only a people of the Book. They wanted nothing to do with mere traditions. They wanted only the Truth. It was a yearning that, for most of us, lies near the heart of the spiritual quest.

But the sweeping claim to have escaped the taint of all human tradition does not result in a tradition-less or culture-free faith. It results only in a faith even more vulnerable to unconscious traditionalism. So first we must simply recognize that we are part of a human tradition. And that is a big step. But once we take that step, we immediately face another crucial step: we must critique our tradition. We must do so simply because it is in part a human tradition, and human traditions—or so many of our forbearers believed—are always tainted. If we are unable to criticize our traditions, we will simply remain captive to them. We will harbor illusions or pretensions, and thus tend to absolutize our own limited tradition.

Critical engagement with the past also forces us to deal with other traditions in a new way. As we have seen, a critical attitude toward the past means that we take Christian traditions other than our own with great seriousness. We do not treat them condescendingly or sneer at them or say to ourselves, "How could people be so blind! How could they be so stubborn or stupid!" Rather, we grant them what we ourselves wish to be granted: sincerity and zeal, honesty and intelligence. With sympathy and imagination, we witness their struggles to take Scripture seriously and to follow God faithfully. We attempt to hear their questions, not simply to make them answer ours.

2.2.2. *Reason for the Choice of Critical Synthesis*

The desire of tribal theologians to construct a tribal theology in tribal terms is valid and necessary. But in such endeavor some seem to assume the existence of a pure Christian message uncontaminated by Western theological and cultural garb. Some theologians believe that the basic message of Jesus as developed in the church got mixed up with Western culture, which they argue is good for the West but is irrelevant and ineffective in a non-Western context. Considering the development of Christianity in this way is to assume that there exists a timeless essence of Christianity that can be separated from its theological expressions.[42] But such a presupposition is unrealistic because there is no pure biblical message independent of and uninfluenced by cultural coating and expressions. Every message is expressed in some cultural and linguistic terms. Therefore, a wholesale rejection or acceptance of all theological developments in the West may be unwarranted and is not helpful in the development of a tribal theology. Another presupposition is that the best way for the indigenization of Christianity in tribal context is to articulate

42 R. Ruether, "Feminism and Jewish-Christian Dialogue" in *The Myth of Christian Uniqueness..*, 139 and translated into Asian expressions by R. S. Sugirtharajah, *Frontiers in Asian Christian Theology: Emerging Trends* (New York, NY: Orbis books, 1994, 4-5.

the message and the meaning of Jesus Christ through the cultural traditions of the tribal people.

Then the questions are: are we not falling into another contingent expression? Can tribal cultural religious concepts adequately express the same nuances of Christian concepts? For example, can *Zawlbuk* express the meaning of the Church and *Tlawmngaihna* the meaning of the love of God? Therefore, a give and take attitude is indispensable for the growth of a balanced theology and ecclesiology in Mizoram, accepting both the historical development of theology in the tradition of the Church and leaving space for new attempts at reformulating the contents of Christian faith suited to the cultural and religious situation of tribal culture in Mizoram.

The church as we find it in the New Testament is a community of believers in Jesus Christ who proclaimed their faith, celebrated it in signs and symbols and lived the same in their cultural milieu in communion with one another. Every genuine encounter between the Gospel and a new culture enriches the culture and give new expressions to the Gospel, which in turn provide new self-understanding of the Church. Faith in Jesus Christ in a tribal context must find expression in tribal cultural and linguistic terms and it must be seen in the life, practices and celebrations of the people.

The church's self-understanding grows as it lives its life in history. Therefore, there is a wide scope for the growth and development of a tribal understanding of the Church. The Gospel must become an intelligible and effective sign of God's salvation and a leaven for transformation of every society, including the tribal society, according to the designs of God in Jesus Christ. Only a tribal ecclesiology can render the church an intelligible and effective sign of salvation and communion in Mizoram to the tribal culture. Only a tribal ecclesiology can lead the tribal Church to dialogue and identify itself with tribal cultures through inculturation and liberation of the poor.

3. Approach to Synthesis of Early Christian Traditions and Mizo Cultural Traditions

We now turn to the synthetic task of applying the results of our investigations and of formulating a relevant ecclesiology for tribal culture based on the insights gained from our discussion of the Church in early Christian traditions and Mizo cultural traditions. In our approach to synthesize the two traditions, we will follow two ways: First, we will identify the new insights from both traditions that will help us to correct or reconstruct and enrich Mizo Christian understanding of the Church. Secondly, we will interpret the nature and function of the Church with the help of tribal cultural symbols and thought forms as we intend to formulate Mizo tribal ecclesiology. What follows are the new insights that we gain from both traditions.

3.1. New Insights from the Ecclesiology of the Early Christian Traditions and Mizo Cultural Traditions

We have discussed at length about the origin, nature and functions of the Church in early Christian traditions starting from the very inception of Christianity until the fourth century in chapter one, and we have also thoroughly analyzed Mizo cultural traditions in chapter two. Therefore, our task now is to identify new insights that we gain from these two traditions for formulating tribal ecclesiology.

3.1.1. *New Insights from the Ecclesiology of the Early Christian Traditions*

From our investigation of the ecclesiology of the Church in the first four centuries, the new insights and resourceful findings for tribal ecclesiology may be summed up as follows: (1) The Church as the community of believers in Christ; (2) The Church as local Christian community; (3) The Church as mother; (4) The Church as the community of service, loving and caring community; (5) The Church as incarnating and suffering community; (6) The Church as prophetic and liberating people movement; (7) The Church as non-hierarchical, non discriminatory.

3.1.1.1. The Church as the Community of Believers in Christ

The early Church was a pre-institutional religious movement. Its small communities lacked the worldwide organization, uniform pattern of internal authority, socio-political influence, or even a national or ethnic identity. It was genuinely a minority movement. The primary characteristic of this church was that it was made up of group of people in a place who received the Gospel of Christ.[43] It was also a missionary movement. Church and mission were synonymous. The community lived through mission and for mission. Every believer lived in obedience to Christ so that others, seeing their exemplary lives, would want to follow Christ also. It was a mission measured by being rather than doing. The whole church was missionary.[44]

3.1.1.2. The Church as Communion of Local Christian Congregations

The church during the period of antiquity existed as a number of local congregations, scattered over the Mediterranean region. The Church's life was synonymous with the local Christian community. Judaism and the Church of Jerusalem, and later the Grecco-Roman civilization, greatly influenced the form of life of the early Christian communities. The Church was founded in different lands with varied religious and social backgrounds. The spreading of the Gospel to the various cultural centers demanded an adaptation to the local culture in the presentation of the message and the organization of the community. However, Christians, irrespective of their race and color, were united in their faith in Jesus Christ, the Lord and Son of God. Unity and plurality were evident during the foundational period of the Church. Their faith in Jesus was based on the witness of the Apostles. Charles Gore has rightly mentioned that the unity of

43 See Chapter I, page, 57.

44 See Chapter I, page, 57.

the church, as it is seen in the New Testament and in the subsequent history of the church, was guarded especially by three bonds: "first by the authority of the common faith or word of God, secondly by the need to seek the gifts of God in the sacraments of the society; thirdly, by the obligation of adherents to the Apostolic ministry."[45]

3.1.1.3. The Church as Mother

Cyprian and Augustine used the metaphor of the Church as the mother[46] who gives birth and nurtures Christians and provides a safe home for her children. Augustine said, "You are safe who have God for your Father and His Church for your mother."[47] For Augustine, the Church gives birth through baptism and it is the Church who gives birth to all, either within her pale or beyond it. Augustine also acknowledges that many of the children whom this mother brings forth prove to be sinners. Repentance is always possible and reconciliation always offered. But there is no second baptism; sinners are purged by faithful discipline and truthful confession. They must return to their mother.

3.1.1.4. The Church as a Community of Service, Loving and Caring

The Church in antiquity was a community of service. In other words, the Church was a loving and caring community. During its first three hundred years the Church suffered persecutions beyond description and was neither wealthy nor powerful. Yet the most striking image of the Church in its own community was that it loved and cared for the unfortunate both inside and outside the church, which was beyond its neighbors' expectation. The Church's "organization of alms" was so impressive to the Emperor Julian that he imitated Christians by establishing "numerous hostels in each city so that strangers may

---

45 Charles Gore, *The Holy Spirit and the Church* (London: John Murray, 1924), 136.

46 See Chapter I, page, 73 & 83.

47 See Chapter I, page, 83.

enjoy our benevolence, not only our own people but also others who may need money."[48] The Christian community may have inherited the traditions of alms giving from the Jews. Moreover, the united acts of charity during the Palestinian famine in the middle of the first century were impressive. In the late first century and early second century, alms giving was regarded as equal to repentance from sin as and better than fasting and prayer.[49] In the church the rich and the poor lived together interdependently as one body. The rich supplied the poor with material needs and the poor prayed for the rich. In the Shepherd of Hermas, we read:

> When the rich man rests upon the poor and gives him what he needs, he believes that what he does for the poor man can find a reward with God, for the poor is rich in intercession and confession, and his intercession has great power with God.[50]

In the second and third centuries, Christian charity was rather highly organized and the president or bishop of the church played the role of protector of guardian of the entire community of the poor. In short, one could say that the early Church was the Church for the poor and unfortunate.

3.1.1.5. The Church as the House Church

From the structural institutional point of view, the early Church was "the house church."[51] The believers of Jesus Christ regularly had a house meeting for fellowship, reading Scripture, prayer and the Lord's Supper. The house church pattern allowed more freedom for the Church to fulfill its mission in a particular given situation. It could move easily in accordance with the circumstances. More

---

48 R. M. Grant, *Early Christianity and Society* (New York: Harper and Son, Publishers, 1977), 144.

49 Grant, *Early Christianity and Society*, 128.

50 Ibid., 130.

51 J. Foster, *The First Advance* (London: SPCK, 1972), 20.

importantly, the house church implies the truth that the Church is the place for life. It implies further that Christian faith or religion is for the whole life of human beings and as necessary as a house, as simple as a house, and as intimate a place for human relationship as a house.

The house church faded away quickly during and after the Constantinian period. The Church, having gained favour from the government, gradually became institutionalized. To be Christian was not always "to be ready for Christ at any cost" as before, but rather "to be privileged in the church and government." The Church became a powerful institution and rigidity prevailed. To be in the Church one had to conform to the institutionalized Church.

3.1.1.6. The Church as Incarnating and Suffering Community

The founder of the Church is the incarnated Lord Jesus. Jesus of Nazareth, son of a humble carpenter, who took human form and lived with the outcasts and died a cruel death on the cross in the midst of human beings whom He was to redeem. The early Christian community realized this truth and made a great attempt to live accordingly. The early Christians were accused of awakening the women, children and slaves to a new consciousness of their condition. This fact implies that the early Christians showed concern for people of low social status. They suffered with the people. But on the other hand, they were accused also of being separated from the whole community. This vivifies the fact that the early Church did not regard itself as a part of the whole community but rather as a distinct community. From the political, social, and religious point of view the early church was rather aloof from society. But in the philosophical arena, several church leaders made serious attempts to see Greek philosophical teachings as a bridge between the Hellenistic world and the Hebraic world. For instance, the philosophic theologian Origen attempted to plant Hebraic Gospel seeds in Hellenistic philosophical soil. Accordingly, one can say the Church did incarnate itself into the world of ideas. The early Church in the hands of the converted Greek philosophical Logos had now become visible in the man called Jesus Christ of Nazareth. The Church did not minimize the significance of the local heritage where the Gospel was brought in, but rather enlivened it. In this sense, the Church was enabled to see God's involvement in all human cultures and histories. In the process of the so-called Hellenization of Christianity, we can see the incarnating reality. The theological formation of the first five centuries was in fact an incarnating process of the Gospel to the mind of the Greco-Romans.

On the other side, the Church is a suffering servant. The Lord Jesus incarnated Himself in human history not by being the master of those in that history, but rather the servant or even more precisely the suffering servant. He came not to be served but to serve until His death on the cross. The incarnated church, therefore, is none other than a servant or suffering servant in society.

The story of persecution tells us that the church of the first four hundred years was a persecuted church of the suffering servant. The story of monasticism is not merely the story of aloofness of the church from a society but rather the story of the servant church. The monks were called to live and work together not for themselves but for others. Basil the Great is an explicit example of monks united for service, "Basil linked the monk's life with service of the needy. Basil tells us that after he became bishop of Caesarea he provided a series of great buildings just outside the city for the work done by monks. There was a guesthouse for travelers, a hospital with doctors, nurses, and attendants... There were so many of these buildings that people called them 'the New City.'"[52]

3.1.1.7. The Church as Non-Structured, Non-Discriminatory to Superstructure

During the first four centuries we saw the process of the development of the ecclesial structure from a non-structured, simple community of believers to a well-established hierarchical Church.

The New Testament speaks of various ministries as functions in the church for the common good and for the building up of the

52 Foster, *The First Advance*, 51-52.

community. Inferior and superior, higher and lower, are concepts alien to the perspective of the New Testament, which views ministries in their relation to community and in their diversity. In the church each one has his function; not everyone can do everything (1Cor. 12: 27–30).

However, beginning in the third century, the emphasis was placed on the visible and organizational set up of the church and the importance of the priestly dimension, which contributed to the transformation of the ministerial structure into a predominantly hierarchical structure with higher and lower positions as on a ladder.

The conversion of the Emperor Constantine in the fourth century brought profound changes in ecclesiastical life. As K. M. George opines, "the situation in which the pagan culture was the dominant power in the face of which the Christian Church as a minority community had to defend itself was reversed."[53] The emperor Constantine considered himself "bishop of external affairs of the Church."[54] To be able to cope with the state on a more equal footing, the church had to develop an organizational structure beyond the local level. Modeled on the administrative structure of the Roman Empire, the Romanist conception of authority gave most prominence to centralization.[55]

The poor believers of Jesus Christ were moving to a body that reflected the imperial glory. Christianity, which had previously been an exclusive faith, maintaining a strict separation between the Church and the world (state), began to integrate into society, structurally and to a great extent ideologically, being open to the contemporary philosophies.

---

53 K. M. George, *The Early Church, Defending the Faith, Witness and Proclamation: Patristic Perspectives* (Geneva: WCC Publication, 1996), 26.

54 John E. Lynch, "Power in the Church: an Historico-critical survey" *Concilium* 197 (April 1988): 14.

55 Charles Gore, *The Holy Spirit and the Church* (London: John Murray, 1924), 201.

3.1.1.8. Evaluation of the Findings from the Ecclesiology of the Early Christian Tradition

The above findings of our investigation reveal to us that the Church in its antiquity was composed of the believers of Jesus Christ who had never thought of the church becoming the imperial church with superstructure. However, as Christianity spread to the Greco-Roman world and grew in size, it was shaped and reshaped by different cultural environments. The self-understanding of the Church varied from one culture to another since it is expressed through the worldview and thought of the recipients' cultures. Therefore, no cultural expression of the church can claim superiority or universality over others. However, in all these early ecclesiologies, we also have seen the common ground or basis wherein every local expression of the church attempted to be faithful to Christ and the Apostolic tradition. Hence, the findings may encourage all Christian communities to have their own expressions of the nature and functions of the Church that are also faithful to Christ and the Apostolic traditions.

3.2.2. *New Insights Drawn from Mizo Cultural Traditions*

3.2.2.1. Communitarian Understanding of God

It is interesting to note that the Mizo understanding of God or gods can be explained as communitarian, in the sense that there is no hierarchy in their understanding of the family gods. Even though they have the idea of a supreme spirit and spirits, these spirits are remembered according to their functions. This communitarian understanding of God has some similarity with the doctrine of the Trinity in Christianity, particularly, with regard to the functions of the three gods, *Pathian* (Holy Father), *Khuanu* (goddess) and *Vanchung nula* (maiden or daughter). Hminga has commented that the Mizos seemed to think of *Pathian* as living in the heaven with a family just like a human family, *Pu Vana* (the grandfather Heaven), *Khuanu*

(Pathian's wife or Mother goddess) and *Vanchung nula* (maiden in heaven above):

> ...just like the Christian doctrine of Trinity-Father, Son and Holy Spirit, the traditional Mizo concept had a triune god idea in the Pathian family-grandfather, a wife and a daughter.[56]

It is reasonable to say that belief in this communitarian God (reality) deeply influenced the Mizo people to sustain a communitarian understanding of humanity.

3.2.2.2. Communitarian Understanding of Humanity[57]

Humanity among the tribal people was perceived more in terms of the community, rather than of the individual. For tribal people, a person's humanity could not be realized unless she or he was in community. To be truly human, one must be in communion with others. In traditional tribal society, those who lived in one village usually belonged to one particular tribe or clan. They were closely related to one another and maintained a particular system of social organization based on family ties and blood relationship. Particularly among the Mizos, every village had a chief, under whose leadership the village became a well-knit community. The chief ruled over the village, and a council of elders, appointed by the chief himself, assisted him in administration. Although the chief held absolute authority over the village, his mode of life and dress were not different from those of the common people. Similarly, though chieftainship was hereditary, there was not a particular chiefly clan among Mizos. Any person could become a chief provided he had followers. Therefore, among the Mizos, if the chief acted "in a cruel manner, his subjects would be likely to migrate to another village with a more benevolent ruler."[58]

56 McCall, *Lushai Chrysalis*, 46.

57 See Chapter II, 130-133.

58 Kipgen, *Christianity and Mizo Culture*, 59.

3.2.2.3. Agent of Community or Communitarianism.

As has been already discussed, the vital cultural traditions that uphold and strengthen the community consciousness among the Mizo people are the institution of *Zawlbuk*, the philosophy of *Tlawmngaihna* and the egalitarian principle. The other two elements can be integrated into the primary agent of Mizo community, *Zawlbuk*. We shall now examine in brief the significance of *Zawlbuk* for tribal ecclesiology.

3.2.2.3.1. Ecclesiological Significance of the *Zawlbuk*

As we have already discussed the nature and functions of the *Zawlbuk* in detail in chapter two, it is not necessary here to repeat the details in this section except for drawing some theological insights from it. The nature and functions of *Zawlbuk* which we have dealt with may be summed up as follows: (1) *Zawlbuk* was the Mizo community home (ii) *Zawlbuk* was the refuge of the Village (iii) *Zawlbuk* was community center for education (iv) *Zawlbuk* was the guardian of social ethics (v) *Zawlbuk* was recreational centre. In what follows we will take a look at what theological insights we can draw from the *Zawlbuk*.

In order to draw theological insights from the institution of *Zawlbuk*; Thanzauva made a critical comparison of the nature and functions of the *Zawlbuk* in Mizo traditions with the nature and functions of the contemporary Church. His findings are highlighted as follows:

1. *Zawlbuk*, a community home is limited in its membership and concern. Membership of the institution of *Zawlbuk* was open only to the villagers and the bachelors; however, inclusive in the sense that it admitted all the bachelors irrespective of caste, class and clan, in some cases (other tribes) even the women in the village. The Church is universal in its concern and membership. Its membership is open to all, and it is concerned for a wider human community but exclusive in the sense that it rejects members of other denominations and other faiths.

2. The community home, *Zawlbuk*, is the keeper or guardian of tribal culture, traditions and values, and an instrument for the welfare of the village community; whereas the church is the custodian of Christian faith and an instrument of the Kingdom of God.
3. The community home is a large building that was built at the heart of the village, specifically near the house of the village chief. It is the community home that integrates and unites the community in a village. So, also the church is a big building at the heart of the village used for worship. It integrates its members who attend the church.
4. The community home contributes towards integration, peace, security and harmony of the village community. The church contributes towards integration of the members of its own denomination and Christian community.
5. The community home is for young men and an institute for training. It is in and by the Church that the spiritual life of the community of believers is nurtured. The church also educates its members through its formal and informal agencies.
6. The community home teaches and keeps a high ethical principle of *Tlawmngaihna* and strict discipline. The church also teaches ethical life and imposes strict rules for its members.[59]

Thanzauva's critical comparison reveals that the institution of a community home lacks a universal concern. Its contribution towards the harmony, welfare and peace of the village community, however, was greater than the contribution of the Church. The limitation of a community is its exclusivist nature, which needs to be broadened. At the same time the church should also realize that the local community matters most. The church is a believing community formed out of, and existing in, the concrete local community. Having seen the place of *Zawlbuk* in Mizo society, Thanzava came to the conclusion that

59 Thanzauva, *Theology of Community*, 140-141.

the institution of *Zawlbuk* is the forerunner of the Christian church and therefore, the spirit and functions of this institution need to be incorporated into tribal ecclesiology.[60] The theological significance of the *Zawlbuk* may be outlined as follows:

3.2.2.3.1.1. *Zawlbuk* as Local Church

As has been mentioned, *Zawlbuk* is the community home that keeps the justice, peace and communion of the entire community in the village. Theologically, it is not wrong to say that it is the local *ecclesia*, or God's ecclesial instrument or an agent of the Kingdom of God to keep and transform Mizo society. Therefore, we may say that ecclesiologically *Zawlbuk* advocates, as Lesslie Newbigin,[61] Hans Kung[62] and Leonardo Boff[63] suggest, local church ecclesiology. Unlike the present Mizo ecclesiology, which has an orderly centralized structure,[64] *Zawlbuk* ecclesiology stresses the primacy of the local church and gives more importance to the communion of local Christian community.

3.2.2.3.1.2. *Zawlbuk* as an Agent of the Kingdom of God

Zawlbuk, by its nature and functions, testifies that the local church should be committed to the cause of the well being of the local Christian community for the realization of the Kingdom of God in tribal context. In other words, the church in the *Zawlbuk* model of ecclesiology should be the servant and guardian of the tribal community. The essence of the church in *Zawlbuk* ecclesiology is a

---

60 Thanzauva, *Theology of Community*, 140 & 144.

61 L. Newbigin, *The Household of God* (London: Friendship Press, 1954), 117. Newbegin advocates the primacy of local church.

62 Hans Kung, *The Church* (London: Search Press, 1973), 85. Kung said that the local church is not a small cell of the whole, it is the real church.

63 Leonardo Boff, *Ecclesia Genesis: The Basic Communities Reinvent the Church* (Maryknoll: Orbis Books, 1986), iff.

64 Presbyterian and Baptist Church of Mizoram are highly centralized, every local church is under its Headquarters Offices.

community of believers who take responsibility for the realization of the Kingdom of God here and now.[65]

3.2.2.3.1.3. *Zawlbuk* as the Institution and Practitioner of the Ethics of the Kingdom of God

The greatest gift of the institution of Zawlbuk is *tlawmngaihna*.[66] The nature and functions of the community home clearly reveals that the separation of *tlawmngaihna* from the *Zawlbuk* is not possible, because *tlawmngaihna* is taught and nurtured in and by the community home. At the same time, the existence of *Zawlbuk* is possible only because of the *tlawmngaihna*. In other words, it is the *tlawmngaihna* that gives power and life to the *Zawlbuk,* in return, it fosters and perfects *tlawmngaihna*. In the light of the relationship between the *Zawlbuk* and *tlawmngaihna*, we may say that the true nature of the Church is expressed through its ethical engagement, and ethics is essential for the life of the Church.

Thanzauva, in his book, *Theology of Community*, has given theological validity to *tlawmngaihna* and its significance for social transformation. For him, "*tlawmngaihna* is a message of Jesus Christ hidden in the tribal culture. It is an active love in action."[67] He, without any hesitation, compares *tlawmngaihna* with the love of God, and said, "If Love is the essence of the Gospel teaching, *tlawmngaihna* is the hidden gospel written in the hearts of the tribal people before they embrace Christianity."[68] Here, Thanzauva has interpreted the Pauline understanding of Love in 1 Corinthians 13:4–7 as *Tlawmngaihna*, which he believes to be the true and appropriate interpretation for Mizo Christians. *Tlawmngaihna* is a self-giving love, which sets aside self-glorification and seeks the welfare of community (others). Thanzauva further argues, "If Jesus Christ is the expression and embodiment of God's love, the incarnation, the ministry and the cross of Jesus Christ may be perceived as paramount

65 Thanzauva, *Theology of Community*, 145.

66 A detailed analysis of *Tlawmngaihna* is seen in Chapter II, 148-161.

67 Thanzauva, *Theology of Community*, 128.

68 Ibid.

act of *tlawmngaihna.*"[69] Therefore, he calls Jesus the *tlawmngai* par excellence.[70]

As has been mentioned, *tlawmngaihna* is a community ethics essential for the sustenance of harmony and integrity of the Mizo community. This principle of *tlawmngaihna* is in essence the Kingdom principle and essential for the realization of the Kingdom of God. *Tlawmngaihna* is truly the praxis of love or love in action. *Tlawmngaihna* may also be considered as a communitarian discipleship, a commitment to the cause of community.[71]

3.2.2.3.1.4. *Zawlbuk* as the Sign of the Kingdom of God

It is the institution of *Zawlbuk* that keeps the basic structure of Mizo Community alive.

Egalitarianism is an absence of racism, caste discrimination, and classism. H. L. Malsawma has rightly pointed out that it was *tlawmngaihna*, the core and living blood of Mizo social life, that knits the individual and family together in an integrated caste-less society where safety is ensured.[72] One of the prominent characters of any egalitarian society is sharing. Sharing is possible for Mizo community because of *tlawmngaihna*, giving oneself for others.

This egalitarianism in Mizo society is very much in line with the life of the early Christian congregations when believers shared together all that belonged to them and also with the biblical teaching that we all are children of God. As children of God it should be possible for us all to come to gather to praise and worship God.

As has been mentioned the *Zawlbuk* is not only the instrument to establish a harmonious society, but *Zawlbuk* itself is a community of fellowship, which teaches and practices mutual trust, sharing of joy and sorrow and mutual help. Therefore, we may also say that *Zawlbuk* is the sign of the Kingdom of God. The life in and

---

69 Thanzauva, *Theology of Community*, 129.

70 Ibid.

71 Ibid., 129-132.

72 H. L. Malsawma, *Sociology of the Mizos* (Guwahati, Delhi: Spectrum Publications, 2002), 64-65.

of *Zawlbuk* implies that the Church should be a community of fellowship that is free from any alienating structures and advocates and practices reciprocity, equality and freedom. In the *Zawlbuk* model of ecclesiology, the local congregation or the church will become the visible body of Christ, the community, guided by the principle of *tlawmngaihna*, which motivates each member of the local congregation to put the interest of the community before their own individual interest and to labour together as a community to realize the Kingdom of God here on earth.

3.2.2.4. Evaluation of the Findings from Mizo Cultural Traditions

The findings from Mizo cultures affirm the idea that God has been revealed to every culture. Even though it is primitive or illogical in the eyes of some modern cultures, the value of Mizo cultural traditions, their understanding of God, humanity and their social cultural institution, *Zawlbuk*, is beyond our estimation. However, it was due to Western cultural hegemony that these cultural values became ignored or distorted. The findings reveal that these precious traditions can be meaningfully interpreted with the help of the Gospel or vice versa and incorporated in the doctrine of the Church, so that the church may become the real Church of tribal people.

4. Conclusion

Our discussion in this chapter reveals that the proposed method of critical synthesis is viable for finding a relevant ecclesiology out of the two traditions. The discussion also reveals that the insights drawn from both traditions are relevant for developing Mizo Tribal ecclesiology.

Chapter 5

Towards a Tribal Ecclesiology
Zawlbuk as a Model of Tribal Ecclesiology

1. Introduction

We now turn to formulate tribal ecclesiology based on the findings in chapter four from both the doctrine of the Church in early Christian traditions and Mizo cultural traditions, the *Zawlbuk* and its essential aspects, *Tlawmngaihna* and Egalitarianism. The formulation is guided by the intent of the research to make tribal ecclesiology biblically grounded, theologically credible and contextually relevant.

2. *Zawlbuk* as a Model of Tribal Ecclesiology

The insights drawn from the two traditions in the previous chapter and particularly our discussion about the ecclesiological relevance of the institution of *Zawlbuk* recommends us to use the *Zawlbuk* model of ecclesiology for Mizo Christian communities. However, it is to be noted that this *Zawlbuk* ecclesiology is a synthesis of the early Christian traditions and Mizo cultural traditions. In other words, *Zawlbuk* ecclesiology is an ecclesiological interpretation of Mizo cultural tradition with the help of the early Christian tradition, and at the same time it is also an interpretation of the doctrine of the Church with the help of Mizo cultural traditions. We shall now highlight the fundamental features of this new tribal ecclesiology: the basis, structure and image of the church in tribal ecclesiology

2.1. Basis of Tribal Ecclesiology: Kenosis of Jesus and Tlawmngaihna

As the early Church borrowed ideas and concepts from its cultural environment to express and communicate the faith, Mizo people too have to find Mizo tribal concepts and symbols to express the life and witness of the church in tribal context. Often the context itself suggests the most appropriate theological model or idea that needs to be given prominence. For instance, in tribal context in Northeast India where poverty is rampant, people are fighting for liberation from alienation, ethnic conflicts, and denominationalism. The motif of Christ's self-emptying (Phil. 2:5–11), which is revealed as *tlawmngaihna* in Mizo culture, seems to be the most appropriate basis for tribal ecclesiology—the life, witness and worship of the Church in Northeast India in general and Mizoram in particular. Today, the church in Mizoram has become highly institutionalized with powerful centralization; it often overlooks the needs of the community. The Mizo church needs to recover the original nature of the Church in the early Christian traditions as a loving and caring community. Therefore, any formulation relating to the doctrine of the Church should be based on the *kenosis* of Jesus Christ, the perfection of Mizo *tlawmngaihna*.

2.2. Koinonia/Egalitarianism: A Model for the Structure of the Tribal Church

The word *koinonia* expressed what church and Christianity actually stood for. Over against the organizational structure of Judaism and the dominance of the law and the legal authorities, Christians felt that they were all equal as disciples of Christ.

The word *koinonia* indicates what is "common" in the Greek language in contrast to what is private. In the "common life," which refers to all sorts of relationships, a whole cultural outlook was embodied implying justice, order, what is fitting or beneficial, friendship, communal economy and equality for citizens of a city. Plato spoke of how "heaven and earth and gods and people comprise the *koinonia* and friendship and orderly behaviour and self control and justice."[1] The word *koinonia* also means fellowship with others in the group.

The Hebrews on the other hand found their identity on the basis of God's call, election, liberation, and fulfillment of promises of the Covenant. But one did not speak about any fellowship with Yahweh, who was considered very much in the fashion of one of those Middle Eastern monarchs who demanded complete loyalty from the subjects. He was so far above people that even His name could not be uttered by human beings. People referred to Him by heaven above where God was seated in all His glory. Righteousness was an attribute of Yahweh who worked for the salvation of Israel. Since there was no question of "fellowship" with God, the root *koinonia* did not have a Hebrew equivalent. The Hebrew root *chabr* produced a term, *chaburah*, which referred to an elite fellowship or group like that of the Pharisees and Essenes in a town or village committed to a stricter observance of the law.[2]

Here we are appropriating the interpersonal relations within the Trinitarian community and tribal communitarianism as a pattern for the tribal Christian community or church. The inner life of God is a communion of love that is personal and relational, and this love is *kenotic* (in Mizo *tlawmngaihna)* or self-emptying.[3]

1 Cited in John B. Chethimattam, *Towards a Theology of Intercommunion* (Bangalore: C.I.I.S & Dharmaram Publications, 2001), 171.

2 Ibid.

3 Thomas P. Looney, "Koinonia Ecclesiology: How Solid a Foundation?" *One in Christ* 36 (2000), 151.

Within the Trinitarian community, there is neither an ontological superiority nor an ontological subordination. The three persons are in mutual, interpersonal and intimate communion without losing individual identity. For each, therefore, to be equally God, each must dynamically make room for, without in any way diminishing, the others.[4] The tribal church is to be characterized by this *koinonia, mutuality* and reciprocity, the dynamic process of making room for another around oneself emphasizing relatedness and communion.

In liberation and tribal theologies, understanding the Trinity as community based on the equality, mutual relatedness, and self-offering of the divine persons lays the foundation for restructuring the human community in ways that are more just and inclusive. Thus, God as community challenges the hegemony of human authoritarianism and entrenched injustice.[5] Leanardo Boff contends that just as the divine persons are joined together by communion, if we are to follow such a model for the Church, we must be true to our source, because it is from this source that the Church's life and oneness spring. He says:

> In the Church community a consideration of the Trinitarian communion ought to present the concentration of power and open the way for a broad, egalitarian participation on the part of all. Not everyone can do everything. Each person performs his or her own task, but in communion with everyone.[6]

---

4 Michael Lawler, "Perichoresis: New Theological Wise in an Old Wineskin," Horizons 22 (1995), 52-53. See also Robert Kress, "Unity in Diversity and Diversity in Unity: Toward an Ecumenical Perichoresic Kenotic Trinitarian Ontology," *Dialogue and Alliance* 4/3 (1990), 69; Jurgen Moltmann, "The Inviting Unity of the Triune God," *Concilium* 177 (1985), 50-58.

5 Nonna Verna Harrison, "An Orthodox Approach to the Mystery of the Trinity: Questions for the Twenty-first Century," 60.

6 Leanardo Boff, "The Liberating Design of God," in *Mysterium Liberationis: Fundamental Concepts of Liberation Theology*, edited by Ignacio Ellacuria and John Sobrino (Maryknoll, NY: Orbis Books, 1993), 401.

The leading exponent of communion ecclesiology, Jean Marie Tillard, says, "The Church of God is nothing else but the communion of the Disciples of Christ Jesus as, through the Spirit, it is understood in the whole relationship of the Father and the Son."[7] It is the role of the Holy Spirit to bring about such unity in the community and, therefore, the Spirit is the source of all communions.

The idea of communion is present in the works of the New Testament. One of the distinctive components of this concept is that of being in communion while being diverse. This ecclesiology of communion invites us to accept the diversity underlying the unity. The import of this idea of unity in diversity is quite evident in the writings of many contemporary theologians. For instance, Macquarrie believes that the richer the diversity, the stronger is the unity and interdependence. He highlights the necessity of defending this diversity in unity against uniformity just as much as against divisiveness.[8] According to Kasper, God's love endures and reconciles the paradoxicality without minimizing it, and one of the characteristics of love is to establish unity in the midst of diversity. "Love means unity and fellowship with the other person, who is affirmed in his otherness, and thus unity and reconciliation in persistent duality."[9]

The early Church was convinced that their communion was brought about by God, in and through Jesus Christ and the Holy Spirit. This is why Pentecost manifests the nature of the church.[10] The gift of tongues to the apostles, which valorizes the languages of the world, shows that the church is not limited to one nation or language or culture. It is open to all the diversities of the human race by virtue of its catholicity. The post-Pentecost community is to be a

7 Jean Marie R. Tillard, *Church of Churches: The Ecclesiology of Communion,* translated by R. C. de Peaux (Collegeville: The Litergical Press, 1992), 52.

8 John Macquarrie, *Principles of Christian Theology* (New York: Charles Scribner's Sons, 1966), 360-361.

9 Walter Kasper, *Jesus the Christ* , translated by V. Green (London: Burns and Oates, 1976), 168.

10 J. M. R. Tillard, *Church of Churches: The Ecclesiology of Communion*, translated from French by R. C. De peaux (Minnesota: The Litugical Press, 1992), 3.

communion of the human multitude with its diversity, whose unity is expressed precisely in this diversity; and whose profound, invisible link is the Spirit of the Lord.[11] However, this communion was not a merely spiritual matter, and had to be manifested in action. This is why Acts shows the first Christians sharing goods among themselves and especially with those in need.

Similarly, for Mizo tribal theology, the structure of community and the structure of communion are rooted in their understanding of God. Their understanding of God is very much in tune with their settled agrarian lifestyle. The Mizo community reflects a structure and communion based on equality and mutuality. They are based on the way God deals with creation. The community home, *Zawlbuk* and its essential components, *tlawmngaihna* and egalitarian philosophy offer us a paradigm of life: a life of communion based on service. It does away with a life built on master-servant relationship. A life of service is possible only when interdependence of all that exists is accepted. Service means to work for the enhancement of the other's life. To serve others entails taking care of the other's wellbeing. Since such one is engaged in serving the other, a relationship of master-servant is overcome and all become equal. In other words, the Mizo community is a communion of kinship where all are at the service of one another.[12]

Hierarchical structure and hierarchical communion give rise to the pyramidal structure. In this case, hierarchical relationship must open itself to an egalitarian structure and mutually beneficial relationships among believers. The dynamics of communion among all members need to be characterized by mutual service, self-sacrifice, equality and sharing. In addition, structures that foster equality, collective decision making and its execution need to be evolved.

A tribal church, which is to be truly catholic, will be truly holistic, not only embracing all categories of people but also enabling all to participate fully in its corporate ministry and decision-making processes. There is inadequate lay involvement, particularly that

11 Tillard, *Church of Churches,* 8 & 6.

12 Laltluangliana, *Mizos of North East India*, 22.

of women, in the leadership of most of the tribal churches. People feel excluded by hierarchical structures and bureaucratic processes. The gifts of the Spirit bestowed on Christ's people go un-received. The church as a foretaste of the Kingdom remains unrecognizable. The church's self-understanding, structures and styles of leadership need to be reshaped by the recognition that in each place it exists among and for a particular group of people. Special attention must be given to the role, status and place of women in the church, taking into account the cultural and theological constraints that distort the church's life.

2.3. The Images of the Church in Zawlbuk Ecclesiology

2.3.1. *The Church as a Communion of local Christian Community*

The attribute 'local,' derived from the Latin 'localis' and 'locus' has several nuances, all indicating place in some form.[13] Whether the distinctive elements of the local church are place or geography, people or community, environment or anthropology, they are interrelated and are essential elements that give identity to the local church. However, one speaks of the local realization of the church, place is automatically implied. But where is the local church to be found? To speak of the local church as a territorial or geographical entity might lead to juxtaposing it with a diocese. To limit the local church to a human or cultural space calls for further precision, for it could imply a local church organized on the basis of language, class, caste, race, ideology.[14] The *Zawlbuk* ecclesiology advocates a communion of local Christian community that embraces all groups of people who follow Jesus Christ.

13 Localis means Local, of the place; locus implies places, isolated, particular; loca (neuter) refers to a country, place, region, portion of the earth, of a property. See Monteiro, *Church and Culture*, 29.

14 Monteiro, *Church and Culture*, 29.

2.3.2. *The Church as inclusive community free from discrimination*

The task of *Zawlbuk* ecclesiology is to build a just and harmonious community free from discrimination, where love dominates human relationships, where women are free to live out the gifts God has given to them.

The church-in-movement becomes an institution with its hierarchical structure. Eventually, this institutional church becomes identified with the body of Christ. Hence, the humble image of Christ the Good Shepherd is replaced with Christ the King.[15] The Western institutional model of the church transplanted into tribal areas during the modern mission era has become more and more solidified, particularly in Mizoram. A critical understanding of the past should enable us to get rid of the distorted elements from our past in order to recapture the original experience of Jesus Christ and mould a true church relevant to the tribal people. As followers of Jesus Christ in the early Church and the inmates of *Zawlbuk*, the tribal church becomes a community of freedom and equality, equality at all levels.[16] The Christian community is open to all without any form of discrimination whatsoever, a community centred solely on the principle of *tlawmngaihna* (the law of love).

2.3.3. *The Church as a community of sharing and service*

The church in *Zawlbuk* ecclesiology should become a community of sharing and service. Following Jesus, the Servant God who came "not to be served but serve,"[17] and the principle of *tlawmngaihna,* which is meant for others, the tribal church becomes essentially a community of service and a community freed from selfishness and greed.

The church in antiquity is remembered for its sharing and service to the needy. However, problems arose when the church became

15 Jacob Kavunkal, "Evolution of the Understanding of the Christian Identity in the course of the centuries," in *The Church in India in Search of a New Identity*, edited by Kurien Kunnumpuram SJ, Errol D'Lima SJ and Jacob Parappaly MSFS (Bangalore: N.B.C.L.C, 1997), 91.

16 Matthew 23:8-10.

17 Matthew 10:45.

wealthy and the people around were getting poorer, particularly during the Middle Ages. John Wyclif attacked the church because of its exceeding wealth and irresponsible use of it. The church was no longer the voice of the poor but rather became the exploiting church. The church was no longer the voice of the poor but the collaborator with the powerful noble rich. The church was no longer standing side by side with the poor beggar Lazarus, but rather sitting at the table with the rich, clad in purple. The church became a tax collector, and its members the taxpayers. The forgiveness of sins was something to be sold and bought. At the same time, in the midst of these problems the church by no means completely lost its uniqueness that is her servanthood. Martin Luther attempted to regain it in his phrase:

> "A Christian man is the most free lord of all, and subject to none: a Christian man is the most dutiful servant of all and subject to every one... He is a servant because by love to bring his life into conformity to the will of God and to be helpful to his neighbor."[18]

Therefore, the church is only the church when it exists for others. To make a start, it should give away all its property to those in need. The clergy must live solely on the free offerings of their congregations, or possibly engage in some secular calling. The church must share the secular problems of ordinary life, not dominating, but helping and serving.[19]

Harvey Cox in his book, *The Secular City*, wrote, "The church's task in the secular city is to be *diakonos* of the city, the servant who bends himself to struggle for its wholeness and health."[20] Robinson pointed out further that the church should not build its own institutional structures but rather incarnate itself into the structures of the world to do service. The house of God for him is not the church

---

18 A. Walker, *A History of the Christian Church* (New York: NY: Scribner's Sons, 1959), 309.

19 A. Dulles, *Models of the Church* (New York, NY: Doubleday & Co. Inc., 1974), 88.

20 Harvey Cox, *The Secular City* (New York, NY: Macmillan, 1965), 134.

but the world. The church is the servant, and the first characteristic of a servant is that he lives in someone else's house, not his own.[21] The church lives in the world and serves God in the world at any cost.

2.3.4. *The Church as catholic, communion of churches*

As the ecclesiology of the early Christian traditions suggests unity in diversity, the church in *Zawlbuk* ecclesiology is capable of breaking down barriers to communication and communion. By the common sharing of riches, the members of different churches will become a genuine community of love, capable of living and working together and thus fulfilling their common mission. We need to extend this sharing of fellowship and mission to other ecclesial communities. This will call for an ecumenical spirit that will demand from us the renunciation of a narrow-minded catholicity and the relinquishing of our absolutist claims in dealing with other Christian communities. In the interests of all tribal Christians as well as the universal Church, the church should be able to work together with other Christian communities.

3. Conclusion

We have made an attempt to construct a relevant ecclesiology for Mizo tribal Christians based on the insight drawn from select early Christian traditions and Mizo cultural traditions. For Mizo Christian ecclesiology, the study proposes a *Zawlbuk* model of ecclesiology, *Tlawmngaihna* becomes the basis of tribal ecclesiology and egalitarianism becomes the new form of the tribal church structure. This *Zawlbuk* ecclesiology also offers the Mizo Church a new identity.

21 J. A. T. Robinson, *The New Reformation*? (Philadelphia: Westminster Press, 1965), 92.

General Conclusion

Recapitulation and Findings

India is a sub-continent that has many religions and cultures. This diversity within India itself is far beyond what a singular theology or theological approach can deal with. There can be no end of contextualization if people are really concerned for constructing a relevant theology. If we want Christianity to take root in the local culture, we must encourage and support any theological reflection done in the local context. As there is no single, monoculture theology that is universally applicable to all peoples for all time, tribal Christians also need to construct a theology that is relevant for them.

In the past few decades, we have seen a number of volumes containing the faith statements or theological writings of tribal people. These writings of tribal theology are concerned about the question of how to define Christ in a tribal context in a way that is both understandable and meaningful. In other words, tribal theology attempts to help tribal Christians understand and confess Christ in their own contexts. Furthermore, tribal theology allows for greater realization of the significance of the power of Christ for their liberation from all kinds bondage. However, in spite of all these efforts, the church in Mizoram appears to be still predominantly

Western almost in every aspect. The foundation of tribal cultures is shifting, and in the emerging context the people are finding that the operational ecclesiology no longer provides adequate answers to the questions they face. In this regard, much of the gospel presentations are becoming trivialised and church life is becoming marginalized. Unless tribal theology becomes the theology of the tribal church one cannot expect any positive result of it in the life of the tribal community, because tribal theology without including ecclesiological shifts is incomplete. Therefore, this study sought to construct a relevant ecclesiology for tribal Christians in general and Mizoram in particular. Such ecclesiology is based on early Christian traditions and Mizo cultural traditions. These two must be linked, as tribal ecclesiology has to be faithful to both the early Christian traditions as well as tribal cultural traditions.

The book identifies two major weaknesses of the existing ecclesiology in Mizoram: first, the uncritical acceptance of ecclesiology from the Western church traditions resulting in the proliferation of denominational churches and division of Mizo Christians; second, the general uncritical rejection of the local cultural traditions making the Church superficial and unable to respond to people's problems. Hence, in order to address these problems, the author selects the early Christian traditions and Mizo cultural traditions for the area of research and proposes a method of critical synthesis for formulating a relevant ecclesiology in the tribal context.

It reveals that the early Church existed as a number of local congregations scattered over the Mediterranean region. The Church's life was rooted in the local Christian community. Judaism had greatly influenced the Church of Jerusalem, and later the Grecco-Roman civilization greatly influenced the form of life of the early Christian communities. The Church was founded in different lands with varied religious and social background. The spreading of the Gospel to the various cultural centers demanded an adaptation to the local culture in the presentation of the message and the organization of the community. Nevertheless, Christians were united by their faith in Jesus Christ, the Lord and Son of God. Unity and plurality in ecclesiology was evident during the foundational period of the Church. Their faith in Jesus was based on the witness of the Apostles. Furthermore, ecclesial structure during these four centuries developed from non-structured, simple community of believers to a well-established hierarchy.

The primary self conceptions of the early Church centred on the spiritual reality of mystery, the body of Christ, the people of God, and the communion with God in Jesus Christ, which transcends all space and time. In addition, communion was the heart and essence of the Church in the New Testament and in the first four centuries of Christianity. The inner reality of the Church is the divine communion or participation in the life of the Triune God in and through Jesus Christ. The vertical communion is attained sacramentally in a historical human community. Additionally, the divine communion is the ultimate basis for the human communion. In short, the vertical or divine communion leads to the horizontal human communion and vice versa. In the early church, the communion of the local church was primarily expressed and realized in the Eucharistic celebration. Such participation led to real communion in life by sharing both spiritual and material things as well as building up community at a deeper level common sharing of goods and properties as an expression of the communion at all levels.

Similar to these fundamental aspects of early Christian communities, Mizo people too have the most essential aspects of Mizo culture, namely, the institution of *Zawlbuk, Tlawmngaihna* and Egalitarianism. In order to develop a relevant tribal ecclesiology, critical examination of the potentialities of the elements of Mizo culture for the construction of tribal ecclesiology must be accomplished. These cultural elements were essential for the Mizo community in the past and are richly loaded with theological potentialities that can be incorporated in tribal ecclesiology. Indeed all these three aspects of Mizo cultures are compatible with the teaching of Jesus Christ and the early Christian traditions.

Furthermore, the ecclesial tradition received from Western Christianity is inadequate to address the problems facing the contemporary Mizo society. The fundamental problem of the existing ecclesiology in Mizoram, as previously mentioned is its uncritical adoption of Western church traditions in addition to its failure to take the Mizo cultural traditions as sources of ecclesiology. These failures are shared by both the Western missionaries as well as the native leaders. Indeed, the Baptist Church of Mizoram and the Presbyterian Church of Mizoram have no difference in their ecclesiology compared to their Western counterparts. In response, members who were not satisfied with these two churches because of their indifference to local culture and identification with Western ecclesiology formed other denominations. In order to bring the Mizo church back to its original relevance to the Mizo Christians, a reconstruction of ecclesiology is necessary.

In order to offer the best ecclesiology that is biblically grounded, theologically credible and contextually relevant to the tribal Christians, the study proposes a *Zawlbuk* model of ecclesiology. In this *Zawlbuk* model of ecclesiology, *Tlawmngaihna* becomes the basis of tribal ecclesiology and Egalitarianism becomes the model of the church structure. In *Zawlbuk* ecclesiology, the tribal Mizo Church receives a new identity: the church as a communion of local Christian community; the church as egalitarian community; and church as a community of sharing and service.

For Mizo Christians, *Zawlbuk* can be used as a model for Mizo church. In other words, the nature and functions of the church can be best explained through the nature and functions of the Mizo traditional institution of *Zawlbuk.* Thus, a tribal ecclesiology for the tribal Christians in Mizoram is the construction of a contextual ecclesiology using the early Christian traditions and the Mizo social cultural traditions.

Appendix

Questionaire Regarding the Relevance of the Existing Ecclesiology of the Baptist and Presbyterian Church in Mizoram

These questionnaires will be used for personal research and study purposes only and is completely anonymous. There is no right or wrong answer. Your answer is correct if it expresses your true opinion. Please put a tick mark ( ) on or before your selected answer.

A. Profiles of Respondents

1. How old are you?

   a. ______________20-30

   b. ______________ 31-40

   c. ______________ 41-50

   d. ______________ 51 and above

2. Gender
   a. ____________ Male
   b. ____________ Female

3. What is your educational qualification?
   a. ______________ Class X
   b. ______________ Class XII
   c. ______________ B.A
   d. ______________ M.A and above
   e. ______________ Other

4. What is your marital status?
   a. _______________ Single
   b. _______________ Married
   c. _______________ Widow and Widower
   d. _______________ Other

5. How do you view your economic status?
   a. _______________ Wealthy
   b. _______________ Rich
   c. _______________ Middle/Medium
   d. _______________ Poor
   e. _______________ Very Poor

6. What is your present position in the church?
   a. _______________ Pastor
   b. _______________ Elder
   c. _______________ Deacon
   d. _______________ Women leader
   e. _______________ Youth leader

B. The evaluation of the ecclesiology of the churches of Mizoram

1. The churches (BCM & PCM) of Mizoram and the early Church ecclesiology

1.1. Do you agree that the churches of Mizoram have continuity with the early church?

Agree / Disagree / Can't decide

1.2. In which area do you think the churches of Mizoram maintain unity (continuity) with the early church tradition?

- Apostolic faith
- Ecclesial Structure
- Mission
- No continuity
- No idea

1.3. Do you agree that the churches of Mizoram seriously take the ecclesiology of the early church for their life and ministry?

Agree / Disagree / Can't decide

1.4. What do you mean by the Church?

____ a community of believers

____ Holy people

____ called out people

____ a group of Christian sect

____ Christian institution

1.5. Do you agree that it is necessary for the churches of Mizoram to study the early Christian Traditions?

Agree / Disagree / Can't decide

2. The churches (BCM & PCM) of Mizoram and the Western Missionary ecclesiology

2.1. Do you agree that the churches of Mizoram are the offspring of Western Missionaries?

Agree / Disagree / Can't decide

2.2. Do you agree that that the churches of Mizoram are eastern duplicates of Western churches?

Agree / Disagree / Can't decide

2.3. Do you agree that the Baptist Church of Mizoram and the Presbyterian Church of Mizoram are the duplicates of the English Baptist Church in England and the Presbyterian Church of Wales respectively?

Agree / Disagree / Can't decide

2.4. Do you agree that for Mizo Christians, it is good to follow the Western church tradition?

Agree / Disagree / Can't decide

2.5. Do you agree those institutionalisms, individualism, division in multiple sects are due to the influence of the Western Missionary church traditions?

Agree / Disagree / Can't decide

3. The churches (BCM & PCM) of Mizoram and the Mizo Context

3.1. Do you agree that the churches of Mizoram are suited to the Mizo cultures?

Agree / Disagree / Can't decide

3.2. What type of church authority do you prefer most for the Mizo Churches?

_______ Shared leadership (Pastors and Elders)

_______ Authoritarian Leadership

_______ Democratic leadership

_______ Charismatic leadership

3.3. Do you agree that the churches of Mizoram effectively address the problems of the present Mizo society?

Agree / Disagree / Can't decide

3.4. Do you agree that the churches of Mizoram are strong enough to transform the Mizo society?

Agree / Disagree / Can't decide

3.5. In which area do you think the churches of Mizoram need to improve most?

_______ the theology or doctrine of the church

_______ Ministerial structure

_______ Worship

_______ Contextualization or inculturation

4. The churches (BCM & PCM) of Mizoram and Inculturation

4.1. Do you agree that the true Church of God is rooted in local culture?

Agree / Disagree / Can't decide

4.2. In your opinion which one is more prominent about the impact of the church on Mizo Christians?

_______ Unity among the Mizo society

_______ Division in the society

_______ Can't decide

4.3. Do you agree that the Mizo cultural traditions can be incorporated to the ecclesiology of Mizo Christians?

Agree / Disagree / Can't decide

4.4. Do you agree that the Mizo cultural traditions, *Zawlbuk*, *tlawmngaihna* and egalitarian trait are compatible with the Gospel?

Agree / Disagree / Can't decide

4.5. Do you agree that Mizo Christians need to develop Mizo Christian theology by using Mizo worldview and traditions?

Agree / Disagree / Can't decide

5. Envision for The Mizo Christian ecclesiology

5.1. Do you agree that the churches of Mizoram need to reconstruct their ecclesiology?

Agree / Disagree / Can't decide

5.2. Do you agree that Mizo Christian ecclesiology should be faithful to early church tradition?

Agree / Disagree / Can't decide

5.3. Do you agree that Mizo Christian ecclesiology should be faithful to Mizo culture?

Agree/ Disagree / Can't decide

5.4. Do you agree that Mizo Christian ecclesiology should address the problems of Mizo society?

Agree / Disagree / Can't decide

5.5. Prioritize the mission of the churches of Mizoram

- soul winning
- transformation of society
- church planting
- sending missionaries to other faiths
- ecumenism among Mizo Christians

Bibliography

1. Sources related to the Mizo people and their culture

Agarwal, A. K. *Modernisation of the Mizo Society*. New Delhi: Mittal Publications, 2003.

Allen, B. C. *Lushai District Gazetteer*, Vol. X. Allahabad: The Pioneer Press, 1906.

Baptist Church of Mizoram. *Zoram Baptist Kohhran Thurin Puanchhuah (Baptist Confession)*. Serkawn: Baptist Church of Mizoram, 1988.

Baptist Church of Mizoram. *Constitution and Rules of Baptist Church of Mizoram*. Serkawn: The Publication Board of BCM, 2001.

Chaltuahkhuma. *History of Mizoram*. Aizawl: R. D. Press, 1987.

Chapman E. and M. Clark. *Mizo Miracle*. Madras: CLS, 1968.

Chatterji, N. *The Earlier Mizo Society*. 2nd Reprint. Kolkata: Firma KLM Private Limited on behalf of Tribal Research Institute Art & Culture Department, 2008.

________ *Zawlbuk as a Social Institution in the Mizo Society*. Aizawl: Tribal Research Institute, 1975.

________ *Puan - The Pride of Mizoram*. Aizawl: Tribal Research Institute, 1979.

________ *The Mizo Chief and His Administration*. Aizawl: Tribal Research Institute, 1975.

________ *Zawlbuk as a Social Institution in the Mizo Society*. Aizawl: Tribal Research, 1975.

Dahrawka, P. S. *Mizo Thawnthu*. Aizawl: Thankhumi, Chhinga Veng, 1981.

Darchhawna. *Mizoram District Gazetteers*. Guwahati: Eastern Press and Publication, 1989.

Dokhuma, James. *Zoram Kohhran Tualto Chanchinte* (Histories of the Indigenous Churches of Mizoram). Aizawl: D. Buanga, 1994.

Hluna, John Vanlal. *Church and Political Upheaval in Mizoram*. Aizawl: Mizoram History Association, 1985.

Hminga, C. L. *The Life and Witness of Churches in Mizoram*. Serkawn: The Literature Committee of Baptist Church of Mizoram, 1987.

________ *Mizoram Baptist Kohhran Chanchin*. Serkawn: BCM Publication Board, 2003.

Hrankhuma, F. and Joy Thomas, eds. *Christ among the Tribals*. Bangalore: Fellowship of Indian Missiologists, 2007.

Khiangte, Laltluangliana, ed. *Mizo Songs and Folk Tales*. New Delhi: Sahitya Akademi, 2002.

Khuanga. "The role of Christianity in the socio-economic praxis of Mizoram." In *Towards a Tribal Theology: The Mizo Perspective. Edited by K. Thanzauva*. Aizawl: Mizo Theological Conference, 1989.

Khup Za Go. *Chin Chronicles*. Churachandpur: L & R Printing Press, 1988.

Kipgen, Mangkhosat. *Christianity and Mizo Culture*. Jorhat: MTC, 1996.

________ *A Critical Historical Study of Bible Tanslation among the Zo People in North East India*. Imphal: BCPW, 1996.

Lalbiaknema, C. *Zawlbuk Titi* (Memoirs of the Zawlbuk). Aizawl: Mizoram Publication Board, 2000.

Lalbiakthanga. *The Mizos*. Guwahati: Purbadesh Mudran, 1978.

Lalchawimawia, C., comp. *British Rule in Mizoram,* Vol. 1: *Missionary and the Government* (1891-1968). Aizawl: C. Lalchawimawia, 2010.

Laldena. *Christian Missions and Colonialism.* Shillong: Vendrame Institute, 1988.

Lallawmzuala, K. "Sem sem dam dam, ei bil thi thi." In *Hmatiang Sawnin.* Edited by Lalrinawmi Ralte. Bangalore: Bangalore Mizo Association, 2001, 286-289.

Lalrema, Clement. *Mizoram Leh Khawvel Thlirna.* Aizawl: Modern Book Store, 1991.

Lalsawma. *Revivals, the Mizo Way.* Aizawl: Lalsawma, 1994.

Lalthangliana, B. *India, Burma Leh Thailand a Mizo Chanchin.* Aizawl: Remkungi, 2001.

________ *Mizo Chanchin.* Aizawl: Remkungi, 1976.

Lianhmingthanga, comp. *The Mizo Folk Tales.* Aizawl: Tribal Research Institute Department of Art & Culture Mizoram, 2006.

Lianzela. *Economic Development of Mizoram.* Guwahati: Spectrum Publications, 1994.

Lloyd, J. Meirion. *History of the Church in Mizoram.* Aizawl: Synod Publication Board, 1991.

________ *On Every High Hills.* Aizawl: Synod Publication Board, 1984.

Malsawma, H. L. *Sociology of the Mizo.* Guwahati: Spectrum Publication, 2002.

Mizoram Baptist Kohhran Chanchin Pawimawh Lawrkhawm, Part I. Serkawn: Baptist Church of Mizoram, 1985.

Mizoram Baptist Kohhran Chanchin Pawimawh Lawrkhawm, Part II and Part III. Serkawn: Baptist Church of Mizoram, 1986.

Pachuau, Lalsangkima. *Ethnic Identity and Christianity: A Socio-Historical and Missiological Study of Christianity in Northeast India with Special Reference to Mizoram.* Frankfurt am Main: Peter Lang, 2002.

Presbyterian Church of Mizoram. *Kohhran Thurin leh Thunun Dante* (Church Doctrine and Disciplinary Rules). Fifth ed. Aizawl: Synod Literature & Publication Board, 1994.

Provost, James H., ed. *The Church as Communion*. Washington, D. C: Canon Law Society of America, 1984.

Ray, Animesh. *Mizoram Dynamics of Change*. Calcutta: Pearl Publishers, 1982.

Rokhuma. "Moral Degradation and the Role of the Church." In *Ground Works for Tribal Theology in the Mizo Context.* Edited by Rosiamliana Tochhawng, K. Lalrinmawia and L. H. Rawsea. Delhi: ISPCK, 2007.

Saiaithanga. *Mizoram Kohhran Chanchin*. Aizawl: Mizo Theological Literature Committee, 1969, Reprint, 2001.

Thanga, L. B. *The Mizos: A Study in Racial Personality.* Guwahati: United Publishers, 1978.

Thanzauva, K, comp. *Reports of the Foreign Mission of the Presbyterian Church of Wales on Mizoram,* 1894-1957. Aizawl: The Synod Literature and Publication Boards, 1997.

Thanzauva, K, ed. *Towards a Tribal Theology: The Mizo Perspective.* Jorhat: MTC, 1989.

Thanzauva, K. *Theology of Community: Tribal Theology in the Making*. Aizawl: Mizo Theological Conference, 1997.

__________ *Transforming Theology.* Bangalore: Asian Trading Corporation, 2002.

Vanlalauva, H. *Doctrine of God: John Calvin's Doctrine of God with Special Reference to the Indian Context.* Delhi: ISPCK, 2006.

Vanlalchhuanawma. *Christianity and Sabaltern Culture, Revival Movement as a Cultural Response to Westernization in Mizoram.* Delhi: ISPCK, 2006.

Zairema. *God's Miracles in Mizoram: A Glimpse of Christian Work among Head-Hunters*. Aizawl: Synod Publication Board, 1978.

Zaithanga, V. L. *From Head Hunting to Soul-Hunting*. Aizawl: Synod Printing Press, 1981.

Periodicals

Lalnghakthuami. "A Theological Examination of the Mizo Festivals." *Journal of Tribal Studies* X/2 (July-December), 30-50.

Lalthuama. "Tlawmngaihna." *Thu leh Hla*, No. 4 (April 2000), 20-25.

Pachuau, Lalsangkima. "In Search of a Context for a Contextual Theology: The Socio-Political Realities of Tribal' Christians in Northeast India." *National Council of Churches Review* CXVII/11 (1997), 760-772.

_______. "Tribal Identity and Ethnic Conflicts in Northeast India: A "Tribal" Christian Response." *Bangalore Theological Forum* XXX/1 (July 1999), 157-167.

Unpublished Thesis

Hminga, C. L. "Christianity and the Lushai People: An Investigation of the Problem of Representing Basic Concept of Christianity in the Language of the Lushai People." M. A. Thesis, Manchester University, 1963.

Ramliana, P. L. "A Study of Poverty in Mizoram with Special Reference to Mamit and Lawngtlai Districts." PhD Thesis, submitted to Mizoram University, Aizawl, 2009.

2. Sources related to other Tribal Groups in India

Agarwal, A. K. *Economic Problems and Planning in North East India.* New Delhi: Sterling Publishers Pvt. Ltd, 1987.

________ *The Growth of the Baptist churches in Meghalaya.* Guwahati: Christian Literature Centre, 1978.

Aier, K. I. *Introducing the Council of Baptist Churches in North East India.* Guwahati: CBCNEI, 1978.

________ *Future Nagaland: A Socio-Politico-heological Vision for the Nagas.* Mokokchung. Wati Aier, 1988.

Alem, O. *Tsungremlogy: Ao Naga Christian Theology.* Mokokchung: Clark Theological College, 1994.

Areeplackal, Joseph. *Spirit and Ministries: Perspectives of East and West*. Bangalore: Dharmaram Publications, 1990.

Bareh, H. M., ed. *Encyclopedia of North East India*. New Delhi: Mittal Publications, 2001.

Downs, F. S. *The Mighty Works of God. A Brief History of the Council of Baptist Churches in North East India. The Mission Period,* 1836-1950. Guwahati: Christian Literature Centre, 1971.

________ *History of Christianity in India: North East India in the Nineteenth and Twentieth Centuries.* Bangalore: The Church History Association of Bangalore, 1992.

________ *Christianity in North East India*. Delhi: ISPCK, 1983.

Dozo, P. *The Growth of the Baptist Church in Chakhesang Naga Tribe*. Kohima: Nagaland Missionary Movement, 1978.

Hembrom, T. *The Santals*. The *Anthropological-Theological Reflections on Santal and Biblical Creation Traditions.* Calcutta: Punthi Pustak, 1996.

Hutton, J. H. *The Angami Nagas*. London: Oxford University Press, 1991.

Jagatdeb, L. "Tribal Development in India: A Critique." In *Tribal Development in India.* Edited by R. N. Pati and Basantibala Jena. New Delhi: Ashish Publishing House, 1989, 151-170.

Jajo, C. *Christian Life in a Tribal Context in Manipur*. Calcutta: Swapna Printing Works, Pvt. Ltd., 1990.

Keitzar, Renthy, ed. *Good News for North East India: A Theological Reader*. Guwahati: The Christian Literature Centre, 1995.

________ ."Tribal Theology in the Making." In *New Horizons in Ecumenism: Essays in Honour of Bishop Samuel Amirtham.* Edited by K. C. Abraham. Bangalore: BTESSC & BTTBPSA, 1993.

Khup Za Go. *Chin Chronicles*. Churachandpur: L & R Printing Press, 1988.

________ *A Critical Historical Study of Bible Tanslation among the Zo People in North East India*. Imphal: BCPW, 1996.

Lasetso, Razouselie, ed. *Grarnering Tribal Resources for Doing Tribal Christian Theology*. Jorhat: Eastern Theological College, 2008.

Leeuwen, Gerwin van, ed. *Searching for an Indian Ecclesiology.* Bangalore: Asian Trading Corporation, 1984.

Longchar, A. Wati. *The Traditional Worldview and Modernity: Focus on North East India.* Jorhat: N. Limala Longkumar, 1995.

Longchar, A. Wati, ed. *The Tribal Worldview and Ecology*. Jorhat: TSC, 1998.

________ *Doing Theology with Tribal Resources: Context and Perspective.* Jorhat: TSC, ETC, 1999.

________ *Encounter Between Gospel and Tribal Culture*. Jorhat: TSC, 1999.

________ *An Emerging Asian Theology: Tribal Theology: Issues, Method and Perspective.* Jorhat: TSC, 2000.

Lorrain, Reginald A. *Five Years in Unknown Jungles*. London: Lakher Pioneer Mission, 1912, Reprint, 1988.

Milton, Sangma. *History and Culture of the Garos*. New Delhi: Book Today, 1981.

________ *History of American Baptist Mission in North East India* 1836-1950. Delhi: Mittal Publications, 1987.

Minz, Nirmal. *Rise Up My People, and Claim the Promise. The Gospel among the Tribes of India.* Delhi: ISPCK, 1997.

________ "The Study Tribal Religion in India." In *Revisioning India's Religious Traditions.* Edited by David Scott and Israel Selvanayagam. Delhi: ISPCK, 1996.

________ "A Theological Interpretation of the Tribal Reality in India." In *Reading in Indian Christian Theology,* Vol. I. Edited by R. S. Sugitharajah and Cecil Hargreaves. Delhi: ISPCK, 1993.

Miri, Sujata, ed. *Rationality and Tribal Thought*. New Delhi: Mittal Publications, 2004.

Mundu, John. *The Ho Christian Community: Towards a New Self-Understanding as Communion.* Delhi: Media House, 2003.

Nungshitula. *The Naga Images of the Human Being.* Jorhat: Tribal Study Centre, 2001.

Prasad, R. N. and Puthenpurakal, J. *Baptist Mission in Nagaland,* Shillong: Vendrame Missiological Institute, 1984.

Puthenpurakal, J, ed. *Impact of Christianity on North East India.* Shillong: Vendrame Institute Publications, 1996.

Rao, O. M. *Focus on Northeast Indian Christianity.* Delhi: ISPCK, 1994.

Rennel, J. "Upon the religions, Manners, Laws and Customs of the Cucis of the inhabitants of the Tripura Mountains." Quoted in J. H. Lewin. *The Hills Tracts of Chittagong and the Dwellers Therein.* Calcutta: Bengal Printing Co, 1869.

Shimray, Shimreingam, ed. *Tribal Theology: A Reader.* Jorhat: TSC, 2003.

Sinha, A. P. "Politics and Economic Development in the Hill District of Assam." In *Tribal Situation in India: Proceedings of a Seminar.* Edited by K. Suresh Singh. Shimla: Indian Institute of Advanced Study, 1972.

Snaitang, O. *Christianity and Social Change in North East India.* Shillong Vendrame Institute, 1993.

Vidhyaarthi, L. P. and B. K. Rai. *The Tribal Culture of India.* Delhi: Concept Publishing Company, 1977.

Shashi, ed. *Encyclopaedia of Indian Tribes,* 1994 ed. Vol. 10: Tribal Culture, Custom and Affinities. New Delhi: Anmol Publications Pvt. Ltd., 2004.

Periodicals

Aleaz, K. P. "A Tribal Christian Theology from India." *Journal of Tribal Studies* VII/2 (July-December 2003), 290-305.

Keitzar, Renthy. "Tribal Perspective in Biblical Hermeneutic Today." *India Journal of Theology* 31/3&4 (July-December 1982), 293-313.

Longchar, A Wati. "Gospel and Culture Interaction in NEI." *Journal of Tribal Studies* III/1 (January-June), 69-77.

Prasad, R. R. "Tribal Development in India: Strategies and Programmes." *Journal of Rural Development* 7/1 (1988), 81-103.

Yimchunger, T. Lakiumong. "Re-Perusal of the Term "Tribe" and its Redeemable Humanized Potentiality: A Liberative Perspective." *Journal of Tribal Studies* X/2 (July-December 2006), 1-14.

3. Sources consulted for Early Christian Traditions (ecclesiology)

Aulen, Gustaf. *The Faith of the Christian Church.* London: SPCK, 1954.

Bagatti, O. F. M. Bellarmino. *The Church from the Circumcision: History and Archaeology of the Judaeo-Christians.* Jerusalem: Franciscan Printing Press, 1971.

Balchin, John F. *I Want to Know What the Bible Says About the Church.* Eastbourne: Kingsway Publications, 1979.

Barnard, L. W. The *Background of St. Ignatius of Antioch.* London: BRILL, 1963.

Battenhouse, R. W. *A Companion to the Study of St. Augustine.* Oxford: University Press, 1955.

Bethune-Baker, J. F. *An Introduction to the Early History of Christian Doctrine: To the Time of the Council of Chalcedon.* London: Methuen & Co. Ltd., 1962.

Brent, Allen. *Ignatius of Antioch: A Martyr Bishop and the Origin of Episcopacy.* London: T&T Clark International, 2007.

Brook, Wes Howard. *The Church before Christianity.* Maryknoll, NY: Orbis Books, 2001.

Brown, Raymond E. *The Community of the Beloved Disciples.* New York, NY: Paulist Press, 1979.

________ *The Churches the Apostles Left Behind.* London: Chapman, 1984.

Burge, G. M. *The Annointed Community.* Grand Rapids: Eerdmans, 1987.

Campenhausen, Hans Von. *Ecclesiastical Authority and Spiritual Power in the Church of the First Three Centuries.* Peabody: Hendrickson Publishers, 1997.

Campenhausen, Hans Von. *The Fathers of the Greek Church.* Translated by Stanley Godman. Stuttgart: W. Kohlhammer, 1955.

Cayre, F. *Manual of Patrology and History of Theology.* Nottingham: Guillelmus Can. Collingwood, D. D, 1935.

Clarke, G.W., trans. *The Letters of St. Cyprian of Carthage.* Vol. II (Letters 28-54). Edited by Johannes Quasten, Walter J. Burghardt, and Thomas Comerford Lawler. New York, NY: Newman Press, 1984.

Corwin, Virginia. *St. Ignatius and Christianity in Antioch.* New Haven: Yale University Press, 1960.

Cyprian. *The Lapsed, the Unity of the Catholic Church.* Translated by Maurice Bevenot. Edited by Johannes Quasten and oseph C. Plumpe. London: Longmans, Green and Co, 1957.

Danielou, Jean and Henri Marrou. *The Christian Century,* Vol. I*: The First Six Hundred Years.* London: Darton, Longman and Todd, 1979.

Deferri, Joseph, ed. *The Fathers of the Church,* Vol. 56. Translated by Donald A Gallagher and Idella. Washington, D. C: The Catholic University of America Press, 1966.

Donaldson, James and Alexander Roberts. Eds. *The Ante Nicene Fathers.* Vol. I. Grand Rapids: WM. B. Eerdmans Publishing Company, 1956.

Dunn, James D. G. *Unity and Diversity into the New Testament.* Philadelphia: The Westminster Press, 1977.

Eno S.S, Robert B. *Teaching Authority in the Early Church.* Wilmington: Michael Glazier, Inc, 1984.

George, K.M. *The Early Church, Defending the Faith, Witness and Proclamation: Patristic Perspectives.* Geneva: WCC Publication, 1996.

Ghost, G. K. *Tribal and Their Culture in Assam, Meghalaya and Mizoram*. Vol. I, II, III. New Delhi: Ashish Publishing House, 1992.

Gonzalez, Justo L. *A History of Christian Thought.* Vol. 1. Nashville: Abingdon Press, 1983.

Graowski, S. J. *The Church: An Introduction to the Theology of St. Augustine.* London: Herder, 1957.

Hanson, R. P. C. *Tradition in the Early Church*. London: SCM Press Ltd., 1962.

Harris, Carl Vernon. *Origen of Alexandria's Interpretation of the Teacher's Function in the Early Christian Hierarchy and Community.* New York, NY: The American Press, 1966.

Harrison, Everett F. *The Apostolic Church.* Grand Rapids: William B. Eerdmans Publishing Company, 1985.

Holmes, Michael W, trans. & ed. *The Apostolic Fathers in English.* Third Edition. Grand Rapids, Michigan: Baker Academic, 2006.

Jay, Eric G. *The Church: Its Changing Image through Twenty Centuries.* Vol. 1. London: SPCK, 1977.

Jervell, J. *Luke and the People of God.* Minnesota: Augsburg, 1972.

Johnston, George. *The Doctrine of the New Testament.* Cambridge: University Press, 1943.

Jurgens, Williams A. *The Faith of the Fathers.* Vol. 1. Bangalore: Theological Publication in India, 2000.

Meeks, W. A. *The First Urban Christians, The Social World of the Apostle Paul.* London: Yale University Press, 1983.

Meier, J. P. *The Vision of Christ: Christ, Church and Morality in the First Gospel.* New York, NY: Paulist Press, 1979.

Minear, Paul. *Images of the Church in the New Testament*. Philadelphia: Westminster Press, 1960.

Pelikan, Jaroslav and Valerie Hotchkiss, eds. *Creeds and Confessions of Faith in the Christian Tradition*, Vol. I, II, III. New Haven: Yale University, 2003.

Quasten, Johannes, Walter J. Burghardt and Thomas Comerford Lawler, eds. *Ancient Christian Writers: The Letters of Cyprian of Carthage*, Vol. 2. Translated by G. W. Clarke. New York, NY: Newman Press, 1984.

________ *Ancient Christian Writers: Origen.* Translated by R. P. Lawson. London: Longmans, Green and Co, 1959.

________ *Ancient Christian Writers: St. Cyprian.* Translated by Maurice Bevenot. London: Longmans, Green and Co, 1957.

Roberts, Alexander and James Donaldson. Eds. *Ante-Nicene Fathers.* Vol. V. Buffalo: The Christian Literature Company, 1886.

Roberts, Robert E. *The Theology of Tertullian.* London: The Epworth Press, 1924.

Schillebeeckk, E. *Ministry, Leadership in the Community of Jesus Christ.* New York, NY: Cross road, 1981.

Schmaus, M. *The Church its Origin and Structure.* London: Sheed & Oates, 1974.

Schnackenburg, R. *The Gospel According to St John,* Vol. 3. New York, NY: Crossroad, 1982.

Sebastian, J. Jayakiran. "*Baptisma Unum in Santa Ecclesia*": *A Theological Appraisal of the Baptismal Controversy in the Work and Writings of Cyprian of Carthage.* Delhi: ISPCK, 1997.

Tannehil, Robert, C. *The Narrative Unity of Luke-Acts: A Literary Interpretation, Vol. 2: The Acts of the Apostles.* Minneapolis: Fortress Press, 1995.

Theissen, Gerd. *Social Reality and the Early Christians.* Minneapolis: Fortress Press, 1992.

Wiles, Maurice and Mark Santer, eds. *Documents in Early Christian Thought.* Cambridge: Cambridge University Press, 1975.

Dictionaries / Encyclopedias

Bornkam, G. "Presbyteros." *Theological Dictionary of the New Testament*, Vol. VI. Grand Rapids: Eerdmans, 1973.

Briggs, Charles A. "The New Testament Doctrine of the Church." *The American Journal of Theology* 4/1 (January, 1900), 1-22.

Douglas, J. D., Peter Toon, Walter A. Elwell, eds. *The Concise Dictionary of the Christian Tradition, Doctrine, Liturgy & History.* Grand Rapids: Regency Reference Library, 1984.

Ferguson, Sinclair B, ed. *New Dictionary of Theology*. Leicester: Inter-Varsity Press, 1988.

Hastings, James. *Dictionary of Apostolic Church.* New York, NY: Scribner's Sons, 1916.

Johnston, George. "The Church and Israel: Continuity and Discontinuity in the New Testament Doctrine of the Church." *The Journal of Religion* 34/1 (January, 1954), 26-36.

Periodicals

Barnard, L.W. "The Background of St. Ignatius of Antioch." *Vigiliae Christianae* 17/4 (December, 1964), 193-206.

Bratton, Fred Gladstone. "Origen, The First Christian Liberal." *Journal of Bible and Religion* 8/3 (August, 1940), 137-141.

Brent, Allen. "Ignatius of Antioch and the Imperial Cult." *Vigiliae Christianae* 52/1 (February, 1998): 30-58.

Brown, Raymond E. "The Unity and Diversity in New Testament Ecclesiology." *Novum Testamentum* 6/4 (November, 1963), 298-308.

Christie, F. A. "Review: An Interpretation of Irenaeus." *The American Journal Theology* 21/1 (January, 1917), 129-130.

Clarke, G. W. "Cyprian's Epistle 64 and the Kissing of Feet in Baptism." *The Harvard Theological Review* 66/1 (January, 1973), 147-152.

Collins, Judy Schindler, Ft. "The Rise of One Bishop Rule in the Early Church: A Study in the Writings of Ignatius and Cyprian." *Baptist Reformation Review* 10/2 (Second Quarterly 1981), 3-9.

Ferguson, Everett. "Origen and the Election of Bishops." *Church History* 43/1 (March, 1974), 26-33.

Greenslade, S. L. "Review: Augustine's City of God." *The Classical Review* 8/ 3 (December, 1958), 261-262.

Haroutunian, Joseph. "The Church, the Spirit, and the Hands of God." *The Journal of Religion* 54/2 (April, 1974), 154-165.

Hefner, Philip. "Theological Methodology and St. Irenaeus." *The Journal of Religion* 44/4 (October, 1964), 294-309.

Kasemann, Ernst. "Unity and Diversity in New Testament Eccelesiology." *Novum Testamentum* 6/4 (November, 1963), 290-297.

Moffatt, James. "An Approach to Ignatius." *The Harvard Theological Review* 29/1 (January, 1936), 1-38.

Pagels, Elaine. "Irenaeus, the 'Canon of Truth," and the 'Gospel of John": "Making a Difference" through Hermeneutics and Ritual". *Vigiliae Christianae* 56/4 (November, 2002), 339-371.

Rabinowitz, Celia E. "Personal and Cosmic Salvation in Origen." *Vigiliae Christianae* 38/4 (December, 1984), 319-329.

Richardson, Cyril C. "The Church in Ignatius of Antioch." *The Journal of Religion* 17/4 (October, 1937), 428-443.

________ "The Condemnation of Origen." *Church History* 6/1 (March, 1937), 50-64.

Sanderlin, George. "St. Augustine and the Twentieth Century." *The Classical Journal* 49/3 (December, 1953), 132-135.

Schindler, Judy. "The Rise of One Bishop-Rule in the Early Church: A Study in the Writings of Ignatius and Cyprian." *Baptist Reformation Review* 10/2 (Second Quarterly 1981), 3-9.

Soares-Prabu, George. "Radical Beginnings: The Jesus Community as the Archetype of the Church." *Jeevadhara* 15 (1985), 307-325.

4. Other Books and Writings

Adolfs, Roberts. *The Grave of God: Has the Church a Future?* Translated by N. D. Smith. London: Burns and Oates, 1967.

Amaladoss, Micheal. *Life in Freedom: Liberation Theologies from Asia.* Maryknoll, NY: Orbis Books, 1997.

Amirtham, Samuel and John S. Pobee, eds. *Theology by the People: Reflections on doing Theology in Community.* Geneva: World Council of Churches, 1986.

Araya, Victorio. *God of the Poor: The Mystery of God in Latin American Liberation Theology.* Maryknoll, NY: Orbis Books, 1987.

Areeplackal, Joseph. *Spirit and Ministries: Perspectives of East and West*. Bangalore: Dharmaram Publications, 1990.

Balasundaram, F. J. *Contemporary Asian Christian Theology*. Bangalore: ISPCK, 1995.

Balasurya, T. *Mary and Human Liberation*. Colombo: Religious Publications, 1997.

Best, Ernest. *One Body in Christ*. London: SPCK, 1955.

Best, Thomas F. and Martin Robra, eds. *Ecclesiology and Ethics: Ecumenical Ethical Engagement, Moral Formation and the Nature of the Church*. Geneva: WCC Publications, 1997.

Best, Thomas F., ed. *Faith and Order at the Crossroads*. Geneva: WCC Publications, 2005.

Bianchi, Eugene C. and Rosemary Radford Ruether, eds. *Democratic Catholic Church*. New York, NY: Crossroad, 1992.

Boff, Leonardo. *Church, Charism and Power.* London: SCM, 1985.

________ *Ecclesiogenesis: The Base Communities Reinvent the Church.* Maryknoll, NY: Orbis Books, 1986.

________ *Holy Trinity, Perfect* Community. Maryknoll, N.Y: Orbis Books, 2000.

Buhlmann, Walbert. *The Church of the Future: A Model for the Year, 2001* Maryknoll, NY: Orbis Books, 1986.

Chopp, Rebecca S. and Sheila Greeve Davaney, ed. *Horizons in Feminist Theology: Identity, Tradition, and Norms*. Minneapolis: Fortress Press, 1997.

Coalter, Milton J, John M. Mulder and Louise B. Weeks. *The Reformed Tradition: Presbyterians and Mainstream Protestantism*. Louisville, Kentucky: Westminster/John Knox Press, 1992.

Cobble, James F. Jr. *The Church and the Power: A Theology of the Church Structure*. Peabody: Hendrickson Publishers, 1988.

Cook, Guillermo. *The Expectation of the Poor: Latin American Basic Ecclesial Communities in Protestant Perspective.* Maryknoll, NY: Orbis Books, 1985.

Costa, Ruy O., ed. *One Faith, Many Cultures: Inculturation, Indigenisation, and Contextualization*. Maryknoll, NY: Orbis Books, 1988.

Cox, Harvey. *Religion in the Secular City: Towards a Postmodern Theology*. New York: Simon and Schuster, 1984.

Crollius, Roest. "Inculturation." In *Following Christ in Mission: A Foundational Course in Missiology.* Edited by Sebastian Karotemprel. Bombay: Pauline Publications, 1995, 110-119.

Deenabhandhu, M. "Ecclesia in the Light of the Dalit Experience: An attempt towards an Indian ecclesiology with the experience of the Malas and Madigas in Dommeru and Jonnada in Andhra Pradesh as a point of engagement." *D. Th Thesis*, SATHRI, 2001.

De Schrijver. Georges. "Paradigm Shift in Third World Theologies of Liberation: From Socio-Economic Analysis to Cultural Analysis?" In *Liberation Theologies on Shifting Grounds: A Clash of Socio-Economic and Cultural Paradigm*, 3-83. Edited by George De Schrijver. Leuven: University Press, 1998.

Doyle, Dennis M. *Communion Ecclesiology: Vision and Versions.* Maryknoll, NY: Orbis Books, 2000.

Dulles, Avery. *Models of the Church*. New York, NY: Image Books, 1987.

________ *A Church to Believe In: Discipleship and the Dynamics of Freedom.* New York: Crossroad, 1982.

Duquoc, Christian. *Provinsional Churches: An Essay in Ecumenical Ecclesiology*. Translated by John Bowden. London: SCM Press, 1986.

Epps, Dwain C. *The Churches in International Affairs: Reports* 1995-1998. Geneva: WCC, 2004.

Evans, G. R. *The Church and the Churches: Toward an Ecumenical Ecclesiology*. Cambridge: Cambridge University Press, 1994.

Everett, William J. *God's Federal Republic*. New York, NY: Paulist Press, 1988.

Fackre, Gabriel. *The Church: Signs of the Spirit and Signs of the Times*. Grand Rapids, Michigan, 2007.

Flannery, Austin. *Vatican II: More Postconciliar Documents*. Bombay: St. Pauls, 1990.

Ford, David F., ed. *The Modern Theologians: An Introduction to Christian Theology in the Twentieth Century*. Second edition. Oxford: Blackwell Publishing, 1997.

Forrester, Duncan. *The True Church and Morality: Reflection on Ecclesiology and Ethics*. Geneva: WCC Publications, 1997.

Fuellenbach, John. *Church: Community for the Kingdom*. Maryknoll, NY: Orbis Books, 2002.

Furer-Haimmendorf, Christopher von. *Tribes of India: The Struggle for Survival.* Berkeley: University of California Press, 1982.

Gadamer, George. *Truth and Method*. New York, NY: Seabury Press, 1975.

George, K. M. *Interfacing Theology with Culture*. Delhi: ISPCK, 2010.

Gelder, Craig Van and R. Hunsberger, eds. *The Church between Gospel and Culture: The Emerging Mission in North America*. Grand Rapids, Michigan: B. Eerdmanns Publishing Co., 1996.

Getui, Mary N., ed. *Theological Method and Aspects of Worship in African Christianity*. Nairobi: Action Publishers, 1998.

Gibbs, Eddie. *Church Next: Quantum Changes in How We do Ministry*. Downers Grove, Illinois: Inter Varsity Press, 2000.

Giles, Kevin. *What on Earth is the Church? A Biblical and Theological Inquiry.* London: SPCK, 1995.

Goizueta, Roberto S. *Liberation, Method and Dialogue: Enrique Dussel and North American Theological Discourse*. Atlanta: Scholars Press, 1988.

Gore, Charles. *The Holy Spirit and the Church.* London: John Murray, 1924.

Gregorios, Paulos Mar (Varghese, T. Paul). *Be Still and Know.* Madras: CLS, ISPCK & LPH, 1971.

________ *Freedom and Authority*. Madras: CLS, ISPCK & LPH, 1924.

________ *The Church and Authority*. New Delhi: ISPCK, 2001.

Greenwood, Robin. *Transforming Liberating Church Structures for Ministry*. London: SPCK, 2002.

Greinocher, Norbert and Norbert Mette, eds. *Christianity and Cultures.* Maryknoll: Orbis Books & London: SCM, 1994.

Grenz, Stanley J. *Theology for the Community of God.* Grand Rapids, Michigan: William B. Eerdmans Publishing Company, 2000.

Gutierrez, Gustavo. *Theology of Liberation*. Maryknoll, NY: Orbis Books, 1998.

Hasselgrave, D. J. *Communicating Christ Cross Culturally.* Michigan: Zondervan Publishing House, 1979.

Hebblethwaite, Peter. "Liberation theology and the Roman Catholic Church." In *The Cambridge Companion of Liberation Theology.* Edited by Christopher Rowland. Cambridge: University Press, 1999.

Heelas, Paul, Scott Lash and Paul Morris. *Detraditionalisation-Critical Reflections on Authority and Identity.* Oxford: Blackwell, 1996.

Hesselgrave, David J and Edward Rommen. *Contextualization: Meanings, Methods and Models.* Grand Rapids, Michigan: Baker Book House, 1989.

Jeanrond, Werner G. "Hans Kung." In *The Modern Theologians.* Edited by David F. Ford. Malden and Oxford: Blackwell Publishing, 1997, 162-178.

Kalu, Ogbu U., ed. *African Christianity: An African Story*. Trenton, NJ: Africa World Press, Inc., 2007.

Kasemann, Ernst. *New Testament Questions for Today.* London: SCM, 1967.

Kavunkal, Jacob. "Evolution of the Understanding of Christian identity in the course of the centuries." In *The Church in India in Search of a new Identity.* Edited by Kurient Kunnumpuram, Errol D' Lima and Jacob Parappally (Bangalore: N.B.C.L.C, 1997), 85-108.

Kee, H. *Community of the New Age.* Philadelphia: Westminster, 1977.

Kloppenburg, B. *The Ecclesiology of Vatican II.* Chicago: Franciscan Herald Press, 1974.

Komochak, Joseph A., May Collins and Dermot A. Lan, eds. *The Dictionary of Theology.* Wilmington: Michael Glazier, 1987.

Kung, Hans, ed. *The Church and Ecumenism: Theology in the Age of Renewal.* New York, NY: Paulist Press, 1965.

__________ *The Church.* Kent, Britain: Burns & Oats, 1992.

LaCugna, Catherine Mowry. *The Theological Methodology of Hans Kung.* New York, NY: Scholars Press, 1982.

Lam, Matthew L. *History, Method and Theology: A Dialectical Comparison of Wilhelm Dilthey's Critique of Historical Reason and Bernard Lonergan's Mett-Methodology.* Missoula, Montana: The American Academy of Religion, 1978.

Leeuwen, Gerwin van, ed. *Searching for an Indian Ecclesiology.* Bangalore: Asian Trading Corporation, 1984.

Leith, John H. *Introduction to the Reformed Tradition.* Louiseville: Westminster John Knox Press, 1981.

Leonard Allen, C. *The Cruciform Church: Becoming a Cross-Shaped People in a Secular World.* N.d: Abilene Christian University, 1990.

Longchar, A. Wati. *The Traditional Worldview and Modernity: Focus on North East India.* Jorhat: N. Limala Longkumar, 1995.

Luzbetak, Louis J. *The Church and Cultures: New Perspectives in Missiological Anthropology.* Maryknoll, NY: Orbis Books, 1988.

MacDonald, Timothy. *The Ecclesiology of Yves Conger*. Lanham, NY: University Press of America, 1984.

Mannion, Gerard. *Ecclesiology and Postmodernity: Questions for the Church in Our Time*. Collegeville: Liturgical Press, 2007.

Mannion, Gerard. "A Virtuous Community-The Self-identity, Vision and Future of the Diocesan Church." In *Diocesan Dispositions and Parish Voices in the Roman Catholic Church. Edited by* Noel Timms. Chelmsford: Matthew James, 2001.

Manthodath, Jacob. *Culture, Dialogue and the Church: A Study on the Inculturation of the Local Churches according to the Teaching of Pope Paul VI*. New Delhi: Intercultural Publications, 1990.

McDougall, Eleanor. *St. Augustine: A Study in His Personal Religion*. London: SCM Press, 1930.

McKelvey, R. J. *The New Temple*. Oxford: Oxford University Press, 1969.

Meeks, M. Douglas. "The Future of Theology in Commodity Society." In *The Future of Theology: Essays in honour of Jurgen Moltmann,* 253-266. Edited by Miroslav Volf, Carmen Krieg and Thomas Kuchrz. Grand Rapids: Wm. B. Eerdmans, 1996.

Meyendorff, John. *Living Traditions*. Crestwood, NY: St Vladimir's Seminary Press, 1978.

Miller, Donald G. *The Nature and Mission of the Church*. Richmond, Virginia: John Knox Press, 1962.

Mohler, James A. *The Origin and Evolution of the Priesthood*. New York, NY: Albha House, 1970.

Morris, Paul. "Community Beyond Tradition." In Paul Heelas, Scott Lash and Paul Morris, *Detraditionalisation. Critical Reflections on Authority and Identity. Oxford: Blackwell, 1996, 223-249.*

Monteiro, Evelyn. *Church and Culture: Communion in Pluralism*. Delhi: ISPCK, 2004.

Neendoor, Thomas. *Communion: An Ecclesiological Analysis of the Concept of Communion of the Thomas Christians in the Light of the*

Idea of Self in Emmanuel Levinas. Kottayam: Oriental Institute of Religious Studies India Publications, 1998.

Niehbur, H. Richard. *The Social Sources of Denominationalism.* New York, NY: Living Age Books, 1957.

Niebuhr, Richard. *Christ and Culture.* New York, NY: Harper and Brothers Publishers, 1956.

Obeng, Emmanuel Adow. " Synthetic and Praxis Model in African Theology". In *Theological Method and Aspects of Worship in African Christianity.* Edited by Mary N. Getui. Nairobi: J.N.K. Mugambi and Carroll Houle, 1998, 41-54.

O'Donnel, D. *Ecclesia: A Theological Encyclopaedia of the Church.* Collegeville, Minnesota: The Liturgical Press, 1996.

Panicker, John, ed. *Joint International Commission for Dialogue between the Catholic Church and the Malankara Orthodox Syrian Church. Papers and Joint Statements* 1989-2000. Kottayam: Joint International Commission for Dialogue, 2001.

Pathil, Kuncheria. *Indian Churches at the Crossroads.* Rome: Center for Indian and Interreligious Studies (CIIS), N.D.

Pelzel, Morris and Thomas P. Walters, eds. *Ecclesiology: The Church as Communion and Mission.* Chicago: Loyola Press, 2001.

Pierard, Richard V. "Introduction." In *Baptists Together in Christ 1905-2005: A Hundred-Year History of the Baptist World Alliance.* Edited by Richard V. Pierard. Falls Church, Virginia: Baptist World Alliance, 2005, xv-xviii.

Pinto, Joseph Prasad. *Inculturation through Basic Communities: An Indian Perspectives.* Bangalore: Asian Trading Corporation, 1985.

Powers, Ward. *The Ministry of Women in the Church.* Adelaide: SPCK, 1996.

Provost, James H., ed. *The Church as Communion.* Washington, D. C: Canon Law Society of America, 1984.

Pullapilly, Cyriac K., et al., eds. *Christianity and Native Cultures: Perspectives from Different Religions of the World.* Indiana: Cross Cultural Publications, INC, 2004.

Reader, John. *Local Theology: Church and Community in Dialogue.* London: SPCK, 1994.

Rennel, J. "Upon the religions, Manners, Laws and Customs of the Cucis of the inhabitants of the Tripura Mountains." Quoted in J. H. Lewin. *The Hills Tracts of Chittagong and the Dwellers Therein.* Calcutta: Bengal Printing Co, 1869.

Roozen, David A. "Denominations Grow as Individuals Join Congregations." In Church and Denominational Growth. Ed. David A. Roozen and C. Kirk Hadaway. Nashvile: Abingdon Press, 1993, 15-35.

Sanneh, Lamin. *Translating the Message: The Missionary Impact on Culture.* Maryknoll, New York: Orbis Books, 1989.

Sapir, E. *Culture, Language and Personality.* Berkeley: University of California Press, 1962.

Scheuerer, Franz Saver. *Interculturality: A Challenge for the Mission of the Church.* Bangalore: ATC, 2001.

Schilling, Harald, *Doctrine of the Church* (Ecclesiology). Abak: The Equipping The Saints Trust Samuel Bill Theological College, 1998.

Segundo, Juan Luis. *The Community Called Church.* Maryknoll, NY: Orbis Book, 1973

Shorter, Aylward. *Towards a Theology of Inculturation.* London: Geoffrey Chapman, 1988.

Snyder, Howard A. *The Community of the King.* Downers Grove: Inter Varsity Press, 2004.

Sobrino, Jon. *The True Church and the Poor.* Maryknoll, NY: Orbis Books, 1984.

Stanley, Brian. *The Bible and the Flag: Protestant Missions and British Imperialism in the Nineteenth and Twentieth Centuries.* Leicester: Appolos, 1990.

Sugirtharajah, R. S. *Frontiers in Asian Christian Theology: Emerging Trends.* New York, NY: Orbis Books, 1994.

Tavard, George H. *The Church, Community of Salvation: An Ecumenical Ecclesiology*. Collegeville: The Liturgical Press, 1992.

Thornbury, John. The *Doctrine of the Church: A Baptist View*. Lewisburg: Heritage Publishers, 1971.

Thomas, Norman E., ed. *Classic Texts in Mission and World Christianity.* New York, N.Y: Orbis Books, 1995.

Thoppil, James. *Towards an Asian Theology: The Understanding of the church in the Documents of the FABC (*1970-2000). Bangalore: Oriens Publications and Asian Trading Corporation, 2005.

Thurian, Max, ed. *Churches Respond to BEM: Official Responses to the "Baptism, Eucharist and Ministry" Text*, Vol.1. Geneva: WCC, 1986.

Tolbert, Malcolm O. *Shaping the Church: Adapting New Testament Models for Today*. Macon, Georgia: Smyth & Helwys, 2003.

Torres, Sergio and John Eagleson, eds. *The Challenge of Basic Christian Communities*. Bangalore: Trading Corporation, 1984.

Uffenheimer, Benjamin. *Creative Biblical Exegesis: Christian and Jewish Hermeneutics through the Centuries*. Sheffield: JSOT Pr., 1988.

Vanek, Noel D. "*Re-Theologizing" The Meaning of Membership in a Local Church: A Lay Study Process*. Princeton: UMI, 1996.

Vaus, D. A. de. *Surveys in Social Research*. Jaipur and New Delhi: Rawat Publications, 2003.

Vorster, W. S., ed.. *Denominationalism - its Sources and Implications: Proceedings of the Sixth Symposium of the Institute for Theological Research (UNISA) held at the University of South Africa in Pretoria on the 8th and 9th September 1982.* Pretoria: University of South Africa, 1982.

Walls, Andrew F. *The Cross-Cultural Process in Christian History*. Maryknoll, NY: Orbis Books and T&T Clark Edinburgh, 2002.

WCC/Faith and Order. *The Nature and Purpose of the Church*. Geneva: WCC/Faith and Order, 1998.

________ *Common Witness: A Study Documents of the Joint Working Group of the Roman Catholic Church and the World Council of Churches*. Geneva: WCC, n.d.

West Charles C. and David M. Paton, eds. *The Missionary Church in East and West*. London: SCM Press Ltd, 1959.

Zizioulas, John D. *Being as Communion: Studies in Personhood and the Church*. Crestwood: St. Vladimir's Seminary Press, 1985.

Dictionaries / Encyclopedias

Davies, J. G., ed. *A Dictionary of Liturgy and Worship*. London: SCM Press Ltd, 1972.

Ferguson, Sinclair B, ed. *New Dictionary of Theology*. Leicester: Inter-Varsity Press, 1988.

Rahner, Karl, ed. *Encyclopedia of Theology*. London: Burns and Oates, 1975.

Sunquist, Scott W, ed. *A Dictionary of ASIAN Christianity*. Grand Rapids: William B. Eerdmans Publishing Company, 2001.

(*The Columbia Encyclopedia*, 5th ed., s.v. "Augustine")

Periodicals

Amaladoss, Michael. "Challenges of Mission in the 21st Century." *Theology Digest* 47 (2000), 15-20.

________. "The Future of the Church's Mission in India." *Jeevadhara* 17 (1987), 377-386.

________. "Mission in a Post-Modern World: A Call to be Counter-cultural." *Indian Missiological Review* 18/3 (1996), 13-21.

Anderson, B. "The Babel Story: Paradigm of Human Unity and Diversity." *Concillium* 1 (1977), 63-70.

Anthonysamy, S. J. "Christian Mission in the Context of Many Religions Today: A Biblical Perspective." *Indian Missiological Review* 18/2 (1996), 9-19.

Arbuckle, Gerald A. "Inculturation Not Adaptation: Time to Change Terminology." *Worship* 60 (1986), 511-520.

Best, Thomas F. "Ecclesiology and Ethics". *The Ecumenical Review* 47/2 (April 1995), 127-141.

Boeve, Lieven. "Critical Consciousness in the Postmodern Condition." *Philosophy and Theology* 10 (1997), 449-469.

Boff, Leonardo. "Salvation in Jesus Christ and the Process of Liberation." *Concilium* 6 (1974), 78-91.

Bulthelezi, Manas. "The Church as a Prophetic Sign." In *Church, Kingdom, World: The Church as Mystery and Prophetic Sign*, 138-144. Edited by Gennadios Limouris. Geneva: World Council of Churches, 1986.

Bunleigh, John H. S. "What is Presbyterianism?" *Evangelical Quarterly* 23 (January 1951), 8-18.

Carter, David and Paul Fiddes. "Article Review and Response: Baptist Ecclesiology". *Ecclesiology* 1/3 (2005), 87-100.

Chathanatt, John. "Globalization Virus: An Ethical Scanning." *Third Millenium* 3/3 (2000), 6-23.

Chenu, Marie-Dominique. "Vatican II and the Church of the Poor." *Concilium* 104 (1977), 56-61.

Clark, F. X. "Inculturation: Introduction and History." *Teaching all Nations* 4 (1978), 211-235.

Crowe, Desmond. "Inculturation: Challenge to the Local Church." *East Asian Pastoral Review* 3 (1981), 204-299.

________ "Consultation on Inculturation." *East Asia Pastoral Review* 2 (1981), 145-152.

De Messa, J. M. "Pastoral Agents and Doing Christology." *Eastern Asian Pastoral Review* 29 (1992), 110-231.

Dules, Avery. "Catholic Ecclesiology since Vatican II." *Concilium* 6 (1986), 3-13.

Dulles, Avery. "A half century of Ecclesiology." *Theological Studies* 50 (1989), 419-442.

Fletcher, Henry. "Quest for Synthesis." *Modern Churchman* 7 (1964), 229-232.

Fossman, Vem. "The breaking in of the future: The Problem of indigenization and cultural synthesis." *International Review of Mission* 52/206 (April 1963), 129-143.

Greaves, Richard L. "The Puritan-Nonconformist Tradition in England, 1560-1700: Historiographical Reflections." *A Quarterly Journal Concerned with British Studies* 17/4 (Winter 1985), 449-486.

Haroutunian, Joseph. "The Church, the Spirit, and the Hands of God." *The Journal of Religion* 54/2 (April, 1974), 154-165.

Hinson, E. Glenn. "Baptist Approaches to Spirituality." *Baptist History and Heritage* XXXVII/2 (Spring 2002), 6-31.

Jathanna, O. V. "Ecclesiology in Context: Reflections from and Indian Perspective in the Light of Current Ecumenical Deliberations." *Bangalore Theological Forum* XXVIII/3&4 (September-December 1996), 3-24.

Jo, Yong-Hun. "Globalization as a Challenge to the Churches in Asia Today." *Asia Journal of Theology* 14 (2000), 355-370.

Johnson, Robert C. "A theologian of Synthesis (P. Tillich)." *Theology Today* 15 (April 1958), 36-42.

Kovesi, Julius. "Marxist Ecclesiology and Biblical Criticism." *Journal of the History of* Ideas, 37/1 (January-March 1976), 93-110.

Kress, Robert. "The Church as Communio: Trinity and Incarnation as the Foundation of Ecclesiology." *The Jurist* 36 (1976), 127-158.

________ . "Unity in Diversity and Diversity in Unity: Towards an Ecumenical Perichoresic Kenotic Trinitarian Ontology." *Dialogue and Alliance* 4/3 (1990), 66-70.

Lodberg, Peter. "The History of Ecumenical Work on Ecclesiology and Ethics" *The Ecumenical Review* 47/2 (April 1995), 128-139.

Lynch, John E. "Power in the Church: An Historico-critical Survey." *Concilium 197* (April 1988), 13-21.

Mering, Norman H. "Some thoughts on Baptist Polity." *Review and Expositor* 52 (1955), 451-459.

Mohler, James A. *The Origin and Evolution of the Priesthood.* New York, NY: Albha House, 1970.

Mudge, Lewis. "Ecclesiology and Ethics in Current Ecumenical Debate". *The Ecumenical Review* 48/1 (January 1996), 11-27.

Mueller, Gustav E. "The Hegel Legend of 'Thesis-Antithesis-Synthesis." *Journal of the History of Ideas* 19/3 (June, 1958), 411-414.

Porter, Andrew. "Church History, History of Christianity, Religious History: Some Reflections on British Missionary Enterprise since the Late Eighteenth Century." *Church History* 71/3 (September, 2002), 555-587.

Prior, Charles W. A. "Ecclesiology and Political Thought in England, 1580-c. 1630." The *Historical Journal* 48/4 (December, 2005), 855-884.

Puthanangady, P. "Theology of Inculturation." *Word and Worship* 20 (1987), 303-315.

Raiser, Konrad. "Ecumenical Discussion of Ethics and Ecclesiology." *The Ecumenical Review* 48/1 (January 1996), 3-10.

Schindler, David L. "Communion Ecclesiology and Liberalism." *The Review of Politics* 60/4 (December, 1998), 775-786.

Smith, Susan. "Gospel and Culture." *Missiology: An International Review*, Vol. XXXIV//3 (July 2006), 337-348.

Soares-Prabu, George. "Radical Beginnings: The Jesus community as the Archetype of the Church." *Jeevadhara* 15 (1985), 307-325.

Starkloff, Carl F. "Inculturation and Cultural Systems." *Theological Studies* 55 (1994), 66-81.

Sullivan, James C. "Baptist Polity as I see it." *Faith and Mission* 2/1 (1984), 109-110.

Victoria C. "Miller, Ecclesiology, Scripture, and Tradition in the Dublin Agreed Statement." *The Harvard Theological Review* 86/1 (January, 1993), 105-134.

Waldo, Beach. "Freedom and Authority in Protestant Ethics". *The Journal of Religion* 32/2 (April, 1952), 108-118.

Wamble, Hugh. "Landmarkism: Doctrianaire Ecclesiology among Baptists." *Church History* 33/4 (December, 1964), 429-447.

Wright, John H. "The Church: Community of the Holy Spirit." *Theological Studies* 48 (1987), 25-44.